DATE DUE

FF 13 05			

Demco, Inc. 38-293

The Economics of the European Union and the Economies of Europe

Larry Neal
University of Illinois at Urbana-Champaign

Daniel Barbezat
Amherst College

New York   Oxford
OXFORD UNIVERSITY PRESS
1998

Oxford University Press

Oxford   New York
Athens   Auckland   Bangkok   Bogota   Bombay
Buenos Aires   Calcutta   Cape Town   Dar es Salaam
Delhi   Florence   Hong Kong   Istanbul   Karachi
Kuala Lumpur   Madras   Madrid   Melbourne
Mexico City   Nairobi   Paris   Singapore
Taipei   Tokyo   Toronto   Warsaw

and associated companies in
Berlin   Ibadan

Copyright © 1998 by Oxford University Press, Inc.

Published by Oxford University Press, Inc.,
198 Madison Avenue, New York, New York 10016

Oxford is a registered trademark of Oxford University Press

Library of Congress Cataloging-in-Publication Data
Neal, Larry, 1941-
The economics of the European Union and the economies of Europe /
Larry Neal, Daniel Barbezat.
p.   cm.
Includes bibliographical references and index.
ISBN 0–19-511067–6 (cloth : alk. paper)—
ISBN 0–19-511068–4 (pbk. : alk. paper)
1. European Union. 2. European Union countries—Economic
conditions.
I. Barbezat, Daniel.   II. Title.
HC241.N4 1998
330.94'0559—DC21   97–4221
                                                        CIP

3 5 7 9 8 6 4 2

Printed in the United States of America
on acid-free paper

Contents

v

Preface

This is a textbook on the European Union by two American economic historians. It attempts to integrate economic analysis, political logic, and historical interpretation in an effort to convey an American perspective on the movement toward European integration, the external constraints it faces and has faced, and the interplay of national concerns, both economic and political, within the vision of a united Europe.

Beginning with the American perspective on Europe, Part I of the text treats Europe as a natural economic unit, irrationally and temporarily (1945–89) divided into separate political units that attempted to remain as distinct from one another as possible. The political and economic framework of the European Union, which has evolved since 1958 to achieve the economic possibilities of unifying this natural economic unit, is naturally the focus of Part I. To prepare readers, we first describe the abbreviations and acronyms that are used by the European Union officials and present the chronology of the European Union's development since 1945. Two maps then show the current (1997) political status of the economies of Europe with respect to the European Union and their relative economic status in terms of per capita incomes. These illustrate very effectively that economics alone does not explain either the past development or the present concerns of the European Union and the economies of Europe. The underlying economic logic of the EU's mode of operation is examined from an economist's point of view in the individual chapters. These take up the economic developments in the period 1945 to 1958 that led to the formation of the European Economic Community; the logic of the customs union leading into a single market by the end of 1992, the budget difficulties for the EEC that emerged over this period; the origins, growth, and eventual reform of the Common Agricultural Policy; the repeated attempts to move toward a permanent regime of fixed exchange rates within an economic area subjected to repeated external shocks and internal stresses; and the efforts to resolve these difficulties in its external relations with the rest of the world. Time and again, we will see the compromises that have had to be made with the forces of political separatism as the EU has evolved.

Part II, then, tries to illuminate the political and economic diversity of Europe by reexamining the post World War II economic history of the major states and groups of minor states. European readers take these adversarial positions for granted, imbued as they are with the knowledge of centuries of distinctive national development for their particular nation. American readers seem increasingly ignorant of the significance of past European developments and the difficulty with which ethnic animosities have been subsumed into the national political entities now governing in Europe. Non-American and non-West-European readers will find many interesting analogies to their own concerns with respect to economic integration at a regional level and resistance to disruptions from the global marketplace. Each member state of the European Union has its own, overriding, domestic priorities in order to maintain its internal unity and the legitimacy of its government. Understanding the different concerns of the constituent member states is essential for comprehending the motivation of the European Union's policies and for appreciating the extent of its accomplishments to date. Moreover, the economic logic of European unification is viewed quite differently by each current member state of the European Union, as well as by each potential member. Part II attempts to lay bare these differences, using the approach of economic history to analyze the political economy of each constituency. It begins with "the problem of Germany" and continues by dealing with the concerns of the other three major countries as they have come to terms with the increased economic influence of Germany and their own reduced political power in international affairs. The remaining countries of Europe are then divided into groups depending on their economic relationship to the European Union: Belgium, Luxembourg, the Netherlands, and Denmark form one group of small, open, high-income countries; Ireland, Greece, Portugal, and Spain form another group of small, traditionally rather closed, and relatively low-income countries; the European Free Trade Agreement countries as of 1990 are then divided into those that entered the EU in 1995—Austria, Finland, and Sweden—and those that did not—Iceland, Norway, and Switzerland. Turkey, the perpetual applicant that is continually rebuffed, is included in the last group. The final chapter deals with the next wave of potential entrants, divided into the Mediterranean islands of Malta and Cyprus and the transition economies of Central and Eastern Europe.

The basic issue that confronts the EU at each step of its evolution is whether to go deeper or wider—whether to intensify the economic and political integration of the existing set of members or to expand the possibilities of economic expansion and political influence by increasing the number of members. The possibilities for progress in either direction are now greater than ever before, which makes the choice even more difficult. All the factors that have entered the decisions made in the past have to be reexamined more intensely than ever, if we Americans and other non-Europeans are to appreciate the significance of the European actions over the coming years.

The authors wish to acknowledge the help of many individuals and institutions in formulating and presenting the material that follows. Barbezat benefited from his time at the European University Institute in Florence, made possible by a Jean Monnet Fellowship and a grant from the German Marshall Fund. Neal's early experience as a staff economist with the Organization for Economic Cooperation and Development (OECD) has been supplemented by the monthly briefings provided to members of "Team Europe" by the U.S. Delegation of the European Commission in Washington, D.C. The Statistics Directorate of the OECD has granted permission to use their detailed data available on diskettes only for the national comparisons that are presented in Part II. Students at Illinois and Amherst have commented on early versions of most of Part I and, at Illinois, on the lectures that eventually became Part II. Janice Hunter was especially helpful in collecting material and then suggesting how it could be presented most effectively. The anonymous referees for Oxford University Press were very constructive in their suggestions and the editorial efforts of Kenneth MacLeod were exceptional. Colleagues have read and commented on several draft chapters, notably Jeremiah Sullivan at Illinois, Henry Gemery at Colby College, Luciano Pezzolo at the University of Venice, and especially Nick Crafts at The London School of Economics and Political Science for his comments on Part II. Finally, Margaret (Peg) Neal read, proofed, and criticized the entire text to make it as comprehensible as possible to non-economists and non-specialists.

August 1997   L. N.
                                                                                  D. B.

Abbreviations and Acronyms

ACP	African, Caribbean, and Pacific countries
APEC	Asia Pacific Economic Cooperation
ASEAN	Association of Southeast Asian Nations
BLEU	Belgium-Luxembourg Economic Union
CAP	Common Agricultural Policy
CEEC (1948–52)	Committee for European Economic Cooperation
CEEC (post 1989)	Central and East European Countries
CEN	European Standardization Committee
CENELEC	European Electrotechnical Standardization Committee
CET	Common External Tariff
CFI	Court of First Instance
CFP	Common fisheries policy
CFSP	Common Foreign and Security Policy
Coreper	Committee of Permanent Representatives
CSCE	Conference on Security and Cooperation in Europe
DG	Directorate-General
EAGGF	European Agricultural Guarantee and Guidance Fund
EAP	Environmental Action Program
EBRD	European Bank for Reconstruction and Development
EC	European Community
ECB	European Central Bank
ECJ	European Court of Justice
ECSC	European Coal and Steel Community
ECU	European Currency Unit
EDC	European Defense Community
EEA	European Economic Area
EEC	European Economic Community
EFTA	European Free Trade Association
EIB	European Investment Bank
EIF	European Investment Fund
EMI	European Monetary Institute
EMS	European Monetary System
EMU	European Monetary Union
EPU	European Payments Union (1950–58)

EPU	European Political Union (1992 on)
ERM	Exchange Rate Mechanism
ERDF	European Regional Development Fund
ESCB	European System of Central Banks
ESF	European Social Fund
ESPRIT	European Strategic Program for Research and Development in Information Technology
EU	European Union
Euratom	European Atomic Energy Community
GATT	General Agreement on Tariffs and Trade
GDP	Gross Domestic Product
GNP	Gross National Product
IBRD	International Bank for Reconstruction and Development (World Bank)
IGC	Inter-Governmental Conference
IMF	International Monetary Fund
IMP	Integrated Mediterranean Program
JET	Joint European Torus
MCA	Monetary Compensation Amount
MEP	Member of the European Parliament
MFA	Multi-Fibre Arrangement
NATO	North Atlantic Treaty Organization
OECD	Organization for Economic Cooperation and Development
OEEC	Organization for European Economic Cooperation
PHARE	Poland and Hungary: Aid for Reconstruction of the Economy
QMV	Qualified Majority Vote
SAD	Single Administrative Document
SAP	Social Action Program
SDR	Special Drawing Right
SEA	Single European Act
TACIS	Technical Assistance to the Commonwealth of Independent States
TEU	Treaty of European Union
VAT	Value added tax
VER	Voluntary export restraint
WEU	Western European Union

Chronology of the European Union

January 1, 1948: Trade agreement among Belgium, Netherlands, and Luxembourg creates Benelux.

April 16, 1948: Creation of the Organization for European Economic Cooperation (in 1960 to become the Organization for Economic Cooperation and Development, OECD)

May 7–10, 1948: Congress of Europe met in the Hague.

April 4, 1949: Creation of the Council of Europe and the signing of the North Atlantic Treaty (NATO).

May 9, 1950: Robert Schuman, France's Minister of Foreign Affairs, called for integration in European coal and steel sectors.

September 19, 1950: Creation of the European Payments Union (EPU) to aid trade liberalization and make European currencies convertible.

April 18, 1951: Creation of the European Coal and Steel Community (ECSC) with members France, Germany, Benelux, and Italy. Entered force on July 25, 1951.

June 1 and 2, 1955: Messina Conference held, setting into motion the move toward multisectoral European integration.

March 25, 1957: Treaty of Rome signed, establishing the European Economic Community with same members as the ECSC. In addition, the European Atomic Energy Community (Euratom) was created. Both came into force on January 1, 1958.

January 4, 1960: Creation of the European Free Trade Association (EFTA) with members United Kingdom, Denmark, Sweden, Norway, Portugal, Austria, and Switzerland. (Iceland joined in 1970 and Finland became a full member in 1986.)

January 29, 1963: General de Gaulle vetoed United Kingdom's membership application.

July 20, 1963: Yaoundé Convention signed between the Community and eighteen mainly French-speaking African states.

September 12, 1963: Association Agreement signed between the Community and Turkey, coming into force September 1, 1964.

April 8, 1965: Merger Treaty signed, combining the Euratom, ECSC, and the EEC into the European Community with a common Council and Commission. Came into force on July 1, 1967.

July 6, 1965: France boycotted discussions concerning Common Agricultural Policy financing.

January 29, 1966: France returned, after the Luxembourg Compromise, and majority voting replaced unanimity on issues affecting a country's vital interests.

December 18 and 19, 1967: France once again opposed U.K. membership and vetoed any resumption of negotiations on the accession of the United Kingdom.

July 1, 1968: Common customs tariff introduced and the last internal customs duties were eliminated (18 months before the deadline).

September 24, 1969: Arusha Agreement signed between the Community and three English-speaking East African States.

April 22, 1970: Luxembourg Treaty signed creating the own-resource finance system.

January 1, 1971: Second Yaoundé Convention signed between the Community and nineteen African, Caribbean and Pacific (ACP) countries. Came into force January 31, 1975.

June 23, 1971: The six member states reached agreement on the conditions for U.K. membership.

October 28, 1971: Majority vote for accession in the British House of Commons.

January 18, 1972: *Ode to Joy* from Beethoven's Ninth Symphony chosen as the anthem of the EC.

January 22, 1972: Treaty signed on the Accession of Denmark, Ireland, Norway and the United Kingdom.

September 25, 1972: Referendum in Norway rejected EC membership.

December 19, 1972: Association Treaty signed between the EC and Cyprus, coming into force June 1, 1973.

January 1, 1973: Denmark (including Greenland), Ireland, and the United Kingdom became full EC members.

April 1, 1974: New British government pressed for new accession conditions pertaining to finances.

February 28, 1975: Lomé Convention signed between the EC and forty-six ACP states, coming into force April 1, 1976, and ending March 1, 1980.

May 11, 1975: Cooperation Agreement signed between the EC and Israel, coming into force November 1, 1978.

June 5, 1975: Referendum in United Kingdom achieved a majority on retaining membership.

April 25–27, 1976: Separate Cooperation Agreements signed by Tunisia, Algeria, and Morocco with the EC, all coming into force on November 1, 1978.

January 18, 1977: Cooperation Agreements signed between the EC and Egypt, Jordan, and Syria, coming into force in November 1, 1978.

May 3, 1977: Cooperation Agreement signed between the EC and Lebanon, coming into force in November 1978.

July 6 and 7, 1978: At the Bremen European Council, France and Germany presented a scheme for the European Monetary System (EMS).

December 4 and 5, 1978: The European Currency Unit (ECU) created.

March 13, 1979: The EMS replaced the leftover "currency snake." The United Kingdom remained outside the system.

May 28, 1979: Accession Treaty for Greece signed, coming into force on January 1, 1981.

June 7 and 10, 1979: First European Parliament elections by direct universal suffrage, with 410 members being elected.

October 31, 1979: Second Lomé Convention signed between the EC and fifty-eight ACP countries, covering the period March 1, 1980, to February 28, 1985.

April 2, 1980: Association Agreement signed between the EC and Yugoslavia, coming into force April 1, 1983, but later suspended.

January 1, 1981: Greece joined the EC.

June 17–19, 1983: Member states issued a declaration on "European Union" at the Stuttgart Summit. (Genscher-Colombo document served as basis.) Ten member states expressed their wish to move to a European Union.

February 14, 1984: Altiero Spinelli's draft Treaty for the European Union released and approved by the European Parliament.

June 25 and 26, 1984: Fontainbleau European Council set out conditions for the United Kingdom to receive rebates on EU contributions.

December 8, 1984: Third Lomé Convention signed between the EC and sixty-six ACP countries, covering the period May 1986 through February 1990.

June 12, 1985: Treaties on the accession of Spain and Portugal signed, coming into force January 1, 1986.

June 14, 1985: France, the Federal Republic of Germany, and Benelux started process to allow open borders among their countries (the Schengen agreement).

December 2–4, 1985: Based on the Lord Cockfield White Paper, member states agreed, at the Luxembourg Council, to eliminate trade and border barriers by drawing up a Single European Act.

January 1, 1986: Portugal and Spain became members of the EC.

January 21, 1986: Danish Parliament rejected the Single European Act. Other member states refused renegotiations. Single European Act passed Danish referendum by majority of 56.2 %.

February 17, 1986: Signing of the Single European Act (signed by the nine on the 17th and by Greece on the 28th).

March 29, 1988: The Cecchini Report on the Costs of Non-Europe released.

November 1, 1989: Start of the Court of First Instance.

June 14–16, 1989: Approval of the Delors Report on Economic and Monetary Union at the Madrid Summit.

November 9, 1989: Fall of the Berlin wall.

December 15, 1989: Fourth Lomé Convention signed between the EC and sixty-nine ACP countries.

December 18, 1989: Creation of the PHARE program (Poland and Hungary: Aid for Reconstruction of the Economy. Later extended to Bulgaria, Romania, Estonia, Latvia, Lithuania, Albania, Slovenia, the Czech Republic, Slovakia, and the Former Yugoslav Republic of Macedonia).

June 19, 1990: France, the Federal Republic of Germany, and Benelux signed the Schengen Agreement eliminating border checks for people.

July 1, 1990: First stage of economic and monetary union begun—removal of capital controls.

October 3, 1990: Unification Treaty between East and West Germany came into force.

April 15, 1991: Official establishment of the European Bank for Reconstruction and Development (EBRD).

October 14, 1991: Chancellor Kohl and President Mitterrand announced the creation of a combined Franco-German military force.

December 16, 1991: Association Agreements signed between the EC and Hungary, Poland, the Czech Republic, and Slovenia.

February 7, 1992: Treaty of European Union (TEU) signed in Maastricht.

May 2, 1992: Establishment of a European Economic Area (EEA) between EFTA and the EC.

June, 2, 1992: The Maastricht Treaty narrowly rejected (50.7% against) in Denmark.

September 20, 1992: France narrowly accepted ratification of the Maastricht Treaty with a 51.01 percent majority.

December 11 and 12, 1992: The twelve agreed on a compromise for Denmark's ratification of Maastricht.

January 1, 1993: The European internal market, goal of the SEA, officially declared.

February 15, 1993: EC Finance Ministers, while keeping the overall timetable of the EMU, agreed that member states need not fulfill the convergence criteria (debt less than 60% of GDP, deficit less than 3%, inflation under 2%) by the end of 1996.

May 18, 1993: Denmark passed ratification of Maastricht with a majority of 51.8 percent.

July 19, 1993: The Technical Assistance to the Commonwealth of Independent States and Georgia, TACIS, program adopted.

July and August, 1993: Crises in the EMS with massive currency speculation driving rates outside of the set bands.

August 2, 1993: EC finance ministers broaden the exchange rate bands from 2.5% to 15%.

January 1, 1994: The European Union officially begun. Stage II of the EMU began with the European Monetary Institute (EMI), headquartered in Frankfurt-am-Main, beginning operations. It is to help establish the pre-conditions for Stage III, coordinating central banks and establishing the European System of Central Banks.

January 1, 1994: The EEA came into force. Much tighter integration with the EFTA countries, Austria, Finland, Iceland, Norway, and Sweden.

June 12, 1994: Austria's referendum on joining the EU passed with a 66.3-percent majority.

June 24, 1994: Accession Treaties of Austria, Finland, Norway, and Sweden signed in Corfu.

July 15, 1994: Extraordinary summit called in Brussels to appoint Jacques Santer, prime minister of Luxembourg, as president of the European Commission, beginning January 1995.

October 16, 1994: Finland's referendum on joining the EU passed with a 56.9-percent majority.

November 13, 1994: Sweden's referendum on joining the EU passed with a 52.1-percent majority.

November 28, 1994: Norway's referendum on joining the EU lost with a 52.5 % majority. (EFTA continued, then, with members Switzerland, Norway, Iceland, and Liechtenstein)

December 6, 1994: Adoption of the "Leonardo da Vinci" vocational training program.

December 22, 1994: Executive Committee of the Schengen Agreement agreed in

Bonn to the elimination of border checks between the seven signatories (Germany, France, Benelux, Spain, and Portugal), starting March 26, 1995.

January 1, 1995: Austria, Finland and Sweden joined the European Union.

February 1, 1995: Europe Association Agreements enter into force with Bulgaria, Romania, and Czech and Slovak Republics.

March 6, 1995: Council adopted framework for trade and cooperation agreement with the Republic of Korea.

July 17, 1995: Euro-Mediterranean agreement signed with Tunisia. Cooperation Agreement signed with Vietnam.

July 26, 1995: Member states signed Europol Convention, the Convention on Customs Information Systems, and the Convention for the Protection of Communities' financial interests.

November 23, 1995: "Partnership Declaration" adopted at the end of the Euro-Mediterranean Conference.

December 3, 1995: EU and the United States signed new transatlantic agenda and joint action plan.

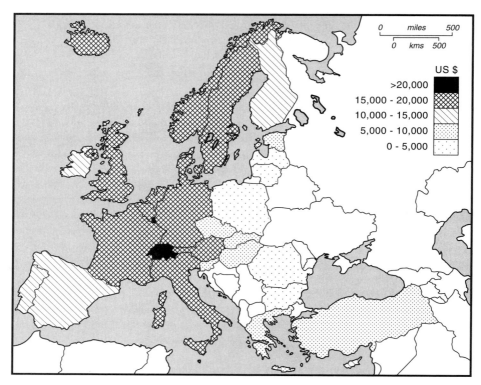

Map 1. The Per Capita Income Levels in Europe, 1992.

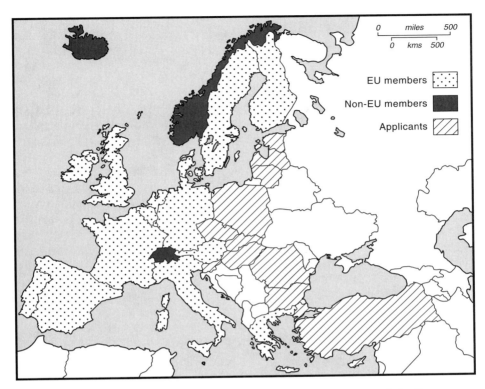

Map 2. Europe: The EU Members, Non-members, Next Members, and the Rest.

PART
I
The Economics of the European Union

CHAPTER 1

The European Union Today:
What Lies Behind It? What Lies Ahead?

World peace can be safeguarded only by creative efforts
which match the dangers that threaten it. The contribution
that an organized and living Europe can make to civilization
is indispensable to the maintenance of peace.

JEAN MONNET, French founder of the European Community, in his
Memoires (Paris, 1976)

[T]he attempt by the European Community, based in Brussels
and led by the French socialist Jacques Delors, [is] to spread
over Europe, like Camembert on a cracker, a superstate
featuring two French specialities—bureaucracy and
dirigisme.

GEORGE WILL, American columnist, in the *Washington Post,*
April 16, 1992

With the declaration of Maastricht in December 1991, the government leaders
of the member states of the European Union reaffirmed their commitment to
achieve a single European market by the end of 1992. On that basis, they also
agreed to move in well-defined stages toward European monetary union over
the remainder of the decade, as well as to follow better delimited paths for
achieving a workable political union. These are important events because they
promise that the economic goals set out in the Treaty of Rome in 1957, which
launched the European Community into existence, will finally be achieved before the year 2000. The EU leaders vowed as well to continue the struggle
toward political union, which has always been the underlying motivation for the
European Union. The chances of success here are less, but not so slight that
they can be dismissed.

THE IRONY OF SHATTERED ASSUMPTIONS

It is ironic, but perhaps not surprising, that the final achievement of the goals of the European Union should occur as the strategic assumptions that underlay their formation have been destroyed by the revolutions of 1989. One assumption was the permanent division of Germany; another was the viability of the Soviet Union as a military superpower opposing American economic power. No attention was paid to possible constraints imposed by the economic or military goals of other players beyond North America, Europe, and the Soviet Union. The limits of potential future membership seemed clear, defined by the number of nations that had accepted Marshall Plan aid as members of the Organization for European Economic Cooperation. The expansion of economic relations, including movements of goods, labor, and capital, was constrained to these countries as well. Now, all of these assumptions are shattered, and the strategy founded upon them is consequently in disarray, even as it appears to be on the verge of achieving its long-sought goals. It will be wonderful material for future economic historians to show how, as the leaders of the European Union approached their goal and had acquired the momentum and confidence necessary to take them the final few steps to achieve it, Central and Eastern Europe became the new center of attention. And it is even more ironic that one of the implicit assumptions of the European Community—the permanent division of Germany—surfaced and was quickly replaced by acceptance of the unification of East and West Germany.

The further breakup of the centrally planned economies of Central and Eastern Europe destroyed at one fell swoop the main economic, as well as political, assumptions on which the European Community had been constructed. This could have ended the initiative, because attention would now have to be devoted to expanding the European Union, instead of intensifying the economic and political relationships within it. Remarkably, it has had just the opposite effect: the incorporation of the former German Democratic Republic bodily within the Federal Republic of Germany expanded the size of the largest country within the EU and intensified the political will of all member countries to complete the Single European Act. The pressures for aid, trade, capital, and employment coming from the former Marxist economies of Eastern Europe reinforced the commitment to define the single Europe on the basis of the EU's current membership, thereby excluding any expansion until the Single Market was implemented at the end of 1992. When the first expansion did occur, it was confined to three neutral countries (Austria, Finland, and Sweden) that had long been among the wealthier nations of Western Europe and had already established intensive trading relationships with the existing members of the European Union.

It is still possible that mistakes from the distant past will be made again, or that policies carried over from the recent past will prove to be mistakes in the new political context. The Danish rejection of the Maastricht Treaty in their referendum in June 1992 was the first harbinger of the political recalculations that had to be made. The subsequent modifications that finally resulted in the ratification of the treaty to form the European Union as of November 1993 created an uneasy mixture of Europeanwide ideals and realistic accommodations to individual national concerns. The accession in 1995 of the three northern countries whose foreign trade was dominated by the German economy intensified the search for ways to reconcile widening with deepening. Widening requires major recasting of the operation of European Union institutions, which is the object of the Inter-Governmental Conference of 1996–97. Deepening requires achievement of the European Monetary Union by the deadline agreed on of January 1, 1999. The two objectives are clearly interdependent, but to make any progress on either, the negotiators in each endeavor have tried to exclude consideration of the other from their agenda.

At this point in the development of the European Union, it makes sense to review the underlying logic of its institutions, both economic and political, and to recapitulate the historical process by which a war-shattered Europe has managed, not only to recover, but also to revitalize and redirect its national economies and to set an example that nations around the world are now trying to imitate. It is necessary for a full comprehension of the European Union to analyze its economics, its politics, and its history.

HISTORICAL BACKGROUND

To gain a historical perspective on current developments and what they augur for the next ten years, it makes the most sense to start with World War II, the initial division of Germany, and with it the division of Europe into East and West. Our story about Europe 1992 and the European Monetary Union in 1999 and expansion of the European Union in the years beyond must begin with the partition of Germany among the four victorious Allies after World War II—the United States, the Soviet Union, Great Britain, and France. Partition was the result of the Allies' refusal to treat Germany as a sovereign state, a refusal maintained technically until 1991, when at last a formal peace treaty concluding World War II was made between the Allies and a German state. Moreover, the original intent of the Allies was to dismember Germany, as well as to deindustrialize, de-Nazify, and democratize it. Doing so, it was thought, would prevent repeating the mistake made after World War I, when a revolutionary government of Germany, always in danger of repudiation by the German nation, was treated by the Allies as the legitimate voice of a sovereign state. Refusal to repeat one mistake of history soon led to another. It is an irony of economics that it was too expensive for any of the victors to sustain the military occupation and partition of Germany. This was realized more rapidly, the more democratic the political system of the particular Allied Power: thus the United States and Great Britain rather quickly combined their zones into Bizonia, and when the French zone was joined to it a bit later, the modern Federal Republic of Germany came into existence. This forced the Russians to create the German Democratic Republic from their zone as a counterpart. The partition of Germany, in turn, led to the division of Europe.

The ultimate economic result of this division of Europe between the two superpowers was to cast Europe as a whole into an inferior position relative to both the United States and the Soviet Union. Quickly, compared with the length of time it had taken to acquire their empires, the West European states lost their colonies. The culminating event for this process was the Suez Crisis of 1956, when the French and British jointly with Israel tried to operate independently of either superpower to retain control of the Suez Canal. They failed to put down President Nasser of Egypt, but they did succeed in gaining the condemnation of both the United States and the Soviet Union. Thereafter, the pace of decolonization accelerated.

THE ECONOMICS OF EUROPEAN INTEGRATION

The bilateral, controlled trade patterns of France, Britain, Belgium, and the Netherlands with their colonies before World War II were permanently disrupted. In this regard, these states found themselves in a position analogous to that of Germany, whose trade with Eastern Europe had been severed irreparably, a result of the policies of the Soviet-bloc countries that insulated their centrally planned economies from foreign trade of any kind. Especially disrupting was the permanent cessation in the flow of agricultural products from Central and Eastern Europe to Western Europe. The Russian refusal to send grain from their zone to the U.S. zone in Germany made the costs of occupation very apparent to the Americans in a short time. The United States reversed its policy, replacing the Morgenthau Plan designed to destroy the German economy with the Marshall Plan designed to restore it. The economic miracles that took place in Europe after 1950 are easily associated with the success of the Marshall Plan.

But, it is well to remember that initially these economic miracles took place only in West Germany and Italy, the first two countries to lose their colonies, despite the distribution of Marshall Plan aid proportionally among the European participants, with much more going to Britain and France than to either Germany or Italy. Other European participants—the Netherlands, Belgium, France, and finally Great Britain—came into the virtuous circle of export surpluses, rising share of investment in GNP, and high, smooth growth rates only as they lost their respective colonies. These losses removed a drain on the domestic economy resulting from the costs of permanent overseas military establishments. The ex-colonies remained as markets for exports from the European countries, but now capital exports from the United States or Great Britain financed these purchases rather than capital exports from the former mother country. So two factors underlay the economic miracles—export-led growth and reduced military obligations.

EUROPEAN ECONOMIC COMMUNITY

The European Economic Community was formed by the Treaty of Rome (1957) and took effect in 1958. It can be seen, in this view of the economic history of

the 1950s, as a successful attempt by countries in Western Europe to institution-
alize and lock in the virtuous circle of export-led growth that they had discovered by responding to the force of circumstances in the aftermath of World War
II. The virtuous circle was in danger of being undermined if the Germans continued to import U.S. food and if the French continued to import U.S. machine
tools. For then the U.S. export surplus would ultimately match the import deficit
of the ex-colonies, and no export surplus would be left for Europe. It would be
better for the French to import their machinery and machine tools from Germany and the Germans their foodstuffs from France. This was accomplished
with a customs union. The benefits of the customs union were seen as *trade
creation* by eliminating tariff barriers with respect to each other and as *trade
diversion*—away from the United States, away from the Soviet Union, and away
from any other trading partners outside the customs union and toward each
other. Both factors, trade creation and trade diversion, worked to increase the
relative importance of trade within the customs union at the expense of previous
trade partners outside the customs union.

The original six members—France, Germany, Italy, Belgium, the Netherlands, and Luxembourg (the last three already joined in their minicustoms
union called Benelux)—found that they had created numerous high-value trade
opportunities by virtue of specializing in the production of goods that all wanted.
Within the sector of household appliances alone, one can cite such examples
as the appearance of Italian refrigerators, German coffee makers, French food
processors, and Belgian washing machines within middle-class homes throughout the EEC. Manufacturers within Europe also gained from economies of scale
and of agglomeration.

Surprisingly, the big losers among former trade partners were the former
colonies, not other industrialized countries. The Third World's share of the total
imports into the EU (including intra-EU trade) fell from 30 percent in 1958 to
18 percent in 1972 and stayed at 17.5 percent in 1985 even after absorbing the
effects of the two oil shocks of the 1970s. The share of imports from African,
Caribbean, and Pacific countries (known in Europe as the ACP), comprising
primarily the poorest of the former colonies, fell from just over 6 percent of all
imports in 1958 to less than 4 percent in 1972 and, despite successive
agreements to reverse this trend, sank to just over 3 percent in 1985.

INTERNAL–EXTERNAL DYNAMICS

Think of a circle representing the EEC. Now divide it into four quarters representing the four economic participants—France and Italy as high-tariff countries, West
Germany and Benelux as low-tariff economic units (neither can properly be described as a "country" at that time) (Figure 1.1a). The intent of the customs union
proposed was to eliminate all internal tariffs within the circle and to strike a common external tariff of 15 percent—the average level of the high French and Italian
tariffs and the low German and Benelux tariffs (Figure 1.1b). Note the political
goal that drove this: success in economic cooperation would lead to increasing political cooperation and eventual regaining of international clout. However, the Dil-

(a)

High and low external tariffs; bilateral countertrade internally

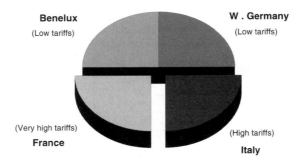

(b)

(c)

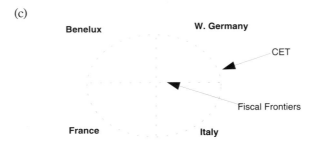

Figure 1.1. Internal and external tariffs among the original six countries of the European Economic Community. (a) Before the Customs Union. (b) The plan for the customs union. CET, common external tariff, = 15%; no internal tariffs. (c) The reality by the mid-1980s. CET = 5%; fiscal frontiers = 5%.

lon Round (1960–62), the Kennedy Round (1964–67), and the Tokyo Round (1973–79)—multilateral trade negotiations under the auspices of the General Agreement on Tariffs and Trade that were initiated by the United States—successively reduced the size of the common external tariff, while the discrepancies of value added tax (VAT) among the sovereign member nation-states led to new fiscal frontiers. By the mid-1980s, the average common external tariff was down to less than 5 percent while the average cost of moving industrial goods across national fiscal frontiers within the EU was nearly 5 percent (Figure 1.1c). The customs union had been eroded on the outside and corroded on the inside!

Another phenomenon that changed the nature of the customs union from its original concept was the import of capital from the United States and Great Britain, as a substitute for the import of goods. This capital came primarily into Benelux and West Germany, whose tariff barriers were the lowest within the Common Market. Within Germany, the capital went primarily to the American zone, which explains the new growth center stretching from Frankfurt to Munich. Along with the capital, labor was also imported from abroad. But the labor came not from the United States or Great Britain but from the ex-colonies, Spain and Portugal for France, Eastern Europe and then Turkey for West Germany, and a combination of these sources for the Benelux countries. (The expansion of industry in northern Italy was facilitated by the immigration of labor from the south of Italy, arguably a different culture if not a different country.) Each country had its own source of guest workers, and these workers were not allowed free movement within the Common Market. Their presence meant that, although workers from the member countries could move freely within the entire EU, such movements became less and less important. Most of the few Germans living in France, for example, are the wives of their French husbands, and most of the few French living in Germany are the wives of their German husbands.

SINGLE EUROPEAN ACT

The successive oil shocks of the mid- and late-1970s had exposed the political weakness of the European Community, because each country followed its own strategy and rejected any idea of cooperating jointly to exploit North Sea oil or to counter the cartel power of the Organization of Petroleum Exporting Countries (OPEC). Expansion of the European Community, which had grown to nine members by 1973, was halted indefinitely. Greece was accepted in 1980 to prevent a relapse to military rule, but the entry of Spain and Portugal was delayed until 1986 despite increased trade and association with each. By the mid-1980s, however, all of the member states were in bad shape, with very high unemployment rates, stagnating labor forces, lower investment ratios, and slow rates of growth. Euro-sclerosis seemed to have set in. The new industrial revolution in computers and telecommunications had bypassed Western Europe.

In 1985, the Commission of the EU, which is the executive branch of the EU in a sense, although it might better be described as the Eurocracy, issued a policy document known as the Single Europe White Paper. This followed the initiative taken by Jacques Delors, the new president of the Commission, and it proposed legislation to the Council, the legislative branch of the EU, to remove the existing nontariff barriers to trade within the Community. Some three-hundred specific barriers were identified that would have to be removed by common agreement. In 1987 the Single European Act (SEA) was passed by the Council, by now representing twelve countries, committing the EU to passing 279 separate proposals, most by a qualified majority rule.

This is not a simple rule—fifty-four of the seventy-six votes distributed among the twelve members of the Council had to be in favor. The four major countries each had ten votes; Spain eight; Belgium, Greece, the Netherlands, and Portugal each five; Denmark and Ireland three apiece; and even Luxembourg got two. The design was to permit any two major countries to block a proposal if they could get one of the small countries to vote with them. Normal matters required only a simple majority, and, as matters progressed on accomplishing Europe 1992, approval of many measures came without formal votes. Once the measures were enacted as "directives" by the Council, however, it remained up to the individual countries to implement them by passing the required domestic legislation to enforce them. This has required constant monitoring effort by the European Commission, which issues regular updates on the progress made or not on each aspect of the Single Market.

What are the nontariff barriers and how are they being reduced?

Government Procurement

The government sector in EU countries is much larger than in the United States. Government units and the various government monopolies—rails, post, telephone, airlines, as well as the military—purchase their supplies from domestic companies within each country to the greatest extent possible. The SEA requires member governments to open up their purchases to other member countries. The United States wants them to open bidding to U.S. companies as well, and this was one of the main agenda items for the Uruguay Round of GATT negotiations completed in 1992, which set up the World Trade Organization.

Technical Standards

There remains much room for further economies of scale in both production and marketing if technical standards are uniform across the EU. The twelve member countries had eighteen different electrical plugs! Uniform standards are still being worked out product line by product line in a lengthy, ongoing process. The United States asked to be informed and to be allowed to sit in on these discussions at industry study level, but the Europeans wanted to get their act together first before allowing any U.S. contribution to the discussions. Nevertheless, most U.S. companies already doing business in Europe are able to keep abreast of the discussions and proposals. The conceptual breakthrough has been to allow products that meet the technical standards of the country of production to be sold without government restrictions in other member countries. The issue, then, comes down to what the minimum acceptable standards are across all countries, and this varies of course by product. Moreover, the issue arises whether the procedure used by a country to set minimum standards is acceptable to the rest of the EU.

Local Content and Rules of Origin

Each country now has various local content laws requiring foreign firms operating within its boundaries to buy fixed percentages of their production supplies from domestic firms. The most recent example was a new rule of origin for computer chips so that they can move freely in the EU only if they have been finished in the EU. This is directed mainly against Japan, but some U.S. firms are also caught in the cross fire.

Physical Barriers

Internal customs stations and passport checkpoints will be eliminated and efforts made to link up transportation routes across national borders. Examples are the construction of the Chunnel to connect France and England, completed in 1995, and to standardize Spanish railroad gauge with French so that trains can move freely across that border. The French autoroutes are finally connected with the Belgium autoroutes, although high French tolls on their superhighways still divert most truck and tourist traffic through southern Germany and Switzerland. Border checkpoints for plant or animal diseases were eliminated inside the EU by the end of 1992, and replaced by checks at collection points within each country. The twelve EC inspectors then employed to monitor processing of beef were, as a result, unable to detect the prevalence of the mad cow disease in British beef at the time.

Fiscal Frontiers

These have been left until the last. The intent is to narrow the ranges of VAT rates to the point that individual states will feel no difficulty in letting goods pass freely, much as cigarette tax rates in U. S. states can vary without states putting up checkpoints, and sales tax rates can also vary but not enough to make it worthwhile for everybody in Illinois to shop in Indiana, for example, or everyone in California to shop in Oregon. The Common Market has a very long way to go in reducing these fiscal barriers. This has been the major sticking point, even though France made a major move to lower its VAT rates to come within the guidelines proposed by the EU Commission. In contrast, Britain needed to raise some of its value added taxes and to make more goods liable to the tax. Denmark and Greece were, and are, the most out of line with respect to their VAT rates, but these countries are too small to resist on their own. It is useful to note that this entire problem could be solved if the European Union simply adopted a rule of collecting VAT at point of origin, rather than destination, as economists originally recommended. Differing tax rates then might create a significant movement of particular industries to the low-tax countries of the EU, but this would be good for increasing the movement of labor and capital across the national frontiers—one of the original goals.

In the summer of 1991, it was announced that an informal agreement had been reached that fiscal frontiers would be eliminated by each country imposing a minimum VAT rate of 15 percent on the goods it chooses to tax. Countries can impose a rate up to any ridiculously high level they wish, but the thought is that they will want to lower these rather quickly to a level close to the minimum rate. Countries can still choose which goods to tax, but if they do tax a particular good, it must be at the minimum rate of 15 percent. As is usual with these kinds of sweeping changes, a prolonged transition period was agreed upon in Maastricht for those countries with categories of goods in low ranges of 2 and 4 percent to either eliminate the VAT entirely or raise it to 15 percent. Nevertheless, the intent was to eliminate fiscal frontiers by the end of 1992 so that pressure would be placed on the individual member states to converge their VAT rates to common levels and to common coverages. In fact, the controls at borders were replaced with controls at distribution centers within each country. These modernized the ability of national tax authorities to monitor the collection of their respective VAT and, ironically but predictably, reduced the competitive pressures to converge their respective rates.

THE POLITICS OF EUROPE 1992

What explains the successes of the EU in reaching agreement against what had seemed until 1990 to be insuperable obstacles? The answer can be broken into two parts: first, a modification of the functional rules that had previously governed EU decision making; and second, a realization that the realities of competition in the global marketplace meant that European firms could no longer be protected by national means alone. The interplay between what political scientists refer to as functionalism and as realism is essential to comprehend if one is to understand the way the European Union has progressed throughout its history. We will return to this distinction in describing and analyzing the structure of the institutions of the European Union. But first it is useful to apply it to the creation of the Single Market by the end of 1992.

The Single European Act of 1987 had a clear "functional" aspect. The EU Commission opted to break down the impediments to internal trade into 279 specific items and to build up momentum by getting member states to agree on many of the easy items first. This would create pressure to achieve agreement on the few remaining obstacles. Basically, France and Great Britain would always take opposing positions; Germany would side with the one to whom the particular issue meant the most or make some commitment to buy off the opposition of the other. That process strategy was at risk for nearly a year—November 1989 to October 1990—because Germany was more concerned then with its own reunification than with settling trade squabbles between the French and British.

There was a "realist" aspect as well to the eventual completion of the Single Market, however. Once the reconstruction of East Germany was well under way and proved to be considerably more expensive than imagined originally, the Germans renewed their commitment to completing the Single Market. This move was interpreted politically as an example of a much larger and politically more significant Germany starting to exercise increased clout. But it might as well be interpreted in narrower economic terms as Germany's effort to get the rest of the EU to share the enormous costs of reconstructing East Germany, of removing Soviet troops, and of opening trade relations with Poland, Hungary, and Czechoslovakia. This move also explains the resistance of the EU to reform its notorious Common Agricultural Policy more quickly or more substantively. Starting from a position of a net loser with respect to that system of agricultural price supports, Germany has over the years become a net gainer. Now with the revitalization of East German agriculture a priority in the reconstruction process that is under way, Germany stands to be a large net gainer if the present rules are allowed to stand.

COMMON AGRICULTURAL POLICY

Note that all the 279 proposals mentioned above had to do mostly with nonagricultural issues. The EU's Common Agricultural Policy (CAP) remained intact and largely unaffected by the SEA. The CAP of the EU has always been a problem for the United States, and it will be a real problem for Eastern Europe. As with the Single Market, there are "functional" and "realist" aspects to the CAP. For many years the CAP has been the major element in the EU's budget and the functional area where European policy cooperation has been carried out most thoroughly. For this reason, it is the single most important part of the functional role played by the EU in the evolutionary process that is intended to culminate in a democratically united Europe. It is the main part of the *acquis communautaire* that the EU insists be accepted by each new member. For countries with a relatively important agricultural sector, the CAP has been a "real" benefit as well, maintaining prices favorable to even the least efficient farming countries.

The standard supply-demand diagram of economics illustrates how the price support policies of the EU maintain high domestic prices of most agricultural commodities in face of lower world prices, and how the effects of the variable levy tariff that the EU puts on agricultural imports imposes deadweight losses on both producers and consumers within the EU. (These concepts are developed in detail in Chapter 6.) The size of this transfer from taxpayers and consumers to producers is substantial and much larger than in the case of the United States. Agricultural subsidies within the EU create overproduction of 19 percent in agriculture as a whole, while U.S. subsidies create only 7 percent overproduction. As inefficient and costly as the EU's agricultural policy is, it has been successful politically and its costs continue to become lower relative to total GDP as agriculture declines in relative importance within the European economy.

Empirical studies show that the CAP redistributes large amounts of income to farmers in the EU, mostly from consumers and some from taxpayers. This transfer is economically inefficient. The mean estimate of the deadweight loss is around 1 percent of GDP of the EU. The distribution of this loss among the member countries is not uniform. The heaviest loser is Great Britain, followed by Italy and Germany. France may lose as well. Ireland clearly gains while Denmark and the Netherlands probably do. The later members (Greece, Spain, and Portugal) are clearly gainers but their access to these gains was phased in gradually. The newest members (Austria, Finland, and Sweden) are net losers since their price supports were even higher than those maintained in the EU. Moreover, with their relatively high per capita incomes overall, they were forced to absorb these losses immediately. Such is the political force of the CAP in driving the EU's progress.

For the rest of the world, the CAP has turned the EU into a net exporter of most temperate-zone commodities. This depresses and destabilizes world prices and makes production in other countries less profitable. It also keeps less developed countries (LDC) from focusing on improvements in agriculture and reduces profits of other exporters. The effect is strongest in wheat, barley, corn, rye, millet, and sorghum. In particular, the CAP means that Eastern Europe will have no market in the foreseeable future for export of their agricultural commodities to Western Europe.

EUROPEAN MONETARY UNION

Under pressure from the United States, the European recipients of Marshall Plan aid agreed to participate in the European Payments Union established in 1950. This allowed for multilateral settlements of the net amounts owed by countries in overall trade deficits to the benefit of countries in overall surplus. The need for convertible foreign reserves, gold or dollars at the time, by each country was thereby reduced. The expansion of trade among the participants must have owed something to the relative ease of making settlements compared with dealing with the sterling or dollar areas. When the European Payments Union was wrapped up in 1958, all the participants made their currencies convertible at fixed, but adjustable, exchange rates as members of the International Monetary Fund. (However, they all kept tight controls on capital movements until the 1990s.) Trade continued to expand rapidly in the following period and especially among members of the European Economic Community.

When the era of fixed exchange rates came to an end in 1971 and all hope of returning to it was forsaken in 1973, the closest European trading partners of Germany tried to maintain fixed parity with the deutsche mark to maintain their beneficial trade relationships with the richest economy in Europe. Failure to do so was associated with marked reductions in growth rates of both national output and foreign trade. Resumption of a regime of relatively fixed exchange rates occurred with establishing the European Monetary System in 1978. This allowed members' currencies to fluctuate with respect to each other within a range of ±2.5 percent and provided for periodic readjustments of the central rates if some currencies were unable to stay within this range. While growth rates of trade and output again fell for all countries concerned in the second oil shock of 1979–80, there was sufficient flexibility in the design of the Exchange Rate Mechanism that the system survived. When prosperity returned in the mid-1980s, readjustments in central rates no longer seemed necessary. The association of fixed exchange rates with expanding trade and increased prosperity is therefore firmly fixed in the minds of most European politicians and their electoral publics. However, professional economists are not persuaded that the connection is theoretically sound, much less empirically proven.

Despite the concerns of economists, political imperatives drove the participants to maintain tight limits on the fluctuations of their currencies relative to the deutsche mark even through the shock of German reunification in the early 1990s. To lock in the perceived benefits, both economic and political, of fixed exchange rates with each other, the majority of the member states agreed to commit to achieving full monetary union by 1999 in the Treaty on European Union, better known as the Maastricht Treaty. To allay the doubts of its feasibility by participants in the foreign exchange markets and especially of German bankers and economists, strict criteria were laid down for countries wishing to join the common currency. They had to keep the price of their money stable with respect to that of the deutsche mark however one cares to measure the price of money, whether by interest rates, inflation rates, or exchange rates. As these are all related in the long run, they are redundant criteria in effect and have been largely achieved in the general disinflation that has occurred worldwide since the early 1980s. More difficult has been the second set of criteria designed to limit the potential quantity of money required by member governments. These are the famous Maastricht limits on governments of 3 percent maximum flows of deficits and 60 percent maximum stocks of debt as a percentage of their country's GDP.

In the face of sustained high rates of unemployment and sluggish growth rates, the concerned governments have deliberately given up using the tools of Keynesian fiscal policy to expand their economies. These were tools that seemed to work incredibly well in the golden age of economic growth from 1950 to 1973, the same period when fixed exchange rates were the rule. Now governments feel they cannot use them until they have managed to achieve a Europeanwide common currency, the "euro." This may be the final irony, of achieving, or trying to achieve, long-sought goals when the assumptions that underlay them have been shattered.

EXTERNAL RELATIONS

The Fourth Lomé Agreement between the EU and the African, Caribbean, and Pacific (ACP) countries was signed in 1989 and extended from the normal five years of the previous agreements to last ten years. These enlarged the number of third world countries given preferential treatment and increased the variety of goods that could be exported by ACP countries to the EU without bumping into quota restrictions. But the agreements still provided only export revenue insurance by the EU to its third world trading partners, not the production subsidies they provide their own farmers and manufacturers. Moreover, strict quotas are retained on the kind of labor-intensive manufactured goods that are the natural first step toward industrialization in third world countries. In other words, the terms that the EU offers the third world do not augur well for the terms they will offer Poland, Hungary, and Czechoslovakia.

Members of the European Free Trade Association (EFTA) (consisting of Iceland, Norway, Sweden, Finland, Austria, Liechtenstein, and Switzerland up to 1995, and now comprising only Iceland, Norway, Liechtenstein, and Switzerland) asked for special treatment and obtained reciprocal trading access under the terms of the treaty that established the European Economic Area. Even so, four of them applied for membership and were eventually accepted by the EU after extensive negotiations. All except Norway then entered on the terms set by the EU. Malta and Cyprus have both applied for membership and the EU Commission has considered their cases seriously, but recommended delays in action. Referendums in Norway, Switzerland, and Iceland have kept Norway (narrowly) out of the EU for the time being and Switzerland even out of the European Economic Area, while Iceland treasures its preferential access to the fishing grounds in its territorial waters. Meanwhile, Turkey is getting increasingly impatient about being kept out, although it appears it will be kept out indefinitely. Even when the most expansionist of the Eurocrats in the EU Commission talk about future members, they mention many countries, including even Bulgaria and parts of what was Yugoslavia, but they do not mention Turkey.

EUROPE'S DRIVE TO UNITY

The economic successes of the European Common Market in the 1960s strengthened European nationalism rather than European federalism, as the European visionaries of the 1950s had hoped. In other words, the functional structure of the European Union, when confronted with the economic reality of the "Golden Age" of economic growth from 1950 to 1973, ended up strengthening the reliance of European nations on their independent policies. The failures of the European nations in trying to confront the economic crises of the 1970s and early 1980s with their individual, separate experiments in national economic policies led to a renewed effort at economic cooperation through the institutional framework of the European Union. This began with the European Monetary System in 1979, gained considerable momentum with the Single European Act of 1987, and culminated with the Maastricht Treaty of 1992 aiming to create European Monetary Union by 1997 or 1999. The shock of German reunification, however, disrupted the momentum for monetary union with crises in the summers of 1992 and 1993. These episodes reflected once again the obstacles that "realistic" economic forces place in the path toward European political union, even as new institutions such as the European Monetary Institute are put into place (beginning January 1994). In such periods, it is a characteristic of the European Union to widen its membership, which may help explain why expansion has typically occurred with two or more entrants at once rather than individual applicants coming in one at a time.

From an outsider's perspective, what is noteworthy about each halting point in the drive for European unity is that the previous achievements remain in place until forward momentum can be resumed. Part of this is by design: there is no provision in the successive treaties for a member state to withdraw and financing of the European Union has always been from its "own resources," rather than contributions from the members. Jean Monnet compared the "functionalist" structure of the European Economic Community's institutions to the raft named Kon-Tiki, which the Norwegian anthropologist Thor Heyerdahl built and used in the 1950s to show how Polynesians could have drifted on ocean currents to arrive in South America. When the economic and political currents are right, the EU moves closer to unity; when they cease or storms arise, the institutional structure remains, ready to resume its course eventually.

THE INSTITUTIONS OF THE EU: HOW TO LOCK IN PROGRESS

The prototype for the institutional structure of the EU was the European Coal and Steel Community (ECSC), to be described in Chapter 2. The economic realist would have dealt with the problem of reviving Europe's coal and steel industries for the purposes of peacetime reconstruction by reviving the International Steel Cartel of the 1930s. It had worked well then, it could work again. The political realist would have noted the danger of financing a potentially revanchist Germany and insisted on control of German coal and steel by Allied powers. Monnet's contribution was to propose a supranational organization, with its "own resources" drawn from its base of activities, its own governance structure representing the political parties concerned, but with a High Authority that prepared, enacted, and executed policy independently of the separate private and public interests involved. It had its "own resources" as well, a levy on the coal and steel output of each member state up to 1 percent of its value. Since 1965, this has been passed on to the European Community, although in the 1990s the ECSC has been allowed to keep some of it to help finance increased subsidies to these declining sectors. The apparent success of the functionalist European Coal and Steel Community was the basis for the European Economic Community agreed upon in the Treaty of Rome in 1957 and the precise model for the European Atomic Energy Community (Euratom) founded at the same time. Its governance structure was incorporated into the European Economic Community's, while its operating structure remained intact until the Treaty of Brussels in 1965, which combined it with the executive branches of the EEC and Euratom.

Realist cynics might argue that the energy supply problem was solved not by the ECSC, however, but by the increased use of cheap petroleum imported from the Middle East. When it began in 1950, coal accounted for 83 percent of the member states' energy consumption and petroleum for only 14 percent. By 1966, coal accounted for under 40 percent and petroleum for 45 percent. Regardless, the ECSC has persisted as a constituent part of the EU to the present day, maintaining a bulwark of advocacy for continued state subsidies to declining coal and steel sectors despite the EU's attempts to coordinate reductions and eventual elimination of such subsidies.

The distinction between these two views of the history of the European Union to date, the functionalist and the realist, is a useful way also to examine the institutions of the European Union. Recognizing that their intent is to form the functionalist framework for eventual political unification, we can categorize the first set of institutions as constituting either a legislative, an executive, or a judicial branch of the structure intended eventually to govern all of Europe. The second set of institutions are more ad hoc, reflecting the intermediate steps that have to be taken by the EU while it maintains a useful economic role for the mutual benefit of all European states.

POLITICAL INSTITUTIONS

The most visible institution and the one with the most promise for the future political development of a united Europe is the *European Parliament.* Elected by direct universal suffrage since 1979, the members of the European Parliament (MEPs) represent specific electoral districts within the European Union, but once elected (elections take place every five years) they arrange themselves by political affinity rather than by nationality. Those seated farthest to the left are the most liberal and those seated farthest to the right are the most conservative, in common with the seating arrangements in most European parliaments. Representation of each country is roughly proportional to its population, but it is undeniable that the smaller states are overrepresented. For example, before the reunification of Germany, while West Germany had the largest population in the European Union (61 million), it elected the same number of MEPs as France (56 million), Britain (57 million) and Italy (57 million), namely 81 for each of the largest four member nations. Luxembourg (1/3 million), the smallest nation by far, had 6 MEPs. The same rate of representation would have entitled West Germany to 183 MEPs! When the population of united Germany approached 80 million and elections were to be held in June 1994, something clearly had to be done if the European Parliament was to remain even symbolic of the democratic possibilities for a united Europe. The solution agreed on was to increase the members from each country except the smallest three, Denmark (remained at 16), Ireland (remained at 15) and Luxembourg (remained at 6). Germany's representation increased by far the most, from 81 to 99, which was close to its proportional increase in population after reunification with East Germany. The other three large nations, however, also increased their representation, from 81 to 87 each. Spain went up to 64 from 60 MEPs, the Netherlands to 31 from 25, and the remaining three countries—Belgium, Greece, and Portugal—each received one more MEP to have 25 apiece instead of their previous 24. The overall membership was thereby increased from 518 (compare to the fixed number of 435 in the U.S. House of Representatives) to 567. How this will be changed with the accession of even more new member states than the three who joined in 1995 on will be determined in the Inter-Governmental Conference of 1996–97 so that new European Parliamentary districts can be drawn up in time for the 1999 elections. In the meantime, Austria was allotted 21 seats, Finland 16 and Sweden 22, to increase the total number to 626. The total number of seats currently available in the new building that houses the Parliament when it is in Brussels is 703, which gives both functionalists and realists something to ponder.

While the European Parliament is elected like a legislature, debates and votes like a legislature, and in every way seems like a legislature, it cannot be said to really be the legislative branch of the European Union. Rather, it is the functionalist version of the legislative branch, acting out all the forms of legislative behavior without having any real power except to delay and annoy the "real" legislators for the European Union. These are the fifteen representatives of the fifteen member states who constitute the *Council of the European Union,* or *Council of Ministers.* The Council consists of the ministers from each member government who have responsibility in their country for the matters being decided upon by the European Union. For example, agriculture ministers attend the sessions when farm policies are being determined, environment ministers when environmental issues are discussed, and foreign ministers when most general matters concerning how the European Union should proceed are voted upon. Voting is weighted according to the economic size of the member states. Before the expansion of the European Union to include Austria, Finland, and Sweden, the total number of votes was set at seventy-six. Each of the four largest countries had ten votes; Spain had eight; Belgium, Greece, the Netherlands and Portugal had five each; Denmark and Ireland three each; and Luxembourg two. With the expansion, Austria and Sweden each received four votes and Finland three. The total of eighty-seven votes possible means that a qualified majority is sixty-two. The reader can work out the various combinations of countries required to constitute a "blocking minority" of twenty-six votes. Determining the rule for a qualified majority vote (QMV in the literature) is one of the primary objectives of the Inter-Governmental Conference of 1996–97. As with the European Parliament, the distribution of votes does not really correspond to economic size, much less population weight, and is deliberately allocated to favor the smaller countries.

What determined the vote distribution here was the move to allow more legislation to be passed at the Community level by eliminating the requirement for unanimity on votes taken over "directives." These are measures that must be enacted by each member state as part of its treaty obligations. A very large number of directives (nearly 300) were required to implement the Single European Act of 1987 and they could never have been passed if unanimity were required on each. The compromise reached was that only a "qualified majority" was necessary, namely fifty-four out of the seventy-six votes. What this meant was that no single major country could veto a piece of legislation desired by the rest of the Union. To block it, a major country would need to persuade one other major country and one of the small countries to vote with it. Alternatively, the small countries could all combine to block a piece of legislation that favored only the large countries. This voting arrangement highlights the essential political fact about the European Union for realists—it is an intergovernmental organization, not a superstate or even a confederation of states, although that is the continued aspiration of the functionalists.

Negotiations over the terms of admittance of the 1995 entrants almost came to an end in the spring of 1994 when Britain led a movement to maintain the blocking minority at twenty-three votes, even after the admission of all four of the applicants would have raised the total number of votes to ninety. The proposal of the European Commission was to raise the blocking minority requirement to twenty-seven votes, maintaining the same percentage (70–71%) previously required for a qualified majority. In the end, the extensive revamping of voting rules that could have been initiated by the British proposal proved too daunting to the other member states to consider seriously. Instead, they backed the Commission's proposal and placated the British (and Spanish who joined with the British for awhile) by the promise that all voting rules and decision-making procedures would be on the table at the 1996 Inter-Governmental Conference. The episode was embarrassing to the British government but it had the virtue of exposing the internal stresses within the European Union as it enlarges and for making clear that it is the Council of Ministers that is the "real" legislative branch of the EU.

The executive branch of the European Union is similarly divided between a "functional" and a "real" institution. The functional equivalent of an executive branch of European government is the *European Commission.* The Commission is the only body that can initiate legislation for the Council of Ministers to vote upon (and the Parliament to issue its opinion). This means identifying Europewide problems and then studying possibilities for confronting them by means of a directive. The Commission, with its twenty members and 17,000 employees, is effectively the most comprehensive and authoritative European think tank. It consults regularly with the relevant bureaucracies, interest groups, and academic researchers and samples public opinion on every issue that might lead to a Europewide initiative. Formally, it must draft legislation in consultation with the *Economic and Social Committee,* comprising 222 members representing employers, employees, and numerous other interest groups, and the European Parliament. If legislation deals strictly with the European Coal and Steel Community (still in formal existence), the Commission must consult with the ECSC Consultative Committee, which is made up of 120 representatives of producers, workers, consumers, and traders in the coal and steel industries.

Once legislation is passed by the Council of Ministers, the Commission is responsible for overseeing its implementation. This means monitoring the individual governments to see if they pass the necessary national legislation to carry out the European Union legislation, initiating infringement proceedings against any member state and issuing cease and desist orders against companies or individuals in violation of Community law. Most important, the Commission oversees the collection and expenditure of funds controlled by the European Union. In this role, however, it is monitored by another institution, the *Court of Auditors.* It is comprised, like the Council of Ministers, of one official from each member state, highlighting once again the intergovernmental organization of the European Union.

It appears that the Commission has executive functions but does not have true executive powers. To enforce its decisions against firms or individuals, for example, it must call on the national enforcement agencies available in their country. To enforce a decision against a member state, it must get a ruling from the European Court of Justice, which in turn relies upon the cooperation of the other member states to enforce its rulings. To help direct this large, often incoherent, body of the European Commission into effective actions that promote the vision of a united Europe, the member states established the *European Council* in 1974. This is composed of the heads of government of each country plus the president of the European Commission. They meet twice a year and discuss strategic issues of mutual concern. If they decide something should be done at the European Union level and propose an initiative to the Commission, it is clear that the legislation, once presented properly by the Commission, will be passed by the Council of Ministers. They, after all, are responsible to the heads of their respective governments who initiated the legislation in the first place. Moreover, the heads of government possess full enforcement powers to carry out the directives that they caused to be passed. The European Council, then, can be considered the "realist's" version of an executive branch.

The *European Court of Justice* was established in 1952 so that disputes that arose among member states of the European Coal and Steel Community could be aired in front of impartial jurists from each country. It has sixteen judges assisted by six advocates-general. Each member is appointed for six years by a member state and approved by the governments of the other member states, with the sixteenth being the Chief Justice elected among them, so that his or her country has two justices. The Court passes judgment on any legal instrument enacted by European or national institutions that a complainant alleges is incompatible with Community law. Suit may be brought by member states, corporations, or individuals, but must deal with interpretations of Community, not merely national, law. Due to the increase in actions taken to promote competition policy after the Single European Act of 1987, a new court, the *Court of First Instance,* was founded in 1989 with the same composition of one judge from each member state. It hears most of the actions brought by individuals or companies. Appeal can be made, however, from its decision to the European Court of Justice. Given the importance of Communitywide competition policy agreed on in the Single European Act, the Court of First Instance has become increasingly active and effective. So even in the judicial branch of the incipient European government, we can draw a distinction between a functionalist version of the judiciary, the European Court of Justice, and a realist version, now the Court of First Instance.

With the final ratification by all member states of the Treaty of European Union (the Maastricht Accord) in November 1993, a new range of institutions came into existence, designed to deal with the expanded scope of responsibilities assigned to the Union and to further the advance toward an eventual pan-European political structure. Most of these dealt with economic issues with realist goals, but all are strictly functionalist in effect at this early stage of their development.

ECONOMIC INSTITUTIONS[1]

The most important economic institution is the *European Monetary Institute,* which began operations in January 1994 and is based in Frankfurt, Germany. This is a symbol of the European Union's determination to have a common currency by the end of the century. Its objective is to strengthen the coordination of monetary policies within the Union in order to maintain common price stability and minimum exchange rate fluctuations among the member currencies. It will also make preparations for the European System of Central Banks, intended to administer the common currency and the common monetary policy after 1999. The ESCB will be composed of the *European Central Bank* and the individual central banks of the member states. Once the ECSB is established, the European Monetary Institute will go out of existence, passing all of its assets, liabilities, and staff to the European Central Bank. The ECB will then become analogous to the Board of Governors of the Federal Reserve System of the United States, with comparable rules for determining the composition of the directors to reflect regional and public interests.

Other agencies set up in response to the Single European Act and the Treaty on European Union include the *European Environmental Agency,* located in Copenhagen, starting with a staff of about fifty. It will monitor environmental indicators throughout the Union and report on its findings every three years. In the future it may monitor compliance with European Union environmental regulations and help formulate new guidelines for such regulations. The *European Training Foundation* is based in Turin with a staff of three-hundred people and is intended to provide training assistance to Central and East European countries. It is open to nonmember countries that are also contributing aid to the Central and East European countries (such as the United States). Its work is complemented by the *European Centre for the Development of Vocational Training,* which has been moved from Berlin to Thessaloniki, Greece. The previously existing *European Foundation for the Improvement of Living and Working Conditions,* established since 1975 in Dublin, now has additional tasks assigned to it in light of the concern for a common social policy that was part of the Treaty on European Union. It would seem to overlap considerably, however, with the mandate of a new agency created in response to the EU Social Charter in 1989. This is the *Agency for Health and Safety at Work,* to be based in Bilbao, Spain.

Another new agency is the *Office for Veterinary and Plant-Health Inspection and Control,* to be established in Dublin. This is a response to the loss of border controls after 1993 so that control on plant and animal health can still be maintained. Although agriculture was not explicitly covered in the Single European Act, much of existing agricultural policy within the EU was affected by the regulatory changes that were necessary to achieve the four freedoms of movement of goods, people, capital, and service. So in March 1994 the European Parliament published a report welcoming the establishment of (note that technically it could not legislate anything into existence) the *European Centre for the Validation of Alternative Methods* (to animal testing).

Lisbon managed to get the *European Centre for Drugs and Drug Addiction,* which will be very small and limited to acquiring information on use and control of drugs throughout the Union. It will not overlap with the Europol Drugs Unit, which is part of the *European Police Unit* based in The Hague. London will be the home for the *European Agency for the Evaluation of Medicinal Products,* which will oversee and implement the "future system" for market authorization for new pharmaceuticals in the EU. Its work will be analogous to that of the Food and Drug Administration in the United States.

Spain gets the *Office for Harmonisation in the Internal Market,* composed of the Community Trademark Office and the Community Design Office. This office administers applications for trademarks that will be recognized throughout the EU. Related to its functions is the *Common Appeal Court for Community Patents,* based in Luxembourg. The *Institute for Prospective Technology Studies,* a new unit of the EU's Joint Research Centre, will be based in Seville.

The future of these institutions is uncertain, but most will survive indefinitely whether or not their functions turn into real exercises of power. The functional range of the agencies and offices illustrates well the positioning of the EU to take advantage of whatever shocks occur to the member states in common so that coordinated Europeanwide responses seem appropriate. The structure is in place to move forward to fulfill the vision of a united Europe, whenever the circumstances warrant. The geographical dispersion of these new institutions, however, may indicate a growing problem for the future development of the EU. How can it maintain an effective decision-making structure that each member government finds comfortable while providing through its policies a net economic benefit to each national economy? That has always been the challenge for the Community; to assess its chances for meeting the even more daunting challenges that lie before it now, it is useful to see what were the challenges it confronted from the beginning and how it has overcome them to date.

Endnotes

1.   For more details, see Vivienne Kendall, "The new Union institutions," in *European Trends,* 2nd Quarter 1994, Economist Intelligence Unit, London, pp. 63–70.

Bibliography

Bainbridge, Timothy with Anthony Teasdale. *The Penguin Companion to European Union.* London: Penguin Books, 1996. Everything you need to know and a lot besides in case you are merely curious or confused about exactly who does what and why in the European Union.

Dinan, Desmond. *Ever Closer Union? An Introduction to the European Community.* Boulder, Colo.: Lynne Rienner Publishers, 1994. A lively narrative of the political and economic issues arising in the course of the EU's development from 1945, from a Euro-enthusiast's point of view.

EUROPA. http:\www.europa.eu.int. The European Union's World Wide Web site for authoritative updates on all aspects of EU activities. Unfortunately, like the publications of the EU, the quality and the frequency of updates varies considerably by topic and by directorate.

Eurostat. *Basic Statistics of the European Union. Comparison with the Principal Partners of the European Union.* 32nd edn, Luxembourg: Statistical Office of the European Communities, 1995. Compact and quite complete with graphics as well. Refers to the numerous publications of Eurostat, not all of which are easily located or even available.

Laffan, Brigid. *Integration and Co-operation in Europe.* London: Routledge, 1992. Political scientist from Dublin. Nice discussion on functionalism and realism.

Leonardi, Roberto. *Convergence, Cohesion and Integration in the European Union.* New York: St. Martin's Press, 1995. Political science treatment of convergence issues with focus on Italian experience.

McDonald, Frank and Stephen Dearden, eds. *European Economic Integration.* 2d ed. London and New York: Longman, 1994. Collection of chapters on every aspect of the EU by faculty members of the Manchester Metropolitan University. More an encyclopedia or reference work than a textbook.

Tsoukalis, Loukas. *The New European Economy, The Politics and Economics of Integration.* 2d rev. ed. New York: Oxford University Press, 1993. More politics than economics.

van der Wee, Herman. *Prosperity and Upheaval: The World Economy 1945–1980.* London: Penguin, 1991. Still the definitive overview of developments worldwide written from the perspective of a cosmopolitan European. Look for the update when translated from the Flemish edition.

Wallace, William. *Regional Integration: The West European Experience.* Washington, D.C.: Brookings Institution, 1994. Good on all the organizations—EFTA, EU, WEU, etc.

Williams, Allan M. *The European Community: The Contradictions of Integration,* 2nd ed. Oxford: Blackwell, 1994. Historical approach. Nicely done if a bit dull.

CHAPTER 2

European Economic Integration, 1945–1958:

All Plans Lead Toward Rome

The development of the European Union follows a long history of European cooperation and rivalry, with various coalitions forming, dissolving, and re-forming again. Although there have a number of attempts to unify Europe, mainly by force, none has been as broadly successful as the EU. Since its beginning in 1958 as the European Economic Community, the EU has proven to be a special international organization and today is a powerful player in the international economy. To understand its formation and operation, we must first put the postwar European integration into the proper framework.

Over the nineteenth century, Europe developed a complicated political and economic structure, with each nation experiencing rapid technical and economic change.[1] It was also a period of European colonial expansion, so that regional changes extended beyond the European continent, altering the pattern of trade in raw materials and industrial products. Europe exhibited a vast array of international arrangements among industries and governments, including some with the rapidly growing United States. The structure was not static; it was forced to change with various shocks up until 1913. For example, with the birth of unified nation-states in Germany and Italy after 1870, the balance of power shifted in Western Europe with Germany becoming an industrial leader. (Germany was founded in 1872 after the Franco-Prussian war, and Italy, the youngest European nation, was created in 1878 with the victory of Garibaldi and his thousand volunteers.) The shocks of the nineteenth century pale by contrast with the traumas endured by Europe in the twentieth century. First the Great War of 1914–18, then the postwar hyperinflations in the losing countries, the Great Depression of 1929–33, the development of separate trading blocs in the 1930s, and then the Second World War and the division of Europe after 1945, all shook the economic and technological foundations of European unity to pieces. It is only after 1989 with the collapse of the Soviet Union, the remarkable changes in Eastern Europe, the reunification of Germany, and their effects on the European Union, that the process of building a continentwide political architecture for Europe has resumed.

WORLD WAR I TO WORLD WAR II

The First World War marked the end of the nineteenth century and shattered the fragile European system of the preceding century, leaving little in its place. The economic structure after 1920 had to be created anew, under new governments and even new political boundaries. After the war, Germany gave up Alsace, the Lorraine, and the Saar to France, and under conditions of the Versailles Treaty surrendered its ability until 1925 to control its own commercial policy with respect to its old Zollverein members, Belgium and Luxembourg.

The interwar years were both politically and economically unstable. France, for example, had over a dozen prime ministers between 1925 and 1935. In Germany, the deep depression of the early 1930s helped foster radical parties, such as the National Socialists (Nazis). Throughout Europe, governments and firms both attempted to work together to establish new working structures within which to conduct national business and international relations. The United States played a major role in this process through loans and foreign aid, administered through the Dawes Plan and the Young Plan. However, with its own problems after 1929, the United States lost interest in cooperative arrangements with Europe. Its trade with Europe fell to historic lows.

During the interwar years, the Europeans themselves had limited cooperation. No real progress could be made toward rebuilding the prewar pattern of trade within Europe until a full five years after the end of the war. Then the rapid adoption of the gold exchange standard from 1924 through 1929 allowed a rapid expansion of trade to take place, but on quite a new basis from the nineteenth century. The Soviet Union had withdrawn from the international economy after 1917. The new successor states formed out of the remains of the Tsarist, Ottoman, Austro-Hungarian, and German empires all attempted to achieve either self-sufficiency or find new trading partners in order to establish an economic basis for their independence. With the collapse of the gold-exchange standard system in 1931, all of Europe lapsed back into a series of bilateral agreements that tended to distort and limit overall trade compared with the multilateral trade and payments system that was emerging in the period 1924–29. The pattern of trade with countries outside Europe was permanently altered also as a result of the loss of colonies by Germany and Turkey.

In the 1920s, there were men like Aristide Briand of France and Gustav Stresemann of Germany who proposed the creation of a European Union within the framework of the League of Nations—their aim was to promote European cooperation while leaving national sovereignty intact. In fact, President Wilson had originally envisioned the League facilitating this sort of international cooperation.[2] However, with the weakness of the League and the sweeping changes of the collapse of the gold-exchange standard and the Great Depression of 1929–33, no real movement was made.

Much more was done by industrialists themselves. Already by the mid-1920s, industrial cooperation had begun with the formation of scores of international cartels.[3] One of the most important was the International Steel Cartel (ISC). The original members of the cartel were France, Germany, Belgium, and Luxembourg. Formed after the Locarno Agreements[4] and the return of Germany's right to conduct commercial policy with respect to the other future members of the cartel, the ISC limited imports between members and set quota limits on total steel production. The International Steel Cartel collapsed with the world depression in the early 1930s but was reformed in 1933 with the International Steel Export Cartel. This latter cartel set quotas only on exports and created exclusive sales agreements with major importing countries in order that the cartel members could price discriminate across markets. It was recreated after the war within the Entente de Bruxelles in 1953. It is no happenstance that the first customs union[5] after 1950 was the European Coal and Steel Community (ECSC), created by the founding members of the ISC with the addition of the Netherlands and Italy.

From this interwar experience, the steel industries learned how to adapt agreements and their behavior to changes in both national and international markets. They were able to operate their national cartels within the context of the international agreements, while all the time working with exclusive import organizations in important third markets. Although the agreements were international in character, they did not limit the passionate European nationalism, far from it. The agreements were made with a keen eye to preserving the national power of their constituent members. This experience formed an important basis for the early European integration after 1945.

POST-WORLD WAR II

After the Second World War, as in the First World War, European nations were eager to establish some common grounds for working together to rebuild Europe and, in contrast with the First World War, to secure peace this time. During the end of the war and directly afterward, men like Jean Monnet of France and Winston Churchill of Great Britain were calling for the reconciliation of Western Europe within the context of some sort of "United States of Europe."[6]

The United Nations Economic Commission for Europe was concerned with creating an organization for the unification of all Europe, East and West. However, as the "cold war" began, this goal was soon abandoned and the West took the path toward the EU while the East formed the Council for Mutual Economic Assistance (Comecon). This division between the East and the West made the policies of the Soviet Union and the United States essentially important for the determination of the organizations within Europe.

The initial conditions of the European economies after World War II were not horrendous. Europe's resource base in 1945 was not as damaged as is often claimed. In neither capital, labor, nor land did Europe suffer intractable constraints. Although the image of utter devastation still persists, the physical damage was concentrated on infrastructural investment; mainly transport and housing. The impact on productive capital was much less. Europe's industrial capacity was most likely larger in 1947 than in 1938; for example, the Netherlands, a relatively badly damaged country, had an estimated industrial machinery capacity substantially greater than that of 1939 just eighteen months after the end of the war.[7]

Not only were capacities increased, they were also better adapted, in some respects, to the needs of the postwar era. In fact, even the break with traditional overseas suppliers stimulated investment through the replacement of imported goods, for example, synthetic fibers and rubber. Utilities were expanded so that by 1947 oil refinery capacity was one-third higher than in 1938. Without taking Europe's initial conditions into account, it is impossible to understand Europe's rapid industrial recovery and it is very easy to overestimate the success of the economic policies followed. As Table 2.1 shows, already in 1948 most Western European countries had surpassed their industrial outputs of a decade earlier. The notable exception was West Germany, which rapidly caught up after the economic reforms after 1947. Note also that all the countries posted very rapid growth rates through 1951.

Although manufacturing expanded remarkably, serious problems still existed. Basic industries, such as coal and steel, struggled to recapture prewar levels. Moreover, the neglect and destruction of transport caused major bottlenecks. Available railway stock was 75 percent of the prewar level and merchant shipping less than half (24 million tons were lost out of a fleet of 44 million). The greatest absolute losses, however, were in housing. About 16 percent of European dwellings were destroyed; their replacement produced the housing investment boom of the 1950s.

The war had little impact on the size of the available labor force. By 1947 Western Europe had surpassed 1938 levels of employment by 4 percent. Even war-torn countries like Belgium and Denmark increased by 17 percent and by 31 percent, respectively. Rather than reducing the total size of the labor force,

TABLE 2.1
Production Indexes of the Six Member States of the European Community

	1938	1947	1948*	1949	1950	1951
Belgium	82	93	100	100	102	118
France	92	85	100	109	112	124
W. Germany	192	65	100	144	182	218
Italy	103	96	100	110	127	144
Luxembourg	69	75	100	96	101	121
Netherlands	88	83	100	112	123	129

*1948 = 100

Source: United Nations, *Economic Survey of Europe Since the War: A Reappraisal of Problems and Prospects* (Geneva, 1953), p. 239.

the war did have an effect on its age and sex distribution and on its regional distribution. The latter was the result of the changes in territory and the migrations spurred by the hostilities and their aftermath.

The war's effect on agricultural land was felt most in Eastern Europe. This and the political changes of the 1940s radically altered the trading relationships of Western Europe, especially German trade. Agricultural production was not severely weakened within Western Europe but recovery was much slower than it had been for industry. Whilst the poor harvests of 1947 reinforced a more negative image, especially with American policymakers of the Marshall Plan, it has to be remembered that this was a serious but isolated incident and that output rebounded quickly. All the same, it was not until 1950 that prewar levels of production were finally restored. European countries responded to these changes with elaborate and extensive governmental involvement that, to some extent, still exists today, both at the national level and at the common EU level.

Perhaps the greatest influence of the war on postwar European economies was to alter their trading relationships, both with each other and with the rest of the world. The lack of a multilateral trading system saddled Europe with a serious balance-of-payments disequilibrium. Europe's commercial problems stemmed from several different sources. The war had witnessed the liquidation or destruction of foreign property holdings. In 1950–51, earnings from this source were, in real terms, less than a quarter what they had been in 1938, and that in itself was a substantial improvement over the previous years. Besides this, countries were rapidly incurring new debts to finance reconstruction. For example, the United Kingdom incurred debts to the United States and Canada of $1 billion, and in 1947 borrowed $4.4 billion from the United States and $1.25 billion from Canada. France borrowed $1.9 billion the same year.

Unable to increase earnings from services to foreigners (e.g., tourism, shipping, insurance, or finance), the European countries were forced to expand their commodity exports. But not to just any foreign customer. The absence of domestic supplies or of imports from traditional European sources, especially Eastern Europe and West Germany, increased their dependence on the dollar area. The dollar deficit increased enormously compared with their prewar experience and it could not be offset by export earnings to colonies or to Eastern Europe. The scarcity of earnings in hard (convertible to dollar) currencies forced the European countries to restrict imports and to control trade through bilateral agreements, augmented with quantitative restrictions and exchange controls.

The effects of these problems, and the measures chosen to cope with them directly after the war, were to reduce the relative levels of trade among the countries to possibly the lowest level in the twentieth century. During the 1930s, when trade was already hindered by restrictive commercial policies, intra-European trade was nearly 50 percent of total trade. By 1948, at the start of Marshall Plan aid, this figure had fallen to less than 35 percent. However, ten years later intra-European trade had surpassed the 1938 level and was at an historic high. The 1950s not only exhibited a dramatic increase in trade, but also a general transformation of the European economy. Immediate postwar recovery was rapid, but growth continued at historically unprecedented levels; gross domestic product from 1949 to 1959 rose annually 7.4 percent for West Germany, 6 percent for Austria, 5.9 percent for Italy, and 4.5 percent for France. The productivity gap between Europe and the United States had closed since U.S. growth was at about 3 percent. By the time Europe was ready to launch its customs union, it was already a highly integrated economic region.

RECOVERY EFFORTS

What happened over the 1950s to generate the conditions for this spectacular recovery? To combat their initial structural problems, the European countries worked together in a variety of international agreements and organizations. A massive recovery program was launched and the 1950s was an era of reorganization and growth. The rest of this chapter examines these policies. Briefly, they can be summarized as (1) an emphasis on economic integration, aided by U.S. backing; (2) reinforcing growth that eased the integration by lessening intersectoral conflicts as factors were reallocated among them; and (3) establishing a framework for multilateral trade within Europe based on fixed, but realistic, exchange rates. All of them can be seen as approaches to solving what was called the dollar shortage problem.

THE DOLLAR SHORTAGE

The dollar shortage can be understood most clearly in terms of a standard supply-demand portrayal of the foreign exchange market. The European need for imports from the United States translates then into a demand curve for dollars in the foreign exchange market where dollars are bought and sold. The demand curve had been shifted out for every country in Europe thanks to the wartime destruction and the military diversion of civilian production facilities. The supply curve of dollars, in turn, is based on the U.S. demand for imports from Europe. Thanks to the high tariffs in the United States and the plentiful supply of domestic products available as substitutes for European goods, not to mention the unavailability of European consumption goods anyway, the supply curve of dollars had been shifted inward. Both situations could be expected to change as conversion occurred on both sides of the Atlantic from a war economy to a civilian economy. A complication had been added, however, by the Bretton Woods agreement, signed in July 1944. This committed all the signatories to fixed exchange rates with the dollar, whose value in turn was defined in terms of gold at $35 per ounce of pure gold. Each country joining the International Monetary Fund, which was set up by the Bretton Woods agreement, had to pay in its share of the capital stock that gave the IMF its initial supply of operating funds. Part of the share could be paid in terms of the country's own currency, but part had to be paid as well in either gold or dollars. To minimize their cost of acquiring the necessary gold and dollars, each country naturally tended to overvalue their own currency, which they could produce at will, in terms of the dollar. This also had the advantage of decreasing the cost to them of acquiring dollars in the foreign exchange markets in order to pay for imports from any other country, as the dollar was clearly the currency preferred by any exporter in the world for receiving payment. The fixed exchange rate set at this time acted as a price ceiling that kept the price of dollars in terms of, say, pounds sterling, from rising high enough to equilibrate supply and demand. Each European nation, then, was trapped in a situation of continued excess demand for dollars.

The resulting situation is portrayed in Figure 2.1, where the solid lines for the supply curve of dollars, the demand curve for dollars, and the price ceiling set for dollars in terms of a European currency depict the situation in 1945. The dotted lines show how the situation could have looked in 1950, after a substantial amount of recovery had taken place in Europe, Marshall Plan aid had been distributed in large quantities, and all the European currencies had devalued, most by the same 30.5 percent that the British pound had been devalued. Each program was an attack on the problem from one of the three possibilities: increase the supply of dollars, decrease the demand for dollars, remove or at least raise the price ceiling on dollars. Any one approach could have solved the problem on its own if pursued vigorously enough. All three were used, in fact, and each approach proved effective. It shows the dollar shortage could have been eliminated by 1950 using any of the strategies.

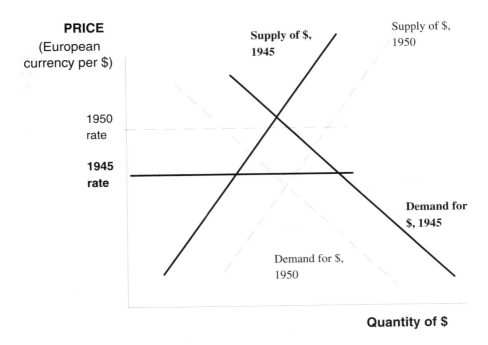

Figure 2.1. Dollar shortage, 1945, 1950.

In fact, the opinion more and more of economic historians is that the dollar shortage was eliminated sometime between 1950 and 1952. However, policymakers in both the United States and Europe continued to think a dollar shortage existed until 1958. The shortage rather quickly turned into an increasing dollar surplus, thanks to the continued use of the same strategies to eliminate the dollar shortage that were initiated after 1945. By 1971, the dollar surplus was so overwhelming that the United States abandoned its commitment to convert dollars into gold, and in 1973 all the IMF countries abandoned their commitment to fixed exchange rates as well. Whenever and however the shortage was eliminated, it is useful to think of the programs described below as attacks on the problem of the dollar shortage using one of the three basic approaches.

THE MARSHALL PLAN

In 1947, the United States began its concerted program for Europe. At Harvard on June 5, Secretary of State George Marshall proposed his now famous aid program to Western Europe, using memoranda drawn up by policy planning staff workers Dean Acheson, George Kennan, and Will Clayton. However politically motivated, the plan was operated through economic means and the United States wanted Western Europe to coordinate internationally to manage and distribute the funds. To this end the Organization for European Economic Cooperation (OEEC) was formed in 1947–48 by the Committee for European Economic Cooperation. With the Marshall Plan, the United States began its active role in attacking Europe's structural problems under the title of the European Recovery Program (ERP). Of course, this was not the beginning of postwar U.S. aid to Europe. In the first two years after the war, the United States contributed about $4 billion in aid through the United Nations Relief and Rehabilitation Administration (UNRRA) and other programs. Although these figures are similar to the aid under the Marshall Plan, they were given on an ad hoc basis, so that European countries could not count on aid from year to year.

The Marshall Plan transferred about $12.5 billion to Europe in grants, loans, and conditional aid, distributed mainly in the first two years of the program. Grants accounted for $9,199.4 million, loans for $1,139.7 million. Conditional aid was awarded as backing the intra-Western European payments agreement of 1948 and came to $1,542.9 million.[8] It was administered by the Economic Cooperation Agency (ECA) on the American side and the Committee for European Economic Cooperation (CEEC) and its successor the Organization for European Economic Cooperation (OEEC), which were created to allocate the aid and attempt to solve Europe's problems collectively.

The allocation of aid was determined by the size of the dollar deficit on foreign trade, not by any measure of national income. It was aimed at providing needed imports for reconstruction, thus freeing domestic funds for capital formation. About 17 percent of the aid was spent directly on "machinery and vehicles"; the rest was spent on raw materials and agricultural products. In addition, the aid and its distribution provided a means for direct U.S. influence in the reconstruction programs of the OEEC countries because the money freed by the aid was spent only with ECA approval. This ensured that the market orientation of the OEEC countries was maintained, while allowing the OEEC countries to commit funds to large projects because they could be sure of the availability of future funds. Countries are not willing to change their domestic structures and policies if they cannot be sure about the fundability of projects and the stability of international arrangements.

The impact of the Marshall Plan has been the subject of some debate over the last ten years. Certainly, Marshall Plan aid did not cause the supergrowth of the 1950s; it simply was not large enough. Table 2.2 presents the aid in terms of selected countries' gross domestic capital formation.

Note that both Germany and Italy received relatively large sums, but all the countries received the bulk of their money in the first two years of the program. Eichengreen and Uzan[9] calculate that out of each dollar of Marshall Plan aid about two-thirds went to increase production and the rest went to investment. Although the returns to European investments were high, these authors estimate that the aid, in total, would have contributed to annual economic growth about one-half of 1 percent; that is, about 2 percent over the four years of Marshall Plan aid. This is an important contribution, but does not explain the rapid growth rates of the period.

However, Marshall Plan aid did have important effects. On the microeconomic level, it stimulated output by promising a flow of imported raw materials in the future, allowing industry to use existing stocks more freely.[10] In addition, it removed the impact of important bottlenecks, as in coal and transport. Resource allocation risk was reduced so that expansion with given resources was less costly, especially for large-scale, lumpy investments such as electric power plants. On a macroeconomic level, the aid, and the assurance of aid, stimulated trade by removing the dollar constraint from payments. The ERP financed the European Payments Union, which made a very important contribution to the establishment of multilateral payments for European trade. Also, Marshall Plan aid reduced the tension of the costs of structural adjustments by as much as one-half by increasing the pie from which the distribution was taken.[11]

TABLE 2.2
Ratio of U.S. Aid to Gross Domestic Capital
Formation (percent)

	1948	1949	1950	1951
United Kingdom	9.0	11.2	9.8	2.0
France	13.9	11.9	10.4	7.8
Germany	31.4	21.8	10.7	6.8
Italy	26.6	33.6	9.5	8.7

Source: Charles S. Maier, *American Historical Review* 86 (2), 1981, p. 342.

Thus, Marshall Plan aid helped Europe avoid the serious social strife confronting nations attempting to make large-scale structural adjustments rapidly. This provides an important lesson for developing countries today as they attempt their own domestic and regional adjustment programs. On an institutional level, the ERP created the organizations that oversaw the entire European integration effort. Through the ECA and the OEEC the necessary groundwork was laid for the completion of the common market at the end of the 1950s.

Along with these early economic measures, Europe was also unifying on defense issues, also largely inspired by the United States. Already in 1948 the Treaty of Brussels brought together the United Kingdom, France, and Benelux in a mutual assistance treaty. (However, this was after they had abandoned most of Eastern Europe, which had similar treaties with these countries, so the Treaty of Brussels could not have meant too much to the participants.) This treaty served to separate the signatories from Germany, while addressing the new threat from the Soviet bloc.

To further this movement toward political unity, in 1949 the Council of Europe was created to start the movement toward a pan-European dialogue. However, it was virtually powerless in anything but very broad cultural and political objectives. It did create the European Convention for the Protection of Human Rights and Fundamental Freedoms on November 4, 1950. This not only laid down a practical minimum standard of human rights to be applied in member states but also established a system for legal remedy, empowering the institutions set up under the Convention—the European Commission of Human Rights and the European Court of Human Rights—to condemn infringements of human rights by the signatories.

EUROPEAN PRODUCTIVITY AGENCY

While tentative gains were being made politically, the productivity gap between Europe and the United States was still a major concern of the OEEC Council and the United States. In 1952 the U.S. Congress approved Benton-Moody aid for ten OEEC countries to receive $100 million and the OEEC $2.5 million in order to fund a European productivity campaign. Countries receiving the grants paid 8 percent as counterpart funds in national currencies to the new agency. In response the OEEC Council established the European Productivity Agency (EPA) in March 1953 to work with the newly created National Productivity Centres in the OEEC countries. In 1952 eleven of the seventeen OEEC members had productivity centers to disseminate information and coordinate productivity programs. The total capital of the EPA from the direct U. S. grant and the members' counterpart funds was FF 3.5 billion. Until the Treaty of Rome, the United States contributed an average $1.5 million each year on an ad hoc basis to encourage certain projects it deemed important. The Council was the supreme governing body, but the agency was run by a Productivity and Applied Research Committee (PRA) along with an advisory board made up of representatives from national producer, labor, and technical organizations. The budget of the EPA was allocated over twelve areas, including business management techniques, applied research, agriculture, and underdeveloped areas.

The overall effectiveness of the EPA was first hampered by a lack of clear direction and then by a breakdown in communication with the national productivity centers; a clear definition of its aims and contact with the national centers was first necessary before it could begin sponsoring projects. Once these links were firmly established, the projects could be funded. As countries had to contribute their own counterpart funds, they were careful in their requests. This, coupled with American supervision, kept the allocation and use of funds under tight control. Through the 1950s the EPA sponsored a great number of programs that effectively impacted regional or sectoral problems through applied research and extension programs, general scientific education, and vocational training.

EUROPEAN PAYMENTS UNION

While Marshall Plan aid and the EPA helped Europe recover, and a general dialogue of integration had begun among the European nations, a persistent problem facing Europe was its external imbalance. The war had witnessed the liquidation or destruction of foreign property holdings. In 1950–51 earnings from this source were, in real terms, less than a quarter what they had been in 1938, and that in itself was a substantial improvement over the previous years. To combat these external structural problems, the European countries worked together in a variety of international agreements and organizations. Initially, they were not effective in solving the problems, nor in uniting Western Europe in order to attempt solutions. A Committee on Payments Agreements first suggested a pooling of such debts so that countries would have to settle in dollars or gold only if the bilateral agreement between them so specified.[12] This would have the effect of preventing creditors picking their debtors according to their creditworthiness. In addition, it suggested that countries approaching dollar points (point at which payments had to be made fully in dollars or gold) with certain countries could have their debts rescheduled over a longer period, thus reducing the dollar flow to creditors.

An agreement was signed by eleven countries on November 18, 1947. France, Benelux, the Bizone of Germany, Austria, Portugal, Norway, Sweden, Denmark, the United Kingdom, Greece, and the French zone of Germany were full members. Switzerland and Turkey sent statistics only. Ireland, which had no payments agreements, and Iceland, which had one, were "occasional" members and did not agree to automatic adjustments. The agreement established a first- and second-category compensation system. "First-category compensations" were the only automatic operation of the arrangements; each pair of countries settled its debts through its net positions with other countries, using the surplus with one country to pay a debt on another, so long as the first country owed the other. For example, if France owed Germany $2 million and Germany owed Netherlands $6 million and the Netherlands owed Belgium $10 million and Belgium owed France $10 million, then the French debt to Germany would automatically be canceled and each successive debt would be reduced by $2 million—a net "saving" of debt payments of $8 million.

A second category of compensation increased the balance available of a member country's currency, but gave that country veto rights over the use of its currency. For example, suppose that by the terms of a payments agreement Belgium agreed to hold sterling balances up to the equivalent of $5 million while England agreed to convert anything over that amount into dollars. Belgium was already holding $4 million in sterling. Norway owed Belgium $2 million and had sterling equal to that amount. If Norway paid Belgium in sterling, Belgium would hold $6 million in sterling and the British would be obliged to change $1 million of it into dollars. Because sterling holdings of Belgium increased in order to clear the trade with Norway and this would increase Belgium's claims on Britain, Britain could refuse permission to the transaction.

Over the period of these agreements, the participants had debts among themselves of $762.1 million. The clearing, however, amounted to only $1.7 million, just 2 percent of the total. The figure was kept so low partly because certain countries were creditors to the whole group and others net debtors to it. Net debts of this sort amounted to about $400 million. Second, only France, Italy, and Benelux, and later the Bizone of Germany, agreed to first-category compensations with the rest of the group. A system of "drawing rights" was also established. These were gifts from one country to another, matched by "conditional aid" from the United States. If deficits were forecast, the surplus country granted the amount to the deficit country and, in turn, received compensatory aid from the United States. This, then, was a "little Marshall Plan," Diebold says, for it "added to the real resources currently devoted to the recovery of intra-European trade and thereby brought about a further distribution of American aid, in addition to the allocation of dollars."[13] American conditional aid, through the Marshall Plan, financed about one-third of the total intra-European imbalance. Of course, this meant that the imports were gifts, so there was no real incentive to correct the deficits.

The 1947 Agreement did not solve Europe's payments problems. Its successors in 1948 and 1949 both provided perverse incentives and were directly tied to the many bilateral trade agreements within Europe (105 for fifteen countries). This made an overall working system impossible. Of course, maintaining convertibility in these circumstances was also very difficult. For example, if a country did not limit its convertibility, others might manipulate controls to engineer a surplus with it and thus obtain dollars. Switzerland had this problem and reacted by restricting convertibility of its currency to its own citizens and to other hard-currency countries.

Responding to these problems, and under American pressure, the OEEC members established the European Payments Union (EPU) on September 19, 1950, and applied retroactively to July 1, 1950. It was to facilitate trade and establish a multilateral payments system by helping to clear country imbalances and establishing fully convertible currencies. Under the EPU, a country's position was determined by its debts to or from all the other members and dollar/

gold payments were established by a uniform formula. Debits were paid by central banks on a sliding scale partially in domestic currency and partly in hard currency up to a "quota." After that payments were entirely in dollars or gold, unless some special arrangement was made. The quotas totaled $3,950 million and were calculated for individual countries on the basis of 15 percent of the value of their total merchandise trade. Originally the largest quotas were the United Kingdom 27 percent of total, France 13 percent, Belgium and Luxembourg 9 percent, Netherlands 8 percent and Germany 8 percent. The United States provided $350 million, of which some was given to countries with "structural" problems, leaving the initial capital of the EPU at $271.6 million.

According to the original agreement, by the time a country had reached its quota limit, it would have paid 40 percent in gold and 60 percent in domestic currency. The system of increasing gold payments improved the incentives from the former agreements: gold or dollar losses would now move countries to cure persistent deficits, and growing credits would make surplus countries reduce their surpluses. The exact distribution of credit to gold as debt or credit increased is shown in Table 2.3.

The 60:40 balance was subsequently altered because it seemed too "soft" on debtors and because the skewed operation of the system (whereby debtors paid in gold at a lower rate than creditors were paid out for the first 80 percent of the quotas) increased its costs. In mid-1954, the coverage was changed to 50:50 and in 1955 to only 25:75.

Already by 1953, a number of members permitted multilateral currency arbitrage: currency transactions could be carried out on ordinary foreign exchange markets, not just by central banks as before. In addition, eight EPU members agreed to standardize the spreads between the official buying and selling limits of their currencies at about 0.75 percent on either side of parity

TABLE 2.3
Increasing Gold Payments with the European Payments Union

Percent of quota		Payments by debtors		Payments to creditor	
		Credit	Gold	Credit	Gold
1st	20	20	0	20	0
2nd	20	16	4	10	10
3rd	20	12	8	10	10
4th	20	8	12	10	10
5th	20	4	161	0	10
Total	100	60	40	60	40

Source: William Diebold, Jr., *Trade and Payments in Western Europe: A Study in Economic Cooperation 1947–51* (New York: Harper, 1952), p. 95.

and to permit banks to deal with each other in any of the eight currencies. These measures, in addition to the increased dollar/gold requirement to settle payments, moved the members closer to convertibility. In 1955 the EPU members further agreed that when sufficient members so decided (the members so deciding had to hold at least half of the EPU quotas) they could make their currencies fully convertible. On December 27, 1958, this moment finally arrived. Belgium and Luxembourg, France, Germany, Italy, the Netherlands, and the United Kingdom held more than the required one-half of all EPU quotas and announced that they would make their currencies externally convertible; sixteen non-EPU members announced that they would follow and allow convertibility. The EPU had completed its mission of establishing a working multilateral trade and payments system for Europe and the wider world.

As a temporary scheme to build a sustainable multilateral payments system out of the restrictive bilateral agreements and trade restrictions before 1950, the EPU was a great success. There were, of course, breakdowns along the way: for example, the agreement suspensions by Germany in 1953. But without the EPU or a similar payments union, the members of the OEEC could not have unilaterally freed payments and would have been forced to retain their trade and exchange controls in order to save scarce hard currencies for their import requirements. Even the united OEEC trade liberalization program could not have stimulated trade because payments would still have been restricted. The EPU allowed intra-European trade to expand while maintaining Europe's trade with the dollar and sterling areas.

The final net positions of each member country, along with the cumulative total EPU balance sheet, help explain how the payments actually worked and to what extent credit was used to ease trade flows by each of the participating nations (Table 2.4). From these data it is clear that the major creditors were Belgium and Germany, with Germany far and away the most important lender.

TABLE 2.4
Cumulative Positions of Member Countries, 1950–58

Surplus positions*		Deficit positions*	
Belgium	+ 1234	Iceland	− 44
Switzerland	+ 39	Italy	− 435
Netherlands	+ 581	Turkey	− 481
Germany	+ 4581	Denmark	− 272
Sweden	+ 146	France	− 2953
		United Kingdom	− 1479
		Greece	− 317
		Austria	− 58
		Norway	− 360
		Portugal	− 173

*Surplus (+) or Deficit (−), in millions of units of account.
Source: Bank of International Settlements, *Annual Report,* 1958–59.

This dominant financial position of Germany continued throughout the EEC's development and is still evident in the current talks on the extension of European monetary cooperation. The major deficit countries were France and the United Kingdom, with deficits many times greater than those of any of the other countries. The total position of the cumulative bilateral positions is given in Table 2.5.

The total net bilateral transactions were $46.5 billion (the total after all debits and credits were offset). The total commercial transactions, of course, were many times greater. The multilateral compensations were cleared through the EPU at the end of each month and were the amounts by which each country's surpluses with some members were offset against its deficits with others. The difference between the total clearing and the monthly compensations shows the cumulative total over the whole period of each member's monthly deficits and surpluses with all other members as a group. The payments over time were those consolidated deficits or surpluses that were later—perhaps very many months later—offset by corresponding surpluses or deficits. The total of multilateral trade not cleared each month was $26.4 billion (1–2), of this only $12.6 reversed itself over time. The rest was settled under "special payments" or in direct credit and gold. The "special" payments category includes settlements by positions initially allocated as grants, by transfers from initial holdings of national currencies, by the net effect of interest due to or from the Union, and by adjustments in connection with special gold credits. Imbalances that had not been multilaterally offset, had not reversed themselves over time, or had not been specially settled or adjusted were necessarily paid by credit received or granted and not yet repaid or by transfers of gold not yet reversed.

Of course, a multilateral payments union would not ease trade if frontier barriers, like quantitative restrictions (QRs) and tariffs, were not removed. The Americans saw the decontrol of goods and service trade and the construction of a payments union as a single issue; policies with respect to one must be matched in the other. Piecemeal relaxation of import quotas had been under way since 1947, but progress had been neither geographically nor sectorally

TABLE 2.5
Total Bilateral Positions Within the EPU 1950–58 (billions of dollars)

Total (deficits + surpluses) of which:	46.5	100%	
Multilateral compensations	20.0	43%	
Compensations over time	12.6	27%	
Special settlements	0.5	1%	
Balance of which settled in:	13.4	29%	
Gold	10.7	23%	(80%)
Credit	2.7	6%	(20%)

Source: Managing Board of the EPU, *EPU Final Report,* Paris, 1959, p. 39 (as cited in Jacob Kaplan and Günther Schleiminger, *The European Payments Union Financial Diplomacy in the 1950s,* Oxford: Clarendon Press, 1989, p. 349).

even. Quotas had largely been removed on essential raw material imports and had been left intact on manufactures and foodstuffs. In 1948 trade liberalization proceeded, with Britain removing 66 percent of its quotas, France 18 percent, and Belgium 78 percent. Countries conducted trade under private compensation agreements, which were not under the liberalization. In addition, surplus countries like Belgium, Germany, Switzerland, and Italy were excluded from import liberalization by Denmark, the United Kingdom, Norway, the Netherlands, Ireland, and Austria.

At the end of January 1950, the OEEC Council decided that after establishment of the EPU, members were to remove additional QRs on private trade with other members until 60 percent of goods were freed. They could, of course, maintain them toward nonmembers. The restriction to private trade was introduced to avoid the charge of interfering with national as opposed to international policy. However, by exempting (semi-) governmental import agencies, which were particularly prevalent in agriculture, the impact of the experiment was dampened from the start. This bias in the operation was compounded by dropping the initial obligation to remove QRs evenly over broad product categories once the targets were raised further: an overperformance in raw materials, for example, could compensate for an underachievement in agriculture. Moreover, the base year for the calculations also presented difficulties. If the base was a year in which imports of certain categories of goods were virtually nonexistent but a fairly liberal quota regime was applied elsewhere, the target of removing QRs from imports worth 60 percent of the total in that year might be relatively easy. Furthermore, the liberalization code allowed countries with balance-of-payments difficulties to reimpose restrictions if necessary, causing a rebound effect on its trading partners and undermining the EPU's "discipline" in the process. Finally, the whole operation excluded tariffs, considered the preserve of GATT, so that quantity restriction removal was often accompanied by the (re)imposition of (partially) suspended tariffs. But this at least made the trade barriers transparent and subject to reciprocal reduction under the negotiations going on under GATT. As the CEEC put it, "As quantitative restrictions are progressively eliminated, tariffs will re-emerge as the principal factor influencing the flow of trade between the participating countries."[14]

On October 27, 1950, the OEEC Council agreed that by February 1951 members should remove QRs on 75 percent of imports from other members. Because of the dissent over agriculture, the target applied only to the total and not to each category. In addition, there was an attempt to construct a common list of products to liberalize so that there would be a unified market, but that came to grief due to the price shocks caused by the outbreak of the Korean War. Further progress was slowed down by successive balance-of-payments crises in West Germany, in the United Kingdom, and in France which compelled their governments to suspend temporarily their liberalizations. This crisis atmosphere inhibited discussions on the timing of a further advance. It was also inhibited by the hardening attitude of so-called low-tariff countries toward the failure to tackle tariffs, and therefore to deal with all frontier barriers to trade.

Finally, as QR removal advanced, it threatened to touch the hard core of protectionism around politically, socially, or strategically vital sectors.

Despite these problems, in January 1955 the OEEC adopted the target of 90 percent liberalization; the low-tariff countries made the renewal contingent on progress on the tariff front. The target was indeed renewed, and when France attained it in December 1958, private trading within Western Europe had, to all intents and purposes, been purged of quantitative restrictions. There remained residual quota discrimination against the United States and, of course, state trading in agriculture was widespread. Nonetheless, for an experiment with such tentative beginnings, the achievement was remarkable.

THE EUROPEAN COAL AND STEEL COMMUNITY

While trade was being liberalized and a multilateral payment system created, the coal and steel sectors of Western Europe were slowly recovering from the war. These were key industries that had figured prominently in governmental recovery programs, such as the Monnet Plan. It was not by accident that the first major broad-based sectoral integration plan was the European Coal and Steel Community (ECSC). Coal and steel were important traded goods, essential industrial inputs, easy to control because they were largely homogeneous products, and had a long history of international cooperation. The first international agreements date from the mid-nineteenth century, and the entire Western European steel trade in the 1930s was controlled by international arrangements. It was also no accident that it came when it did and from whom; the French proposal came when France was finally convinced that it would not be able to establish some sort of international control of the Ruhr and that German reindustrialization was a reality and a major objective for the United States.

After negotiations beginning in Paris in June 1950, a draft of the Treaty of Paris was initialed on March 19, 1951, by representatives of France, West Germany, Italy, Belgium, the Netherlands, and Luxembourg, the same countries that would sign the Treaty of Rome six years later. The Treaty was officially signed and agreed to on April 18, 1951, and the European Coal and Steel Community came into effect in July 1952. The British chose not to join the ECSC, and Clement Attlee, prime minister during the negotiations, summed up the British position that would carry over to the British response to the EEC. He said: "We on this side are not prepared to accept the principle that the most vital economic forces of this country should be handed over to an authority that is utterly undemocratic and is responsible to nobody."[15]

The ECSC was created to stabilize prices, ease the distribution of coal during the postwar boom, provide new markets for iron ore and steel, and coordinate competition. To these ends, all import and export duties, subsidies, and other discriminatory measures were immediately abolished on the trade of coal and steel. Internally, the ECSC was administered by an organization similar to that of the future EEC. It was controlled by the High Authority, a supranational organization composed of nine independent members assigned by the member nations. It cooperated with a Consultative Committee, made up of thirty to fifty-one members from producer, worker, consumer, and dealer unions, and with a Special Council of Ministers, in which each country had one vote. The High Authority was responsible to a Common Assembly composed of seventy-eight members of the national parliaments. Although the High Authority was the most powerful governing body, the Council could block HA decisions and the Assembly could force the resignation of HA members. Because members had very different dependencies on nonmembers, policies with respect to them were left uncontrolled.

The impact of the ECSC is hard to judge. The immediate removal of trade controls differed from the transitional periods common in most European agreements, and thus avoided the indefinite postponement of their removal. However, the actual impact of the tariff removal sounded better than it was: tariffs and quotas were less important in determining trade flows than in the past. In coal there were international agreements and tariffs did not really play a role, except in Italy with a 15 percent rate. For steel, Italian tariffs remained at 11 to 23 percent ad valorem until 1958; France and Germany suspended tariffs before the Treaty was signed. Thus, the only tariffs actually removed by the treaty were the low Benelux tariffs.

The ECSC's impact on pricing was certainly more important. It eliminated dual pricing within the ECSC and created a base-point pricing system. Although price controls and subsidies were not fully abolished, even small progress on this front eased trade. In addition to dual pricing, the discriminatory transport price policies of the ECSC members were eliminated. By volume, coal and steel were two of the most important traded goods, so reduction of cross-border rates of about 30 percent made a major impact in decontrolling transport. The opening of the coal and steel trade did expand imports of steel products into France and the Saar. They jumped from 27.7 thousand tons in 1952 to 117.6 thousand in 1953—a period of low demand with trade barriers in effect for the first few months. In fact, throughout the 1950s, total intracommunity trade grew much faster than production or trade with nonmembers; intra-ECSC trade in treaty products increased 171 percent from 1952 to 1957, while production increased only 43 percent and extra-ECSC trade only 51 percent (Table 2.6). In addition to these concrete effects, the ECSC set the pace and structure of the debate over the next common market for the ECSC six: the European Economic Community.

AGRICULTURE

The other sector that was targeted for integration plans was agriculture. Europe had clear problems with this sector; the protection and control of agriculture was even stronger after 1945 than in the 1930s. During the war, governments had run agriculture virtually as national corporations in order to guarantee food supplies. This had made agricultural self-sufficiency afterward a national prior-

TABLE 2.6
Growth of Steel Trade of ECSC Members

	Intra-ECSC trade	Crude steel	Steel exports to third countries	Intra-ECSC trade in non-treaty goods
1953	138	95	102	111
1954	200	105	102	125
1955	271	126	121	150
1956	243	136	145	179
1957	271	143	151	193

*1952 = 100

Source: William Diebold, Jr., *The Schuman Plan: A Study in Economic Cooperation, 1950–1959* (New York: Praeger, 1958), p. 577.

ity. Nonetheless, production still lagged behind population growth: in 1950–51 overall production had reached prewar levels, but the population had already grown by 12 percent. Within cereals, wheat and rye production rose 4.2 percent and oats and barley rose 1.5 percent. The European excess demand had to be made up by imports from the leading world exporter, the United States, and this contributed substantially to the total dollar deficits; the relative share of imports from the dollar area almost tripled from 1934–38 to 1950–51. In circumstances of import dependence, governments usually resorted to monopoly importing agencies. These administered "equalization" taxes paid by importers to make up the difference between the import price and the domestic target price; this had the same effect as a sliding duty but was not a tariff. (These would, of course, become the variable levies of the CAP; see Chapter 6.) Through such measures, governments avoided decontrol from the OEEC liberalization scheme (state trade not included) and the GATT (the equalization was a domestic tax, not a tariff). A different forum was needed to attack agricultural controls.

After a meeting of the OEEC's agricultural ministers in March 1952, it was clear that the supranational plans of Dutch minister Mansholt were unacceptable even to the six. So between 1953 and 1955 a series of ministerial meetings, the so-called Green Pool negotiations, were held to discuss collective agricultural policies and to look for means to promote trade in foodstuffs. Three product groups were discussed: cereals, dairy products, and fruits and vegetables.

Cereals were the most traded agricultural products but were mainly imported from the dollar area, accounting for about 40 percent of OEEC foodstuffs deficit. After it was clear that a multilateral trading arrangement was impossible, countries moved to bilateral agreements, with each country protecting its domestic producers. Dairy products were the second largest traded category and were heavily supported by governments. The United Kingdom had massive deficits, mainly with non-OEEC countries. However, the unique nature of U.K. controls made them difficult to address. Moreover, other countries were unwilling to give up their own domestic controls. The legacy of this early failure was clearly evident in the butter mountains and milk lakes of the CAP later. The final area was fruits and vegetables, which were protected whenever domestic harvests were ready. These "calendary" controls made countries race to sell their own surpluses before the seasonal closing of the markets.

Overall, the Green Pool had little impact on reducing governmental controls and freeing trade, and in 1955 the operation was wound up. Even when there was a willingness to increase imports, it would not be at the expense of national production. The European control of agricultural products during the slump of the 1930s, immediately after the war, and even through the dollar shortages of the early 1950s did have an economic rationale. However, with these crises, powerful agricultural domestic groups were formed. One "lesson" learned from this experience was that leaving agricultural ministers alone to decide agricultural policy left them at the mercy of these pressure groups. A second was that agriculture by itself offered insufficient trade-offs to secure substantial progress. A possible third was that the only way to neutralize national agricultural policies was to replace them with a single supranational policy. All three "lessons" were subsumed into the negotiations that were to lead to the Treaty of Rome. Subsequent history showed that they were only imperfectly learned.

REGIONAL TRADE AGREEMENTS

As well as sectoral integration, regional schemes were attempted also. The oldest postwar experiment in regional integration in Western Europe was the agreement between Belgium and Luxembourg (whose own economic union, the BLEU, dated back to 1921) and the Netherlands, which has coexisted with many organizations quite well. It was founded on a monetary agreement concluded in 1943 and a customs union treaty signed a year later by the three governments-in-exile in London. Before the war they had conducted approximately 10 percent of their trade with each other, although there was an increasing imbalance in favor of the BLEU. The greater wartime damage in the Netherlands served to accentuate the Dutch deficit; from 1947 to 1951 the deficit grew 202 percent.

Despite the difficulties, the customs union came into force in January 1948, when all tariffs were abolished and a common external tariff (CET) was created. However, trade was still impeded by the widespread imposition of quotas, especially on the side of the Dutch. To remove these, even if only toward the BLEU, threatened merely to aggravate the deficit. Progress was made possible only by two further measures. First, Belgium granted ever greater credit extensions (which it was willing to do if it meant securing the Dutch market from Germany while the latter's industry was still being kept artificially low) and eventually the problem was subsumed into the European Payments Union. Second, the Dutch were able to secure preferential access to the Belgian agricultural market. They had wanted completely free access, as this would have helped remedy the deficit, but they had to make do with a provision that left Belgium's domestic protectionism intact.

Agriculture remained a continuous source of irritation within Benelux. The original deal had been made when the Dutch position had been weak. Attempts by the Netherlands to strike a better bargain floundered on the opposition of the Belgian farmers' unions and, after 1951, on concerns about the Belgian balance of payments. The turnaround in the situation was remarkable as Belgian industries felt increasing pressure from Dutch competition. Further trade relaxations agreed to by the partners were, to some extent, undermined by secret protocols permitting import limitations if the pressures became too acute.

With the disappearance of overall balance-of-payments problems, the countries began also to free capital controls and signed a convention to that effect in July 1953. In January 1956 an agreement was reached on the mobility of labor and, in 1958, the final arguments about the unification of excise duties were resolved. At that point the partners signed a treaty of economic union. Ironically, just two months earlier, the Treaty of Rome had come into force spelling the end of the trade preferences that had sustained the Benelux experiment since the war.

There is a tendency to underplay the Benelux achievement, especially since it became overshadowed by larger unions. This has been reinforced by the revelation in the archives of the domestic rivalries and international wrangles that accompanied its creation and functioning. Yet there was a considerable shift in commercial relations. From 1948 to 1958 the relative share of imports from the Netherlands into BLEU doubled, while BLEU's share in the Netherlands increased 40 percent. The Netherlands' exclusive rights in the BLEU made a major impact on its trade and helped to swing the Dutch deficit around. Benelux shows that smaller unions can exist within larger ones.

PRECURSORS OF THE EEC

From very early on, plans were made to extend these regional and sectoral arrangements and to create a global customs union for Europe. Countries had tried "little European" unions, for example, the FINEBEL between France, Italy and BLEU, and the Franco-Italian Customs Union, but each of these came to naught. The necessary economic and political framework did not exist and the plans were not undertaken. The first major plan for a European customs union was in the negotiations for the Marshall Plan, under the heading of the European Customs Union Study Group (ECUSG). However, the ECUSG never moved beyond the preparation of some technical reports. Its work was hampered by the fact that no political decision had yet been taken about the future of the West German economy. Without that, its "assessments of the impact of a Western European customs union remained a purely hypothetical exercise."[16] France would not consider a union of which Germany was a member from the start; the Netherlands and Denmark would not join one of which it was not. To make matters worse, the United Kingdom had decided not to join because it felt that membership would interfere too much with the exercise of domestic policy. Within a year most governments had lost any illusions that the attempt at a sixteen country customs union would succeed.

Nonetheless the experts produced a "final" report at the end of 1948. Its upbeat message, that there were "fewer difficulties in the way of the formation of a Customs Union than might have been expected,"[17] was curiously at odds with its contents. It argued that particular measures for individual industries were better than general measures (though the individual solutions to facilitate integration often had an overtly protectionist or cartelistic tint). It also suggested that not all measures needed to be taken together. It distinguished between those industries that would be relatively easy to integrate and those that would not. The latter were more numerous and included foodstuffs and iron and steel. Nobody was remotely interested. The ECUSG lingered on for a while until its technical work on collecting customs data could be transferred to another body. Forty years later, it is difficult to disagree with Diebold's dismissive judgment of the ECUSG as "pretty much a backwater of European economic cooperation."[18]

This illustrates the importance of political relations in the implementation of economic programs. Also, it shows that important players need to be addressed politically. For most of Europe it was not an easy political decision to include Germany in their plans so soon after the war. However, once the various organizations were operating (the OEEC, the EPU, the ECSC) with Germany as an important member, German relations were no longer a constraint to broader integration plans, and the countries finally could discuss meaningfully a broad economic union.

Endnotes

1. For a description of this process, see Alan Milward and S. B. Saul, *The Development of the Economies of Continental Europe: 1850–1914,* London: Allen & Unwin, 1977.

2. Thomas Knock, *To End All Wars: Woodrow Wilson and the Quest for a New World Order,* New York: Oxford University Press, 1992, especially pp. 162–165.

3. The International Chamber of Commerce in 1937 issued a report on international cartels, whose products included such products as lightbulbs, cocaine, cotton, and iron and steel. See the International Chamber of Commerce's report on Ententes Internationales. Congrès Berlin, Document no. 4, 1937.

4. These were the agreements of 1925 that ended the French occupation of the Ruhr and granted Germany sovereignty over the area.

5. We discuss this in more detail in the next chapter, but here is a brief definition: A customs union is an agreement between at least two countries that abolishes restrictions on goods and factors (land ownership, labor migration, and capital movements) and creates a common trade policy among members toward nonmembers.

6. See Winston Churchill's speech in Geneva in 1946 and Jean Monnet's letters in Washington.

7. J. L. van Zanden and R. T. Griffiths, *Economische geschiedenis van Nederland in de 20e eeuw,* Utrecht: Het Spectrum, 1989, pp. 186–187.

8. A. S. Milward, *The Reconstruction of Western Europe, 1945-*51, London: Metheun, 1984, p.95.

9. Barry Eichengreen and Marc Uzan. "The Marshall Plan: Economic effects and implications for Eastern Europe," *Economic Policy,* vol. 15, 1991.

10. See Knut Borchardt and Christoph Buchheim "The Marshall Plan and economic key sectors: a micro-economic perspective," in Charles Maier, ed., *The Marshall Plan and Germany,* New York: Berg, 1991.

11. J. Bradford De Long and Barry Eichengreen, "The Marshall plan: history's most successful structural adjustment program," CEPR Discussion Paper No. 634, p. 45.

12. These bilateral agreements caused all sorts of distortions. For example, often goods were "tied in" to contracts so that in the postwar period luxury goods such as expensive textiles, cosmetics, perfumes, jewelry, gourmet foods, wines, and even vacuum cleaners were extensively traded.

13. W. Diebold, *Trade and Payments in Western Europe: A Study in Economic Cooperation, 1947–51,* New York: Harper, 1952, p. 44.

14. Committee for European Economic Cooperation, *Report,* Summer 1947 para. 87.

15. Prime Minister Clement Attlee, in response to the Schuman Plan. Quoted in Michael Palmer, et. al., *European Unity: A Survey of the European Organizations,* London: Allen and Unwin, 1968, p. 258.

16. Asbeek Brusse, *West European Tariff Plans, 1947–1957. From Study Group to Common Market,* Ph.D. dissertation, Florence, 1991, p. 49.

17. Ibid., p. 56.

18. W. Diebold, *The Schuman Plan: A Study in Economic Cooperation, 1950–1959.* New York, Praeger, 1959, p. 317.

CHAPTER 3

The Customs Union:
A Step Forward or a Step Backward?

With international trade becoming a larger part of world economic activity, trade relationships have become ever more complicated and disputed. The multilateral, overarching GATT framework that has guided trade over the past fifty years has been increasingly challenged by regional "minilateral" arrangements, as in the recently ratified NAFTA.[1] Perhaps the most important example of this type of arrangement is the European Community, which is currently widening by incorporating more countries and deepening by integrating more fully in new sectors. Why are countries interested in these agreements and should nonparticipating countries be concerned about them? This chapter explains the consequences of unions, both for their members and nonmembers.

Before analyzing them, we must first set out some common terms. *Bilateral arrangements* are made between two countries only; we saw the difficulties these type of agreements can have on trade in the previous chapter. *Multilateral arrangements* are among a large group of countries, not conditioned on any regional requirement. *Minilateral* or *regional agreements* are among a selected group of countries, and may or may not spread to more countries. Among these type of relationships between or among countries, the nature of the actual agreements can differ in degree of integration. The first step along the way is the free trade area. This is an area in which the countries agree to eliminate tariffs within the area only; they retain their own policies toward nonmembers. The next step is the customs union, in which countries add a common external policy to the free trade area. When factors of production (land ownership, labor, and capital) are allowed to flow freely within a customs union, you then have a common market. This is what the Treaty of Rome envisioned and is what the EC is still moving toward. Once in a common market, countries can add the common determination of fiscal and monetary policy. This forms the basis for an economic union and is what the Maastricht Treaty attempts to achieve.

BACKGROUND

By 1957, the export-led economic miracles of West Germany, Italy, and the Netherlands were well recognized, as was the relatively slow growth of France, Great Britain, and Belgium. The Belgian economist, Alexandre Lamfalussy, explained why the sluggishness of the British and American economies compared with the successes of the European Continent predated the formation of the European Community.[2] In each case where a European country had achieved the "virtuous circle" of sustained high rates of growth of total output, Lamfalussy found that exports had grown much more rapidly than either imports or total product. This led to large and growing export surpluses, which provided the firms in the export sector the financing they needed to sustain continued high rates of investment. Lamfalussy noted that this worked only if home demand was also strong, as a result of governments pursuing full-employment policies. As this was universal practice then among all industrial democracies, including the slow-growing economies of Great Britain and the United States, the importance of export surpluses was not so much to provide financing for additional investment as to remove balance-of-payments concerns for governments. Great Britain and France in the 1950s repeatedly ran into balance-of-payments problems, which led Great Britain to restrict home demand, including investment, and led France to devalue or maintain import restrictions and exchange controls. Both strategies reduced investment, reduced export competitiveness, and kept growth slow.

The link between high ratios of investment to total output and high rates of growth of total output that Lamfalussy found in his empirical data fit very nicely with the Keynesian growth theory that dominated economic thinking in the 1950s. According to this view of the economy, the rate of growth of output was determined by the rate of growth of the capital stock, a consequence of a fixed capital-output ratio that was supposed to characterize modern industrial economies. The rate of growth of the capital stock was determined in turn by the share of investment in total national product, which in its turn was limited by the share of savings in total national income.[3] The Harrod-Domar growth model formalized these relationships in the expression $s/k = g$; the warranted rate of growth of total product for a nation, g, was equal to the product of its savings rate, s, and the inverse of its capital-output ratio, k. Export-led growth had the salutary effect of increasing a nation's savings rate by tapping into the funds of foreign customers *and* of decreasing its capital-output ratio by increasing the productivity of its capital stock. The two factors combined to give exporting countries significantly higher rates of growth than importing countries.

Export-led growth appeared to be driving the economic miracles of Germany and Italy, with the Netherlands benefiting from its preferred position as the gateway for the external trade of a revitalized German economy. Belgium and France lagged noticeably behind, even though they were associated with the export leaders through the European Coal and Steel Community. The idea of a customs union among the members of the ECSC was appealing to the laggards, France and Belgium, so they could imitate the success of the leaders, and it was also appealing to the leaders, so they could exploit naturally contiguous markets that they had not yet begun to penetrate and so keep their export booms continuing. Both sets of countries anticipated benefits from trade creation among the member countries. The United States and Great Britain were less enthusiastic about the prospects, as were the Scandinavian states. They foresaw dangers of trade diversion because their export markets in Europe would be diminished.

PART I: THEORY

Creating a customs union is a partial liberalization of trade and should have positive welfare effects for the member countries and the nonmember countries. Insofar as tariffs are reduced, this should create trade and yield a welfare benefit, yet if a low-cost producer is excluded from the tariff reduction, then trade will be *diverted* from the low-cost producer and welfare will be lost. The two phenomena, *trade creation* within a customs union and *trade diversion* from former trading partners now outside the customs union, are most easily analyzed in a comparative statics framework.[4] We begin with a highly stylized portrayal of the French economy in the mid1950s, in the course of gradually substituting high tariffs for the quantitative restrictions (QRs) it had maintained after World War II. Figure 3.1 represents France as a high-cost producer of any manufactured good, *M*. This good is available at much lower prices from either

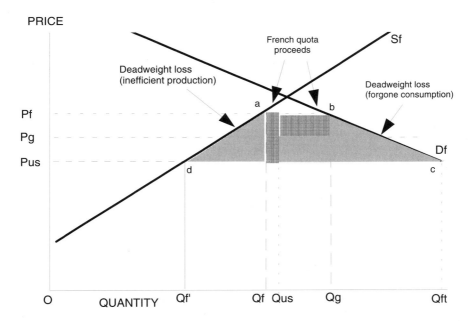

Figure 3.1. Efficiency and political economy of quantitative restrictions.

Germany or at even lower prices from the United States. Initially, France permits very small amounts in from the United States (thinking it has a dollar shortage), setting an American import quota of ($Q_{US} - Q_F$). France permits larger amounts from Germany, setting the German import quota at ($Q_G - Q_{US}$) (using credits it has received for agricultural exports to Germany), making total imports ($Q_G - Q_F$), total consumption OQ_G, and French domestic production OQ_F. This diagram can be analyzed in two different ways: (1) using positive economics to examine the efficiency of this situation of limited foreign trade; and (2) using normative economics to examine the equity, or distribution of benefits, among the various groups involved.

EFFICIENCY OF QUOTA RESTRICTIONS

French producers benefit from the restriction of imports, but at the expense of French consumers who are kept from enjoying the lower prices available from either the German or U.S. producers. Nevertheless, French consumers enjoy some of the benefits of foreign trade, as the price at which the market will absorb the U.S. and German imports in addition to French domestic production, P_F, is lower than the price at which the market will absorb the supply that can be provided by the high-cost French producers alone. Moreover, the French government can extract the difference between the French price and the prices the U.S. and German producers receive for their exports by charging the American firms $P_F - P_{US}$ and the German firms $P_F - P_G$ for per unit import licenses. Thus, the government receives the areas shown as "French quota proceeds."

If France had a free trade policy, it would import from the United States, making the domestic price P_{US} and consumption Q_{FT}. If the government, however, forces the price P_F through quotas, consumption falls to Q_G. Note that consumer surplus has fallen by $P_F bc P_{US}$. Producer surplus has risen by $P_F ad$-P_{US}, which is an area merely transferred from consumers to producers. The rest of the lost consumer surplus, *abcd,* still must be accounted for. The shaded triangles labeled as deadweight losses give a visual measure of the inefficiency of this trading arrangement. These are areas of lost consumer surplus that are not regained by any French group. The right hand triangle labeled "Deadweight loss (forgone consumption)" is the net loss of the lost consumption. French consumers also lose the benefits of the possible increase in production of other goods, measured by the left-hand triangle labeled "Deadweight loss (forgone production)." In the end, France gets less M and pays more for it.

POLITICAL ECONOMY OF QUOTA RESTRICTIONS

Looking at the various differences between free trade and the quota restrictions, one can see why many policy-oriented economists are less than overwhelming in their enthusiasm for free trade. Their reluctance to push harder for an improvement in economic efficiency stems mainly from recognizing the political

difficulties that policymakers would confront in displacing so much French production $(Q_F - Q_{F'})$ and facilitating the re-deployment of French capital, labor,
and natural resources into production of other, diverse, goods, whose effects
are measured in the deadweight loss triangle on the left. In addition, the government receives revenues from the quota proceeds. Governments are almost
always looking for ways to finance projects without having to tax their citizens
directly. However, the argument for moving from quantitative restrictions to
tariff barriers is much more compelling. With this policy change, the distribution of gains to consumers and producers does not have to be disturbed and
the government itself will end up as the net gainer. This is the result of now
receiving tariff revenues that should be larger than the proceeds it received
from the sale of import licenses.

TARIFF BARRIERS: EFFICIENCY CONSIDERATIONS

Figure 3.2 shows exactly the same demand and supply schedules as in Figure
3.1, as well as the same prices for U.S. and German sources of supply.[5] Now a
uniform tariff is levied on imports, regardless of their origin, and no restriction
is placed on the amount imported. The same deadweight losses occur as before—no surprise—but now the sole foreign source of supply becomes the lowest cost producer anywhere in the world, in this case the United States. (Remember, we are developing our theory in the context of the international
economic situation of the mid-1950s, the golden age for U.S. manufacturing!)

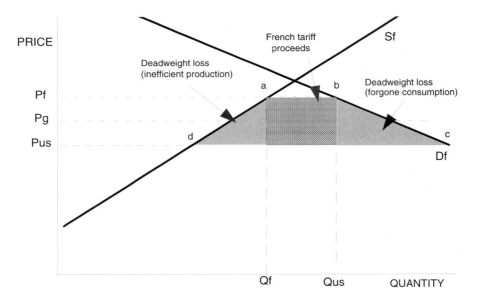

Figure 3.2. Efficiency and political economy of tariffs.

As a result, the French government obtains a much larger amount of tariff revenues than it did under the previous regime of quota restrictions. The only losers in this case are the German producers, who now lose their quota on the French market and have to look for alternative buyers for their output either in Germany or in other foreign countries (such as the United States)—or go out of business.

CUSTOMS UNION: COMPARATIVE STATICS

It is precisely this situation that a customs union is designed to prevent. Instead of driving German industry further away from cooperation with French industry and looking to increased trade opportunities in Scandinavia and overseas, a customs union would bring German and French industry closer together, albeit at the expense of tariff revenues for the government. Inside a customs union, which erects a common external tariff around the member countries while removing all tariffs on trade among themselves, both French and German firms would enjoy the same level of tariff protection from U.S. and British competition. In the French market, the German producers are given an artificial advantage over the U.S. producers by having no tariff levied against their imports, while the full tariff remains in force against the United States, Britain, Japan, or any potential competitor outside the customs union. French firms receive the same advantage on the German market.

EFFICIENCY ANALYSIS

Using the same supply and demand schedules as shown in Figures 3.1 and 3.2, Figure 3.3 illustrates the efficiency effects of such a customs union, which maintains the same tariff as before on U.S. imports, but now eliminates it entirely for imports from Germany. Because German producers are more efficient than their French counterparts in the production of this particular good, the total imports rise substantially, and the final price paid by French consumers falls to the level of the German price. Much of the deadweight loss triangles we saw in Figures 3.1 and 3.2 are now eliminated. These are counted as net gains to the French economy, but note that they are captured entirely by French consumers. French producers lose as part of their former production is now taken up by German imports. The French government loses all of its tariff revenues that it received previously, because now all the imports are coming from the lowest price source, which has become, thanks to the differential tariff on U.S. goods, Germany. And German imports pay no tariff under the rules of the customs union. Part of the lost tariff revenues are captured, however, by French consumers (and presumably can be taxed back by the French government). It is only the amount marked "Trade Diversion" that is lost, net, to the French economy.

The three shaded areas in Figure 3.3 represent the diverse sources of gains and losses to an importing country that joins a customs union that includes a

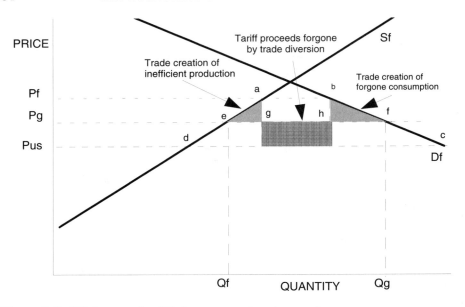

Figure 3.3. Efficiency and political economy of customs unions.

country with more efficient firms than its own. They are *gains from trade creation* and *losses from trade diversion*.

- *Gains from trade creation.* The right-hand triangle results from consumption expansion (as a result of more total units of *M* now available to French consumers) and the left-hand triangle results from production reduction (as a result of French firms now being unable to compete with the more efficient German firms).

- *Losses from trade diversion.* The rectangle representing the net loss of tariff revenues to the French nation also measures the losses from trade diversion—the cost to the French of importing now from a more expensive foreign source than previously. The height of the rectangle is the difference between the German price and the U.S. price for the good, and the length is the amount previously imported from the United States.

The net effect of moving from a tariff situation to a customs union is the sum of the areas of the two triangles representing the gains of trade creation, minus the area of the rectangle representing the loss from trade diversion.[6] In this case, the net outcome is a loss for France for this particular commodity. The outcome, of course, will vary across the many thousands of commodities that can be traded, so it is useful to summarize the key factors that determine whether the outcome will be positive or negative. The area of the right-hand triangle, the gain from expanded consumption, will be larger the more elastic, or price responsive, is the French demand curve for the product. Likewise, the area of the left-hand triangle, the gain from decreased production, will be larger the more elastic or price responsive is the French supply curve for the product. And both will be larger, the lower is the German price relative to the U.S. price plus the tariff. The area of the rectangle, or net losses of tariff revenues, will be smaller the less was imported in the first place and the closer the German price is to the U.S. price.

EQUITY EVALUATION

Now let's examine the distributional effects of the customs union after it has taken full effect and assuming, as is usual in comparative statics analysis, that no changes in the underlying demand and supply curves have occurred in any of the affected countries. Clearly, French consumers have gained over the situation when France imported from the United States with a tariff of t; consumer surplus rises by area $P_{US} + tbcP_G$. In addition to capturing all of the trade creation gains analyzed above and taking part of the previous tariff revenues away from the French government (the top half of the rectangle $abef$), they have added even more to their total of consumers' surplus at the expense of the French producers, who have now been displaced by the German imports. The French producers have lost a substantial part of their previous market, whether viewed in terms of the absolute quantity produced, share of the total domestic consumption, or, as we prefer to do in this kind of evaluation, in terms of the total producers' surplus they enjoy, which has fallen by the area $P_{US} + tbcP_G$. The American exporters are nowhere to be seen and are clearly big losers, losing export earnings of $P_{US} * (Q_{US} - Q'_F)$. By contrast, German exporters are enormous gainers, with export earnings of $P_G * (Q_G - Q_F)$, and will clearly become more oriented to the French export market than previously.

It appears on this analysis that the political motivation for a customs union had to be the same as that for the European Coal and Steel Community—to reduce reliance on the United States as a source of supply for vital imports in order to reduce pressure on a recovering nation's tenuous supply of U.S. dollars, while at the same time encouraging economic integration of a politically weak and physically diminished German nation into Western Europe. It also appears on this analysis that these political considerations were dominant, rather than economic benefits foreseen. The efficiency gains were dubious and relatively small at best, whereas the equity implications were obvious and required substantial reallocation of net benefits, with all the domestic political difficulties such redistributions entail. For these reasons some authors have argued that the creation of a customs union is always welfare-inferior to unilateral tariff reduction. If a country favors a customs union policy it must be due to political constraints that preclude the adoption of free trade.[7]

If policy makers cannot, for political reasons, create the conditions necessary for maximizing economic efficiency (say, by eliminating all tariff barriers entirely), they can usually improve things nevertheless by creating some of the conditions and settle for "second best" (say, by eliminating all tariff barriers only with some, politically acceptable, countries). The United States accepted the EC's innovation of a customs union, despite its obvious inconsistency with its long-term goals of promoting multilateral trade under the terms of the General Agreement on Tariffs and Trade.[8] The basis was the assurance by the EC that the average tariff rate of the common external tariff would be less, in fact, than the average of the individual countries' tariff schedules before the formation of the customs union. The EEC committed in 1960 to achieving an average 7.4-percent tariff by 1968, which was significantly lower than the British tariff. In the context of the time, the customs union proposed by the original six was moving in the right direction as far as the United States was concerned, and more rapidly than would be possible otherwise. (The further vicissitudes of tariff negotiations are covered in Chapter 8, External Trade Policies.) However, this view that customs unions need to appeal to political justifications has been challenged by Paul and Ronald Wonnacott. They have shown that a customs union can be welfare-superior to unilateral tariff reduction when tariff and transportation costs are considered within the non-member countries.[9] This finding makes the empirical study of each customs union important because not only can the union be welfare-enhancing (if the trade creation outweighs the diversion), it could be the first-best policy open to a group of nations.

All of these analyses are subject to assumptions about the smallness of the country joining the union and the static, one-time welfare effects of the union. In the next sections we relax these assumptions and find that the evaluation of unions is affected.

THE DYNAMICS OF CUSTOMS UNIONS

The primary factor in the growth of European production and trade has obviously been technological progress, which has created new goods not even imagined in 1958, reduced the cost of producing other goods that were available in the United States but not yet in Europe, and reduced the business transaction costs, including the shipping charges, and costs of inventory control and marketing. These effects can only be captured in our static demand and supply graphs by showing an outward shift in both demand and supply, but a larger shift in supply. If the pace of technological progress is the same for all three countries—the importer, the exporter, and the potential customs union partner—then it is clear that trade will expand more rapidly than production, that the importer's consumers and the exporter's producers will reap the largest gains in consumers' surplus and producers' surplus, and that tariff revenues for the importing country's government will increase rapidly as well. All that technological progress does from this perspective is to increase the gains from trade for the winners (the importer's consumers and government, and the exporter's producers) while reducing the size of the losses for the losers (the importer's producers).

But it is clear from the historical record that technological progress has not been evenly distributed across countries, much less among industries within countries. It is also clear that the rapid increases in production typically lead to more rapid increases in productivity (Verdoorn's Law).[10] This means that the exporting country's productivity will grow more rapidly than productivity in the importing country or in the potential partner country in the customs union; this is often referred to as the polarization effect. Economic historians refer to this phenomenon as another example of path dependency, where chance determines which path an economic activity takes at its beginning, but the path determines the course of the activity ever after. Economic policymakers have seized upon it to justify strategic trade policies, which use trade barriers and investment incentives to launch a national industry on a high productivity path (hopefully). Economic theorists have tried to analyze its effects in the simplest way possible by building on traditional trade theory, which means using the concept of economies of scale to modify the shape of the supply curves.

The creation of the customs union can have a number of indirect, or dynamic, effects. The elimination of some protection can increase competition and lower transaction costs while allowing firms to benefit either from decreasing cost industries, for example, sectors with high fixed costs, or from scale economies, like network systems. In addition, any domestic market power is eroded by the increase of competition, which increases domestic welfare by lowering deadweight losses. Thus, the reduction in market barriers can accelerate the process of technological advance referred to above. In fact, the reduction in production costs could, conceivably, move member states' costs closer to world prices, thus lowering any trade diversion and increasing trade creation. One of the areas Europeans point to most frequently is the gains from increasing size, the gains from economies of scale.

DECREASING COSTS/ECONOMIES OF SCALE

Economies of scale in production for a particular industry imply that as inputs are increased, output increases by even a greater amount. Decreasing costs mean that over an observable range of quantity produced in the industry, its average costs fall. Both imply that as the amount produced rises the per-unit costs fall; in other words, the technical efficiency of the firm's production increases. Figure 3.4 shows the effect for our last example of a customs union in which France is the importer, the United States the previous exporter, and Germany the new exporter, thanks to the differential tariff advantage it enjoys inside the customs union of the European Economic Community. As in the case shown in Figure 3.3 with constant returns to scale for the United States and Germany, the German exporters and the French consumers gain substantially at the expense of French producers and government and U.S. producers. The main differences now are: (1) the difference in gains to the winners and losses to the losers are much greater; (2) the cost advantage of the German producers over the French producers widens enormously, thus wiping out all French production and locking the two economies into this particular trade pattern; and (3) the German producers now obtain a cost advantage over the U.S. producers as well, so that France is now importing, as under the universal tariff regime,

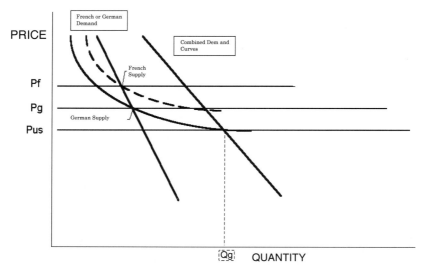

Figure 3.4. Efficiency and political economy of economies of scale.

from the most efficient supplier in the world. The reason for these differences from the constant returns to scale scenario shown earlier is that, thanks to economies of scale, both the French producers and the U.S. exporters who are displaced by the German exporters become less efficient and therefore higher cost as they are forced to produce less than before.

Contrasting the result with that shown in Figure 3.3, one can see clearly the prediction of the kind of result that seems to have been generated by the formation of the customs union called the European Economic Community. The trade has shifted away from previous partners toward partners within the customs union *and* trade has increased within the customs union even more than total production, although that has increased as well. The theory of trade creation and diversion by the formation of customs unions under conditions of economies of scale in production leads to many variations on two themes: strategic trade and technological advantage. Before dealing with these policy issues, however, it is best to anchor our analysis in an accurate appreciation of what has happened to trade patterns and technological progress within the European Community since its formation in 1958.

FROM "SMALL" TO "LARGE"

When countries combine their policies, their global economic relevance changes. While independent, they might have been too small to affect world prices, but combined, they might be able jointly to affect the price. If this is the case, then the rest of the world's received price is forced down and welfare is transferred from the rest of the world to the union. Note that the welfare gains referred to below are not global gains; the terms of trade effects for the union comes at the cost to non-union countries, and so are a type of "beggar-thy-neighbor" policy. Figure 3.5 illustrates how this all works.[11] Suppose a group of small countries[12] are independently conducting their commercial policy and that they each have a specific tariff of t. The horizontal sum of their demand curves for a good is *DEMANDec* and of their supply curves is *SUPPLYec*. Suppose the supply curve of the rest of the world is S_w. Because the countries are each small they face a domestic price of P_w plus their tariff, t; each country's domestic price is thus $P_w + t$. Total imports from the rest of the world into the countries is $(Q_3 - Q_2)$. Now, suppose the countries create a union and combined they face the upward-sloping supply curve, denoted SUPPLY *world*. In this case, the tariff does not simply get added to the intersection of the world supply and domestic demand; instead, the tariff is added vertically to the world supply, resulting in the tariff-included supply curve, *SUPPLY world + tariff*. The intersection of this curve and the domestic demand curve determines the union price, P_{cu}. At price P_{cu}, the quantity demanded rises to Q_4 and union production falls to Q_1. Here, however, foreign producers are receiving a price $P_{cu} - t$, or P'_w. The formation of the union has forced the foreign goods' price down while increasing tariffs so that the domestic economy captures the boxed area, which is the fall in the world price multiplied by the amount of imports—$(P_w - P'w) * (Q_4 - Q_1)$. This is the "terms of trade effect" and represents a transfer

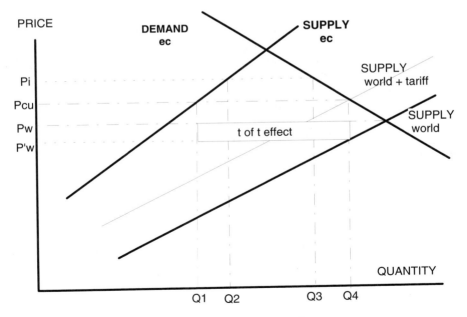

Figure 3.5. Terms of trade (t of t) effect of customs unions.

from the rest of the world to the union. One of the reasons other countries concern themselves with unions is that they must suffer the effects of these terms of trade changes; recall that Japan tried to argue that the North American Free Trade Agreement (NAFTA) might cause such adverse effects to them and opposed the agreement.[13]

PART II: PRACTICE

Given the preceding theory, we would expect the creation of the EEC to increase trade creation more than trade diversion in the member nations. Trade among Western European countries has always been relatively high, and Europe has been a strong industrial area for the whole post World War II period. Indeed, almost all of the estimates of trade creation and trade diversion caused by the EEC show that trade creation far exceeded diversion. This is true for sectoral studies as well as for economy-wide estimates.[14] For example, Bela Belassa's estimates of trade creation for all goods was $11.3 billion, while his estimate of diversion was $0.3 billion.[15] These figures are from a static analysis and ignore the changes through time brought on by the EEC.

The essential feature of a customs union is to change the pattern of trade of the member countries. The EEC has succeeded in doing this to an extent far beyond the wildest expectations of its founding fathers. From having two-thirds of their imports coming from outside the customs union when it was set up in 1958, by 1990 the original six members had over two-thirds of their imports coming from within the customs union, which had doubled its membership to twelve countries. The significance of this change in the pattern of imports (which necessarily has been largely duplicated in the pattern of exports) is often overlooked in view of the even more dramatic increase in the total volume of foreign trade. The rapid growth of West European foreign trade has meant that all trading partners have seen substantial increases in the volume of their exports to the European Community. Whether this has been primarily because of technological progress or institutional changes, or a felicitous combination of the two processes since World War II, is an open question. But there can be no doubt that the change in the geographical pattern of West European trade has been due to the institutional changes created by the European Community.

As is true with most of the initiatives of the European Community, however, this change in trade patterns has historical roots that predate the formation of the customs union. Figure 3.6a shows the growth of imports worldwide over the period 1928 to 1958. The situation in 1928, the last full year of "normalcy" in the interwar period, was that the future founding members of the EC accounted for one-fourth of world imports and of these imports fully three-fourths were from other trading partners. In the 1930s, the figures for 1937 and 1938 evoke the collapse of world trade generally, in which the future EC members shared proportionately. The situation changed dramatically after World War II. (The rise in levels for each series is a result of higher price levels after the war and is not important for the changes in trade patterns.) The exhausted postwar

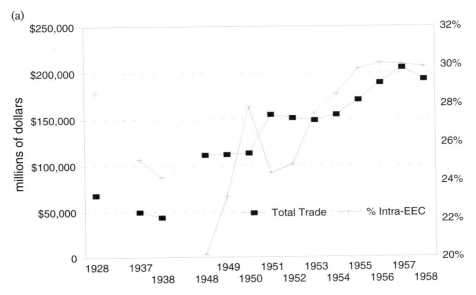

Figure 3.6. (a) EEC Trade, 1928–58 (total in millions of dollars and in percent by EEC6). (b) Growth of imports, 1928–58 (EEC and its members from the rest of the world). (c) Growth of exports, 1928–58 (EEC and its members from the rest of the world).

Source: Statistical Office of the European Communities, *Jahrbuch 1953–1958 des Aussenhandels nach Ursprungs- und Bestimmungslanden,* Brussels, 1959.

economies accounted for only about one-sixth of world imports and five-sixths of their imports came from other trading partners. Their recovery in 1948–50 was reflected in their foreign trade mainly by an increase in their imports from one another. From 1950 on, their imports from the rest of the world grew at about the same pace as world imports generally, but their imports from one another continued to grow more rapidly. By 1958, only 70 percent of their imports came from the rest of the world and now the customs union began to work its effect.

Before examining the vicissitudes of the EC's trading patterns since 1958, it is worthwhile examining Figures 3.6b and 3.6c, which show the growth of imports and exports, respectively, for the original six members over the historical period 1928–58. These show the dominant role of Germany in 1928 and the 1930s, then the collapse of the German economy after its defeat in World War II and the partition of a reduced territory into the four occupation zones. The striking thing is the rapid recovery of a reduced German economy to its prewar preeminence on the European continent by the mid-1950s. Even more striking is the much more rapid growth of exports than imports for the West German economy, which was discussed at the beginning of the chapter. Italy also had a more rapid growth of exports than imports, as did the Netherlands, while

(b)

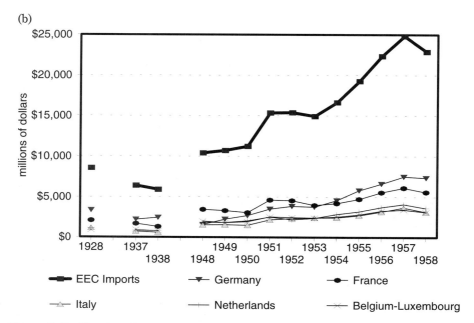

Figure 3.6. *(Continued)*

(c)

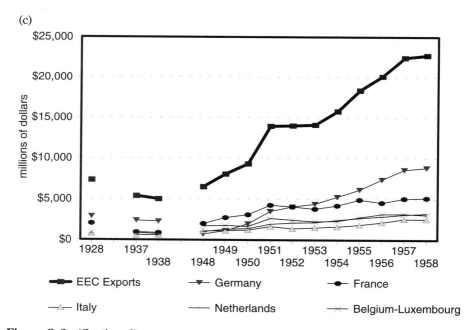

Figure 3.6. *(Continued)*

Belgium-Luxembourg and France both had slightly higher growth rates of imports than exports prior to the formation of the European Economic Community. A more detailed analysis of the trade patterns[16] shows that from 1953 to 1958 the percentage of imports for all the EC members combined fell from every other part of the world, most notably from colonies in Africa and Asia and the sterling area, while rising from North America and East Europe. The rise in the share of imports from the latter two areas was almost entirely due to the new trade orientation of West Germany. This, however, was to come to an end in the 1960s.

Figures 3.7a–d illustrate the changing trade orientation of the four major countries, the four high-income countries, the four low-income countries, and the last three entrants of the EU15 over the entire period 1958–93. The effect of entry into the customs union is clear for the original six, as the share of their trade with each other rose immediately and strongly. The last six members to join show a similar rise in their share of the trade with the EU12 when they enter the customs union—Great Britain, Ireland, and Denmark in 1973; Greece in 1980; and Spain and Portugal in 1986. If we anticipate the addition of the North Sea trio in 1973 and calculate what the share of trade with the outside world would have been if they had been included ten years earlier than they were in fact, it turns out to be around 60 percent also. In other words, the remaining trade of the original six members with the rest of the world was not focusing on the members-to-be, but rather on Scandinavia and North America for Germany, Africa for France, the Mediterranean and Latin and North

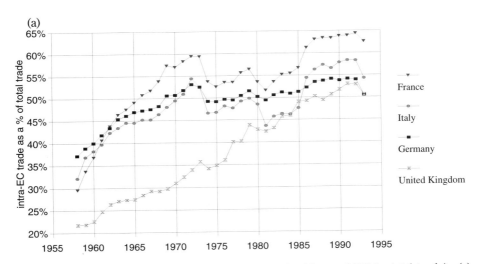

Figure 3.7. Structure of European Community trade (share of EC in total trade). (a) Large countries. (b) High-income small countries. (c) Low-income small countries. (d) Last three entrants of EU15.

Source: Eurostat, *External Trade Statistical Yearbook, Recapitulation 1958.* European Communities: Brussels, 1994, pp. 10–33.

(b)

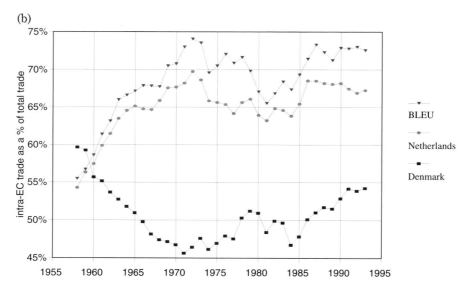

Figure 3.7. *(Continued)*

(c)

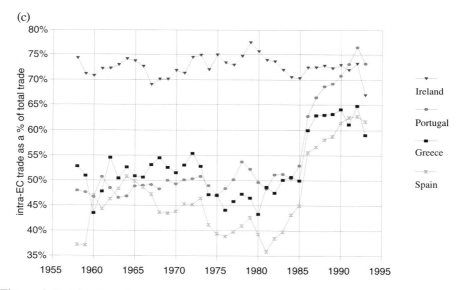

Figure 3.7. *(Continued)*

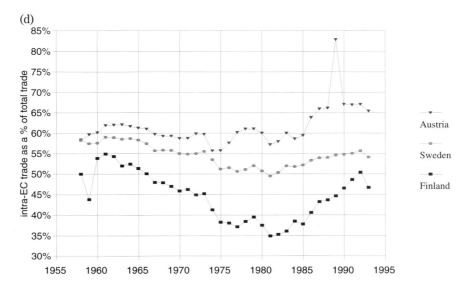

Figure 3.7. *(Continued)*

America for Italy. Britain, meanwhile, concentrated on North America and Ocea-
nia. The major countries in Europe were once again targeting different parts of
the world for their foreign trade initiatives.

The small countries, by contrast, were committed to focusing their trade on
the most aggressively expanding partners, which turned out to be Germany for
the Netherlands and Belgium and Britain for Ireland and Denmark. As might
be predicted, the small countries were the first to show the effects of trading
preferences created by the EEC and the European Free Trade Association in
their trade patterns.

By 1970, the last full year in which the Bretton Woods system of fixed
exchange rates with the dollar as the key currency was in effect, the trading
pattern of the EC6 had dropped its share of imports from the world outside the
customs union to 50 percent, achieving rough equality in their overall trade
between EC members and non-EC members. Again, the same equality shows
up if we include Britain, Ireland, and Denmark, but by 1970 it had become clear
that this was strictly due to an intensification of Irish and Danish trade with
Britain, offsetting their increasing exclusion from the markets of the inner six.[17]

The effects of the customs union on changing the trade pattern of the next
three members to join show up clearly in the figures for 1979. This is all the
more remarkable due to the temporary increase in the weight of imports from
the OPEC countries, caused by the successive oil price shocks of 1974 and
1979. Now the share of imports was greater from within the EC9 than from
outside. But this was the net result of the small member countries focusing on
their trade with large member countries. The large member countries, in turn,
were all less focused on trade within the customs union than were any of the

small member countries. Among the four major countries, a clear pattern emerges with France, Germany, Italy, and Britain, in that order, funneling their imports from within the Community.

During the 1980s, the drop in the price of oil, especially after 1985 when its fall in terms of dollars was augmented by the fall of the dollar with respect to the European currencies, and the expansion of membership to include first Greece (1980) and then Spain and Portugal (1986), combined to continue the change in trade patterns in favor of imports from within the common external tariff area. By 1985 both France and Germany were clearly oriented toward their fellow EC members in their imports, while only Spain among the large countries was still clearly oriented outside the EC. All the small countries, with the exception of Portugal, which had not yet formally joined, and Greece, which was still in its transition period of conforming gradually over five years to the common external tariff, were even more committed to trade within the EC than the large countries. The cases of Ireland and Denmark are especially noteworthy for the progress they had made in re-orienting their imports since 1979. But the pace of reorientation was clearly picking up in the 1980s. By 1990, Spain was almost exactly at the EC12 average of 59 percent of imports from within the EC and Portugal was close to 70 percent. Portugal was now one of the most tightly committed countries to trade within the Community, along with the Netherlands and the Belgium-Luxembourg Economic Union. The last three entrants found their trade with the EC was falling as a share of their total trade until the early 1980s, when more favorable terms were granted to the EFTA countries in general and Finland in particular. This importance of the EU market will certainly continue to increase for them now that they have formally entered the EU as of January 1, 1995.

The countries that had lost their relative share in supplying the markets of these rich and growing economies were the OPEC oil exporters, the centrally planned economies of Eastern Europe, the ACP countries (African, Caribbean, and Pacific—mainly former colonies of the European powers), and Latin America. Even the United States, with the benefit of sharply lowered prices for its goods in terms of the European currencies, lost some of its small remaining share in the EC's imports—from 7.9 to 7.5 percent. Only Japan, the ASEAN countries, and the EFTA countries increased their share of the EC12's imports in the period 1985–90. This continued in an accentuated way the pattern that had begun in the 1950s even before the formation of the European Community. Naturally, these continued and consistent alterations in the pattern of the European Community's trade have raised a variety of policy issues. These will be taken up in Chapter 8.

The process of trade diversion and trade creation has not proceeded evenly, of course, across the various categories of trade goods. Figure 3.8 shows the relative importance in 1991 of intra-EC and extra-EC sources of imports for the major commodity categories. As might be expected from traditional trade theory, based on the principle of comparative advantage that arises from differences in resource endowments, the European Community has not been able to

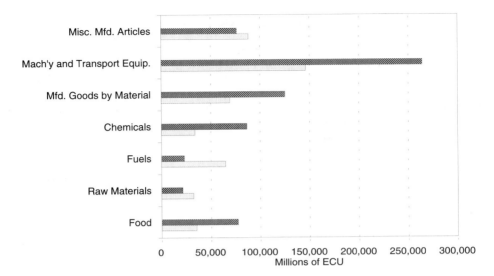

Figure 3.8. Source of trade goods (EU12 imports in 1992).

reduce significantly its reliance on outside sources for raw materials and mineral fuels (Standard International Trade Categories (SITC) 2 and 3). For these primary inputs, the EC still gets 60 and 75 percent, respectively, of its imports from outside the customs union. On the other hand, the possibilities of expanding intra-industry trade that is emphasized in modern trade theory have been realized in the sectors we would expect—chemicals, manufactured goods, and machinery and transport equipment (SITC 5, 6, and 7). What comes as a surprise for any version of international trade theory is the relative self-sufficiency of the European Community in agricultural products. The highest ratio for any of the major categories is reached for beverages and tobacco (SITC 1), although it must be added that this is one of the least significant trade categories. Another high ratio is reached for animal and vegetable fats and oils (SITC 4), but again this is a small category. Food and live animals (SITC 0), however, are not a minor item and this again exceeds the average ratio of self-sufficiency for the imports of the Community. This is an empirical fact that cannot be explained by trade theory or customs union theory. In fact, the common external tariff has never included agricultural goods. Instead of a fixed tariff rate commonly applied by all member states to agricultural imports, the Community early on determined to fix first a set of internal price supports for agricultural products, and then to vary the external tariff precisely enough to protect the domestic agricultural prices from foreign competition. This separate policy for agricultural goods has had striking effects for the economic development of Western Europe and its relationship with traditional trading partners, including the United States, Eastern Europe, and the former overseas colonies. It requires, therefore, a separate chapter of its own.

Endnotes

1. For more on the development of these and other arrangements see Beth Yarbrough and Robert Yarbrough, *Cooperation and Governance in International Trade: The Strategic Organizational Approach,* Princeton, N. J.: Princeton University Press, 1992, especially Chapter 5, which deals with the EC and other forms of mini-laterals.

2. Alexandre Lamfalussy, *The United Kingdom and the Six: An Essay of Economic Growth in Western Europe,* London: Macmillan, 1963.

3. This view of modern economic growth enjoyed a brief moment of glory as the Harrod-Domar theory. Let K = the capital stock of the economy, Y = the total product (or income) of the economy. The capital-output ratio, K/Y, was assumed to be a constant (around 3.0) denoted as k. If $K/Y = k$, then $\Delta K/\Delta Y = k$, and $\Delta K/K = \Delta Y/Y$—the growth rate of K equals the growth rate of Y. The change in capital stock, ΔK, is the same as I, the net investment in the economy. So $I/K = \Delta Y/Y$, the warranted rate of growth, symbolized by g. Multiplying the left-hand side of the equation by Y/Y yields the expression, $I/Y * Y/K = \Delta Y/Y$. But the level of I in any year was constrained by the amount of saving available out of current income, S, so $I/Y = S/Y$, or s, the saving ratio of the economy, and $Y/K = 1/k$, yielding the expression in the text, $s/k = g$.

4. "Trade deflection" is another possible result from selectively eliminating tariffs. Imagine two countries creating a free trade area (FTA), that is, eliminating tariffs between them and retaining separate control of external tariffs. Suppose that the two countries (country 1 and country 2) both import a good from a third country. If the tariff rate for, say, country 1 is higher than for country 2, then both countries before the FTA will import directly from the third country. Once the FTA is created, country 1 will import the third country's good from country 2. The trade from the third country has been "deflected." Once the countries move to a customs union, with a common external tariff, deflection disappears. This sort of problem is most often dealt with by "rules of origin" agreements that often complicate trade. In an EFTA report, the rules are shown to be so complex that many EFTA exporters chose to pay the higher nonpreferential tariff rather than incur the administrative costs necessary to qualify for zero tariffs! See J. Herin, "Rules of Origin and differences between tariff levels in EFTA and the EC," EFTA Occasional Papers, 1986, quoted in Richard Baldwin, *Towards an Integrated Europe,* London: Centre for Economic Policy Research, 1994.

5. Interested students can reproduce these results, either by hand on graph paper or by using a spreadsheet program on a personal computer. The demand curve is assumed to be $Q_d = -3/2P + 13.5$; the supply curve is $Q_s = P - 1.5$; the U.S. price is \$4.00, the German price \$4.75, and the French tariff \$1.50.

6. For the quantitatively oriented student, the areas so calculated from the assumptions underlying the graphs are:

    Left-hand triangle: $1/2$ $(4.0 - 3.25)(.75) = 0.28125$
    Right-hand triangle: $1/2$ $(6.375 - 5.25)(.75) = 0.421875$
    Rectangle: 0.75 $(5.25 - 4.0) = 0.9375$
    Net Gain (Loss): $(0.703125 - 0.9375) = (0.234375)$

7. The generally accepted position has been that if there are no economies of scale or terms of trade effects, then the unilateral tariff reduction is always superior to the customs union. See C. A. Cooper and B. F. Massell "A new look at customs union

theory," *Economic Journal* 75, December 1965, pp. 742–47; H. G. Johnson "An economic theory of protectionism, tariff bargaining and the formation of customs unions," *Journal of Political Economy* 63, Autumn 1965, pp. 256–82; and E. Berglas "Preferential trading theory: the *n* commodity case," *Journal of Political Economy* 87, April 1979, pp. 315–32.

8. Although discriminatory tariffs were not allowed under the GATT per se, they were accepted for the creation of a customs union, and so the EC is perfectly within the bounds of the GATT.

9. They first established this with a specific counter example in Paul Wonnacott and Ronald Wonnacott, "Is unilateral tariff reduction preferable to a customs union? The curious case of the missing foreign tariffs," *American Economic Review* 71, September 1971, pp. 704–14. They recently generalized their finding in Wonnacott and Wonnacott, "The customs union issue reopened," *The Manchester School* 60, June 1992, pp. 119–35. Appendix I explains their counter-position.

10. Formulated by the Belgian economist, P. J. Verdoorn, in "Fattori che regolano lo sviluppo della produttivita del lavoro," *L'industria,* I, 1949, pp. 45–53, and popularized by Nicholas Kaldor in *Causes of the Slow Rate of Economic Growth of the United Kingdom,* Cambridge: Cambridge University Press, 1966.

11. This is a simplified version of a rather complex effect. For a more detailed study of this sort of effect, see Yarbrough and Yarbrough, 1992, note 1, ch. 5.

12. Recall that "small" here simply refers to an agent's inability to affect market outcomes.

13. These worries were largely unwarranted. Mexican trade with Japan is very small, and U.S. trade with Japan would be little affected by the NAFTA agreement.

14. A good overview of these estimates and the effects of the EEC can be found in Michael Davenport's "The economic impact of the EEC," in A. Boltho, *The European Economy: Growth and Crisis,* Oxford: Oxford University Press, 1985, pp. 225–58. A survey of the trade creation/diversion estimation literature is D. G. Mayes, "The effects of economic integration on trade," *Journal of Common Market Studies,* September 1978. Probably the best known estimates are by Bela Balassa, ed., presented in *European Economic Integration,* Amsterdam: North-Holland, 1975.

15. "Trade creation and trade diversion in the European common market: An appraisal of the evidence," in Bela Balassa, ed., *European Economic Integration.*

16. Available in the Statistical Office of the European Community, *Jahrbuch 1953–1958 des Aussenhandels nach Ursprungs- und Bestimmungslandern,* Brussels: EC, 1960. This is also the source for Figures 3.5a–c and the preceding text.

17. These comments are based on the analysis contained in the publication by the Statistical Office of the European Community, *EC-World Trade, A Statistical Analysis, 1963–1979,* Brussels, 1980.

CHAPTER 4

Creating a Single European Market:

Goods, Services, Labor, Capital

The creation of a true common market, with the four freedoms of goods, services, capital, and people, has been the long-term goal of the European Community since the signing of the Treaty of Rome. However, rather than a single market, Europe for most of its post-1945 history has had a fragmented market, with all sorts of nontariff barriers still constraining the flow of goods and the flow of factors, labor, and capital. The jokes about the "uncommon market" stemmed from these barriers among the member countries. In this chapter we look at the effects of nontariff barriers and the controls on inputs, and at the recent attempts, mainly in the form of the Single European Act, to rectify this situation and create a single European market. The SEA marked a new era for the European Economic Community, with virtually every policy area deeply affected. Reforms swept across the gamut of Community action, and for the first time, member nations were seriously engaged in creating a single market.

NONTARIFF BARRIERS

In addition to quantitative restrictions and tariffs as discussed in the last chapter, all sorts of nontariff barriers (NTBs) can distort trade. But while tariffs are so-called "transparent" barriers to trade because exporters can see through them to the domestic market, nontariff barriers are far more difficult to discover and to eliminate. For thirty years, only the most blatant nontariff barriers were attacked by the various Generalized Agreement on Tariffs and Trade negotiations. Although small steps were made in the Tokyo Round of the 1970s, only with the most recent Uruguay Round has the international community seriously addressed these sorts of trade barriers. Examples are discriminatory regulations and taxation on foreign firms that make them less able to compete, customs and other border controls that increase cross-border transport costs, and closed or restrictive bidding for public contracts.

The effects of these indirect barriers are very similar to the effects of transparent barriers, except that governments do not directly receive revenue from them. Basically, they have the same economic distortions—reducing consumer surplus and decreasing allocative efficiency. As with the tariff case, domestic producers benefit, but only at the cost of the economy as a whole. In a survey from 1987 conducted in the twelve member states by G. Nerb, 20,000 firms ranked the seriousness of the barriers. On average, they were ranked in three tiers, in order of most to least important:

1. Technical standards and regulations, administrative barriers, and frontier formalities
2. Freight transport regulations, value-added tax differences
3. Capital market controls, public procurement, and the implementation of Community law

These were the areas targeted by the Single European Act.[1]

THE SINGLE EUROPEAN ACT—EUROPE 1992

The much publicized "Europe 1992" program was initiated with the European Commission's 1985 White Paper, supervised by Lord Cockfield (then the Commission vice president), which was designed to identify market barriers and to propose changes to eliminate them. It was to be used as a guideline and not "to harmonize or standardize at any price." Even approximations of the proposals would be a significant movement toward unity.[2] The structure of the plan was a brilliantly constructed piece of international relations. It set a tight, specific timetable, which ensured that individual members would be less likely to stall on efforts; otherwise they would be left behind. In addition, its acceptance was to be made under qualified majority voting in the Council of Ministers so that the program would not get bogged down before even starting. Finally, the program was to be implemented by attaining hundreds of small, specific workable steps so that the momentum from the document would be carried through. The success of the SEA, still within the context of member states pursuing their own national interests, has been ascribed to its qualified majority voting rule and the overall reduction in special interest group conflicts.[3] To this we would add the tight schedule and the breakdown of goals into bite-sized pieces.

The countries formally adopted the White Paper with the signing of the SEA in February 1986, which entered into effect on July 1, 1987, after each member state had ratified it. The document identified three areas of constraints that needed attention by EC competition policy: (1) physical barriers, such as customs and border controls; (2) technical barriers, such as product safety rules, public procurement policies, and limits on types of labor and capital flows; and (3) fiscal barriers, such as different tax rates and laws.

Before 1985, horribly bureaucratic paperwork was required to move goods across national boundaries, and cargoes were subject to many inspections required for health and safety reasons. As a simple example, if a truck (lorry) made a 750-mile trip within the United Kingdom it would take about thirty-six hours. If, however, the same truck were to go from London to Milan, it would take about 60 percent longer, fifty-eight hours, even netting out the channel crossing. The cost of the London/Milan trip would obviously be higher, even without considering the delay in delivery deadlines, and the costs of inventory management and storage. This difference was mainly due to all the documents required (each in the languages of the countries being crossed!) by border controls, which were needed to ensure that all the various trucking regulations were being observed.

Far more costly, though, were the administrative costs of the barriers. In a study done by the accounting firm Ernst and Whinney, the direct costs of border controls were estimated at ECU 8.4 to 9.3 billion, and of that amount 7.5 billion were accounted for by the administrative costs of cross-border trade.[4] To combat this, the members simply first initiated a common form, called the Single Administrative Document (SAD), and then by the beginning of 1993, eliminated the need for even this document, except for goods deemed for military use. By January 1993, all hauling quotas in and out of a country were abolished, and nondomestic trucks were granted cabotage freedom, that is, they were allowed to carry goods from point to point within the domestic market as long as this was shown not to cause severe harm to domestic truckers. So, by 1993, goods were largely able to flow freely across the EC, something that was only envisioned earlier. However, problems still arise from illegal restrictions on cross-border goods' flows. The number of complaints about unwarranted border restrictions received by the Commission increased from 202 in 1994 to 259 in 1995.[5]

Technical barriers were, of course, difficult to resolve. Through the 1980s, countries largely had their own regulations, affecting goods and, even more importantly, services. In the original EC treaty, technical barriers were forbidden, but countries could impose special regulations for health and safety reasons (Article 36). However, member states were highly regulated, and all sorts of standards and regulations controlled their markets. It was estimated that before the SEA there were over 100,000 different technical regulations and standards in the member states. Regulations can seriously impede trade without being clearly directed toward trade. For example, in the French market prior to passage of the SEA, tile manufacturers pushed stringent standards for tile construction with the national standards authority AFNOR. Although the French were not able to make the standards legally binding, they were required for all public construction, which was 40 percent of the market at the time, and were often required for insurance for builders. These conditions practically precluded far cheaper Spanish and Italian tile from the French market.[6]

The abuse of this safety clause changed with the landmark *Cassis de Dijon* case in 1979. Germany forbade Cassis, a liqueur made from black currants, to be imported as a liqueur because it failed to meet its alcohol-content standards.

The German importer (a certain Rowe-Zentral AG) took this to the Court of Justice and the Court ruled that because *Cassis* met French standards and did not jeopardize German health or safety in its status as a liqueur, it could not be kept out of the German market. This effectively established the "mutual recognition principle" for such cases—lawful products of one member can have access to all members, given no security or safety problems. Because of this decision, many more cases came before the Court. With the push for the Single Market, the Commission published its "New Approach to Technical Harmonization and Standards" in 1985.[7] This established the means for countries to conduct cooperative efforts in setting and policing common standards for goods, indicated by the near ubiquitous CE mark (for *Communauté Européenne*) placed on goods that meet the requirements. These are the standards that are often lampooned by the media—reports, for example, of the standard minimum length for condoms of 6.7 inches. It has been very difficult for the EC to establish rules that are consistent across the member states for all sectors. It would be incredibly more difficult to attempt rules for all products across all sectors. Not surprisingly, the process has been slow and difficult in protected areas such as motor vehicles and pharmaceuticals. However, progress has been made and the convergence of rules and standards has made trade easier and cheaper to conduct.

Another broad area taken under the heading of a "technical barrier" is public procurement, the purchases of the members' governments, and state subsidies. As one would expect, governments, in office at the discretion of the domestic population, buy and subsidize domestic products. In 1992, the Commission estimated that only 2 percent of the 600 billion ECU public market was bought from firms outside the home country.[8] This was an area closely watched by the United States because the growing telecommunications market was controlled by member governments, and the highly competitive U.S. firms were worried that they would not be able to compete in those markets. Although the SEA was very clear on establishing open, transparent bidding across all enterprises, Article 29 allowed members to discard bids with less than half EC content and to allow a 3-percent price preference to EC bids.[9] Government subsidies to firms are also precluded, although member states are often loathe to discontinue financially supporting sectors or providing incentives for business investment. One example was the continued subsidies to Volkswagen in Saxony, which were made in direct disregard for the Commission's block on the payments.[10]

Regulations covering professional and the service sector were also addressed. The banking and insurance industry, for example, has been the target of several formal initiatives from the Commission, designed to allow capital to flow more freely and to facilitate the convergence of the European economies. Economists have argued that harmonizing limited regulations within the framework of the SEA for Europe will reduce the possibility of regulatory capture and collusion that characterized the banking and insurance industry before 1992.[11]

Intellectual property, the bane of GATT law, has also been very difficult for the Commission. The establishment of common rules for a mutually recognized trademark has been nothing short of a battle among the states. The EC has also had difficulty in applying standards for high-tech patents. The rejection in March 1995 by the European Parliament of the draft directive on the protection of biotechnological patents is a recent example that is claimed to put European industry at a competitive disadvantage.[12]

Differences in taxation are at the heart of fiscal barriers. The member countries applied a wide variety of rules for taxation, and of rates for excise taxes and value-added taxes. Of course, these differences distorted trade, as businesses and consumers avoided taxation in high-taxed areas. As standards were harmonized, rules for kinds of goods to be taxed also became more similar. However, trying to get the actual tax rates to converge has proved difficult for the EC. Not only are the rates different, but they differ in how they are actually applied. For example, some countries do not place any tax on purchases of food and clothing; others give reduced rates for such goods.

Before 1992, average VAT rates varied over 10 percent across countries. Countries with high rates and extensive programs, like Denmark, were nervous about accepting Community control of rates and thus were ambivalent about deepening integration. However, in 1991, member states agreed that rates should be harmonized and further agreed to standardize rates at 15 percent or more, to abolish luxury rates, and, for countries with zero rates on special items like food, to allow lower rates for a transition period. As late as mid-1997, however, the new Labour government in the United Kingdom was allowed to reduce its VAT rate on household gas and electricity bills from 8 to 5 percent, instead of eliminating it entirely or raising it to 15 percent as required by the agreement.

The collection of taxes from cross-border sales still posed a problem. The Commission had proposed simply collecting the VAT in the country of sale, but member states opted for payments in the country of destination, forcing buyers and sellers to report their activities to tax authorities and pay their country's VATs on imports from other member states. Before January 1, 1993, if someone bought some good worth more than ECU 600 in one member state and transported it to another, she had to declare the item and could receive a rebate of the VAT already paid, but she then would have to pay the VAT of the country into which she was importing the good. This lengthy, complicated process is no longer applicable as long as the good is for the person's own use and is not for resale. Now such goods can be bought in one country and freely transported to another. Because exports carry with them the exporting country's taxes, the tax authority of the importing country will later bill the exporting country to get its taxes. In short, settling of tax balances between the two states is done by the tax authorities, not the traders. Sales by exporters are monitored inside each country instead of at the borders as before. To coordinate information of sales among traders and states, all member states are linked via a computerized system (VAT information exchange system, VIES) that keeps the VAT registration numbers of all the traders along with their cross-border transactions. The system is still complicated, but actual trading is no longer subject to long delays as shipments are held up at borders. Since the 1992 agreement there has been

some progress toward general harmonization of VAT rates, but delays in installing the new system and double-checking by tax authorities on tax payments
and rebates with businesses has kept transactions costs higher than was intended by the SEA.

In addition to general consumption taxes, certain goods have special taxes,
excise taxes, placed on them, for example, petroleum products, alcoholic beverages, and tobacco. These differences, though, are relatively minor and have
small effects relative to the differences in the VAT rates and bases. Areas in
which the Commission has paid special attention are mineral oils and alcohol.
It is clear that VAT and excise rates do not have to be identical across all the
members for the SEA to become operative; neighboring states in the United
States have different rates with no border controls. The range of rates can be
up to 5 percent apart before cross-border trading starts to become significant in
the U.S. experience. The United Kingdom has long argued to allow market
forces to drive tax rates, not the Commission. In any case, member states have
agreed that excises will not be lower than a set Community minimum rate for
goods covered, for example, for unleaded gasoline (petrol) ECU 287 per 1,000
liters.[13]

In addition to consumption taxes, countries vary as to their corporate taxation. Until 1990, very little was accomplished in this area. However, with the
attempt to decontrol capital movements in the EU, tax distortions were also
examined. In 1990, after decades of consideration, directives on the taxation of
cross-border mergers were issued. Following that, the Ruding Report of 1992
estimated that the variations in tax base assessment and tax rates caused major
distortions and predicted that the market would be slow to correct these fail-
ings. In response, the Commission recommended a corporate tax range of 30
to 40 percent, harmonization of tax base assessment, and the elimination of the
distinction between domestic and foreign companies in cross-border activities.

In fact, corporations have had great difficulty with EU law. The long-
standing proposal for a European Company Statute (ECS) has been held up by
problems across member states agreeing to the conditions of worker participation. The ECS would provide the format for a company that would operate
EU-wide and would be governed by a single Community law applicable in all
member states. Companies established in more than one member state would
benefit greatly, since they would not need to organize each subsidiary differently according to the various different national statutes. The Ciampi Report,
from the Competitiveness Advisory Group, estimates that such organization
costs European businesses about ECU 30 billion a year.[14]

Of course, there has been much slippage among these three areas. At the
outset, 287 proposals were made, but some were either too sensitive or difficult
to undertake, so they were broken down further and the original proposals
evolved to 302. By the beginning of 1996 93.4 percent of the national measures
had been enacted in order to implement the Community's Single Market legislation. However, member states' acceptance of Single Market legislation vary considerably: Denmark, the Netherlands, Spain, and Sweden are substantially
above the Community average of 93.4 percent; Greece, Germany, and Austria

are substantially below. As we saw above, most of the failures to implement measures of the SEA are in the areas of public procurement, intellectual property, and insurance.

LIBERALIZING FACTORS

Of course, once tariffs and nontariff barriers are removed, countries will start specializing in those goods for which they have a comparative advantage, which, of course, will be a function of their factors of production—labor and capital. Trade affects factor costs, and under conditions of perfect competition, factor prices can equalize without any movement of labor or capital between countries. Trade in goods, thus, can be a substitute for factor flows. Conversely, if goods were not allowed to flow, but factors were, the relative scarcities of labor and capital would equalize and trade would not be necessary. In both of these cases, trade and factor flows are substitutes. However, if the reallocation of resources can increase the degrees of comparative advantage because of increasing returns or imperfect competition, then trade would increase, and factor flows and trade would be complementary.[15] Whatever the case, substitutes or complements, forcing countries to eliminate barriers to factor flows further pressures economies to liberalize their markets, reduce regional disparities, and harmonize social policies and conditions.

Labor

In the last chapter, we saw how the elimination of trade barriers affects the flow of goods and services. The underlying assumption was that goods were traded but the factors of production responsible for producing them—capital, labor, and land—remained fixed in each country and did not move across their respective national borders. For labor and capital to be allocated efficiently across regions within each country, however, they must be allowed to move freely from one location to another. If each factor moves to where it can receive the highest return, then total output for the country will be maximized. The same reasoning applies for movement of capital and labor within an economic union made up of different countries. Only with free movement of the factors of production across national borders can total output for the economic union reach its full potential.

Figure 4.1 illustrates this reasoning by contrasting the situation for labor as a factor of production in Germany and Italy during the economic miracle period of the 1950s. (This is described in more detail in Chapters 9 and 11.) The demand for labor in each country is determined by the marginal product of labor (MPL in the figure). Germany's demand for labor decreases from left to right, showing that marginal product falls as the quantity of labor used with a fixed amount of capital and land increases. Italy's demand for labor also decreases with increasing quantity but from right to left. The two countries are juxtaposed so that the supply of labor for each country, taken as fixed in both cases, meets

(a)

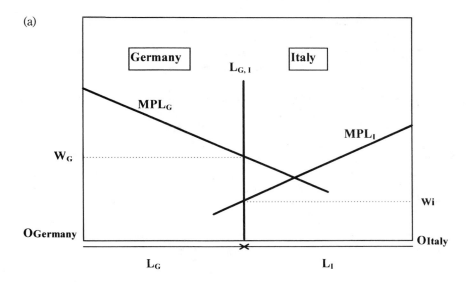

(b)

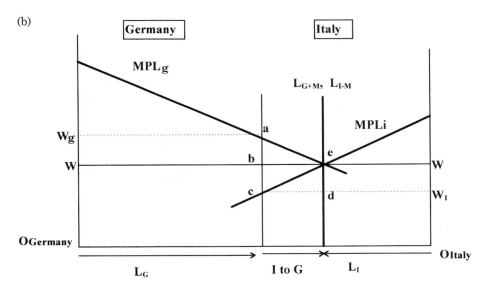

Figure 4.1 Welfare gains and losses with wage equalization. (a) No migration. (b) With migration.

in the center of the diagram. (Read Germany from left to right, Italy from right to left.) The marginal product of labor in Germany was consistently higher than in Italy, mostly because the quality and quantity of capital available per worker was greater in Germany than in Italy. The supply of labor, however, was roughly the same.

Figure 4.1a shows the situation that arises if no migration of labor or capital is allowed between the two countries. The real wage in each country is determined by the intersection of the demand and supply for labor in that country. The result is that real wages are higher in Germany than in Italy. They can remain higher as long as no movement of labor (or capital) is allowed between the two. The implication, however, is that total output of the two countries combined remains less than it could be if labor were allowed to move freely. If some of the Italian workers with low marginal products could move to Germany and produce higher marginal products, for example, the loss of output in Italy would be less than the increase in output in Germany and the total product available would increase. The loss of potential output is given by the area of the triangle in the center of the figure.

In the course of the 1950s, arrangements were made to allow Italian workers to migrate temporarily to Germany. These culminated with the provision for free movement of labor within the European Economic Community made by the Treaty of Rome. Figure 4.1b illustrates the result that could have happened with migration. Equilibrium would be reached by equalizing the marginal products of labor in each country and paying labor the same real wage (W) in both Germany and Italy. This could be done simply by moving the required number of workers from Italy to Germany (I to G in Figure 4.1b). Total output for the two countries combined would then rise by the amount of the triangle.

Of course, the additional product may not be shared equally between the two partner countries, although the figure is drawn deliberately to show that as a possibility. Even with equal gains to each country, however, political conflicts will arise within each country the way the gains will be distributed initially. The entire gain to Germany, for example, has gone to the owners of capital, not labor. (This is the area of the triangle above the new real wage, W.) Moreover, the laborers in Germany would have seen their real wage fall from W_G to W so the entire area of the rectangle, W_GWba, that had previously been distributed to labor would now be redistributed to capital. Obviously, business owners in Germany would find this attractive and be enthusiastic supporters of labor migrants and, later, guest worker programs. Equally obviously, labor unions would oppose immigration, at least of workers competitive with their members. (They might, however, accede to increased numbers of workers in occupations or sectors that were complementary to those of their members. In this case, they could share in the gains that would accrue to owners of capital.)

On the Italian side of the diagram, by contrast, all the gains of increased output go to the workers (the area of the triangle below the new wage W). In addition, the remaining workers in Italy also gain at the expense of Italian capitalists as their real wages rise due to the decreased supply of workers remaining in Italy. The total redistribution of Italian product from capital to labor is given by the area $W_ f ce W$ (W now on the Italian axis to the right hand side of the diagram). No wonder Italian labor unions favor outmigration of competitive laborers, while Italian capitalists are displeased by the resulting increase in real wages.

Of course, nothing as extreme as depicted in Figure 4.1b was allowed to happen in practice, even though the Treaty of Rome is explicit about attaining the freedom of movement of labor for both employed workers and self-employed workers.[16] Workers in the "public sector" have special status, however, and the prohibition of national discrimination does not extend to workers who can be shown to be directly or indirectly involved with the "exercise of public authority," or with "state matters." Given the size of the civil service in most European countries, these exceptions have kept a large portion of the European labor force out of a "common market." In general, though, the EC had attained free movement quickly for individuals and by 1970 for manufacturing and agricultural workers. However, countries had very different welfare and social security systems, different health insurance systems, and different educational systems. All of these made moving very risky and costly for workers and for families.

In Article 8A of the Single European Act, member states agreed to create common policies for political asylum, immigration, visas, and police measures (terrorism, drug smuggling, etc.). Although each of these was addressed in various conventions, only those relating to border formalities were enacted under the Schengen Agreement. In 1985, France, Germany, and Benelux agreed to allow the free movement of persons along their borders, and in 1993, Italy, Spain, Portugal, and Greece had become members. However, all sorts of strategic and security issues plague Schengen, and it has not been fully functioning.

Given all these attempts to eliminate the restrictions on labor, the experience of labor flows within the European Union (see Table 4.1) has been consistent, with trade and migration acting as substitutes for one another, rather than as complements. While trade among the member countries has expanded rapidly, migration of labor to countries within the EC9 has been mainly from external sources—Greece, Spain, Portugal, Turkey, Eastern Europe, and North Africa. These have gone into sectors in each country where labor unions have been weakest, usually services or unskilled manufacturing jobs. There has been in practice relatively little intra-EEC labor migration. The costs of migration are large, especially in Europe. Population density is very high and housing is expensive; which makes relocating very costly. In fact, in most member states, the cost of housing has increased far more than the average price level. In addition, changing countries often means changing languages and cultures, not to mention the actual costs of moving.[17] Differences in social protection across countries—unemployment compensation, health benefits, pension, and so on—also restrict labor flows. This is one of the reasons the member states have rekindled the attempt to establish a common social policy. In 1994, the Council was unable to reach an agreement on the establishment of freedom of cross-border membership of pension funds.

TABLE 4.1
Stock of Foreign Population in European Countries in 1993

	1993 ('000s) Total foreign population	Of which EU nationals	EU as percent of foreign pop'n	EU as percent of total pop'n
Austria	277.5	19.1	6.9	0.4
Belgium	920.6	543.5	59.0	5.4
Denmark	189.0	31.2	16.5	0.6
Finland	55.6	..	..	..
France*	3596.6	1311.9	36.5	3.5
Germany	6878.1	1535.6	22.3	2.8
Italy	987.4	153.0	15.5	0.4
Luxembourg†	119.7	85.9	71.8	31.8
Netherlands	779.8	187.7	24.1	1.8
Spain	430.4	192.1	44.6	0.5
Sweden	507.5	..	..	..
United Kingdom	2001.0	720.0	36.0	1.9

*Figures are for 1990, † Figures are for 1992

Source: SOPEMI, *Trends in International Migration Annual Report, 1994.* Paris: OECD, 1995. SOPEMI is the French acronym for "Continuous Reporting System on Migration."

Capital

The basic argument for allowing free movement of capital is virtually the same as for labor, except that the price of capital is the interest rate, not the wage rate. With capital mobility, interest rates converge, as did wage rates, and national welfare increases. Willem Molle shows that if capital controls are removed while tariffs are retained, the negative impacts of tariffs are increased. This indicates that eliminating capital controls should proceed with tariff reductions and not be a substitute for them. He also shows that once trade and factor mobility are liberalized, quantity restrictions such as import quotas or voluntary export restraints have a smaller impact, which helps to explain their popularity in the 1980s.[18]

Global capital mobility has increased dramatically over the past twenty years, and with the recent changes in capital controls, the movement of capital has accelerated. This has had deep effects in the ability of countries to control exchange rates and on the consolidation and merger activity of European firms. Capital constraints have long been the means for countries to carry out their monetary coordination. Capital controls, like those used by France and Italy in the 1980s, prevented financial institutions from making loans to foreigners and precluded nationals from holding foreign currency assets, including foreign bank accounts. Foreigners could move funds in and out of the countries, so the capital controls were not as restrictive as the exchange controls that were broken down by the European Payments Union in the early 1950s. In fact, although interest rate differences were higher and more volatile in countries with controls, average capital outflows were not any smaller than those from countries without controls.[19]

Through the 1980s, these capital controls effectively kept foreigners' portfolios devoid of controlled currencies and kept residents from selling their countries' currencies. When a revaluation was expected, the supply of credit was very inelastic, making interest rates rise sharply. This made it unnecessary for monetary authorities to raise interest rates to defend their currencies. The Commission decided in 1988 to lift capital controls by July 1990. In 1990, when they were removed, foreigners took on formerly controlled currencies to enjoy the higher interest rates than those available in the deutsche mark and dollar market. The liquidation of these positions played a major role in the 1992 crisis and the collapse of the European Monetary System (EMS). Responding to the crisis by reestablishing the controls was a solution exactly opposed to the Single European Act and one that violated the Maastricht Treaty, which stated that temporary controls were allowed only if capital movements were to "cause, or threaten to cause, serious difficulties for the operation of economic and monetary union."[20] As T. Padoa-Schioppa put it, it was inconsistent to pursue free trade, full capital mobility, fixed exchange rates, and independent monetary policy. In the long-run, he said, "the only solution to the inconsistency is to complement the internal market with a monetary union."[21]

While the deregulation of capital markets certainly affected the EMS and the ability of countries to conduct cooperative monetary policies, it has made very important changes in the way Europe does business. Financial deregulation has provided welfare benefits for both European and American firms.[22] In banking, the European Commission pushed for a harmonization of regulation across members, for "home control," and for mutual recognition among regulatory authorities. A branch bank should be the regulatory responsibility of the country in which it was located, and the main (home) bank should be monitored by the regulatory agency in its home country. The so-called Second Banking Directive was adopted in 1989 and entered into force in the beginning of 1993. Insurance and brokerage firms were also placed under similar rules, with the attempt to make cross-border sales less burdensome, both for the companies and for their customers. Common rules were created to standardize practice while following the basic format of harmonization, home control, and mutual recognition. However, financial services across frontiers are still inhibited by widely different fiscal regimes, which precludes true financial integration.[23]

Not surprisingly, mergers and acquisitions (M&As) have increased since the announcement of the SEA. European firms turned their attention to the internal market in anticipation of reaping the benefits of a substantially larger market. For example, for U.K. firms, in 1986 three times as many cross-border acquisitions were completed with the United States; by 1992 the situation had reversed, and there were twice as many acquisitions or U.K. firms in Europe as in the United States. Given the significant deregulation of the service industries such as banking and insurance, it should not be surprising that a large number of the operations were in services, dominated by banking. M&A activity peaked in 1989, the year before the German unification shock, which increased exchange rate and tax rate uncertainties, and the adoption of merger regulation. Until 1989, Community control of industrial concentration was done by applying Articles 85 and 86 of the Treaty of Rome. These encouraged the formation of large firms if they increased economic efficiency and left the determination of whether that was the case up to the individual member states. The new regulation gave the Commission the exclusive responsibility to oversee mergers of a Communitywide dimension; smaller mergers would still be the work of the member states. "Communitywide dimension" was taken to mean an aggregate worldwide turnover of more than ECU 5 billion, or Communitywide turnover of each of at least two of the parties is more than ECU 250 million or the parties concerned do not have more than two-thirds of their Community turnover within one and the same member state.[24] Through 1994, of 164 reported mergers, only one merger was prohibited by the Community, the Aérospatiale-Alenia/de Havilland merger. In eleven other cases, the merger was deemed potentially harmful and firms had to agree to conditions to decrease dominant positions. As would be expected, 71 percent of all the cases were cross-border mergers, rather than combinations within member states.

Figures 4.2 through 4.4 show figures for foreign direct investment for the EC12. Countries are grouped by size and development. What is striking is the similarity among the countries. From 1986 through 1990 there was increased foreign direct investment in these countries, both reflecting the anticipated

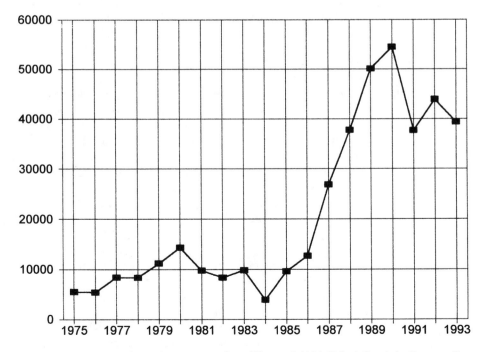

Figure 4.2. Foreign direct investment (in millions of 1994 U.S. dollars) in France, Germany, Italy and the United Kingdom, 1975–93.

Source: IMF, Balance of Payments Statistical Yearbook, various issues.

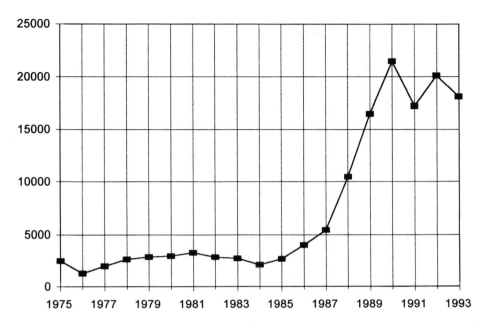

Figure 4.3. Foreign direct investment (in millions of 1994 U.S. dollars) in Benelux and Denmark, 1975–93.

Source: IMF, *Balance of Payments Statistical Yearbook,* various issues.

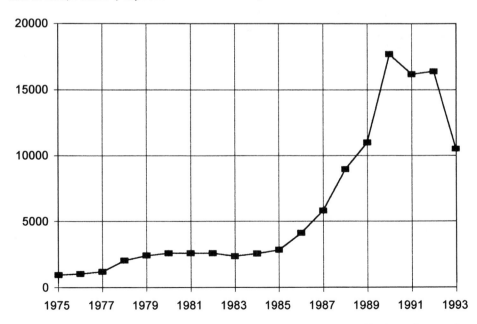

Figure 4.4. Foreign direct investment (in millions of 1994 U.S. dollars) in Greece, Ireland, Portugal, and Spain, 1975–93.

Source: IMF, *Balance of Payments Statistical Yearbook,* various issues.

gains from the single market and the fears of third countries who did not want to be shut out by a "Fortress Europe." The falloff after 1990 shows the impact of the EMS crises and the German unification shock.

Deregulation of capital markets has not stopped at EU borders; The Commission has also pushed for the removal of obstacles to foreign direct investment from nonmembers. In March 1995, the Commission adopted a communication on a "level playing field for direct investment worldwide."[25] The Commission has also started to work with the World Trade Organization and the OECD for the opening of negotiations to establish multilateral investment rules.

CONCLUSION

The Single European Act, which has also been referred to as the Delors Plan, addressed eight basic areas, seven of which extend and complement the changes in direct market liberalization. The SEA's components were:

1. Competition policy. Create an internal market comprising an area without internal frontiers in which the free movement of goods, persons, services, and capital is ensured in accordance with the provisions of the Act. (Especially targeted were the administrative and legal constraints on small and medium-sized businesses, with a Commission task force created to guide deregulation.)

2. Work toward a monetary union to reduce the transactions costs of currency conversions (though this was not a legally binding part of the 1992 initiative).

3. Address the disparity between the poorer and richer states. If markets were to be opened, protected, generally poorer, areas might initially be hard hit. To address these asymmetric shocks, member states agreed to double regional and social programs funds by 1992.

4. Increase production efficiency throughout the Community by encouraging and coordinating technical research.

5. Harmonize environmental laws and contribute toward the cooperative attempt to protect human health and the environment. (Denmark's objections that its own standards were higher than those of the other EC members were met by a clause stating that the Act need not prevent member states taking "more stringent measures" than the EC norm.)

6. Increase Community policy in the social dimension.

As one can see, the many elements extend beyond simply eliminating nontariff barriers, because it was seen that in order for the market to be freed from restrictions permanently, the Community would have to initiate supporting policies, the so-called back-up policies. These would ensure that the asymmetries of gains and losses from market deregulation (structural funds) would be alleviated, that firms would respond to the competitive environment (support for R&D), that people would feel freer to relocate across national boundaries (social policies), and that firms would not have to cope with varying environmental legislation (environmental policy). This process of deepening integration led straight to the Treaty on European Union (TEU), also known as the Maastricht Treaty. This treaty formalized the conditions of the monetary union (more about this in Chapter 7), changed parliamentary action, and established the outline for a common foreign and security policy. In a sense, the Community felt that the TEU was a culmination of the process of establishing the Single Market in 1993. Whereas the SEA was more a consolidated reform, taking elements already existing and forcefully putting them together, the TEU was a constitutional reform, changing the nature of the integration process.

As the SEA was intended to eliminate market protection in the member states and to deepen integration, we would expect that there would be a great deal of creative destruction of less competitive firms. In areas with heavily protected industries, the removal of protective measures should cause unemployment and large allocative shifts. Realizing this, the Community supported the operation of the SEA with a complete reform and expansion of the structural and regional funds. Since the expansion in this area would necessitate contractions in others, the Community looked for areas to contract. This caused a reassessment of the budget and a complete overhaul of all the major expenditure categories of the Community.

It would be difficult to overestimate the impact of the SEA on the Community. Whatever the exact monetary impact, the push to complete the 1992 project has affected every branch of the Community's policies and fundamentally changed the nature and allocation of the Community budget. The decade from 1986 through 1996 is one of the most dynamic in the history of the European Community. Almost all major policies have undergone serious reforms. In the next chapter, we examine how this has proceeded.

Endnotes

1. G. Nerb, *The Completion of the Internal Market: A Survey of European Industry's Perception of the Likely Effects.* DG for Economic and Financial Affairs as quoted in M. Emerson et al., "The Economics of 1992," *European Economy* 35, Brussels, March 1988, p. 44.

2. See the *Bulletin of the EC,* no. 6, 1985, p.18.

3. See Ludger Schuknecht. "The political economy of current European integration," in Hans-Jürgen Vosgerau, ed., *European Integration in the World Economy,* New York: Springer-Verlag, 1992, pp. 677–702.

4. Costs per consignment were estimated at an average of ECU 67 for imports (with a low of 26 for Belgium and a high of 130 for Italy) and ECU 86 for exports (with a low of 34 for Belgium and a high of 205 for Italy). See Emerson et al., note 1, p. 48.

5. European Parliament, "Report on the Status of the Single Market," Brussels, 1996, section 1.

6. Emerson et al., note 1, p. 53.

7. For an analysis of this "new approach" see Jacques Pelkmans, "The new approach to technical harmonization and standardization," *Journal of Common Market Studies* 25, no. 3, March 1987.

8. Desmond Dinan. *Ever Closer Union? An Introduction to the European Community,* Boulder, Colo: Lynne Rienner Publishers, 1994, p. 345.

9. Ibid., p. 346.

10. The Commission attempted to block subsidies of DM 241m ($163m) to VW plants in Saxony. While Germany was trying to reverse the decision, Saxony had already disbursed DM 92m. "Bonn and EU resort to court," *Financial Times,* September 12, 1996, p. 2.

11. Xaxier Vives, "Banking competition and European integration," in Alberto Giovannini and Colin Mayer, eds. *European Financial Integration,* New York: Cambridge University Press, 1992, p. 18.

12. Commission of the European Communities, *The Single Market in 1995,* Brussels, 1996, section 1.

13. For the list of minimum rates for all the covered items, see the DG10 website, address http://europa.eu.int/en/comm/dg10/incom/xc5/ewfqa/ewfq0902.htm#09.02.00.

14. CEC, note 12.

15. See, for example, J. R. Markusen. "Factor movements and commodity trade as complements," *Journal of International Economics* 14 (May 1983), pp. 341–56.

16. See Article 7 for the general commitment to forbidding discrimination and Article 48 for details on how it is applied to various types of workers.

17. In much of Europe, kinship has an important monetary component. For example, in highly bureaucratic areas, like Italy, having familial ties makes a big difference. A friend of mine, Primo DiVito from Florence, needed a cataract operation. At the local hospital, he would have had to wait three years to get national insurance to pay for it, or pay about $5000 at a local private clinic. Instead, he called his sister, who knew one of the doctors, and he was in within three weeks for the operation. Had he recently moved to Pisa, he would have known no one and would have had to wait or pay for his operation. These sorts of clan benefits are worth a lot to most Europeans, even in a pecuniary sense.

18. See Willem Molle, *The Economics of European Integration,* Brookfield, Vt.: Dartmouth, 1994, pp. 170–3.

19. See Peter B. Kenen. *Economic and Monetary Union in Europe: Moving Beyond Maastricht,* Cambridge, Cambridge University Press, 1995, p. 169. For the measure of outflows see Daniel Gros and Niels Thygesen, *European Monetary Integration: From the European Monetary System to Monetary Union,* Harlow, U. K.: Longman, 1992; and for interest rate differentials and volatility see Michele Fratianni and Jürgen von Hagen, *The European Monetary System and European Monetary Union,* Boulder, Colo.: Westview Press, 1992.

20. Kenen, note 19, p. 170.

21. T. Padoa-Schioppa, "The European monetary system: a long-term view," in Francesco Giavazzi, Stefano Micossi, and Marcus Miller, eds. *The European Monetary System,* Cambridge: Cambridge University Press, 1988, p. 376.

22. For a theoretical account of the impacts of financial deregulation, see Alberto Giovannini and Colin Mayer, note 11.
23. Commission of the European Communities, *The Single Market in 1995*. Brussels, 1996, section 1.
24. European Commission, "Competition and Integration: Community Merger Control Policy," *European Economy* 57, 1994, p. 11.
25. Commission of the European Communities, *General Report on the Activities of the European Union, 1995,* Brussels, 1996, point 755.

Bibliography

Commission of the European Communities. *The Single Market in 1995*. Brussels, 1996. An outstanding reference with detailed accounts of the current status of the implementation of the SEA throughout all aspects of Community policy.

Cecchini, Paolo. *1992: The Benefits of a Single Market*. Brookfield, Vt.: Gower, 1988. Oft quoted report from the "Cost of Non-Europe" Steering Committee, based on the findings from M. Emerson et al.

Dinan, Desmond. *Ever Closer Union? An Inroduction to the European Community*. Boulder, Colo: Lynne Rienner Publishers, 1994. Detailed account in Chapter 12 on the process of forming the single market. Very good reference.

Emerson, Michael. et al. "The Economics of 1992," *European Economy* 35, March 1988. Dated in its attempt to estimate the economic impact of the SEA, it is still an excellent source in clarifying the issues and providing the theoretical context in which to analyze the liberalization program.

Giovannini, Alberto and Colin Mayer, eds. *European Financial Integration*. New York: Cambridge University Press, 1992. Good collection of articles, especially on integration and its effects on banking, corporate finance, mergers and capital flight.

Ulman, Lloyd, Barry Eichengreen, and William Dickens, eds. *Labor and Integrated Europe*. Washington, D.C.: Brookings Institution, 1993. Several good articles within a collection of articles European labor markets.

CHAPTER 5

The Budget of the European Union:
Accounting for Unity

As the breadth and depth of the European Union have grown over the years, so has its budget. How the Union receives and then spends money tells us a lot about its priorities and conflicts. Over the past ten years, the deepening and widening of the Community has meant many changes for both the process and the allocation of the budget. This chapter reviews that process.

BUDGETARY PROCESS

The initial budget is drafted by the Commission and sent for review to the Council. The Council amends or accepts the proposed budget by qualified majority and then sends it on to the Parliament. The shared responsibility for the budget has grown out of demands that the EU become more democratic and open in its decision making. (The cloistered discussions between the Commission and the Council had created a "democratic deficit," which undermined the legitimacy of the EU in general.) The Parliament examines the document and either simply approves it; proposes modifications to compulsory spending, spending that arises directly from the European treaties, and/or passes amendments for new, noncompulsory spending. If the Parliament accepts the budget, the process is over. If not, the amended budget is returned to the Council, which reconsiders, either accepting or rejecting parts of the Parliament's changes. The Council then sends the document back to the Parliament, which reads it for a second time. If the Parliament accepts the proposed budget this time with three-fifths of the votes cast, the official budget is complete. If, however, the Parliament rejects the budget, the Council must reintroduce one. A second rejection has happened only three times, all during the budgetary crisis years of the early 1980s—first for the 1980 budget, then for the 1982 supplementary budget, and finally for the 1985 budget. After 1985 a series of reforms has quieted the budgetary process and only recently have problems arisen again. The expanded role of the Parliament reflects the Community's efforts to close the democratic deficit of decision making by giving more power to the institution that most represents the citizens of the member states, the Parliament.

EARLY HISTORY AND ORGANIZING PRINCIPLES

In the Treaty of Rome that established the EEC, member states agreed to make financial contributions in fixed proportions to fund the needs of the Community. Unlike the ECSC Treaty, which allowed its High Authority to create taxes, the EEC did not have its own resources; rather, it relied on contributions to match its expenditures. With the plans for the Common Agricultural Policy in the early 1960s, member states recognized that the EEC's budget required its own financing. In 1965, proposals were made to establish the EEC's own resources through new levies. However, France vehemently opposed this and the proposals failed. This caused severe problems in the EEC as France blocked any attempt to complete a program by refusing to vote—the so-called empty chair *(chaise vide)* policy.

Although the Merger Treaty of 1965 changed the budgetary procedure somewhat, the next major reform came in 1970. This is the most important budgetary reform of the EC as of 1996. In the Luxembourg Agreements of 1970, member states established the current framework of the EC budget by granting it the power of fiscal autonomy. The EC could now raise fiscal revenues through agricultural levies, custom duties. and the value added tax (VAT), even though the revenue was actually collected by the member states. However, the VAT contributions would only be phased in over a transition period. Given these changes, it was clear, and clearly stated in the Treaty, that the role of the Parliament would have to be expanded; however, Parliament's powers have been expanded very slowly and only recently have reforms actually brought the Parliament direct power in budgetary determinations.[1]

Throughout its development the budgetary process has been guided by six organizing principles:

- *Unity.* All revenue sources and expenditures of the Union need to be shown in a single, unified budget. (The activities of the European Investment Bank are held outside the budget, as are the common foreign and security policies proposed under the Maastricht Treaty.) Before 1965, this was not a concern of the Community, but as expenditures became more varied and own resources were added, a clear, unified budget was necessary.

- *Universality.* Revenues may not be assigned to particular expenditures; revenues and expenditures are entered in full in the budget without any adjustment against each other.

- *Annuality.* Each year estimates are made for expenditures and revenues for the financial year, which runs from January 1 to December 31. Of course, provisions are made for carry-over funds and payments.
- *Equilibrium.* The budget must be balanced—expenditures must equal revenues; the EC does not issue its own debt. This was part of the original EC treaty (Article 199) and has been reinforced in the reforms of 1970, 1985, 1988, and 1994. The problem here, felt most recently in the last recession, is that when GDP resources are less than predicted, deficits are incurred. These are funded by member state contributions. Passing negative balances on to the next year for payment severely limits spending, since own resources are capped. This problem has been avoided by rolling over negative balances from one year to the next while retaining spending. Clearly, this is not a long-run solution and proposals are being considered to address this problem.
- *Specification.* Although receipts can not be specified for particular expenditures, when the budget is proposed, spending must be specified across all headings and subheadings.
- *Common Unit of Account.* The budget is denominated in units different from the member states' national currencies. From 1958–60, the EEC used a gold parity unit in accord with the Bretton Woods Agreements, the Unit of Account (UA).[2] Following the breakdown of Bretton Woods in the early 1970s, a new unit was needed; and finally, in 1977, the EC adopted a basket currency called the European unit of account (EUA).[3] Then, from 1981 on, the European Currency Unit (ECU) has been used, which is similar to the EUA but is subject to regular revisions.[4] When looking at EC budget data over time it is always important to recognize that the units of measurement may differ according to the different accounting epochs.

These principles are the basis for any reform of the budget. They both constrain and guide member states in their negotiations over payments of revenues to the Community and their receipts from Community expenditures.

REVENUES

In 1995, total revenues were 76 billion ECU (including carry-over funds), which is about 1.2 percent of the EU's total GDP. The European Community received these funds mainly from contributions of member states' value added taxes (VAT), through tariff revenues and levies, and through direct contributions from member states based on their GDPs. Table 5.1 shows figures in nominal terms for total payments (without netting out collection costs), broken down by major category for the years 1975, 1980, 1985, 1990, and 1995. Figure 5.1 shows the relative weights of the revenue sources (net of collection costs) from the period 1971 through the projections for 1997. Over time, the percentage of cus-

TABLE 5.1
EC Revenues by category (in ECU millions)

	Custom duties and ag. levies	%	VAT contributions	%	GDP-based funds	%	Total
1971	1,296	55.6	—		—		2,329
1975	3,741	58.5	—		—		6,385
1980	7,908	48.1	7,258	44.2	—		16,432
1985	10,489	37.4	15,218	54.2	—		26,079
1990	12,161	26.1	27,440	59.1	95	0.2	46,469*
1995	14,454	19.3	39,183	52.2	14,191	18.9	67,827*

*These are the totals without netting out the costs incurred gathering the revenues.[5]
Source: CEC, *The Community Budget: The Facts in Figures* (Brussels, 1996), pp. 38–39.

toms duties, and agricultural levies[6] in total revenues has fallen from a high of over 90 percent in 1974 to a projected 16.9 percent in 1997. This reflects the shift from external to internal trade within the union, increased self-sufficiency in agriculture, and an overall decrease in tariff rates. Collecting the EC's revenues at its external borders was disadvantageous to countries like the Netherlands, Belgium, Ireland, and the United Kingdom because it linked revenue to port of entry, the so-called Rotterdam effect. To maintain revenue levels and appease the countries listed above, the EEC had to shift to an internal source for income. The VAT contribution was raised from 1 percent of gross value-added tax receipts to 1.4 percent. With the relative fall in custom duties and the increased contribution rate for the VAT, the VAT has become the main source of revenues, accounting now for over half of all revenues. However, the VAT is inherently regressive because the proportion of consumption to GDP is higher in poorer countries, which makes the VAT base a relatively higher proportion of GDP for these countries. High-saving, net-exporting countries, by contrast, have a relatively lower VAT base. To redress this inequity among member states a new category, "GDP-based resources," was instituted as part of the 1988 reform. The collection of these resources is determined by member GDP size in relation to VAT contributions. Its importance will grow because the VAT rate paid by members will fall .08 percent per year, from the 1994 1.4 percent to 1 percent by 1999.

It is only obvious to wonder what the net positions of the members are, whether they are paying more or less than they are receiving. Of course, such a calculation does not address whether the countries are net beneficiaries from their membership because the payments and receipts measured in the budget do not address all the indirect effects of the union. These data simply show the fiscal stance of the members. However, these figures are very important politically because they are tangible data to demonstrate the value or the cost of membership to citizens of member states. Figure 5.2 shows the net payments of the countries for 1985, 1990 and 1994. Note that, with the exception of Lux-

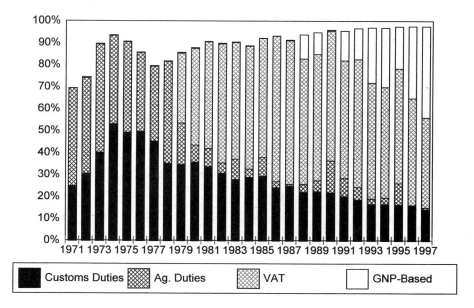

Figure 5.1. Revenues by category as a percentage of total revenues (1971–97).*

*For 1996, the percentage is taken from the budget, and for 1997, the projected budget. The percentages do not add to 100% because of other country contributions.

Source: CEC, *The Community Budget: The Facts in Figures* (Brussels, 1996), pp. 38–39.

embourg in 1994, the original six are either close to being payment neutral or are net contributors, while the poorer countries Portugal, Greece, Spain, and Ireland are net receivers. Both France and Germany have made serious financial contributions to the EU since 1990. With the reform of the Common Agricultural Policy and the increase in structural funds, the French have moved from being net receivers to becoming large net payers. Denmark, with a per capita income 108 percent of the EU average, is a net receiver, while the United Kingdom, with a per capita income at about the EU average, is a net payer and has been throughout its membership.

Not surprisingly, the United Kingdom bitterly opposed the way payments were collected and demanded a partial rebate of its payments. As a net food importer, the United Kingdom did not benefit as a whole from the relatively large agricultural spending from the Common Agricultural Policy, although its small agricultural sector benefited. The United Kingdom was never happy with the VAT and its appropriation by the EC. In all member countries the base from which the VAT contribution is calculated is determined by the "revenue method." This takes not the actual receipts collected by a government, but calculates what would have been collected had it taxed a given range of goods and services at standard rates. Because the United Kingdom exempted from VAT a

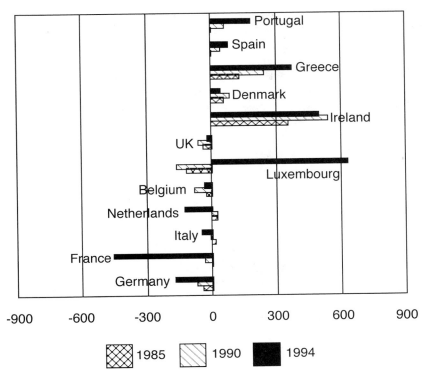

Figure 5.2. Net payments (−) or receipts (+) from the EU to member states (ECU/capita).

Source: Court of Auditors, *General Financial Position of the Community,* Brussels, various years.

large range of goods, especially food and medicines, its financial contributions to the EU were large relative to its actual tax collections.

These problems surfaced early; already by 1975 they were at the core of the referendum concerning whether the United Kingdom should continue its membership. Although the problem was addressed by the Dublin Councils of 1975 and 1979, a solution was finally found at the Fontainebleau Summit in 1984. For 1985, the U.K.'s VAT contribution was reduced by ECU 1 billion. From 1986 on, the members agreed that 66 percent of the difference between the U.K.'s share of VAT payments and its percentage share of allocated expenditure would be refunded by way of a reduction in the U.K. VAT base. This reduction in the U.K. contribution is made up by all the member states in accordance with their respective share of VAT payments, with the exception of Germany, which pays two-thirds of its normal share. This special arrangement, made only for the United Kingdom, is known as the U.K. Rebate.

While the United Kingdom was claiming it was paying too much, the EC as a whole was not receiving enough to sustain its spending. After a series of budgetary crises over the 1980s, the Brussels Agreement of 1988 changed the structure of payments and reformed revenues. It was here that the VAT contribution was increased and that GDP resources were added, which attempted to apply an appropriate VAT contribution based on the difference between each member's GDP and the targeted VAT base. Along with raising the rate of the VAT, the EC needed to appease countries such as the United Kingdom that had complained bitterly about its tax contribution. In addition, countries with low per capita incomes were also upset about having to pay more while sustaining the shock of decontrolling their economies under the Single European Act. The EC responded by placing a cap on the VAT base of 55 percent of a member's GDP. This was amended in 1994 to a cap of 50 percent for countries whose per capita GNP is below 90 percent of the Community average (Spain, Greece, Ireland, and Portugal). Capping the VAT has benefited the United Kingdom, Portugal, Luxembourg, Ireland, Greece, and Spain.

EXPENDITURES

The Union has been so concerned about its revenues because demands for its expenditures have been increasing. The development of expenditures clearly illustrates the expansion of the Community's functions as integration deepened. Figure 5.3 presents real expenditures per capita, with 1996 used as a base. The per capita expenditure in 1996 was ECU 224 (about U.S. $235.00). As the figure clearly shows, expenditure has been rising over time, taking a series of jumps

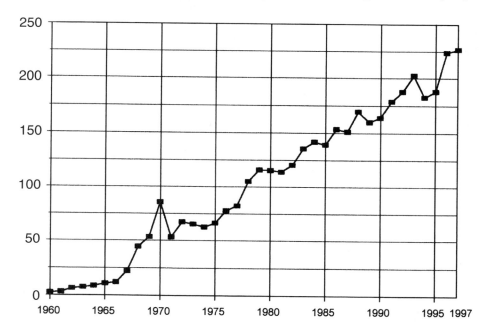

Figure 5.3. Real community expenditures per capita (1996 prices). The figure for 1996 is based on the official budget and for 1997 on the financial perspective (see Table 5.3).
Source: CEC, *The Community Budget: The Facts in Figures* (Brussels, 1996), pp. 35–36.

at the end of the 1960s and early 1970s as the Common Agricultural Policy was initiated and set running. The growth of real expenditures per capita has been relatively stable over the period 1975–97.

While the Community spending has grown steadily, the allocation of spending has changed over time (Figure 5.4). Traditionally, most of the money went toward agricultural subsidies (EAGGF in the figure), as this was one area where member governments were happy to give control over to the Community. In the mid-1980s, however, the agricultural expenditures often overshot their anticipated levels. This happened because final outlays depended on the levels of agricultural output that occurred near the end of the fiscal year and the market prices farmers faced at harvest time. Often output was higher than predicted, so prices were lower than expected, and the combined result of higher output and lower prices increased the subsidies that had to be paid out. Gradually, the proportion of agricultural supports has been reduced, but the corresponding rise in structural funds has been directed primarily to rural areas.

Table 5.2 shows the amounts and proportions of total spending for the vari-

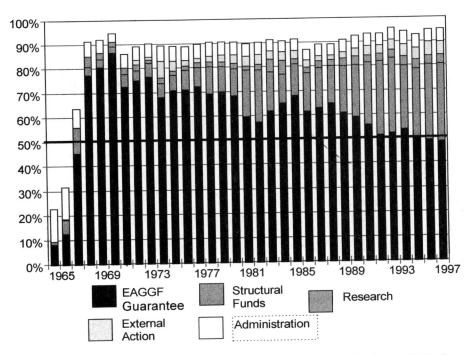

Figure 5.4. Community spending broken down by category, 1965–97. EAGGF, European Agricultural Guarantee and Guidance Fund.*

*The percentages do not add to 100 percent because of payments to categories not covered in the five given.

Source: CEC, *The Community Budget: The Facts in Figures* (Brussels, 1996).

TABLE 5.2
Total Spending on Various Categories, 1952–79,* and 1994

	1952—1979 spending (mill EUA)	%	1994 spending (mill ECU)	%
Administration	4,382.2	6.3	3,565.0	5.9
Agriculture	54,740.3	78.8	33,605.0	55.7
Regional/structural policy	2,074.0	3.0	15,966.0†	26.5
Energy and industrial policy	1,848.3	2.7	3,165.0	5.3
Social policy	2,466.12	3.5	543.4	0.9
External action	235.5	0.3	3,151.8	5.2
Other	3,762.9	5.4	307.9	0.5
Total	69,509.3	100.0	60,304.9	100.00

*Spending includes carry-overs from 1952–67 on cooperative spending for the various categories.
†Now includes payments to the European Social Fund, previously in the category "Social Policy."
In most recent budget reports, "Energy/Industrial Policy" and most of "Social Policy" are found in the category, "Internal Policies."

Sources: Daniel Strasser. *The Finances of Europe.* The European Perspectives Series (Brussels, 1980), pp. 398–99 and the *Bulletin of the European Community,* 1995.

ous categories from 1952–79, compared with 1994. For the first period, the years 1952–58 are covered by the European Coal and Steel Community spending. Table 5.3 presents the financial perspective for the EU15 until 1999. As the data show, the trends shown in Table 5.2 are projected to continue through the end of the 1990s. By the end of the century, agricultural spending should be at about 45 percent, with structural policies growing to almost 36 percent.

As the tables show, the administrative area has taken only between 5 and 6 percent of the total budget. Within the administration, the various institutions are allocated funds in proportion to the size of their staffs. In 1996, the Commission had a staff of 20,831, 70 percent of the total, and was allocated about 67 percent of the funds paid to "Administration." The Parliament, with a staff of 4,095, 13.8 percent of total EC staff, received about 20 percent of administrative funds, while the smaller Council received around 10 percent of the total. The Court of Justice and the Court of Auditors took up the rest.

TABLE 5.3
Financial Perspective for EU15, 1996–99 (millions of 1992 ECU)

	1996	%	1997	%	1998	%	1999	%
Administration	3,859	4.9	3,974	4.9	4,033	4.8	4,093	4.7
Agriculture	37,245	47.3	37,922	46.8	38,616	46.0	39,327	45.2
Structural Policies	26,026	33.1	27,588	34.0	29,268	34.9	30,945	35.6
Internal Policies	4,914	6.2	5,117	6.3	5,331	6.3	5,534	6.4
External Action	4,847	6.1	5,134	6.3	5,507	6.6	5,953	6.8
Total	78,692	—	81,047	—	83,954	—	86,952	—

Source: CEC, The Community Budget: The Facts in Figures (Brussels, 1996), p. 62.

AGRICULTURAL POLICY

Clearly, the main area of Community spending has been for agriculture, mainly for the guarantee portion of the European Guarantee and Guidance Fund, the financial arm of the Common Agricultural Policy. Cereals, dairy, and meat products receive about 70 percent of the total payments. Guarantee payments, which are basically subsidies for agricultural products, of all types still make up the majority of EU expenditures, though their weight in the budget has fallen. From over 70 percent of expenditures, payments to agriculture are projected to fall well below 50 percent by the end of the decade. The heart of the financial reform, the Delors Plan of 1988, was to limit growth in agricultural payments to less than 74 percent of the rate of increase in community GDP. In 1992, the reform was extended to align European prices with world prices, set aside land in order to reduce production, and provide direct aid to farmers rather than production subsidies. These reforms, which have shifted toward changing the structure of agriculture and its population, have made a difference. Because of this, guidance and structural payments have benefited; in 1975, the guidance portion of the CAP, whose purpose is structural aid, was 2.87 percent of the budget, while in 1990 it rose to 4.45 percent. In the next chapter, we discuss the development of the Common Agricultural Policy in detail.

REGIONAL POLICY

The need for regional funds has always been with the Community, since there are significant and persistent economic disparities among and within member nations. As we saw in Chapter 3, the creation of a customs union can lead to "polarization," with the dynamic effects of the union actually increasing disparities rather than decreasing them. With the addition of Greece, Spain, and Portugal to the European Community, it became clear that more regional and structural funds would be demanded. In addition, the Single European Act has caused and was expected to cause many regional disturbances, with certain countries and areas within countries being affected more than others. Because of these changes, the Community has only recently formulated a coherent regional policy, and the regional and structural funds have increased dramatically. While in the period before 1979 regional and social funds made up only 6.5 percent of total spending, in 1994 they accounted for 27 percent. Regional spending rose from 5.78 percent of the budget in 1985 to 10.51 percent in 1990, while social spending increased from 5.3 percent to 8.2 percent. By 1994, 26.5 percent of the budget went toward "Structural Operations." These increases reflect the increased effort in responding to the changes demanded by the Single European Act and the significant reforms of the CAP.

The main instruments of these funds are the European Regional Development Fund, the European Social Fund, and the guidance portion of the EAGGF. In 1994 the European Union officially instituted its regional policy by accepting the reform of 1988 under Delors I by committing these funds as well as the European Investment Bank and Financial Instrument for Fisheries Guidance (FIFG) to five objectives:

1. Promote the development and structural adjustment of lagging regions
2. Convert regions seriously affected by industrial decline
3. Combat long-term unemployment
4. Facilitate job training for workers
5. Promote rural development through structural aid rather than supporting continued production

To achieve these ends, members committed more money to each. The first objective received no less than 68 percent of the increased funds allocated. To implement this, the Treaty on European Union created the Cohesion Fund to direct funds to countries that have per capita GDPs below 90 percent of the Community average. The Fund will pay out between 80 and 85 percent of the projects covered so the recipient countries co-pay between 15 and 20 percent. The exact allocations have been specified: the Fund, amounting to ECU 2.25 billion in 1996, will allocate 52 to 58 percent of the total to Spain, 16 to 20 percent to both Greece and Portugal, and 7 to 10 percent to Ireland. These are the four countries with per capita incomes below 90 percent of the EC average.

In addition, special provisions have been made for the former East German provinces, the five new Länder. Although funds have been committed from the Social Fund and the guidance portion of the EAGGF, the Regional Fund contributes about one-half of all aid. This goes mainly to create jobs, increase productivity, and secure cleaner infrastructures in the environmental nightmare that was inherited from the former East Germany. Other funds have been allotted for the rest of eastern Europe. In 1995, 1.5 percent of the budget was allocated for cooperation and structural aid to the east and 1.4 percent is projected for 1996. Programs like Poland and Hungary: Aid for Reconstruction of the Economy (PHARE), which now has been extended to all the countries under association agreements, are scheduled to allocate these funds. The Technical Assistance Information Exchange Office (TAIEO) was opened in January 1996 after long delays. Its task is to coordinate and inform agents both in the east and west on the allocation of funds for technical assistance.

SOCIAL POLICY

Social policy covers a wide variety of activities that are generally covered by the member states. The Union, however, has made important steps to address social problems such as poverty, pensions and social security and health and welfare. Until 1974, when the first social action program (SAP) was instituted, social policy was following the letter of the Treaty of Rome with respect to the labor market—ensuring equal pay for equal work, allowing labor to flow, and so on. Then the European Social Fund was created to finance social programs. Currently, the ESF's funds are a component of the "Structural Funds," making up about ECU 47 billion of the total ECU 156 billion allocated for the period 1994–99. Even though spending has increased for areas such as those affected by industrial decline or long-run unemployment, severe implicit restrictions on social harmonization still exist. Examples are incompatible or nontransferable pensions; significant differences in welfare, unemployment, and health policies, and working conditions. The SAP was drafted to address these sorts of problems, but actually did little to eliminate them. As one can see from Table 5.2, very little financial commitment had been made to the SAP. Other than a short attempt to redress labor problems with the ill-fated Vredeling directive of 1980,[7] the latest move to establish a common social policy was derailed by the British government's refusal to accept its conditions.

The attempt to create a "Social Charter" was largely an attempt to rekindle the SAP within the context of the Single European Act. The Commission's report of 1989 established some fifty measures for the Social Charter, but only seventeen provisions were new. Only twenty-eight of the total needed to be addressed by the Community under the principle of subsidiarity, and since that time eight directives have been passed by the Council, mainly pertaining to working conditions.[8] The Charter itself was not part of the Treaty on the European Union, and Community efforts have mainly been advisory through organizations such as the European Employment Services (EURES) and Handicapped People in Europe Living Independently in an Open Society (HELIOS). Besides employment, the social policy of the Community includes education. Although the educational systems of the member states are different, the Community has attempted to create programs to help coordinate training and education. Along with declaring 1996 the European Year of Life-Long Learning, the Parliament and the Council adopted the "Socrates action program" with funding from 1995 to 1999 of ECU 850 million. This will fund higher education, school education, foreign language learning, open and distance learning, adult education, and exchanges of information across member states. Programs like the ERASMUS on the higher education level, Comenius on the secondary, and Leonardo da Vinci (along with the FORCE, Comett, and PETRA programs) for vocational training will implement the Socrates program.

ENERGY

There is no energy policy per se, although the Single European Act did include the market for energy for liberalization, especially concerning incompatibilities in cross-frontier infrastructure, for example, pipelines, electricity networks, and railroads. In January 1985, the Commission adopted a Green Paper for a European Union Energy Policy that aims at stronger concerted action between decisionmakers and energy policymakers, a more comprehensive approach to national and Community energy policies, and the creation of a definition of the Community's energy policy responsibilities that takes into account environmental matters.[9] In addition, the Community has embarked on a number of projects to enhance and develop electricity and gas networks in various outlying areas and neighboring areas (North Africa to the EU and Russia-Belarus-Poland to the EU)[10] through trans-European networks for energy. The Community supports the research of programs to find new sources of energy and to improve energy-use efficiency.[11] However, even though there have been ambitious programs, the EC has not set energy policy as a priority. Within the payments to the category "Energy and Industrial Policy," energy and the environment took just 0.96 percent of the budget.

ENVIRONMENT

With the economic inefficiencies created by the negative externalities of various forms of pollution, it is only natural that the Community develop environmental regulations. However, by and large, the individual countries have retained their own standards and regulations rather than setting policy jointly through the Community. Although the Treaty of Rome did not mention the environment, environmental policy has been somewhat more focused with five successive five-year Environmental Action Programs (EAPs), starting in 1973. These have established the objectives and rules under which the environment should be regulated by the member nations. Of course, countries range widely on their environmental commitments. On the high end, countries such as Denmark spend almost 2 percent of GDP on environmental protection; on the low end, countries such as Greece spend less than 0.1 percent. The Single European Act explicitly adds harmonization of environmental policy as one of its goals, and this was reinforced by the Treaty on European Union (Articles 130r,s,t). In 1987, the Community established the European Environmental Agency to provide information necessary to assess environmental legislation through the Environmental Information and Observation Network (EIONET). However, due to political squabbles, it began operation only in 1995. In 1992, the Council adopted the LIFE program, which provides money to environmental projects; ECU 400 million was allocated through 1995. In 1993, the rules under which the Commission would actually judge environmental quality were established. Recently, the Community has focused on the limitation and regulation of carbon dioxide emissions through extension of the Rio accords on global emissions. Approximately 6.5 percent of the world's population lives in the EU, and they produce 14 percent of total CO_2 emissions. As with energy policy, however, very few funds have actually been spent on environmental policy.

INDUSTRIAL POLICY

The industrial policy of the Community has been to support research and technological development, competition policy, and the transition of declining industries.[12] The TEU set out four objectives for industrial policy:

1. To speed the adjustment to structural changes
2. To encourage innovation, especially so that small and medium business can develop
3. To encourage an environment to stimulate cooperation that increases efficiency
4. To foster the implementation of research and technological development

The three areas of declining sectors targeted are textiles, shipbuilding, and steel. Although much has been tried in these areas, especially during the economically challenged 1970s, these sectors have not been competitive and have been largely dismantled.[13] As we saw in the last chapter, competition policy has been very important for the Community after 1988 with the unfolding of the SEA. But since most of the emphasis has been on deregulation, this has not been a financially burdensome area for the Community.

RESEARCH AND TECHNOLOGY

Like other areas we have seen, research and technological development policies are coordinated through five-year action programs, designed to give the EU the guidelines to coordinate policies. The SEA makes clear that the emphasis of EU policy should be to support research coordination, open up national contracting, and remove legal and fiscal barriers that impede intermember cooperation. The Community supports technological research in any of three ways. One is to cooperate with large firms or research institutions, paying 50 percent of the total costs for industrial partners and 100 percent of the marginal costs of other partners with the rest of the costs coming from the private consortia. A second is to do its own research under its Joint Research Center (JRC). The JRC consists of eight institutes in six countries with a staff of about 2,000 and a budget of about ECU 300 million. The third is to operate under concerted action. This means that the EU bears the costs of the actual cooperation and leaves the costs of the research up to the private or institutional agents. This last means has been quite effective. It is in this area that the Community can best deal with the market failures inherent in the asymmetry of information between inventors and implementors. By facilitating cooperation among countries and among firms and coupling this with competition policy (discussed below), the EU can increase technological development and lower costs.

The Community operates many programs designed to coordinate and work in these three ways. To organize research it has the Scientific and Technical Research Committee (CREST), for European Research Coordination it has EUREKA, for industrial technologies and advanced materials the BRITE/EURAM programs, for advanced communications the ACTS program, for information technology ESPRIT, and for the dissemination of information the VALUE program. While the Community does have its own research organization, the JRC, which initiates and operates projects; the main emphasis of its policy is to ensure the sharing of information and the coordination of research. The Community is well placed to conduct these types of operations. In 1995, the Community aimed at much tighter coordination of European research and pledged to focus on railroad, automobile, and aircraft research; multimedia and educational software; vaccines and viral diseases; and transport intermodality. Because research and development is an area with seemingly large positive externalities and perhaps some scale economies, we should expect growing expenditures in this area. Indeed, payments for R&D rose from 1.4 percent of the budget in 1975 to 4.3 percent in 1994.

TRANSPORT POLICY

The only common economic policies outside of external trade that were specified in the Treaty of Rome were for agriculture and transport. However, whereas agricultural policy has dominated Community activity, transport policies have mainly been conducted by the member states. States have made these investments due to market failures associated with transport networks. If such networks are left unregulated, they tend to become natural monopolies, but regulators have difficulty in maintaining both economic efficiency and social externalities. Within a customs union, a well-functioning transport system is clearly important. The emphasis is on expanding internal trade and an important part of the delivered price of goods is accounted for by transport costs. Ironically, precisely because of its importance and the political commitments to state enterprises or labor unions that had arisen, member states kept close control of transport policy. States controlled prices and limited entry; they protected national carriers and pursued discriminating subsidies and taxation. Blatant examples of breakdowns in transport networks abounded. For example, on the French/Spanish border, trains had to be stopped and reloaded because the gauges were not compatible—this even though the French had been mostly responsible for building the Spanish rail system!

For the first thirty years of the European Community there was no serious attempt to implement Community control of transport systems. In fact, the European Parliament brought action against the Council for failing to implement a common transport policy in 1985. This forced the Commission and the Council to consider transport seriously in their recommendations for the Single Market. With the push for the Single Market and the reductions in physical barriers, moreover, transport and haulage regulation has become an area of serious interest. The Program for Sustainable Mobility of 1992 laid out five focus areas that will guide transport policy[14]:

1. Promoting the creation of a single market through removing barriers to the movement of goods and persons
2. Removing national and cross-border distortions within the transport market
3. Assisting investment in order to reduce regional disparities

4. Ensuring that transport developments respect environmental conditions

5. Improving transport safety

Since the SEA, the Community has moved strongly toward establishing these goals in the transport sector. For example, the Spanish gauge changes have been nearly completed and the European market is more integrated than ever before.[15] With the so-called Third Package of 1992 (the first two were in 1987 and 1990), the European aviation market is far more open than ever before. An EC operator's license was standardized and restrictions on cabotage were reduced. (Cabotage occurs when a transporter from one country who has delivered goods or passengers to a second country picks up goods or passengers there for delivery elsewhere in the second country or in a third country. If cabotage were allowed, a British Air flight from London to Paris could pick up passengers there and fly them on to Marseilles or Milan.) Full cabotage rights were targeted for April 1997 (with the exception of Greece). Airlines would be free to set their own fares, subject to strict monitoring for signs of "unfair" competition. Although state aids continue and the allocation of take-off and landing slots is tightly controlled throughout Europe, the Community's stance, along with pressures from countries such as the United Kingdom and Luxembourg, has gradually made the European air transport market less restrictive.

The latest aspect of this increased attention to transport is the ambitious creation of so-called trans-European transport networks that target transport infrastructure. The goal is to meld the fifteen independent member state networks into a single European network. Currently, there is still inadequate cooperation. For example, throughout the EU air services are managed by fifty-two air traffic centers, many of them redundant, with twenty different operating systems. The TEU set out the guidelines for creating trans-European networks in transport, energy and telecommunications in Article 129b. The EU will identify projects of common interest, and support them with loan guarantees, interest rate subsidies and technical standardization to make networks interoperable with particular attention to "link island, landlocked and peripheral regions with the central regions of the Community."[16] For transport, the Commission's program is wide-sweeping. It requires 70,000 kilometers of railways, including 22,000 kilometers of new and upgraded track for high speed trains; 15,000 kilometers of new roads, nearly half in poorer regions; 267 airports of common interest and networks of inland waterways and sea ports.[17] The Council endorsed fourteen transport projects at its Essen meeting in 1994.[18]

DEVELOPMENT AID

So-called cooperation payments, which include foreign aid and other international payments, have ebbed and flowed as required by the international community. As we saw in Chapter 3, the importance of trade with developing countries has fallen over the years. The Community has shifted to more internal trade and has, as have other industrial nations, reduced its relative demand for primary products. The Community has a number of special trading arrangements with different areas of the developing world, and we will examine them in Chapter 8. European development policy, as such, has been rather fragmented, with the member states pursuing separate policies. It is really only with the TEU that the member states and the Community have seriously attempted to coordinate overall development policies. Article 130 of the TEU lays down the guidelines for this cooperation of policies toward developing countries: the policies should foster sustainable economic and social development, the integration of the targeted countries into the world economy, and the fight against severe poverty. However, with the internal demands for more structural funds and the demands placed on the Community by the Eastern European countries, aid to other areas will be limited in the future. The Community spends about 3.5 percent of its budget on development, mainly for humanitarian and food aid, controlled by the Commission's European Office for Emergency Humanitarian Aid (ECHO). The Community also cofinances some projects launched by nongovernmental organizations (NGOs) and supports community-based cooperation.

The most important financial contributions for development assistance payments to foreign states are controlled mainly through the Lomé Conventions[19] with the African, Caribbean, and Pacific countries (ACP). These arrangements provide special treatment of some seventy countries throughout the three target areas with special treatment for former colonial areas. The basic features of the convention are direct aid, loans and grants, the System for the Stabilization of ACP and Overseas Countries and Territories Export Earnings (Stabex), and the System for the Stabilization of Export Earnings from Mining Products (Sysmin). Total spending allocated for the most recent convention, Lomé IV, for the period 1990–95 was ECU 12.0 billion. For the period 1995–2000 ECU 14.6 billion has been allocated. Grants account for about 67 percent of the payments, and are primarily connected with structural adjustment programs rather than project financing. Stabex accounts for about 11 percent and Sysmin for about 4 percent. Most of these funds are allocated by the European Development Fund (ECU 10,800 million), which is funded directly by member states' contributions and is separate from the EU budget. The rest of the funds are controlled by the European Investment Bank. The payments to the ACP are about 55 percent of all EU aid, so that even though the money sent to the ACP is not seen in the budget, its impact on spending is clear.

Stabex is funded as a means to stabilize commodity export earnings. ACP states receive subsidies from the Community for targeted products if in a year the received export price is lower than the average of the previous six years, minus the minimum and maximum years. Note that this system is very different from the Common Agricultural Policy. Rather than a price support system, the Stabex is an income maintenance program. The total payments to Stabex are bounded by the level of past income. Stabex-receiving countries cannot expand production and receive more and more subsidies. The Community perhaps could not change the CAP in 1975 but it had certainly learned from it, and since the ACP countries have virtually no political power vis-à-vis the Community, the structure of Stabex was very different from that of the CAP. The actual amount that is given to the affected country is the difference between this reference average and the actual export earnings for the year, less 4.5 percent of the reference level (or only 1% for the least developed areas). This system has changed little since it was begun in 1975, except that now the Community has attached more conditionality to the way funds are spent in the affected country. The Sysmin program is similar, but focuses on mining export sectors. It covers such commodities as copper, phosphates, manganese, iron ore, uranium, and bauxite.

CONCLUSION

Community expenditures were about 1.05 percent of Community GDP in 1995. It is easy to get caught up in thinking that the spending of the Community is dominating member state spending—it does not. Even as a percentage of public expenditure, Community spending was just 2.1 percent of the public expenditures of member states. However, the budget itself shows where the Community has put its priorities and how it has attempted to harmonize member states, so that their own spending sits in line with Community objectives. The Single European Act has marked a large change in the allocation of the budget. New payments for a variety of programs were made, and reductions in traditional payments were carried out, most notably in agriculture. Although agricultural spending has fallen, it still accounts for nearly half of all expenditures, far more than any other area. It is to this sector and area of Community policy that we now turn.

Endnotes

1. The Treaty of 1975 did officially establish Parliament's right to reject the budget (acting by a majority of members and two-thirds of the votes cast), but this was understood procedure after the Luxembourg Treaty of 1970; in 1975 the understood right was confirmed by the Treaty, so it did not really mark a change in Parliamentary policy.

2. The Bretton Woods Conference of July 1944 established the rules for the post-World War II international monetary system. At the conference it was clear that the U. S. dollar would be the international reserve currency and that the institutions of the World Bank and the International Monetary Fund would be needed to fulfill the delegates' plans. The value of a Unit of Account was 0.88867088 gram of fine gold, which was the weight equivalent of the U.S. dollar from 1934 to 1972.

3. The signing of the Lomé Convention led to the need for a new unit in order to achieve greater stability in financing aid. See D. Strasser, *The Finances of Europe* (in Bibliography), pp. 61–64.

4. Essentially, the ECU is a basket currency made up of the member states' currencies

in fixed proportions. Its value in any member currency is then determined by the weighted average value of all the member currencies to the one member's currency. We will discuss the ECU in detail in Chapter 7 when we examine monetary union.

5. Until 1988, member states received a reimbursement of costs incurred in the collection of customs duties and agricultural levies amounting to 10 percent of the total collected, which was entered as a budgetary expenditure. However, now "member states shall retain, by way of collection costs, 10 percent of the amounts paid under duties and levies." (Decision 94/728) This is now entered as a negative revenue in the budget.

6. Included are the glucose and isoglucose levies that protect European sugar markets, much the same as U.S. sugar producers are protected.

7. This attempted to regulate multinational corporations by requiring them to inform workers of European activities as well as non-European activities. Given the high unemployment during the early 1980s and the low levels of international investment, it is not surprising that the response to the directive was hostile.

8. The Community Charter of the Fundamental Social Rights of Workers, the "Social Charter," was adopted in December 1989. It contains twelve items, among them right to a fair wage, right to work in the country of one's choice, and the guarantee of minimum living standards for the elderly.

9. Commission of the European Communities, *General Report on the Activities of the European Union, 1985,* Brussels, 1986, p. 144.

10. In conjunction with this, the EU also signed the "Energy Charter" in 1991 that will help develop the energy sector in the former Soviet Union. New accords have been signed outlining legally binding rules for trade and investment in these countries. For more on this, see the section of the EUROPA website on energy policy, address http://europa.eu.int/en/eupol/energ.html.

11. For example, the Joint Opportunities for Unconventional or Long-Term Energy Supply (JOULE) program, the Program for the Promotion of European Energy Technology (THERMIE), the Promotion of Energy Efficiency (SAVE), and the Community Program to Improve the Efficiency of Electricity Use (PACE).

12. These data do not include the financing of the ECSC, but even if they were included in the category "Energy and Industrial Policy," its percentage would rise to only 5.6 percent.

13. In fact, these are the areas of the most dirigistic programs. The Davignon Plan of 1977 effectively tried to operate a European cartel for steel with recommended quotas and prices, but the second oil shock destroyed any notion of saving the European steel industry.

14. For an excellent guide and analysis of the details of these measures, see Norman Lee "Transport policy," in M Artis and N. Lee, eds., *The Economics of the European Union,* Oxford: Oxford University Press, 1994, pp. 202–37.

15. Note that some of the most dramatic changes have been more indirectly affected by European integration as guided from the EC. For example, the Chunnel, linking the continent with Britain (a dream for over 100 years) was completed mainly through private financing.

16. Treaty of European Union, Article 129b, part 2.

17. Taken from the "TENs for Transport," at the EUROPA website, address http://europa. eu. int/eupol/ten/transp. html.

18. These are: High Speed Train, Paris-Brussels-Cologne-Amsterdam-London, with total investment of ECU 13 billion; High Speed Train/Combined Transport North-South, linking Germany and Italy, with total investment of more than ECU 20 billion; High Speed Train South, crossing Spain and linking Spain to French High Speed Trains, total investment ECU 12.9 billion; High Speed Train, Paris-Eastern France-Southern Germany, total investment ECU 4.5 billion; Conventional rail/combined transport Betuwe line, connecting Rhine/Main to the port of Rotterdam, total investment ECU 3.3 billion; High Speed Train/Combined Transport, Lyon-Turin, Turin-Milan-Venice-Trieste, investment between ECU 13.6 and 14.2 billion; Greek Motorways, Patras-Athens-Thessaloniki-Promahon, and Via Egnatia both along the Bulgarian border, investment ECU 6.4 billion; Lisbon-Valladolid Motorway, along Portugal and into Spain, investment ECU 1.1 billion; Conventional Rail Link, Cork-Dublin-Belfast-Larne-Stranraer, investment ECU 238 million; Malpensa Airport in Milan, investment ECU 1 million; Fixed rail/road link between Denmark and Sweden (consisting of 4-km-long tunnel under the sea, a 4-km artificial island and a 7.5-km bridge), investment ECU 3.4 billion; Nordic Triangle, connecting Norway, Sweden, and Finland, investment ECU 4.4 billion; Ireland-U.K.-Benelux Road Link, investment around ECU 2.9 billion; and West Coast Main Line (U.K.), investment between ECU 600 and 800 million.

19. These superseded the earlier Yaoundé (capital of Cameroon) conventions of the 1960s. Lomé is the capital of Togo. Both Cameroon and Togo are former French African colonies.

Bibliography

General Budget and Policy Areas

Bladen-Hovell, R. and E. Symons. "The EC Budget," in M. Artis and N. Lee, eds. *The Economics of the European Community*. Oxford: Oxford University Press, 1994, pp. 368–87. Excellent, if now somewhat dated, overview of the EC budget with chronology of major financial reforms.

Commission of the European Communities. *The Community Budget: The Facts in Figures*. Brussels, 1996. It can be an arduous task to collect budget data from the Official Journal of the Community; this source gives excellent summary data on all aspects of the budget and its components in figures and tables.

Commission of the European Communities. *General Report on the Activities of the European Union, 1995*. Brussels, 1996. This is the best starting place to learn the most recent changes in EU policies. Well organized and indexed, this is an important research tool.

European Commission. *European Union: Public Finance*. Brussels, 1995. An excellent reference for understanding the details of both constructing and implementing the budget.

Eurostat. *Europe in Figures*. Luxembourg, 1995. Copiously illustrated and documented with data, this is a very clear and succinct overview of current and recent EU history. An excellent guide to any area of the European Union.

Strasser, D. *The Finances of Europe: The Budgetary and Financial Law of the European Communities*. 7th edn., Office for Official Publications of the European Communities, Luxembourg, 1992. Everyone writing about the budget quotes Strasser because it is the best single reference. It also serves as an excellent general guide to the different policy areas of the EC.

Regional Funds and Social Policy

Albrechts, L., F. Moulaert, and E. Swyngedouw. *Regional Policy at the Crossroads*. London: Kingsley, 1989.

Armstrong, H. et al. "Regional Policy," in M. Artis and N. Lee, eds. *The Economics of the European Community*. Oxford: Oxford University Press, 1994, pp. 172–201. A clear examination of Community policy along with a summary of regional policies of the member states.

Armstrong, H. and J. Taylor. *Regional Economics and Policy*. Hemel Hempstead, U.K.: Harvester Wheatsheaf, 1993.

Clout, H., ed. *Regional Development in Western Europe,* 3rd edn., London: John Wiley & Sons, 1987.

Commission of the European Communities. *Guide to the Reform of the Community's Structural Funds*. Brussels, 1989.

Commission of the European Communities. *The Regions in the 1990s: Fourth Periodic Report on the Social and Economic Situation and Development of the Regions of the Community*. Brussels, 1991.

Commission of the European Communities. *A Social Portrait of Europe*. Brussels, 1991.

Commission of the European Communities. *The Community's Structural Fund Operations, 1994–1999*. Brussels, 1993.

Dinan, D. *Ever Closer Union?* Boulder, Colo.: Lynne Rienner Publishers, 1994, pp. 403–13. Good treatment of the impact of Delors I and II on structural funds.

Eurostat. *Social Protection Expenditure and Receipts, 1980–1992*. Luxembourg, 1994. Excellent source for detailed data on the recent history of social protection spending. Very good for seeing how member states have converged or diverged in their spending.

Eurostat. *Social Portrait of Europe*. Luxembourg, 1996. Not as detailed as the expenditure and receipts volume, but a volume with broader coverage of issues. An excellent starting place for just about any issue dealing with the population of the member states.

Eurostat. *Regional Statistics*. Luxembourg, annual. An indispensable guide to the regions within the member states, broken down by sector. A must for any regional analysis.

Purdy, D. and P. Devine. "Social Policy," in M. Artis and N. Lee, eds. *The Economics of the European Community*. Oxford: Oxford University Press, 1994, pp. 269–93. Overview of the nature of social policies within market economies and good review of the framework of EC policy.

Springer, Beverly. *The Social Dimension of 1992: Europe Faces a New EC*. New York: Praeger, 1992.

Steinle, W. "Regional Competitiveness and the Single Market," *Regional Studies* 26, 1992, pp. 307–18.

Industrial, Energy and Research and Technological Development Policy

Peterson, J. "Technology policy in Europe: Explaining the Framework Program and EUREKA in theory and practice," *Journal of Common Market Studies* 29, 1991, pp. 269–90.

Sandholz, W. "ESPRIT and the politics of international collective action," *Journal of Common Market Studies* 30, 1992, pp. 1–24.

Sharp, M. and C. Shearman. *European Technological Collaboration.* London: Routledge & Kegan Paul, 1987.

Stubbs, P. and P. Saviotti. "Science and Technology Policy," in M. Artis and N. Lee, eds. *The Economics of the European Community,* Oxford: Oxford University Press, 1994, pp. 139–69. Description of all the various organizations with an overview of the history of R&D in the Community.

Swann, Dennis. *Competition and Industrial Policy in the European Community.* London: Metheun, 1983. Somewhat dated but classic examination.

Transport Policy

Button, K. "The Liberalization of Transport Services," in D. Swann, ed. *The Single European Market and Beyond.* London: Routledge, 1992, pp. 146–61.

Commission of the European Communities. *The Future Development of the Common Transport Policy.* Brussels: Office for Official Publications of the European Communities, 1992.

Lee, N. "Transport policy," in M. Artis and N. Lee, eds. *The Economics of the European Community,* Oxford: Oxford University Press, 1994, pp. 202–37.

Whitelegg, J. *Transport Policy in the EEC.* London: Routledge, 1988.

Environmental Policy

Commission of the European Communities. "The economics of limiting CO^2 emissions," *European Economy,* Special Edition 1, 1992.

Lee, N. "Environmental Policy, in M. Artis and N. Lee, eds. *The Economics of the European Community.* Oxford: Oxford University Press, 1994, pp. 238–68.

CHAPTER 6

The Common Agricultural Policy:

Economic Efficiency vs. Self-Sufficiency

In most countries, agriculture has traditionally been protected. Governments have treated domestic food supplies as strategic commodities, with high levels of subsidies and external protection. It is not at all clear why governments would want to protect their own farmers to such a degree, but they continue to do so. Farmers make up small proportions of industrialized nations, and food products are easily and cheaply available from many sources in the world commodity market. Western European countries have always been very protective of their farmers. From the abortive attempts of the Green Pool in the 1950s to the difficult trade talks of the GATT Uruguay Round ending in 1993, countries have been unwilling to make serious compromises on agricultural intervention. Ironically, it was the United States that demanded that primary products, especially agricultural products, be exempted from the basic GATT rules.

For farmers, though, it is clear why they want governmental protection. In agriculture, supply fluctuates from year to year, season to season, due to a variety of external causes. The climate, the soil, diseases and pests, and many other variables can cause large differences in production. The demand, in Western Europe at least, is virtually constant. In industrial nations the percentage of income spent on agriculture is small and there is little reason for the demand to change from year to year. Here are the percentages of expenditure on food to total household consumption in 1982:

Belgium	18.3	Denmark	16.7	West Germany	14.6
Greece	35.6	Spain	31.5	France	17.5
Ireland	23.1	Italy	25.6	Luxembourg	14.7
Netherlands	15.1	Portugal	37.0	United Kingdom	14.7

Europe is the leading importer and the world's second ranking exporter of food and other agricultural products. Europe imports about 20 percent of all agricultural imports (the United States about 10% and Japan 11%). This illustrates that the European Union's common agricultural policy has not eliminated imports, nor has it made Europe a relatively closed area for the trade of agricultural goods. For exports, Europe ranks second only to the United States. The Community's share in world export of food and other agricultural products is about 10.5 percent. Although Western Europe's trade with the rest of the world is large, the greatest expansion of agricultural trade has been within the EC. From 1973 through 1984, the percentage of intra-EEC trade to non-EEC trade (imports and exports to nonmember countries) has risen from about 49 percent to about 63 percent.

At the outset of the customs union in 1958, agriculture was heavily protected. Recalling that the average tariff on all imports was intended to be 7.4 percent, it is striking that the average tariff on foodstuffs alone was 14.2 percent.[1] The high level was not the result of a common consensus that foodstuffs should be protected as much as industrial goods; rather it was a necessary outcome of considerable divergence in agricultural problems and policies among the member countries. First of all, the relative importance of agriculture ranged from 23 percent of GDP in Italy to 8.4 percent in Belgium, where the average farmer earned three times as much as in Italy. The range of prices for basic foodstuffs varied widely. Wheat, for example, was much cheaper in France than in either Italy or Germany. The size of farms varied, although most were too small to make mechanization profitable. In Italy, holdings between 0.5 and 5 hectares (1 hectare = 2.471 acres) accounted for 85 percent of all farms, 55 percent of the farms in Germany, and nearly 35 percent of the farms in France.[2] For the United States less than 10 percent of farms were under 5 hectares.[3] Agricultural productivity varied widely as well, with the Dutch using three times as much fertilizer per acre as the French and five times as much as the Italian farmers.[4]

To establish a common market in agricultural goods required a common agricultural policy, but to reach agreement on the essential features of such a policy required a willingness by each country to protect not only its own less efficient farmers but also the less efficient farmers in the partner countries as well. The more efficient countries in agricultural production, France and the Netherlands, wanted to speed up the elimination of internal customs barriers on foodstuffs, while the least efficient, Italy and Germany, wanted to slow down the dismantling of internal tariffs in agriculture until a common agricultural policy was agreed on. It was not until 1962 that a Common Agricultural Policy came into practice, despite the urgency for prompt agreement on agricultural policy expressed in Article 40 of the Treaty of Rome. The CAP was supposed to enable the member states to achieve the five objectives for agriculture that they had enunciated in Article 39. These were:

1. To increase agricultural productivity by promoting technical progress and the optimum use of production factors

2. To ensure a fair standard of living to the agricultural community by increasing their per capita income

3. To stabilize markets

4. To assure the availability of supplies

5. To ensure reasonable consumer prices

In other words, there was something promised for everyone, and it was left for future negotiations to determine who could actually get what was promised them. In fact, the overriding priority held in common was to achieve self-sufficiency in agriculture. This had been a goal throughout Europe after World War I, and with the separation of industrial West Germany from agricultural East Germany the urgency of reaching this goal was intensified. The first four objectives are all compatible with the strategic goal of agricultural self-sufficiency, as inconsistent as they might be with one another in terms of economic practicality. The last goal was inconsistent with the first four, but was left purposely vague to minimize conflict.

During the Stresa Conference in July 1958, the fundamental principles of the CAP were laid down by the participating farmers' federations and the delegations of the Six. By June 1960, the Commission submitted its proposals and in December 1960 the Council adopted three principles:

1. A single market was to be established with free flow of goods, and harmonization of prices and exchange rates.[5]

2. Community preference was extended to European farmers in the form of price supports and export subsidies, but foreign trade would not be eliminated.

3. Joint financial responsibility would be accepted by all members through the creation of a common agricultural fund called the European Agricultural Guidance and Guarantee Fund (EAGGF).

It is clear from the results on trade patterns described in Chapter 3 that the goal of agricultural self-sufficiency has been reached. On that criterion the Common Agricultural Policy must be judged a success. In fact, by 1980 the European Community was exporting more foodstuffs than it was importing, so self-sufficiency in this sense was achieved even before the addition of Greece, Spain, and Portugal to the membership. Over the course of the 1980s, the EC actually became a net exporter, to the extent that traditional exporting nations such as the United States, Canada, and Argentina put considerable pressure on the EC to ease certain features of its policy. Indeed, by the mid 1980s the EC10's share of OECD agricultural exports had risen to 56 percent from 45 percent in the late 1960s, while its share of OECD agricultural imports had fallen to 55 percent from 60 percent over the same period of roughly twenty years. At the same time, the U.S. share of OECD agricultural exports had fallen from 25 percent to 20 percent while its share of imports had remained at about 19 percent.[6]

Although the addition of Greece, Portugal, and Spain did not bring about the export surplus, it did change the distribution of subsidies. In 1980, dairy products (42.1%), cereals (15.3%), and meat and eggs (14.2%) comprised nearly 72% of guarantee payments. In 1990, these three products made up only 45 percent of guarantee payments; the rest of the payments were going to new products grown by the new, more agrarian member countries.

PRICE SUPPORTS VS. INCOME SUPPLEMENTS

The CAP agreed on by the EC6 in 1962 was essentially a price support scheme, in which target prices would be set for each supported commodity that were the same across the entire Community. If the target price was met in each country then there was no impediment to letting the commodity be traded freely among the partner countries. In the early days of the CAP not all agricultural products were included; by 1970, 87 percent were included and by 1986, 91 percent.

The CAP actually uses three types of interventions. The first and most prominent is support prices, which cover about two-thirds of all CAP products. The second, covering about a quarter of all products, is simply external protection. Examples of these products are wines, flowers, eggs, poultry and some fruits and vegetables. The third is special or flat-rate aid for certain products that keeps domestic prices low but supplements farmer incomes. Examples of these products are olive oil, durum wheat, cotton, and tobacco.

Since the Community's farmers were very inefficient relative to those in the United States, Canada, Argentina, Australia, and Great Britain for that matter, the target prices were typically higher than those in the major exporting countries of the world. To protect EC agriculture from competition from more efficient farmers in the rest of the world, a variable levy was assessed on imports at each port of entry. The variable levy was set to make up the difference between the target price and the import price at the particular port of entry. In the initial years when the Community was still a net importer, the variable levy was expected to yield significant revenues, which would be allocated directly to the Community as part of its "own resources." Out of these own resources it would then be able to finance the purchase of surplus production wherever and whenever it occurred in the Community.

Figure 6.1a illustrates this case. Note that the target price is set high enough to encourage a substantial percentage increase in domestic production, even if the farmers still cannot meet the domestic demand for the agricultural good in question. The figure also shows a target price and a threshold price at two different levels. The target price at a major point of distribution, say Frankfurt, is above the threshold price at the port of entry, say Bremen, because of the transportation costs required to ship from Bremen to Frankfurt. The variable levy, then, needs to be set only at the height of the threshold price to give European farmers a protected market in Frankfurt at the target price.

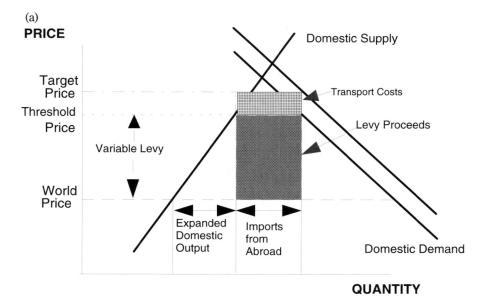

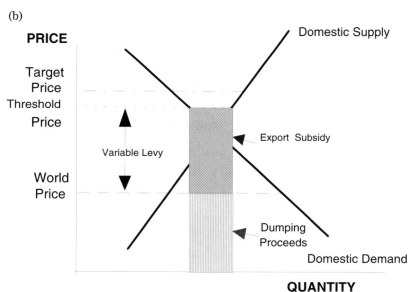

Figure 6.1. The Common Agricultural Policy. (a) Import deficit. (b) Export surplus.

To finance the price support schemes set up for the basic commodities, the EEC established the European Agricultural Guidance and Guaranty Fund (EAGGF). The "guidance" part was intended to help finance technical assistance to European farmers who wished to modernize their operations, thereby increasing their productivity and hence the ability of the customs union to be self-sufficient in agricultural goods. From the beginning, however, the share of the budget allocated to the guaranty part of the fund has dominated, accounting typically for about 95 percent of the total EAGGF budget. As a result of the expense of maintaining above-world-market prices to European consumers, the EAGGF has also dominated the entire budget of the EC. From nearly 90 percent of the EC's budget in the 1968 to 1972 period, it has gradually been trimmed.

The policy goal has been to reduce the guarantee section of the EAGGF and increase the guidance section, while reducing the overall weight of agriculture within the EEC budget. In fact, the total amount of the Guarantee section of the EAGGF is limited (set at 32.5 billion ECUs in 1991) by guidelines set since the Council's budgetary decisions on June 14, 1988.[7] In the beginning of the 1980s the guarantee section of the EAGGF was about 64.3 percent of the total EEC budget, while guidance was about 3.2 percent. In the mid-1980s, guarantee actually increased to 65.3 percent and guidance fell to 2.7 percent. In 1990, though, guarantee had fallen to 54.8 percent and guidance had increased to 3.5 percent. Guidance had increased within the EAGGF from 3.4 percent in 1986 to just over 6 percent in 1990.

Until the mid-1980s, increasing the share of guidance was done by increasing the resources of the EC. Resources were enlarged mainly by increasing the EC's share of the value added tax levied in all member states and, more recently, by levying an additional contribution based on a member state's GDP. (See Chapter 5 on the EU budget.) The bulk of the additional expenditures of the EC has gone to so-called structural funds, which emphasize improving the economy of backward regions within the EC. Because backward regions are typically dominated by the agricultural sector, these funds could be counted as part of the guidance appropriations directed to the improvement of agricultural productivity.

Despite a very small allocation to guidance over the years by the EC, the technical progress of the agricultural sector has been spectacular. In 1960, 15.2 million people were employed in agriculture within EC6; by 1987 that number had dropped to only 5.2 million and the average size of a farm within the EC6 had risen from 12 hectares (one hectare equals 2.471 acres) to just under 20. Over the same period the EC6 grew in total population but went from providing only 85 percent of its own agricultural needs to being a net exporter.[8] It is clear that fertilizers and tractors have increased enormously the productivity of both land and labor in Western Europe, so much so that labor productivity has increased more rapidly in agriculture than in either services or industry.

Despite the relative increase in labor productivity, however, the ratio of farm incomes to incomes in the rest of the economy has remained quite low, typically 50 percent, in France, Italy, and Germany. The exceptions are Belgium and the Netherlands, which had relatively advanced agricultural sectors at the beginning of the 1950s. As a result, outmigration from agriculture to the rest of the economy has been rapid, especially in the 1950s and 1960s, when it was regarded by some as the key factor in the economic miracles of Germany, Italy, and France.[9] The reason rapid increases in relative labor productivity did not lead to increases in relative labor income is that consumer demand for agricultural output did not rise much at all, even though consumer incomes rose rapidly and the price of agricultural goods fell relative to all other goods. This combination of rapid technical progress, which created elastic supplies of foodstuffs, and slow increase in demand, caused by inelastic demand in terms of both income and price, has been far more important than the guidance policy of the EC or of its member governments in achieving the desired goal of self-sufficiency.

However, the EC's common agricultural policy can take most of the credit for overshooting the goal of self-sufficiency in the 1980s. While maintaining price supports as the primary policy instruments, the agriculture ministers of the EC responsible for setting the levels of the support prices became increasingly concerned about narrowing the income gap between farmers and the rest of the economy. The result, predictably, was to set prices high enough to provide respectable incomes for small, inefficient farmers. But these same prices provided incentives for even greater production by the more efficient farmers. It is this response by European farmers that by 1980 led to the situation of export surpluses, shown in Figure 6.1b. In this case, domestic supply exceeds domestic demand at the threshold price and the excess supply has to be bought up and stored, or dumped on the world market. In that case, the difference between the threshold price and the world price is the subsidy rate necessary to induce European farmers to sell their produce on the world market.

British economists recognized the problem that price supports can cause in the agricultural sector when Britain was negotiating its eventual entry into the Common Market. They proposed using a different policy instrument, income supplements called deficiency payments, to achieve closure of the agriculture-industry income gap. Figures 6.2a and 6.2b illustrate how deficiency payments would work in the case of a net importing country and in the case of a net exporting country. The income supplement represents a transfer from consumers to producers via the government, but the net cost to consumers is much less in both cases than it is under a system of price supports designed to keep the same inefficient, high-cost farmers in business. In the case of a net importing country, the cost of the deficiency payments amounts only to the deadweight loss of maintaining inefficient farmers in the economy, a loss that is also sustained under a price-support scheme. Consumers, on the other hand, gain consumers' surplus from purchasing a larger quantity of foodstuffs at the much lower world market price. Only part of this is a net gain in efficiency over the alternative of price supports; the rest represents a transfer to consumers from the government, which now gives up the proceeds of the variable levy, and even more important, a transfer to consumers of producers' surplus from the efficient farmers in the EC.

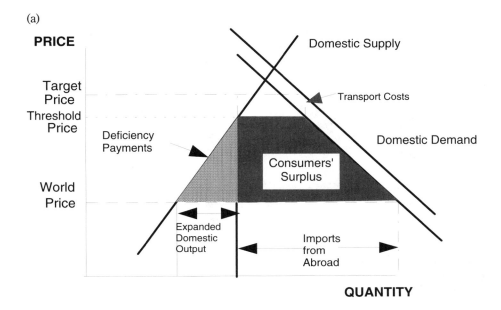

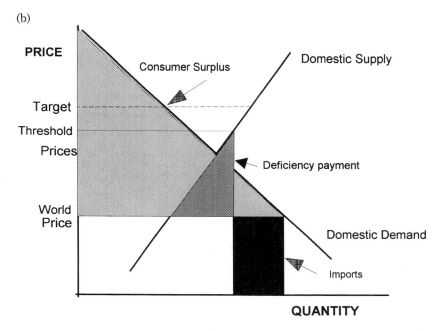

Figure 6.2. The deficiency payment alternative. (a) Import deficit. (b) Export surplus.

In the case of a net exporting country, the system of deficiency payments has even greater advantages over price supports. Again there is a transfer to consumers' surplus from producers' surplus, with some of the consumers' surplus being offset by the deficiency payments, which must come out of general government revenues (see Figure 6.2b). There is a net cost to the society—the amount of deficiency payment made to producers for the excess production that is induced by the height of the price support. Previously this was exported, now it is consumed domestically, and consumers still import additional quantities at the lower world price. The efficient producers lose their producers' surplus and the government loses its dumping proceeds, but it lays out a much smaller amount of money to only the most marginal of the agricultural producers.

If we draw the implications of this analysis for the political economy of changing from price supports to deficiency payments, we can see that once a system of price supports has been functioning for some time, there arises a vested interest among prosperous producers and dedicated bureaucrats to maintain price supports as the existing agricultural policy. In 1992, the EC's commissioner of agriculture, Ireland's Ray MacSharry, proposed shifting from price supports to deficiency payments for the smallest farmers in the EC. To gain the assent of the ministers of agriculture from the member states, he had to propose increasing the actual expenditures on agricultural subsidies during the transition period. Even so, the proposal met with violent protest by Continental farmers, leading at one point in the summer of 1992 to a virtual blockade of Paris by farmers parking their tractors and self-propelled combines on the Boulevarde Périphèrique.

Nevertheless, the EC did adopt the bulk of his proposals in May 1992 (see Box 6.1). The MacSharry reforms were as much a response to international pressure to reform European agricultural subsidies (e.g., GATT negotiations in the Uruguay Round) as to internal pressures. Support prices were lowered, representing a gain to EU consumers (and the EU's budget) and, of course, a loss to EU farmers. To compensate farmers, the EU decided to grant direct income payments (surprise!), subject to farmers reducing their use of inputs. For example, cereal producers will set aside at least 15 percent of their arable area; livestock producers will limit their herd sizes. In addition, special provisions were made to ease the transition out of agriculture for existing farmers.

The welfare effects of these changes are, predictably, difficult to determine. The reduction of EU production support should raise world prices because the reforms should lead to a virtual "vanishing of cereal exports."[10] Domestic European prices, though, should fall, increasing welfare for EU consumers. For EU producers, however, it is more complicated. Special exceptions are made for small producers in both the arable and livestock sectors, so they are not hit by the reductions. They are not the source of the CAP's tendency toward overproduction. This stems from the larger, more efficient farms. For them, the reduction in support prices reduces producer surplus, but the set-asides represent welfare gains. If the compensation payments are large enough, farmers could actually gain from the reforms! In addition, as American policymakers have

---

BOX 6.1   THE MACSHARRY REFORMS

Arable Sector

(i)   A reduction of about one third in the cereal intervention price, which is to fall by 1995–96 to 1000 green ECU per ton, in three steps. An important degree of protection remains through the threshold price of 155 green ECU per ton.

(ii) Elimination of price support for oilseeds and protein crops.

(iii) Compensation through direct area payments based on historical base areas and regional yields, subject to 15 percent rotational set-aside for such crops grown by all except small farmers (under 92 tons of cereal equivalent).

Livestock Sector

(i)   A 15% reduction in intervention prices for beef from July 1993, in three steps.

(ii) Compensation through direct headage payments (premiums) subject to a maximum stocking rate [two livestock units (LU) per fodder hectare] by 1996;

(iii) Increased male bovine and suckler (beef) cow premiums subject to individual limits per holding and to regional reference herd sizes which, if exceeded, reduce the number of eligible animals per producer. There are extra "extensification" headage premiums if a producer reduces the stocking rate below 1.4 LU per fodder hectare.

(iv) A reduction in the ceiling for normal beef intervention buying from 750,000 to 350,000 tons by 1997.

Accompanying Measures

(i)   Implementation through member state programs with 50 percent of the cost (75% in less developed regions) borne by the CAP budget.

(ii) An agri-environmental package aimed at more extensive means of production and the use of land for natural resource protection and public leisure.

(ii) Aid for forestry investment and management with up to twenty years' compensation for income loss.

(iv) Various forms of compensation for early retirement, including lump sum or annual payments, for farmers and farm workers over age 55.

Source: EC Commission, Directorate-General for Economic and Financial Affairs, "EC agricultural policy for the 21st century," *European Economy, Reports and Studies,* No. 4, 1994, pp. 3–40.

---

found, farmers set aside the least productive land and use retained land more intensively, resulting in output falling less than the area of cultivated land (this is known as slippage.) Given this, the budgetary effects are also ambiguous; if producers actually benefit, then the CAP budget could increase from the reforms. All depends on the relative reduction in overall support.

It is interesting, in the light of this analysis, how entrenched has become the interest of the prosperous, large farmers in Great Britain in maintaining the price support system of the Common Agricultural Policy, now that they have been adapting to it for twenty years. From accounting for 27 percent of the OECD's agricultural imports in the late 1960s before entering the EC and adopting the Common Agricultural Policy, Great Britain's share had dropped to 11 percent in 1985. Meanwhile, its share of the OECD's agricultural exports had stayed constant at 6.4 percent. The implication is that Britain, in common with the original members of the EC, moved sharply toward self-sufficiency in agricultural products. This is borne out by Table 6.1, which compares the self-sufficiency ratios for Great Britain and the other EC member countries in various commodities for 1970–74 and 1985.

Table 6.1 brings out more interesting aspects of the CAP than merely the incentive it gave to Britain's efficient farmers to expand enormously their output. The self-sufficiency in sugar enjoyed by the EC6 in the early 1970s, of course, derived both from their protection of sugar beet farmers, especially in Belgium and France, and from the inclusion in the EC of Martinique and Guadaloupe as overseas territories of France. Sugar beets were introduced in southern Belgium and northern France at the beginning of the nineteenth century as part of Napoleon I's policy to circumvent the blockade by the British navy of France's access to its sugar islands in the Caribbean, namely Martinique and Guadaloupe. Once Denmark, Ireland, and the United Kingdom adopted the same tariff protection for sugar beets in their agricultural policy, however, their self-sufficiency rose sharply toward the EC6's levels.

The same story is repeated for butter and meat. It is interesting that price supports are not used for vegetables and fruit, and that deficiency payments have been the accepted policy for producers of oilseeds. In these categories of foodstuffs, dominated by smaller truck farmers located near cities or owning small orchards, the EC has not attempted to reach self-sufficiency. The self-sufficiency ratios of the member states changed very little from 1970 to 1985, and that of the United Kingdom actually declined.

To conclude, the agricultural policy of price supports, carried on with enthusiasm, even extravagance, by the European Community since its foundation, when coupled with the technological progress made possible by mechanization and the application of scientific research to the cultivation of crops and the rearing of livestock, has achieved the original goal of self-sufficiency. Indeed, it has gone right on to overshoot the goal and create increasingly unmanageable surpluses. The price paid for self-sufficiency has been an increasing sacrifice of economic efficiency.

COST OF CAP TO EUROPE

There are two ways of viewing the loss of efficiency. One is to see how much more the economy is paying for agricultural products than it would if it abandoned price and income supports altogether and relied on the productive capacity of the world's farmers to provide its consumers with the food they demand. This criterion asks how much extra the society is paying for its agricultural *product.* The other measure of efficiency is to determine how much more the

TABLE 6.1.
Self-Sufficiency Ratios in Various Foodstuffs for EC and Members, 1970–74 and 1985

	Cereal		Sugar		Butter		Meat		Vegetables, fruit	
	1970–74	1985	1970–74	1985	1970–74	1985	1970–74	1985	1970–74	1985
Belgium	41.6	60.6	184.2	231.0	104.9	...	119.5	130.3	96.9	93.8
Denmark	97.7	133.5	121.1	238.9	327.8	198.0	322.6	322.5	60.9	59.3
France	158.8	215.3	153.9	211.4	113.2	127.9	95.4	98.5	97.0	92.4
Germany	78.0	99.5	95.5	131.9	105.6	111.9	86.2	90.7	47.9	47.3
Greece	...	110.3	...	84.8	...	...	...	71.3	...	143.0
Ireland	70.8	101.8	107.7	141.4	202.2	...	172.2	198.9	85.5	65.7
Italy	67.8	81.6	72.5	77.3	65.3	...	78.9	80.6	114.6	124.3
Netherlands	31.3	31.0	112.2	164.3	361.7	...	167.1	183.9	139.2	143.5
U.K.	65.3	138.7	34.8	63.7	18.3	73.1	69.7	81.6	62.6	49.7
EC Total	89.7	127.1	91.5	131.7	101.5	112.6	94.8	102.1	91.6	94.1

Source: IMF, The Common Agricultural Policy of the European Community, Occasional Paper No. 62, November 1988, pp. 28–30.

society is paying to maintain the incomes of its farmers than the farmers are receiving. This criterion asks how much extra the society is paying for its agricultural *producers.*

Every advanced industrial country, including the EC, the United States, and Japan, is guilty of an inefficient agricultural policy on the first criterion. The OECD's economists attempted to measure this kind of inefficiency by calculating producer subsidy equivalents in each member country for a range of agricultural products. The producer subsidy equivalent is what would be needed to compensate producers for the removal of all agricultural producer support policies (price supports and deficiency payments) as a percent of the value of output at world prices.[11] On this measure, the United States was guilty of raising its average producer subsidy equivalent (PSE) to 28 percent of agricultural output in 1984–86 from an equivalent of only 16 percent in 1979–81. Japan also raised its PSE over the early 1980s, but at much higher levels—from 57 percent to 69 percent! The EC fell between these extremes, merely raising its average PSE from 37 percent to 40 percent.[12] The EFTA countries' agricultural policies give even higher PSEs than the ECs. The question arises, why are rich countries willing to pay so much extra for their food supplies?

Part of the answer is surely the institutional inertia that keeps policies in operation well after the political forces that created them have lost their power. When price supports were initiated in the 1930s and reinstated in the immediate postwar years, agriculture accounted for a very large share of the jobs in the EC economies. By 1957, agriculture's share of total civilian employment was still 35.6 percent in Italy, 16.3 percent in Germany, 24.6 percent in France, and 12.8 percent in the Netherlands, and over 7 percent in Belgium.[13] This obviously translated into a great deal of political power, which could be used to enact government programs very favorable to agriculture. By 1985, however, agriculture's share of civilian employment had fallen to 11.2 percent in Italy, 5.5 percent in Germany, 7.6 percent in France, 4.9 percent in the Netherlands, and only 2.9 percent in Belgium.[14] Clearly, the political clout of the agricultural sector has diminished sharply over the life span of the European Community. It is likely that agriculture's continued political success depends on the nature of the institutional arrangement devised for supporting it.

If the agricultural supports come from the European Community, into which each member country has paid a share of its value added tax and of its total GDP, then the incentive for each is to get back as much in payments as possible. Because agriculture outlays account for 70 to 90 percent of the EC's budget, setting price supports at levels that subsidize a member country's farmers is clearly the best chance for that country to retrieve its contribution. A similar situation exists in the United States where each lightly populated state in the Great Plains has two Senators to vote in favor of agricultural price supports. In Japan as well, the power of the ruling Liberal Democratic Party resides disproportionately in the rural areas populated by small farmers.

Another part of the explanation for the political success of agricultural interests in modern industrial societies, however, surely must be that the cost of supporting agriculture at an excessive rate has fallen relative to the enormous growth of the rest of the economy. Agriculture's share of the GDP of the EC10 had fallen to only 3.3 percent by 1985. An overpayment of 40 percent, even if made to the entire agricultural sector, would amount to only 1.3 percent of GDP.

Finally, for all the overpricing of foodstuffs that the CAP has created for the EC's consumers, their food prices have still risen less than the prices of their nonfood goods and services, and food expenditures have fallen even more as a share of household budgets. So the political pressures to undo the CAP have been steadily abating, thanks to the combination of technical progress on the supply side and price and income inelasticity on the demand side. In the last analysis, the costs to any society of inadequate food supplies are far more daunting to consider than the costs of excess food supplies.

The second measure of inefficiency of agicultural support programs—the difference between what society pays and what farmers receive—indicates, however, how much money a society can save by changing the kind of policy it uses to support the agricultural sector. Economists have made an exercise out of calculating the benefits to producers of agricultural supports of different kinds and then comparing them with the costs, whether in the form of higher consumer prices or in government expenditures. For example, comparing the United States, the EC, and Japan in 1986–87 gives the results shown in Table 6.2.

These data show that agricultural support is not only a European problem— the transfer ratios in both the United States and Japan are similar to that of the EC. Note, however, that the financing of the supports is different. In the United States, taxes paid for the subsidies, while in the EC and in Japan consumers have paid farmers through higher prices. The EC has both relatively large tax and consumer costs because domestic prices are kept high and the EC pays for export restitutions, financed through taxes.

In 1980, British economists estimated the costs to consumers of the excess prices they were paying for foodstuffs in the EC, the costs to governments of the subsidies made in whatever form, and the amount of extra income actually received by producers. The results are worth reproducing in full (Table 6.3),

TABLE 6.2
Measures of Agricultural Policy Inefficiency

Countries	Producer benefits	Consumer costs (Billions of US $)	Taxpayer costs	Transfer ratio
USA	26.3	6.0	30.0	1.37
EC	33.3	32.6	15.6	1.45
Japan	22.6	27.7	5.7	1.48

Source: V. O. Roningen and P. M. Dixit, *How Level is the Playing Field: An Economic Analysis of Agricultural Policy Reforms in Industrial Market Economies,* ERS, FAE Report 239. (Washington, D.C., United States Department of Agriculture, 1989).

TABLE 6.3
Welfare Effects of the CAP by Country in 1980 (in millions of U. S. dollars)

Country	Consumers	Taxpayers	Producers	Net	Transfer Ratio
EC9	−34,580	−11,494	30,686	−15,388	1.50
Germany	−12,555	−3,769	9,045	−7,279	1.80
France	−7,482	−2,836	7,237	−3,081	1.42
Italy	−5,379	−1,253	3,539	−3,093	1.87
Netherlands	−1,597	−697	3,081	787	0.74
Belgium	−1,440	−544	1,624	−320	1.22
United Kingdom	−5,174	−1,995	3,461	−3,708	2.07
Ireland	−320	−99	965	546	0.43
Denmark	−635	−302	1,736	799	0.54

Source: IMF, *The Common Agricultural Policy of the European Community. Principles and Consequences,* Occasional Paper No. 62, Washington, D.C.: IMF, 1988, p. 40.

because they show that consumers and governments were consistently paying much more than producers were receiving.

On this criterion, the consumers and taxpayers of the EC paid 1.5 times the amount of extra income received by agricultural producers. Surely, a more efficient redistribution scheme could be devised, if there were the political will to do so.

Moreover, the transfer ratio varied widely among the member states. Tiny Ireland and Denmark benefited greatly because their agricultural sectors, which had concentrated on their comparative advantages for supplying the huge British market, now had the protected markets of the EC6 to exploit. Britain, on the other hand, suffered the worst transfer ratio of all the member states. The substantial losses that Britain took from adopting the CAP meant that membership in the EC continued to be a net economic loss for it well after the difficult years of the 1970s. This factor, more than the clash of personalities of Margaret Thatcher, the British prime minister in the 1980s, with Guiscard d'Estaing and François Mitterrand, the French presidents in the 1980s, accounts for the continued pressures exerted by the British government to reform both the CAP, if only marginally, and, failing that, the EC budget process.

Britain insisted on increasing expenditures for regional policy, especially for areas of industrial decline which were of special concern to Britain, and of allocating expenditures of the EC among member states more in line with the origin of EC "own resources" from the member states. Britain failed to get full satisfaction for its demands, which explains in large part its continued reluctance to join the other major powers in the European Monetary System. By retaining the policy instrument of a flexible exchange rate against its trading partners in the EC, Britain could unilaterally change the financial terms of its membership, or so its policymakers thought.

COSTS OF CAP TO THE REST OF THE WORLD

The welfare effects of the CAP have not been limited to Western Europe. Because the EEC is a large producer of agricultural products, its subsidies affect world agricultural prices, mainly lowering them through reduced demand because of the variable levies and through increased international supplies because of the export subsidies. Figure 6.3 illustrates these effects.

Figure 6.3a depicts the short-run impact, or the impact from reducing European demand through the imposition of a variable levy. On the top is the EC market and on the right side the WORLD market. At the free-trade price of Pf, the EC imports eh tons of goods. However, when the EC imposes a tariff, the price of agricultural products in the EC rises, causing the quantity demanded from foreign sources to fall. This is depicted in the WORLD market by the leftward shift of the world demand of agricultural products; $D_{ROW + NON\text{-}CAP\ EC}$, to $D_{ROW + CAP\ EC}$. We assume that the rest of the world's demand, that is, demand from non-EC countries, D_{ROW}, remains constant, so the leftward shift of the total world demand is caused by the reduction in demand for imports from the EC. This leftward shift, along a constant world supply, means a lower world price, Pf'. The domestic price in the EC is now Ps because of the levy of $Ps - Pf'$, and so imports have fallen from eh to bc. The rest of the world suffers a welfare loss of $ehbc$ from reduced exports to the EC. The welfare change in the EC is ambiguous, *fgkj*, which is a new gain from tariff revenues, minus the deadweight loss triangles (*bfe* + *chg*). Basically, domestic production has risen, the government is receiving additional money, but consumers are paying more for a reduced amount of goods.

In Figure 6.3b, European producers have had time to adjust to the subsidies and supply has become relatively more elastic. This supply response has been dramatic in practice. To illustrate how exports have expanded relative to imports, in 1977 import levies were nearly 70 percent of export subsidies, and by 1984 they were barely 25 percent.[15] This supply response means that the world supply function rotates downward as well, as shown in the WORLD side of the figure. Given the same demand, the price falls. If the CAP keeps Ps as its target price, the EC becomes a net exporter of agricultural products, so the world demand becomes just D_{ROW}, (because D_{EC+CAP} goes to zero in the long run as the EC becomes a net exporter). As a consequence, the world price falls to Pf''. The EC is paying export restitutions (subsidies) of *cxnm;* consumers lose the area *achd* and producers gain *axod*. This time there is a net loss in welfare for the EC that is equal to *csxnm* + *soh*. This is because the export subsidies are a loss, but the triangle *cxs* is netted out as a transfer from government to producers. The triangle *soh* is counted twice because it represents the loss to consumer welfare and is included in the cost of export subsidies. This time there is an unambiguous loss to welfare for the EC.

Looking at the long-run effects on the rest of the world, producers lose by the area $Pf'cqPf''$. But their consumers gain from receiving agricultural products at cheaper prices, so consumers' surplus increases by the area $Pf'brPf''$. So the net gain to the rest of the world is the area *pqr* − *bcp* (the net consumers gain minus the net producers loss). In other words, net exporting countries lose

(a)

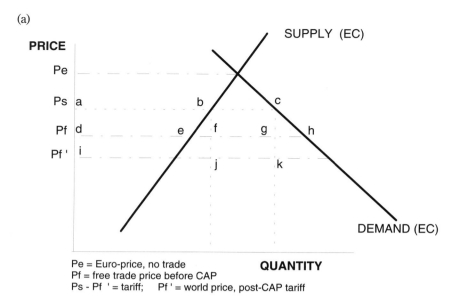

Pe = Euro-price, no trade
Pf = free trade price before CAP
Ps - Pf ' = tariff; Pf ' = world price, post-CAP tariff

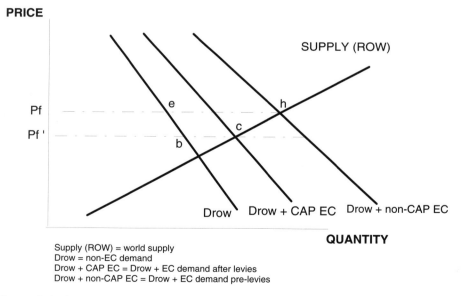

Supply (ROW) = world supply
Drow = non-EC demand
Drow + CAP EC = Drow + EC demand after levies
Drow + non-CAP EC = Drow + EC demand pre-levies

Figure 6.3. Costs of CAP to rest of world (ROW). (a) Short-run. Top: EC. Bottom: Rest of world.

(b)

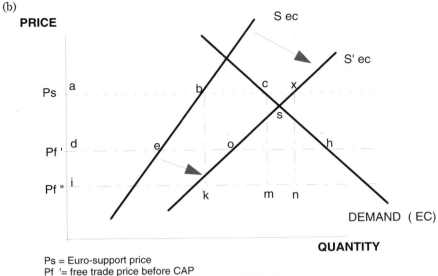

Ps = Euro-support price
Pf ' = free trade price before CAP
Ps - Pf ' = tariff;   Pf " = world price, post-CAP tariff

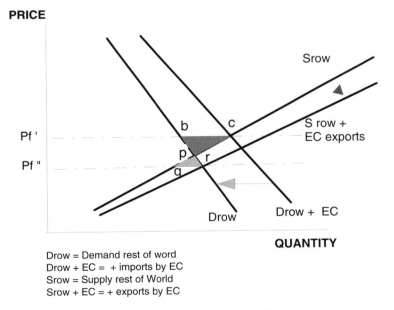

Drow = Demand rest of word
Drow + EC = + imports by EC
Srow = Supply rest of World
Srow + EC = + exports by EC

Figure 6.3. (b) Long-run. Top: EC. Bottom: Rest of world.

from the EC's agricultural policy but net importing countries gain. There has been much concern from traditional agricultural exporting countries as well as from developing countries about the effects of CAP on them. Temperate product (wheat, maize, etc.) producers in developing countries face depressed prices from expanded European exports. Static analysis of third world countries shows that they are net beneficiaries from subsidized food imports because so many of them are net importers. Studies show that real income of developing countries would fall as much as 10.5 percent if the CAP were abolished.[16]

The counterfactual analysis is complicated because estimating the supply response of developing countries is very difficult. Of course, if there were no CAP, supply relationships would change in developing countries and these potential changes are not estimated in partial equilibrium analysis. To trace the dynamic effects of the abolition of the CAP, T. Loo and E. Tower[17] used a four-sector general equilibrium model to predict the changes in real income of six "typical" developing countries. They found that a 10 percent increase in agricultural prices would have raised developing countries incomes by about $26 billion in 1985.[18]

These gains stem from the increase in the terms of trade for food exporters, the efficiency gains from the reallocation of resources, and the tax revenue gains from taxing agriculture. Bela Balassa has shown that developing countries do respond to price changes and that their real incomes rise through trade creation.[19] Peter Svedberg has shown that there has been a long-run positive correlation between exports and real income growth for African countries but is hesitant to be too optimistic about the size of the market response to higher prices.[20] However, it is not at all clear that developing countries could react by increasing production of exportable commodities because of the bottlenecks and institutional constraints of the agricultural sectors in these countries. For example, in sub-Saharan Africa some twenty countries are food crisis countries, meaning that some countries cannot afford to import enough food to feed their people and do not have the internal resources to increase production and distribution of food. David Sahn and Alexander Sarris analyzed the effects of price changes on rural smallholders in sub-Saharan Africa and found that the welfare effects showed an unequivocal pattern of improved social welfare in response to higher prices. But the effects varied greatly from region to region, and did not seem that large in any region.[21] They were very pessimistic about the ability of African farmers to respond to world price changes.

Although the long-term net effects on developing countries are ambiguous, the CAP seems to have dampened overall world trade in agricultural products. Abolition of the CAP would increase world trade by a substantial amount. R. Tyers and K. Anderson estimate that the volume of world trade in products like dairy or ruminant meat (beef, etc.) would rise 34 million tons or 107 million tons, respectively.[22] In addition to dampening world trade, the CAP appears to increase price volatility on world markets. Dimitrios Demekas and co-workers summarized the evidence from various sources and found that "comparing the EC agricultural policies with price support schemes in other countries reveals that the CAP is the most important destabilizing factor in world markets."[23]

Looking at wheat prices, A. H. Sarris and J. Freebairn estimated that over half the excess variability (price changes not accounted for by structural factors like tastes, weather, etc.) was caused by the CAP alone.[24] These price changes make an already unstable market even more difficult to predict, which makes farmers' decisions very hard given the lag in production and inelastic supply for most agricultural products. More important, it increases the political pressure in all countries to protect both their farmers and consumers from volatile food prices. This increases the difficulty of reaching international agreement on agricultural trade issues.

Of course, not only developing countries are affected. Industrialized countries also are affected. Japan, for example, is a clear winner from the CAP. Japan is a major importer of food products, and the Europeans are basically subsidizing Japanese consumption. The Japanese export only a small amount of food products. During the 1980s, Japanese agricultural products (SITC1) made up only 0.3 percent of total exports. Agricultural imports, in contrast, comprised about 14 percent of all imports.[25]

The United States, on the other hand, is a major exporter of food products and for many years has complained about European agricultural practices. Although the United States does subsidize and protect its farmers, the effective rates of protection[26] of European commodities have been much higher. For example, the effective protection rate for dairy farmers in the United States has been 35 percent on cheese and 47 percent on butter—in the CAP the rates have been 276 percent for cheese and 1,328 percent for butter.[27] For the most part, the United States has relied on supply management and storage operations, rather than export subsidies and variable levies. As the leading exporter of agricultural products, the United States would like Europe's protection to fall and their export subsidies to fall. The United States has reacted to the EC's policies by instituting subsidy policies very similar to those of the CAP. The 1985 Farm Bill specifically targeted export markets and allocated $325 million to provide export subsidies in markets in which U.S. producers face foreign export subsidies and an additional $2 billion to expand markets. Furthermore, $5 billion was allocated for short-term export credit guarantees and $1 billion per year for intermediate credit.[28]

As we saw above, these types of support policies are costly and greatly affect world markets; they are not the kinds of policies that maximize U.S. welfare. Therefore, the United States changed its position in the GATT negotiations of the Uruguay Round and pushed for freer trade in agricultural products. Reluctantly, the EC made some concessions, but maintained very long transition periods for limiting the amount it would spend on export subsidies. Fortunately for the EC budget, world wheat prices rose sharply in the mid-1990s, leading to EC restrictions on how much their farmers could export.

The rest of the Western European countries, mainly EFTA countries, are affected indirectly by the CAP. Some of them have joined the EC. In all the EFTA countries, agriculture has been and is highly protected. With the attempts at reforming the CAP, these countries have had problems in reducing protection of their farmers. In a country like Switzerland, say, that has very high protection rates and some national preference for retaining a certain farm sector size, joining the more streamlined EC will be a political nightmare. This has already been evidenced by the lack of support in Switzerland for the European Economic Space (EES) proposed by Delors in 1989. As for the Eastern European countries that have relatively large agricultural sectors, the reform of the CAP puts them even farther away from membership. In March 1993 the EC restricted agricultural imports from the east for "health" reasons, which the east reacted to by increasing protection against EC products.

COMMON FISHERIES POLICY[29]

Although fishing accounts for a very small part of Community GDP, perhaps 1 percent, many regions of member states depend on fishing as their primary income source. The problem among the member states has been to define property rights to what is a common resource. The danger of a common resource is that each fishing boat has an incentive to catch as many fish as possible because if that boat does not do it others certainly will. A classic example of this sort of problem is the overhunting of the American bison. Once herds measured in the hundreds of thousands, but due to eastern demand for bison skins, each hunter killed as many as possible, not even considering the long-run consequences. By the end of the nineteenth century the American bison was almost extinct. To extract a renewable resource optimally over time, agents must coordinate their actions, either by setting rules or by assigning property rights. Since the private negotiation of such agreements is very difficult and would be unstable because of the short-run gains from cheating, a pan-European organization like the Community is ideal for addressing the problem internally and externally with non-EU nations.

The Treaty of Rome recognized this long-run problem and included the structure of a common fisheries policy (CFP) within it. Over the 1950s and 1960s, though, there were few areas that had problems with the size of fish stocks, so virtually no policies were enacted. However, in the beginning of the 1970s problems began to arise as fishing boats had to go farther to sea to catch adequate amounts of fish. With the accession of Denmark, Ireland, and the United Kingdom, all countries with relatively large fishing sectors, member states called on the Community to coordinate internal policies and negotiate agreements with non-member countries, like the Scandinavian countries, Spain, and Canada. In 1973, fishing rights were established for coastal bands six to twelve miles wide for local fishing craft that had traditionally fished those areas, and access to other member state's waters was suspended. This quasi-formal agreement was fully formalized into a real CFP in 1983. This agreement, motivated by the impending addition of Spain and Portugal, created a common system for conservation and management of fishing stocks and provided new measures to provide funds for structural reform.

When Spain and Portugal joined the European Community in 1986, fishing capacity increased by 65 percent and fishing production and consumption by 45 percent. (In British papers of the time, writers referred to the Spanish fishing fleet as the Spanish Armada.) Of course, transitional agreements were made so that the Iberian addition would not completely overwhelm the existing CFP. The old CFP policy was phased into a new, global policy starting in 1991. New measures were taken in 1992 to control fishing hauls. In 1993 the CFP, which previously had been run as a separate policy under the general rubric of agriculture, was folded into the Community's "structural funds." This was an important development because it meant that the EC considered the problem to be not just management of stocks, but rather serious reform of the European fishing industry. Just as the CAP was being reformed so that its funds would support the removal of factors out of agriculture, the same reform was initiated for fishing.

The actual organization of the sector is based on targets for the total allowable catch for a particular year; once the target has been reached the area is closed to fishing. Monitoring and penalties for ignoring these limits are conducted by the member states. However, the Community provides aid to members to strengthen their control and to monitor catches with their own inspectors. In 1993, new measures were added to increase the documentation of catches, sales to processors, and sales to consumers. This added information helps the Community monitor annual catches. In 1995, new fishing licenses were implemented that govern where and how much each vessel can fish. In addition to these measures, the Community has set standards for fish processing and packaging, has allowed price of fish products to be set by supply and demand,[30] and has created producer organizations to help introduce and maintain Community policy.

These new policies are carried out in four areas:

1. Multiannual guidance programs (MGPs), which modernize ships and reduce overall tonnage. The MGP III program, which ended in 1996, called for an overall decrease in shipping tonnage of 10 percent. The new MGP IV, noting the offsetting effect of technical improvements, calls for an additional decrease of 12 percent and larger-mesh nets

2. Financial instrument for fisheries guidance (FIFC), which provides funds for the support of the MGPs and other policies to reform European fishing. The current budget allocation is ECU 2.7 billion for 1994–99

3. Social Policies, which provide the means for new training and job-creation due to the reduction in the fishing industry; this, of course, extends to all the supporting areas of the economy—fish processors, boat yards and so on. These policies are funded out of the European Social Fund and the European Regional Development Fund

4. PESCA Community Initiative, which monitors and maintains the global coordination of policies

Because the waters around the Community have been so heavily fished for so long, European boats now travel regularly into international waters. Some 25 percent of the fish caught for human consumption is taken from international waters. Arranging this right with foreign countries has been relatively expensive for the Community. In fact, 40 percent of CFP spending goes to finance arrangements with non-EC countries, mainly African and Asian countries, North Atlantic countries, and Latin American countries. The Community also participates in the Atlantic Fisheries Organization, the International Baltic Fishery Commission, and the North Atlantic Salmon Conservation Organization.

In the future, the CFP will continue efforts to reduce the size of the fishing sector, provide for the structural reform of affected areas, and conduct management and environmental polices with neighboring states, most notably in the Mediterranean. Unlike the CAP, which created the conditions for overproducing relative to the market, the CFP is engaged in creating policies to reduce production where the market (or rather, the absence of a market) has failed to do so. Over the next decade there will be bitter battles as fishing communities are forced to change their traditional behavior. If the Community were to do nothing, these areas would continue to plead for subsidies and protection, something exactly counter to Community goals. The Community hopes it can guide the structural reform of these areas and supply funds to alleviate regional tensions, so that countries such as Iceland, Norway, and the Baltic states will not continue to be alienated from the rest of Europe but will become more integrated with it through a common fisheries program.

To economists, however, the programs still fall short of the final solution, which would be to assign property rights to access to the North Atlantic fishing grounds and then use the market to allocate usage of the common resource to the most efficient firms. A favorite proposal is for member states to auction off fishing licenses for fairly long periods (say, at least three reproductive cycles of the resource in question). This would provide the revenue required to relocate and retrain the less efficient fishermen who lose out in the bidding. Such proposals immediately raise howls of protest, however, among the fishing community who regard their activity as an entitlement. Only Britain within the EU has tried this approach. Outside the EU, even Iceland will not consider it, although it would benefit this country enormously, both through the increase in revenues and the rescue of its fishing stocks. Until each country in the EU can be persuaded to begin a rational method of allocating access to the common fisheries, no supranational assignment of auction rights is conceivable, much less agreement on how to define property rights to them.

MONETARY COMPENSATION AGREEMENTS

The EC always set the target price for supporting a commodity in terms of a unit of account—a common denominator from which the market price in each member country's currency could easily be calculated. Until the period August 15–December 31, 1971, the unit of account was always the U.S. dollar. This made sense, because each member state was also a member of the International Monetary Fund and therefore had agreed to keep its currency pegged at a fixed exchange rate with the U.S. dollar. This rate was then the exchange rate used to convert the CAP's target price into the currency of each member country. When the dollar floated for the first time in August 1971, its exchange rate varied differently for each European currency. This meant that the fixed exchange rate at which the target price had been converted into a member country's currency, the so-called green rate, diverged from the actual exchange rates each country had with the U.S. dollar. Consequently, countries that had devalued relative to the dollar—France, Italy, Belgium-Luxembourg—found that their farmers now had a support price in terms of their national currency that was lower than the original target price. At the same time, due to the devaluation of their currency, their farmers faced higher prices for all of the inputs and consumption goods that they imported. They were unexpectedly worse off.

On the other side of the coin, countries that had revalued relative to the dollar—Germany and the Netherlands—found that their farmers now enjoyed a support price in deutsche marks or guilders that was higher than originally anticipated. They were unexpectedly better off. The differential rates at which member currencies were varying with respect to the floating dollar, therefore, undermined the calculations and negotiations that had gone into the original determination of the target prices for each supported commodity.

Consequently, it was agreed to adjust after the fact for the unintended consequences of exchange rate fluctuations by creating "monetary compensatory amounts" (MCAs). When a currency has appreciated against the green rate (see Fig. 6.4), levies are imposed on imports at the percentage rate of the appreciation (Fig. 6.4a) and subsidies are paid on exports at the same percentage rate (Fig. 6.4b). These are "positive" MCAs. If a currency has depreciated against the green rate (see Fig. 6.5), "negative" MCAs are imposed, which act as subsidies on imports (Figure 6.5a) and percentage levies on exports (Fig. 6.5b).

In principle, the MCAs should just offset the fluctuations in the support prices caused by fluctuating exchange rates. In practice, they can never be fine tuned adequately to accomplish this ambitious goal. Calculations of the "monetary gap," the percentage difference between the current rate and the green rate, are based on data for the week ending Tuesday. If a change is warranted, and it is not if the percentage difference lies within the margin allowed under the rules of the European Monetary System, then it becomes effective the following Monday. As exchange rates have become increasingly volatile, this delay in adjusting the size of the MCAs can lead to cumulative shortfalls or excesses. As it turns out, the currencies of the Netherlands and Germany have consistently appreciated against the other currencies, so that timing errors in adjustment have tended to cumulate, rather than offset each other.

Moreover, it appears that farmers in the Netherlands and Germany have responded positively to the production incentives implied by the export subsidies and import levies that they have consistently received as a result of the appreciation of the guilder and the deutsche mark. Farmers in Belgium and France, on the other hand, have not decreased production in response to the price losses caused by the export levies and import subsidies they have had

(a)

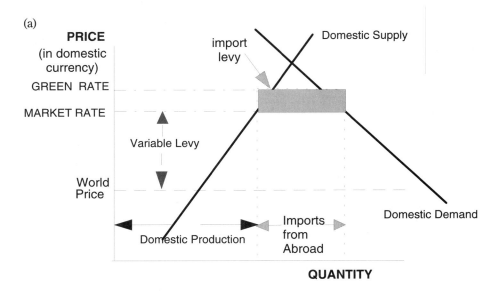

(b)

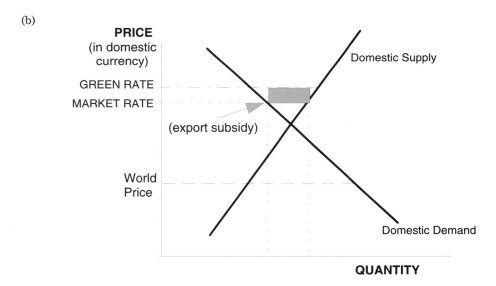

Figure 6.4. Positive monetary compensation amounts. (a) Import deficit. (b) Export surplus.

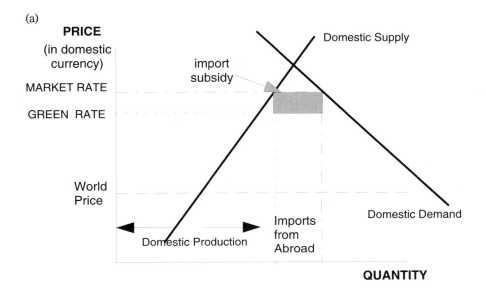

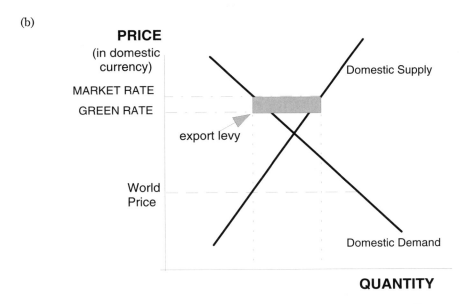

Figure 6.5. Negative monetary compensation amounts. (a) Import deficit. (b) Export surplus.

imposed on them as a result of the depreciation of the Belgian and French francs. Perhaps this is due to the natural tendency of small farmers to increase output in response to an expected fall in price in order to keep total sales revenue the same. Perhaps it is due to measures taken by the national governments to protect farmers from bearing the brunt of the negative MCAs.

Whatever the explanation, the net result of fluctuating exchange rates among the member country currencies combined with the device of the MCAs has been to exacerbate the CAP's tendency to overproduction in agriculture. Moreover, the MCAs have tended to keep the agricultural prices in the Netherlands and Germany consistently higher than in the rest of the Community, undercutting the goal of a common market in agriculture. Table 6.4 shows the experience with MCAs over the period 1974–86, when it was agreed to eliminate MCAs altogether.

The net result of the MCAs has been to encourage the overproduction of food in Europe and increase therefore the cost of the CAP in the EC budget. In addition, the MCAs have shifted agricultural production from the weak to the strong currency countries. As a result, over the 1980s Germany became the largest agricultural producer in the EC and its farmers received the largest amount of aid from the EC. Finally, by requiring variable levies or subsidies on either exports or imports, the MCAs effectively suspend free trade in agricultural products even within the EC customs union.[31]

Various steps have been taken over time to alleviate these problems. Since 1973, a "neutral margin" was deducted from the negative MCAs as a cost-saving measure for the EC budget. In 1979, the neutral margin was extended to the

TABLE 6.4
Monetary Compensation Amounts (percent difference in current and green rates)

	Germany	Netherlands	France	Italy
1974/75	12.0	2.7	−13.3	−16.0
1975/76	10.0	2.0	0.0	0.0
1976/77	9.3	1.4	−17.0	
1977/78	9.3	1.4	−14.9	−17.0
1978/79	10.8	3.3	−10.6	−15.0
1979/80	9.8	1.9	−3.7	−4.0
1980/81	8.8	1.7	0.0	0.0
1981/82	3.2	0.0	0.0	−1.0
1982/83	8.4	5.4	−5.3	−1.4
1983/84	13.0	8.4	−9.5	−5.0
1984/85	7.9*	3.5*	−4.4	−1.8
	6.8†	2.6†		
1985/86	2.9*	2.9*	−1.0	0.0
	1.8†	1.8†		−7.3‡

*Dairy products †All other products ‡After the July realignment

Source: F. Giavazzi and A. Giovannini, *Limiting Exchange Rate Flexibility, The European Monetary System,* Cambridge, Mass.: MIT Press, 1989, p. 17.

positive MCAs. Then in 1984, the positive MCAs were phased out by basing the target price not on the ECU but on the strongest currency in the EMS exchange rate mechanism, meaning in practice the deutsche mark, although a complicated formula was devised to disguise explicit recognition of this fact.[32] This meant that German and Dutch producers would no longer receive export subsidies.

In addition, part of the stock of positive MCAs was "switched over" to negative MCAs in other countries, in an effort to reverse the tendency to shift production to the strong currency countries, Germany and the Netherlands. The final step, of course, is to move toward a regime of fixed exchange rates among the currencies of the member states. This would help many of the problems with trade in agricultural products and in addition would reduce transactions costs in manufactured goods and services. However, other problems would have to be faced if the member states adopted fixed exchange rates with each other, or in the extreme case, a common currency. These will be discussed in the next chapter.

CONCLUSION

Ironically, the CAP has dominated the economic cooperation of one of the most industrial areas of the world. It has been successful in pushing out Europe's supply curve for agricultural products, but at the cost of domestic consumers and domestic allocative efficiency. More than anything, the CAP is ample evidence of the costs imposed by protecting a domestic industry and not having a long-term plan for making it competitive. Since the European Single Market Act was signed in the mid 1980s, the reform of the CAP has proceeded and we can see that the proportion of the CAP in the budget has fallen from a high of nearly three-fourths to just under one-half. This process will continue, aided by the opening of the markets along with the single market legislation. How Europe deals with the rising unemployment that has accompanied the single market process and how it deals with the implementation of the Uruguay Round of the GATT talks will determine what it does with the difficult process of restructuring the agricultural sector that will be necessary with the reduction of EU subsidies for European farmers. As Eastern Europe completes its transition to a market economy, moreover, the issue of restoring traditional trade patterns between East and West Europe will confront EU policymakers with an increasingly difficult dilemma between maintaining the most successful element of the EU's internal integration or meeting the EU's external goal of eventually including all of Europe.

Endnotes

1.   Emile Benoit, *Europe at Sixes and Sevens.* New York: Columbia University Press, 1961, p. 23.

2. Commission of the European Communities, *A Common Agricultural Policy for the 1990s*, 5th ed. Luxembourg: Office for the Official Publications of the European Communities, 1989, p. 12.

3. "Farms and land in farms, by size of farm: 1880–1954," Series K 61–72. *Historical Statistics of the United States*. Washington, D. C., 1960.

4. Benoit, note 1, p. 50.

5. This is an important inclusion and indicates that the EEC was already aware of the problems that exchange rate changes would cause to its pricing policies.

6. International Monetary Fund, *The Common Agricultural Policy of the European Community*, Occasional Paper No. 62, Washington, D. C.: IMF, November 1988, p. 31.

7. EC Council of Ministers Decision 88/377, quoted in Danile Charles-Le Bihan and Daniel Gadbin. "New Trends in the Common Agricultural Policy," in L. Hurwitz and C. Lequesue, eds., *The State of the European Community,* London: Longman, 1991.

8. CEC, note 2, p. 14.

9. Charles Kindleberger, *Europe's Postwar Growth. The Role of Labor Supply,* Cambridge, Mass.: Harvard University Press, 1967. See also John Cornwall, *Modern Capitalism. Its Growth and Transformation,* London: Martin Robertson, 1977.

10. The effects of the reforms have been estimated by ECAM, the EC Agricultural Model. See "The Economics of the Common Agricultural Policy," *European Economy* 5, 1994, pp. 71–112.

11. Organisation for Economic Co-operation and Development, *Report on Monitoring and Outlook of Agricultural Policies, Markets, and Trade,* mimeographed, Paris: OECD, 1988.

12. Ibid., reproduced in IMF, note 6, p. 27.

13. Herman van der Wee, *Prosperity and Upheaval: The World Economy 1945*-1980, translated by Robin Hogg and Max R. Hall, London: Viking, 1986, p. 168 and B. R. Mitchell, *European Historical Statistics 1750–1970,* New York: Columbia University Press, 1978, p. 51.

14. IMF, note 6, p. 34.

15. Dermot Hayes and Andrew Schmitz, "The price and welfare implications of current conflicts between the agricultural policies of the United States and the European Community," in Robert Baldwin, Carl Hamilton, and André Sapir, eds., *Issues in US-EC Trade Relations.* Chicago: NBER, 1988, p. 70.

16. For a summary of studies see Dimitrios G. Demekas et al., "The effects of the Common Agricultural Policy of the European Community: a survey of the literature," *Journal of Common Market Studies* 27, no. 2, December 1988, pp. 137.

17. T. Loo and E. Tower, "Agricultural protectionism and the less developed countries: the relationship between agricultural prices, debt servicing capacities and the need for development aid," paper presented at the Conference on Agricultural Policies and the Non-farm Economy, Washington, D. C., 1988.

18. Quoted in Demekas et al, note 16, p. 136.

19. Bela Belassa. "Incentive policies and export performance in sub-Saharan Africa," *World Development* 18, no. 3, 1990, pp. 383–91.

20. Peer Svedberg. "The export performance of sub-Saharan Africa," *Economic Development and Cultural Change* 39, no. 3, April 1991, pp. 549–66.

21. David Sahn and Alexander Sarris. "Structural adjustment and the welfare of rural

smallholders: a comparative analysis from sub-Saharan Africa," *World Bank Economic Review* 5, no. 2, 1991, pp. 259–89.

22. R. Tyers and K. Anderson, *Distortions in World Food Markets: A Quantitative Assessment.* background paper for the World Development Report, 1986.
23. Demakas, note 16, p. 138.
24. A. H. Sarris and J. Freebairn, "Endogenous price policies and international wheat prices," *American Journal of Agricultural Economics,* 56, no. 2, 1974, pp. 214–24.
25. United Nations, *Trade Statistics,* 1992, p. 472.
26. This is the percentage by which the protected value added exceeds value added without protection.
27. A. J. Yeats. "Agricultural protectionism: an analysis of its international economic effects and options for institutional reform," *Trade and Development,* 3, 1981, quoted in Hayes and Schmitz, note 15, p. 71.
28. Hayes and Schmitz, note 15, p. 87.
29. This section is based on the excellent information in the EUROPA website on the EC fishing policy, address http://europa.eu.int/en/eupol/fish.html.
30. In a concession to fishing fleets, the Community has also established a price floor governing the price of fish caught but not sold. This has not cost the Community much, though, since after fruit and vegetables, fish is the second largest food import into the Community. Most of the European catch is consumed in Europe. The Commission can intervene, however, in the international market if it feel imports are "disturbing" markets too much.
31. Francesco Giavazzi and Alberto Giovannini, *Limiting Exchange Rate Flexibility, The European Monetary System,* Cambridge, Mass.: MIT Press, 1989, pp. 12–19.
32. See Appendix II of IMF, note 6.

Selected Bibliography

Benoit, Émile. *Europe at Sixes and Sevens.* New York: Columbia University Press, 1961.

Charles-LeBihan, Danièle and Daniel Gadbin. "New trends in the Common Agricultural Policy," in L. Hurwitz and C. Lequesue, eds. *The State of the European Community.* London: Longman, 1991, pp. 167–81. A useful description of recent changes in the CAP with a description of the new budgetary process. Students of all levels.

Colman, David and Deborah Roberts. "The Common Agricultural Policy," in Mike Artis and Norman Lee, eds. *The Economics of the European Union.* Oxford: Oxford University Press, 1994. Sophisticated treatment of the economics of the CAP, including the set-asides initiated in 1993, and a description of the pressures for reform both within the EU and from without.

Commission of the European Communities. *A Common Agricultural Policy for the 1990s,* 5th ed. Luxembourg: Office for the Official Publications of the European Communities, 1989.

Commission of the EC. Directorate-General for Economic and Financial Affairs. "EC agricultural policy for the 21st century," *European Economy, Reports and Studies,* No. 4, 1994, pp. 3–40. Nice treatment of the European perspective on the Uruguay Round agreements on agriculture as well as a look ahead to the challenge of incorporating new members into the EU.

Commission of the EC. "The Economics of the Common Agricultural Policy (CAP)," *European Economy, Reports and Studies,* No. 5, 1994. Good treatment of the MacSharry reforms with estimates of their effects.

Demekas, Dimitrios G. et al. "The effects of the Common Agricultural Policy of the European Community: a survey of the literature," *Journal of Common Market Studies* 27, no. 2, December 1988, pp. 113–45. This is an edited version of their IMF Occasional Paper no. 62, 1988 and is an excellent overview, although now see Vol. 39, no. 3, April 1991, pp. 549–66.

Hayes, Dermot and Andrew Schmitz. "The price and welfare implications of current conflicts between the agricultural policies of the United States and the European Community," in Robert Baldwin, Carl Hamilton and André Sapir, eds. *Issues in US-EC Trade Relations.* Chicago: NBER, , 1988, pp. 67–100. A good account of CAP policies during the 1980s with a strong theoretical treatment of the effects of the CAP on the United States. More advanced students.

Hitiris, T. *European Community Economics.* 3rd edn. Hemel Hempstead, U.K.: Harvester Wheatsheaf, 1994. His Chapter 7 on agriculture is a good alternative source for understanding the basics of the economics of the CAP. Students of all levels.

International Monetary Fund. *The Common Agricultural Policy of the European Community,* Occasional Paper No. 62, November 1988.

Loo, T. and E. Tower. "Agricultural protectionism and the less developed countries: the relationship between agricultural prices, debt servicing capacities and the need for development aid," Paper presented at the Conference on Agricultural Policies and the Non-farm Economy, Washington, D. C., 1988. Another general equilibrium model, assessing the impact on developing countries and stressing the impact of the CAP on overall development. More advanced students.

Organisation for Economic Cooperation and Development. *Report on Monitoring and Outlook of Agricultural Policies, Markets and Trade,* mimeographed, Paris: OECD, 1988.

Sarris, A. H. and J. Freebairn. "Endogenous price policies and international wheat prices," *American Journal of Agricultural Economics* 56, no. 2, 1983, pp. 214–24. Important study demonstrating the increased price volatility due to the CAP. More advanced students.

Tarditi, Secondo, et al., eds. *Agricultural Trade Liberalization and the European Community.* New York: Oxford University Press, 1989. Although somewhat dated, given the stage in the reforms of the CAP at the time of its writing, this collection of articles provides strong theoretical analysis of agricultural markets that provide useful models for the analysis of current reforms.

Tyers, R. and K. Anderson. "Distortions in world food markets: a quantitative assessment." Background paper for the *World Development Report,* 1986. A general equilibrium approach to estimate the impact of the CAP on the rest of the world. Interesting for its overall findings, which are summarized well in Demekas et al. above. More advanced students.

Yeats, A. J. "Agricultural protectionism: an analysis of its international economic effects and options for institutional reform," *Trade and Development* 3, 1981. Good for an overview of the development of the CAP over the 1970s with good data on protection levels. Intermediate students.

CHAPTER 7

The European Monetary System:

Deutsche mark über Alles

In December 1991, the leaders of the European Community member states assembled at the Dutch city of Maastricht to sign the Treaty for European Monetary and Political Union. The site was appropriate, for Maastricht is an ancient city founded by the Romans at a strategic point on the river Maas. The river runs downstream through the narrow province of Limburg, a stretch of Dutch territory that was inserted between Belgium and Germany after 1830 in order to maintain a viable connection with the rest of the Netherlands. Maastricht did not flourish, however, until the founding of the European Community made it a crossroads of Dutch, Belgian, and German economic activity, instead of a Dutch bastion protecting Belgium against German encroachment. Just as the history of the city of Maastricht encapsulates the significance of the European Community for peaceful economic development of Europe, so does the Accord of Maastricht embody the consequences of the ongoing search for a common currency for Europe.

The Maastricht Accord for European Monetary Union envisaged three stages for achieving a common currency, the European Currency Unit (ECU), by January 1, 1999 (Table 7.1). The three stages reflected the three alternative routes that had been proposed and at various times attempted in the past. After the breakdown of the Bretton Woods system in 1971, Europe needed to replace the U.S. dollar as the base of the European Unit of Account in keeping accounts among the member states (see Chapter 6 on the development of monetary compensation amounts under the Common Agricultural Policy). One route was to have *competition* among the various currencies to see which proved the most desirable to replace the U.S. dollar. Even by the end of 1971, it was clear the replacement currency would be the German deutsche mark (DM). For several years after the collapse of Bretton Woods, the mark served as the de facto base of EC payments.

A second route was to *coordinate* monetary policy among the various cen-

TABLE 7.1
Summary of Maastricht Treaty for European Monetary Union [1]

Stage 1—Before Ratification of new Treaty (from 1 July 1990)

Liberalization of capital movements inside Community
Multilateral surveillance procedure for economic policy coordination
Strengthened monetary cooperation

Stage 1—After ratification of new Treaty (1993)

Freezing of currency composition of ECU basket
Irrevocable commitment to single currency (ECU)
Reinforced multilateral surveillance in the context of broad guidelines for economic policies and convergence programs of member states

Stage 2—From 1 January 1994

Liberalization of capital movements to or from third countries
Prohibition on direct access to central banks and on privileged access to financial institutions for the financing of public deficits
No bail-out rule for member states
Start of procedure to avoid excessive public deficits (non-binding)
Continued balance-of-payments support
European Monetary Institute (EMI) set up, prepares complete framework for stage 3
Start of process leading to independent central banks

Stage 2—After decision on start date of stage 3 (before 1 July 1998)

Establishment of European System of Central Banks (ESCB) and European Central Bank (ECB) and adoption of necessary legislation

Stage 3—1 January 1999 at the latest

Members must meet specific fiscal rules (or show credible progress toward meeting them) to join:
  A government debt/GDP ratio of below 60 percent
  A government deficit/GDP ratio of below 3 percent
  An inflation rate and long-term interest rates within 1.5–2 percentage points of the average of the three lowest inflation and interest rate countries
  Irrevocable fixing of exchange rates to the euro (which will replace the ECU) and to each other, followed by the replacement of the national currencies by the euro (planned for 2002) as the single currency
Single monetary policy conducted by independent ECB
Single exchange rate policy determined between Council of Ministers and ECB
Binding procedure (including sanctions) aimed at avoiding excessive public deficits (the Stability Pact).

tral banks so that a common exchange rate policy with respect to the U.S. dollar and other currencies could be developed. Proponents of this approach, elements of which had been attempted first with the "snake" and then the "snake in the tunnel" episodes in the 1970s, and formalized with the European Monetary System in 1978, were called monetarists in the academic debate that followed.

Their opponents, who argued that monetary policy could not be coordinated successfully without coordination of fiscal policy, and indeed, of overall economic policy, were called economists. They believed the success of a common currency depended on *centralization* of all economic policymaking within the EC. Because most of them did not want to see this happen, economists were mostly opposed to the idea of a common currency, preferring instead to allow periodic changes in the exchange rates among the national currencies, which would be maintained indefinitely.

The three stages proposed at Maastricht for achieving European monetary union can be seen as moving from *competition* among the currencies to *coordination* of their relative amounts to *centralization* of control over the supply of the EC's money stock. This is a composite plan of action, then, for the European Community member states to move from independent management of their separate national currencies to a common currency managed jointly.

Two questions arise naturally: why have a common currency at all, and, How should it be managed once it exists? The answer to the first lies in the theory of common currency areas. The answer to the second lies more in the history of the European currencies than in the theory of common currencies.

THEORY OF OPTIMAL CURRENCY AREAS

The optimal area for a common currency to be used depends on the degree to which real resources can be transferred within it in response to shocks. In the original formulation of the problem, due to Robert Mundell,[2] the question hinged on the *mobility of labor and capital.* Could the factors of production, labor, and capital move easily from a depressed area within the common currency zone to a more prosperous one? If so, the zone should continue to use a common currency. If not, however, the depressed area should be allowed to depreciate its local currency relative to the rest of the zone. This would stimulate local demand for its idle capital and labor by making its products cheaper relative to the rest of the zone. Depreciation would also make imports from the rest of the zone more expensive, decreasing local demand for output of the rest of the zone. This would help spread the effects of the shock to the local area's trading partners. Mundell, a western Canadian, felt that western Canada should have a separate currency from eastern Canada, given the difficulty of getting labor and capital to move from east to west in that country.

Countering this conjecture, Ronald McKinnon[3] argued that if the local area was already open to trade with the rest of the currency zone, then local labor and capital would realize that the devaluation had reduced their real wages and

real returns. They would raise their nominal wages and rates of return sufficiently to offset the effects of the devaluation. The size of the optimum currency
area, then, depended on the *intensity of trade* within it. On McKinnon's criterion,
Canada was too small for a single currency and should join the United States,
where so much of its trade was directed.

A third criterion has emerged with the increasing importance of the welfare
state in industrialized countries, especially in Europe. This is the extent to
which shocks to a local area can be softened by the effects of *fiscal transfers*
within the common currency zone. Within the United States or any Western
European country, for example, a depressed region suffers reduced income.
This reduces the amount of income tax and sales tax that it generates, as well,
but this can be seen as a reduced drain to the central government on its effective local demand. The depressed area also will see a rise in unemployment,
but this will bring unemployment compensation into the region from the central
government. In this view, fiscal transfers can substitute for mobility of labor and
capital and maintain an area as large as the United States, or Canada, as an
optimum currency area. Using the example of the German Economic and Monetary Union, between East and West Germany, Paul de Grauwe has argued that
"the issue of whether two countries (or regions) constitute an optimum currency area is ultimately a political one."[4] That is, the political will to form the
union and withstand whatever fiscal transfers are necessary to maintain it can
be as important as the underlying economic conditions. The EU shows a similar
commitment as it expands its structural funds in response to the increased integration via the completion of the internal market and the anticipated arrival of
the EMU. Given its small revenue base, however, it is currently inconceivable
that it could take on the scale of transfers that might be required in the face of
a shock that reduced income in just one of the smaller countries.

On the three criteria, the countries of Europe fail both in terms of mobility
of labor and capital and in terms of fiscal transfers. European labor markets are
more rigid than those in the United States; wage elasticities with respect to
unemployment rates are very low in Europe, suggesting that shocks caused by
the currency union could be felt for long periods because wages would be very
slow to adjust. These data are further confirmed by the relatively high rates of
long-term unemployment in Europe.[5] Only in terms of the criterion of openness
and intensity of trade relations do the countries of the EC qualify as constituting
an optimum currency area. Countries with larger intracommunity trade will
likely benefit more from the reduced exchange rate variability and the reduction in transactions costs that will be brought about from monetary union. However, countries differ significantly on their openness.[6] It is clear that the smallest countries are most likely to benefit by a common currency with their larger
trading partners. Further, the small countries outside the European Community
that find their trade is carried on overwhelmingly with one or more large countries within the EC will also find it beneficial to join in the common currency.

The various theories suggest the possibilities of substitutability of economic
shock absorbers—substituting price level changes for changes in location of
factors of production in the Mundell theory, substituting trade flows for factor

flows in the McKinnon counter-theory, or substituting fiscal flows for market-driven flows of income in the last case. If exchange rate flexibility is removed, national policymakers will have to rely on other means to absorb shocks to the economy. The degree of substitutability for any particular set of countries at any particular period of their history is, of course, an empirical question. To answer that we have to turn to the history of the search for a common currency among the countries of Western Europe since World War II.

THE EUROPEAN PAYMENTS UNION

As part of the general effort of the United States to "stretch" the effectiveness of a limited Marshall Plan, the European Payments Union was established in 1950.[7] Instead of each European country trying to sell in dollars to its trading partners and buy from them in their own national currency, the EPU made net exporters to the rest of Europe receive payment half in dollars and half in the national currencies of their debtors, while the net importers from the rest of Europe paid an increasing proportion of their debts in dollars as the size of their deficits increased. The key condition for the direct U.S. support, at least, and for keeping accounts consistent among the European trading nations, was that the European currencies maintain fixed exchange rates with the U.S. dollar, and hence fixed cross-rates with each other. No real danger of excessive foreign indebtedness or speculative runs on a country's limited foreign reserves was posed by these fixed exchange rates, because each country maintained capital controls and most restricted convertibility of their currency even for current account transactions.

The European Payments Union proved to work very well,[8] partly because of the export boom for European manufacturers started by the U.S. financing of the Korean War, partly because of the $500 million of capital provided it at the outset by the United States, and partly because the persistent debtors in the scheme—Greece, Turkey, and Austria—were bailed out with direct aid from the United States. On the other side of the ledger, Germany, Italy, and the Netherlands were well into their export-led economic miracles, which generated increasingly large surpluses and dollar reserves for them.

In sum, the EPU did not owe its success to the regime of fixed exchange rates; rather, its success gave a boost to the confidence of central bankers that a regime of fixed exchange rates could be maintained. With the establishment of the European Economic Community in 1958, France went to convertibility on current account of the *nouveau franc* created by DeGaulle as a symbol of the new direction to be taken by the Fifth French Republic. The United Kingdom likewise restored convertibility on current account to the pound sterling. Both nations maintained controls on large-scale movements of funds on capital account, however. By 1960, the EPU was formally wound up, replaced by a much looser European Monetary Arrangement, and its $500 million of initial U.S. capital was set aside to make loans to the less developed members of the newly formed Organization for Economic Cooperation and Development (OECD).

This comprised all the European nations receiving Marshall Plan aid (the OEEC) plus now the United States and Canada.

THE BRETTON WOODS ERA (1958–71)

With the resumption of currency convertibility by the leading nations of Europe in 1958, the multilateral settlement of trade imbalances envisioned in the original Bretton Woods Agreement of 1944 could be realized. Indeed, the following ten years saw the full flowering of the possibilities for trade expansion. France and the Netherlands joined in the export-led growth parade initiated by Germany and Italy, while those two leaders continued to grow rapidly. On the other side of the world, Japan freed the yen, and it too began its export-led ascent to economic supremacy. Underlying this expansion in world trade and world output was a system of fixed exchange rates, with all European currencies pegged to the U.S. dollar. Figures 7.1a and 7.1b show that this golden decade was initiated by a minor devaluation of the German mark and the Dutch guilder in 1961 and ended in 1969 with a devaluation of the French franc and a revaluation of the German mark. The initial decade of the European Economic Community, in short, with its enormous expansion of trade among the member countries, was one of fixed exchange rates and effectively a common currency within the customs union.

As a result of their common adherence to the rules of the International Monetary Fund, which meant maintaining fixed exchange rates with respect to the U.S. dollar, the member states of the EC did not have to pay explicit attention to the questions of exchange rates with one another, or move toward a common currency as mandated by the Treaty of Rome. By 1968, however, the expansion of trade between France and Germany had developed into increasing trade deficits for France, which led to the first disruption of the regime of fixed exchange rates within the EEC.

Part of the explanation for France's increasing trade deficits lies in the nature of demand for food and clothing relative to consumer and producer durables. France exported mainly food and clothing, with relatively low income elasticities of demand, whereas Germany exported mainly durables, both for consumers and producers, which have relatively high income elasticities of demand. Necessarily then, Germany's exports to France expanded more rapidly than France's exports to Germany even though both countries had similar rates of growth of population and of real per capita income.

This long-run trend in real trade balances, which favored Germany over France, was enhanced by the differences in monetary policy between the two countries. The Banque de France continued to be directed by the Minister of Finance even under the Fifth French Republic, which meant that it had to respond to any monetary demands made on it by the central government. Under DeGaulle's rule, these demands were kept much lower than had been the case under the Fourth French Republic, but they still exceeded the pressures faced by the completely independent Bundesbank in West Germany. There, the con-

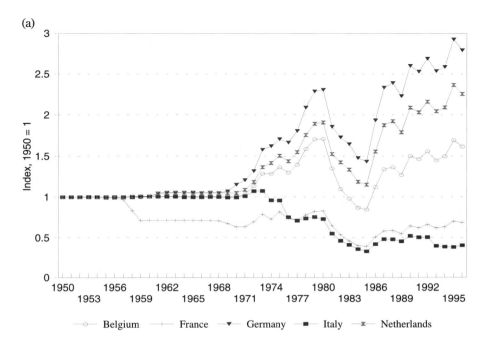

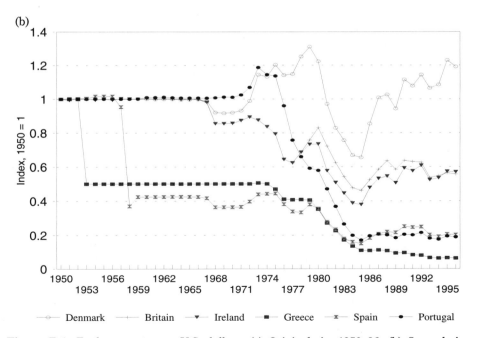

Figure 7.1. Exchange rates on U.S. dollars. (a) Original six, 1950–96. (b) Second six, 1950–96.

stitution of the Federal Republic of Germany required the Bundesbank to hold none of the debt of the central government, so the government could not force it to increase the money supply. Moreover, German experiences with hyperinflation after both World War I and World War II made the political pressures much stronger in Germany than in France to restrain any tendencies to let the money supply grow more rapidly than output.

Finally, widespread unrest in France in May 1968, culminating with a general strike by organized labor and political dissatisfaction expressed by university students, forced the French government to increase wages, permit a rise in prices, and accommodate all this with substantial increases in the French money supply. All this culminated with a one-time realignment of the French and German exchange rate at the end of 1968.

Before further realignments were necessary within the European Economic Community, however, the Bretton Woods era of fixed, but adjustable, exchange rates was terminated by the United States. This occurred in August 1971 when President Nixon ordered the Federal Reserve System of the United States to cease paying out gold to central banks of foreign countries when they wanted to cash in part of their holdings of U.S. dollars. Closing the gold window, as this action was termed, enabled the United States to float the dollar against all other currencies, letting it rise or fall depending on the state of the balance of payments. In the 1970s, as Figure 7.1 shows, this meant that the dollar fell in terms of the amount of most European currencies it could buy.

With respect to the currencies of the original six members of the EC, however, the dollar fell at differing rates, most against Germany, then against the Netherlands and Belgium, and least against Italy. This meant that the exchange rates within the EC changed as well, creating uncertainty among traders and consternation among the bureaucrats charged with administering the price supports of the Common Agricultural Policy.

THE SNAKE

In 1969, in response to the acrimony generated over the realignment of the French and Germany currencies, which was carried out bilaterally, the EC had already launched an ambitious effort to achieve economic and monetary union. Based on the Werner Report in 1970, a plan was introduced to achieve a common currency by 1980 in three stages. Stage I, to begin in 1971 and last for three years, would achieve a "concertation" of national macroeconomic policies with a goal of narrowing exchange rate fluctuations among member currencies within a smaller range than authorized by the IMF (then still ± 1 percent). Stage II would create a European Monetary Cooperation Fund controlled by the governors of the individual central banks, which would use its resources to intervene in the foreign exchange markets to minimize exchange rate variations among member currencies. Stage III would see the evolution of this fund into a European central bank managing a common Community currency by 1980.[9] Any resemblance between the Werner Plan of 1970 and the Delors Plan of 1990 is more than coincidental!

Of course, the collapse of the Bretton Woods system in August 1971 forced Stage I into a series of makeshift arrangements as the individual countries struggled to cope with the final collapse of a managed international monetary system in March 1972, the first oil shock in October 1973, and the second oil shock in 1979. Concertation was largely put aside in favor of domestic political considerations, and achievement of consensus over exchange rate policies was not aided by the accession of three new members in 1973—Great Britain, Ireland, and Denmark. What emerged instead was a system of jointly floating currencies anchored to the deutsche mark, which came to be known as the snake in the tunnel and the snake.

The first stage in the breakup of the Bretton Woods system was the Smithsonian Agreement in December 1971, where a new set of "central rates" among the Group of Ten[10] major industrial countries was agreed on, with temporarily wider bands of 2 1/4 percent on either side allowed. The initial reaction of the EEC Council of Finance Ministers to the Smithsonian Agreement was to state that the EEC currencies would maintain this ± 2.25 percent band with respect to one another, but not with respect to U.S. or Canadian dollars. A bit later, in March 1972, they determined to maintain margins with respect to each other that were only ± 1.125 percent from the agreed central rates (the snake), while keeping within the ± 2.25 percent margins with respect to the other G10 currencies (the tunnel). Britain joined only briefly (May to June 1972) as a token gesture of its commitment to membership in the EC, which began in 1973, but then floated from June 1972 on. Italy left the arrangement in February 1973, just before the entire Smithsonian Agreement broke down and generalized floating began in March 1973. This ended the tunnel, but the snake continued to float, although with a varying membership. By January 1974, France had dropped out of the arrangement, rejoining briefly from July 1975 to March 1976. While Norway and Sweden participated from time to time, the joint float ended up being conducted by Germany, the Netherlands, Belgium, Luxembourg, and Denmark.[11] Obviously, it was the German Bundesbank that was orchestrating this arrangement, and not the European Monetary Cooperation Fund envisioned in the now moribund Werner Report.

While each major country in the EC pursued its own national policy to respond to the first oil shock, the relative success of the German economy and those linked most closely to it in the snake meant that France and Italy, at least, renewed their efforts to imitate the German policy when they were confronted with the second oil shock starting in late 1978 and lasting through 1979 into 1980. This led quickly to the formation of the European Monetary System, a greatly modified version of the Stage II envisioned in the Werner Report.

THE EUROPEAN MONETARY SYSTEM (1979–92)

The inclusion of France and Italy in the joint float with Germany against the dollar and yen required some modifications in the arrangements of the EC. While the formal initiative was launched at the July 1978 meeting of the heads of government of the member countries (the European Council), operation of the EMS did not begin formally until March 13, 1979.[12]

The first innovation was the introduction of a parallel currency to the individual national currencies—the European Currency Unit, or ECU.[13] This is a basket currency, comprising specified amounts of each currency in the EC. When the amount of each currency is assigned a fixed weight in the ECU, a value of the ECU in terms of the national currency units is determined for each country. From this central rate with respect to the ECU, one can easily (with a computer spreadsheet) calculate the bilateral rates with respect to each pair of currencies. Table 7.2 shows the original composition of the ECU, the weights assigned to each currency, and the central rate for each in terms of units of national currency per ECU.[14] In fact, of course, the negotiations focused on the weights to be assigned each currency.

After the weights were agreed on, the ECU was taken as one European Unit of Account, the accounting unit used within the EC for converting pay-

TABLE 7.2
The European Monetary System at the Beginning. Original EMS Setup:
March 13, 1979

	European Monetary System—Bilateral central rates						
	100 BFR	**100 DKR**	**100 DM**	**100 FF**	**100 ITL**	**100 IRL**	**100 HFL**
BFR	. . . .	556.854	1571.64	680.512	3.43668	5954.71	1450.26
DKR	17.9580	. . . .	282.236	122.207	0.617160	1069.350	260.438
DM	6.363	35.4314	. . . .	43.2995	0.218668	378.886	92.2768
FF	14.695	81.829	230.949	. . . .	0.505013	875.034	213.113
ITL	2909.79	16203.26	45731.4	19801.5	. . . .	173270	42199.5
IRL	1.67934	9.351	26.393	11.4281	0.0577135	. . . .	24.3548
HFL	6.89532	38.397	108.370	46.9235	0.23697	410.597	. . . .

	Composition of the ECU in March 1979			
Currency	per ECU	in the ECU	Share (%)	
BFR	39.4582	3.660	9.3	Belgian Franc
DKR	7.0859	0.217	3.1	Danish Krone
DM	2.5106	0.828	33.0	Deutsche mark
FF	5.7983	1.150	19.8	French franc
ITL	1148.1500	109.000	9.5	Italian lira
IRL	0.6626	0.008	1.1	Irish punt
HFL	2.7208	0.286	10.5	Dutch guilder
LFR	39.5	0.14	0.4	Luxembourg franc
UKL	0.6626	0.089	13.3	United Kingdom pound
			100.0	

ments between each country and the EC. Originally equal to one U.S. dollar, by March 1979 the EUA had risen to a bit over $1.30. Taking the exchange rate of the deutsche mark/$ times the $/ECU, for example, yields deutsche mark/ ECU—the initial central rate. Assigning the appropriate weight to each country, depending on the size of its economy and its importance in the trade within the European Community, was a matter of negotiation, with a review to be undertaken every five years. The weight times the central rate of the ECU in terms of the national currency yielded the exact amounts of each currency that, figuratively, would be tossed into the basket to make up each ECU—a new, artificial currency, similar in nature to the SDR (Special Drawing Right) previously devised by the International Monetary Fund for calculating members' quotas in place of the now fluctuating U.S. dollar. But this new currency, it was hoped, would eventually become the common currency of all countries in the European Community.

The next step, after devising the composition of the ECU and determining the central rates of each member currency, was to establish the Exchange Rate Mechanism. While each member country's currency was necessarily included in the ECU, not every member was required to participate in the joint float against the rest of the world with Germany and its closest trading partners. Great Britain opted out entirely; Ireland and Italy were persuaded to participate if they were allowed exceptionally large intervention bands around their central rates—± 6 percent, compared with the ± 2.25 percent agreed on by the other participants.

Great Britain opted out for a variety of reasons, pragmatic and political. Its previous effort at floating with the rest of the EC had aborted after only one month in 1972; as yet its trade with the rest of the Community had not expanded to the extent hoped for when it had joined; and most important, its commitment to development of its offshore oil resources in the North Sea was coming to fruition, foretelling the emergence of Britain as a net oil exporter rather than oil importer, unlike the rest of the EC. The importance of this was that the price of oil was then (and still is) set in U.S. dollars by the OPEC cartel. Germany's tight money policies during the first oil shock of 1973–74 had meant the deutsche mark appreciated relative to the dollar, so the price of oil, while still rising in terms of deutsche marks, did not rise as much as it did in dollars. This was a definite advantage for a net importer like Germany and the rest of the EC, but a definite disadvantage for a net exporter such as Britain.

In the event, the British decision proved right—almost immediately with the launching of the European Monetary System came the second oil shock of 1979–80 set off by the revolution in Iran. This redoubled the price of oil, which had already quadrupled in response to the power of the OPEC cartel in 1973–74.

The British decision forced Ireland and Denmark, two small open economies whose major trading partner had traditionally been Great Britain before they entered the Common Market with Great Britain in 1973, to decide where their future lay. Both opted to stick with Germany in essence, and take their chances on trade with Britain as the pound floated with respect to the deutsche mark. In the short run, this proved especially painful for Ireland, as it found itself priced out of much of its traditional British market and not yet competitive in the rest of the EC. No doubt the economic costs were judged worth bearing for the political independence from Britain that the decision implied.

More important than the short-run costs for these two small countries, however, was the effect of the second oil shock on the stability of the newly created system. The first oil shock had destroyed permanently the Bretton Woods system of fixed exchange rates, set with adjustable pegs to the U.S. dollar, despite the best efforts to realign rates in the Smithsonian Agreement of December 1971. Would the second oil shock destroy the more modest effort of the Europeans to have a limited area of exchange rate stability within the confines of their customs union? Surprisingly, the EMS survived, expanded in membership, strengthened in effectiveness, and eventually induced even Britain to join in late 1990.

The key to its survival in face of the second oil shock, reduced growth, greatly increased unemployment, and political turnover in most participating countries was its flexibility. The Exchange Rate Mechanism was designed to encourage the individual central banks to intervene equally on each side of the market when a particular bilateral rate started to move toward one of the outer bands from the agreed central rate. Table 7.2 illustrates this with the full parity grid, where the upper triangle of rates above the diagonal of 1:1 own rates is perfectly symmetrical with the lower triangle of inverse rates. So if Denmark saw its rate with the Netherlands declining 2 percent from the central rate of 260.438 DKR/100 HFL, for example, then the Netherlands would see its rate rising 2 percent from the central rate of 38.397 HFL/100 DKR as well. The hope was that each central bank would intervene symmetrically as well as in the foreign exchange markets. In this case, the Dutch central bank would sell more guilders, driving down their price, and the Danish central bank would buy back some of its kroners, driving up their price. If each central bank acted in this manner, then very little recourse would be necessary to a central pool of reserves by the central banks with the weaker currencies.

The EMS did establish under the Basle/Nyborg agreements, in fact, such a pool of reserves, called the Very Short Term Financing Facility. These were just mutual credit lines established between each pair of participating central banks. In addition, the "short-term monetary support" and "medium-term financial assistance" facilities, which had been established in 1970 and 1971 under the provisions of the Werner Plan, were expanded from 10 to 25 billion ECU. Finally, a new European Monetary Cooperation Fund was established, each member of the Exchange Rate Mechanism receiving an initial supply of ECUs in return for allocating 20 percent of its combined gold and dollar reserves to the EMCF. Administration of these reserves pooled in the EMCF, however, was left to the contributing central banks in carrying out the swaps necessary to perform their exchange rate interventions.[15] As it turned out, the ECU reserves were used only when exchange rates reached the limits of their bands, and these interventions accounted for only a small part of the total made by the

TABLE 7.3
Dates and Size of EMS Realignments (percent change in central rate with the ECU)

	24 Sep. 79	30 Nov. 79	22 Mar. 81	5 Oct. 81	22 Feb. 82	14 Jun. 82	21 Mar. 83
FF	0.	0.	0.	−3	0.	−5.75	−2.5
DM	2.	0.	0.	5.5	0.	4.25	5.5
IRL	0.	0.	0.	0.	0.	0.	−3.5
ITL	0.	0.	−6.	−3	0.	−2.75	−2.5
HFL	0.	0.	0.	5.5	0.	4.25	3.5
DKR	−2.9	−4.8	0.	0.	−3	0.	2.5
BFR	0.	0.	0.	0.	−8.5	0.	1.5

	20 Jul. 85	7 Apr. 86	4 Aug. 86	12 Jan. 87	22 Jan. 90	14 Sep. 92	17 Sep. 92
FF	2.	−3.	0.	0.	0.	3.5	0.
DM	2.	3.	0.	3.	0.	3.5	0.
IRL	2.	0.	−8.	0.	0.	3.5	0.
ITL	−6.	0.	0.	0.	−3.	−3.5	*
HFL	2.	3.	0.	3.	0.	3.5	0.
DKR	2.	1.	0.	0.	0.	3.5	0.
BFR	2.	1.	0.	2.	0.	3.5	0.
PTA						3.5	−5.0
UKL						3.5	*
ESC						3.5	0.

	23 Nov. 92	1 Feb. 93	1 May 93	6 Mar. 95
FF	0.	0.	0.	0.
DM	0.	0.	0.	0.
IRL	0.	−10.0	0.	0.
ITL	*	*	*	*
HFL	0.	0.	0.	0.
DKR	0.	0.	0.	0.
BFR	0.	0.	0.	0.
PTA	−6.0	0.	−8.0	−7.0
UKL	*	*	(+2.58)	(2.02)
ESC	−6.0	0.	−6.5	−3.5

Source: Ecustat, Supplement 10, "The Evolution of the EMS," December 1995, p. 50.

individual central banks. Most of their interventions were made well within the margins agreed on and, moreover, were made with dollars, not with ECU. The secret of the initial success of the EMS, then, did not lie in the nature or amount of the pool of liquidity it provided for mutual assistance in maintaining exchange rate stability. Rather, it lay in the willingness of the participating members to peg their currencies to the deutsche mark and, when this proved too difficult to sustain without touching the limited reserves available through the EMCF, to realign the rates.

Realignments were frequent in the first few years of the system, occurring in September and November 1979, again in March and October 1981, in February and June 1982, in March 1983, and finally in July 1985. The remaining realignments, until the breakaway of Britain and Italy in September 1992, occurred in the context of new entries coming into the Exchange Rate Mechanism or existing members narrowing their bands from 6 percent (Italy and Ireland initially, and then Spain, Britain, and Portugal as they entered the ERM) to 2.25 percent. (See Table 7.3.)

Typically, however, the size of the realignments was small save for those of one or two members. Initially Denmark had the most troubled currency, then Italy, then Belgium, and finally France. The other members adjusted either up (usually Germany, often the Netherlands, but even Denmark and Belgium by the mid-80s) or remained at their initial central par rate. Given the wide variations in the exchange rate of the ECU with the dollar and the yen during this period, this record was especially noteworthy.

From the middle of 1985 until September 1992, indeed, the EMS was hailed as having achieved its goal of stabilizing exchange rates among member states of the European Community, enabling them to move confidently forward to the next step—establishing a common currency. The success in this period owed everything to the economic benefits obtained by member states when they permitted their central banks to accept the monetary leadership of the Bundesbank. The Bundesbank, in turn, was committed by the German constitution to maintain independence from the central government and to keep inflation under control, meaning under 3 percent annually. In effect, the deutsche mark had replaced the U.S. dollar as the key currency for the rest of the European central banks.

The stability of the exchange rates encouraged the member states to press forward with plans for establishing a European Financial Common Market, allowing free movement of capital among the member states. This required, first and foremost, elimination of capital controls by individual members, at least as far as the capital exported to other member states. It also required elimination of restrictions on ownership by foreigners of financial assets in the EC, at least if the foreigners were also from the EC. The initial effects of this limited deregulation of European financial services was very beneficial to those countries that had had the most tightly controlled financial sectors—France, Italy, and Spain. German and British banks and insurance companies, especially, found previously untapped markets for their efficient operations in mutual funds in Italy, branch banks in Spain, and financial markets in France. Tying their exchange rates firmly to the deutsche mark further encouraged import of fresh capital to these economies. Consequently, all of the EC prospered during the late 1980s. It was against this background of increasing prosperity, renewed foreign investment within the EC generally and especially in the southern tier, financial deregulation, and stable exchange rates that the Delors Plan for achieving, finally, the long-cherished goal of a single currency for the EC was formulated.

COMPETITION

Stage 1, which was already in progress, was to be completed by the end of 1992, when all twelve member states would have committed to maintaining fixed exchange rates with respect to the other eleven currencies. All seemed well until difficulties began to be experienced with ratification of the Maastricht Treaty by the member states. From early 1987 to June 1992, the EMS and the Exchange Rate Mechanism undergirding it enjoyed an unprecedented period of stability in the central parities and in the fluctuations around them. Spain and the United Kingdom joined the ERM; Italy and Ireland moved from wide 6 percent bands for the allowable fluctuations in their currencies to the narrow 2.25 percent bands. Moreover, when uncertainties over the possible outcomes of the Maastricht Summit held in December 1991 began to put pressure on some currencies, coordinated actions were taken by several central banks to maintain stability in the exchange rates. In November, the French and Italians raised their key interest rates and the British were allowed to move closer to the bottom of the 6 percent band. After the Maastricht Summit, the Germans raised their discount rate, countering inflationary pressures caused by the mounting costs of reunification, but all the ERM countries except Great Britain followed suit, again to maintain the stability of the grid of fixed exchange rates with one another.[16] By April 1992, even the Portuguese escudo had joined the ERM and only Greece remained outside the parity grid.

The first alarm occurred in June 1992 when the referendum presented to the Danish electorate by the government failed to elicit the necessary approval by a majority of Danish voters. Not only did this cast in doubt the viability of the political union foreseen by the Maastricht Treaty, it undermined confidence in the future of the EMS as a stepping stone to monetary union. The political difficulties of both Italy and Britain made participants in the foreign exchange markets doubt those two governments could continue to follow the German Bundesbank in maintaining high interest rates. Moreover, the weakening U.S. dollar was putting balance-of-trade pressure on all the European economies. Nevertheless, Germany continued to raise its interest rates, and economic difficulties increased for other member states, especially Italy, Britain, and Spain.

Looming in the near future was the upcoming referendum on the Maastricht Treaty in France, scheduled for September 20, 1992. The rejection of the treaty by voters in Denmark was a disturbance, not a disaster. Voters in Ireland had overwhelmingly approved it; perhaps the Danish government had mishandled the presentation of the treaty to its public.[17] But if the French referendum failed, it would be a disaster. Polls showed that this was quite possible, in fact.

In early September, Finland, which had been pegging its currency, the markka, to the deutsche mark in anticipation of applying for full membership and participating in the advantages of the single market, was forced to abandon the project and float the markka, which fell sharply. The Swedish krone came under heavy attack by speculators, leading to incredible interest rates of 75 percent and then for a spell, 500 percent. On Monday, September 14, the Italian lira was permitted to devalue by 7 percent against the rest of the currencies.[18] Speculative pressures then focused on the British pound. On Wednesday, September 16, the pound sterling was withdrawn (temporarily!) from the ERM, the Italian lira was allowed to float, and the Spanish peseta was devalued by 5 percent against all the remaining EMS currencies. This effectively ended the ERM for those countries and the prospect of uniting all the member state currencies into a common currency, as foreseen by the Maastricht Treaty. The foreign exchange markets had decided the fate of EMU before the French voters had their say.

COORDINATION VS. CRISIS

Nevertheless, the French franc remained steadfastly linked to the deutsche mark despite enormous selling pressures against it. And the narrow approval of the Maastricht Treaty by French voters on September 20 undoubtedly help sustain the French government in its determination to maintain the exchange rate with the deutsche mark. The speculative pressures continued to play against the various currencies that had decided to continue pegging their exchange rate to that of the deutsche mark. At the end of November 1992, both Spain and Portugal devalued their currencies 6 percent against the ECU. On February 1, 1993, the Irish pound finally conceded defeat and devalued 10 percent against the ECU. By May 1993, both Portugal and Spain were forced to devalue yet again.

Meanwhile, the French economy continued to suffer slow growth and rising unemployment while British exports began to rebound and the economy revive, apparently in response to the continued lower value of the pound sterling relative to its trading partners in the Single Market. At the end of July 1993, the crisis culminated when the French government decided it could no longer raise interest rates in defense of the franc and the Bundesbank decided it could no longer extend loans of deutsche marks to the Banque de France. These were starting to increase the supply of German currency circulating in Germany and undermining the Bundesbank's efforts to control inflationary pressures within unified Germany.

The resolution was to allow the French franc to devalue, but not by realigning relative to the ECU, as had been done by Spain, Portugal, and Ireland, or by withdrawing from the Exchange Rate Mechanism, as had been done by Italy and the United Kingdom. Instead, a novel solution was reached—temporary expansion of the allowable limits of fluctuation in the values of the participating currencies to ± 15 percent. This allowed the French franc to devalue, in fact, by as much as had the pound and lira during the September 1992 crisis.

In fact, once the speculators starting taking their profits by buying back the now much cheaper French franc, it rose again to within the original ± 2.25 percent range around its central par rate with respect to the deutsche mark.

CENTRALIZATION VS. DUAL CURRENCIES

The August 1993 solution was viewed as a temporary fix, with the goal of moving toward a common currency still held firm by the French, Dutch, Belgians, and Danes, whose central par rates had remained intact throughout the turmoil. The commitment of the Spanish, Portuguese, and Irish was maintained as well through irregular realignments. At the European Council meeting in December 1993, the composition of the ECU was fixed at its 1989 basket, when the peseta and escudo had been added to it. Hereafter, the ECU is a "hard" unit of account, meaning that in the future any change in a member state's exchange rate can be only a devaluation relative to the ECU. For example, a devaluation of the Italian lira of 7 percent in the future will require it to devalue 7 percent against the ECU, instead of having all the other currencies revalue 3.5 percent against the ECU while Italy devalues only 3.5 percent, as was done in September 1992.

The successive crises of the European Monetary System from September 1992 to August 1993 forced all the member states of the European Union to resolve the ambiguities of the Exchange Rate Mechanism in one way or another. Economists from the United States and Britain were nearly unanimous in proclaiming the EMS dissolved. (And good riddance, because of the confusion it caused in foreign exchange markets, whose sporadic crises caused disruptions to foreign trade.) It would henceforth be better for all countries concerned to allow their exchange rates to fluctuate freely on the foreign exchange markets. This would use the competitive forces of global product and capital markets to constrain policymakers in each country to follow sound economic policies that kept their economies competitive with those of their trading partners. If competitive in the product and capital markets, a country's exchange rate would stabilize in the foreign exchange market. Coordination, in short, would occur spontaneously by individual decision makers responding to the price signals emitted from the common marketplace.

Policymakers in both Germany and France, however, determined that the solution to the periodic instability of an adjustable peg system would be better solved by affirming that existing exchange rates would be locked at some point on the way to a common currency. With only one currency among them, the problems of coordination will be solved once and for all by centralized authority. The "only" remaining question is how that central authority will make and enforce its decisions. The agreement reached at the Brussels meeting of the European Council on October 29, 1993, between Mitterrand and Kohl was to proceed on course with the Delors Plan and begin Stage 2 as planned in January 1994. The Treaty on European Union, better known as the Maastricht Treaty, came into effect in November 1993. The decision to proceed with the next stage of monetary union required by the treaty was taken even as the Exchange Rate Mechanism, which had been characterized by Delors as the "glide path" to a common currency, had crashed.

Instead of a glide path for a common system of currency management that would take off into a common currency centrally managed, the more realistic analogy now was of a convoy of separate ships headed for a common destination but temporarily scattered by stormy seas. Meanwhile, serious construction of the destination site should be undertaken. So the countries remaining in the EMS agreed to maintain their previous central par rates but to allow market rates to diverge up to 15 percent in either direction from them. No longer would central banks have to stand in one place when attacked by foreign exchange speculators betting on either a revaluation or a devaluation. They could easily slip to the other side and let another set of speculators on the opposite side of the market come to their defense. Meanwhile, the creation of the framework for a single currency could go forward.

The first step was to freeze the composition of the ECU, as mentioned. The next step was to proceed with the establishment of the European Monetary Institute, locating it in Frankfurt where the Bundesbank is also located. Stage 2 would be made as short as possible, given the difficulties that had arisen over the long, drawn-out course of Stage 1. The next step, however, was not taken until the Madrid meeting of the European Council in December 1995. By that time, German public opinion was clear in its objection to replacing their deutsche mark with an Ecu. Helmut Kohl had won reelection as German chancellor in the fall of 1994, meaning he would be in power until the elections in October 1998, by which time the terms of entry for countries wishing to join the EMU would be set. He proposed substituting a different name, perhaps the "franken," for the common currency. Jacques Chirac, head of the most nationalistic of the Gaullist political parties, had replaced François Mitterrand as president of France in the elections held in Spring 1995. The compromise name agreed on, to the relief of all, was the "euro." In the transition period of adopting the new currency, therefore, the Germans could refer to their "Euro-marks" and the French to their "Euro-francs" and eventually both would refer to their "euros."

The European Monetary Institute began operation as planned in Frankfurt, starting January 1, 1994. Its function was to assemble a technical staff to monitor the progress of each member state toward fulfillment of the Maastricht criteria and to determine the technical arrangements needed to replace the individual national currencies with the European common currency. The first director was Alexandre Lamfalussy, a naturalized Belgian economist of Hungarian origin, who had begun his career in the European Payments Union and had been the managing director of the Bank for International Settlements in Basle. Lamfalussy's experience and prestige were precisely what was needed for the EMI to establish a credible professional reputation and authority among European central bankers for the staff of the European Central Bank that would follow when the common currency was established. The EMI has begun fulfilling its obligation to: (1) coordinate member state monetary policies with a view to ensuring price stability and to monitor the EMS; (2) prepare for a common currency managed by a future European Central Bank (ECB); and (3) oversee the development of the European Currency Unit. It now publishes monthly updates called *Ecustat,* with occasional supplements on specific issues.

Tables 7.4 and 7.5 display the central par rates of the currencies participating in the European Monetary System as of the end of November 1996 and the composition of the ECU as well. Comparing this with Table 7.2 enables us to see quickly how the system has evolved in nearly twenty years of operation. A more detailed picture, however, is afforded by Figure 7.2, which traces out the annual exchange rate indexes of the EU15 countries over the period 1985–96, whether they were in or out of the EU and whether they were in or out of the EMS.

Greece has never joined the ERM, and once Italy and the United Kingdom dropped out neither had rejoined until Italy reentered on November 25, 1996. Spain and Portugal have joined the EMS but have devalued repeatedly, preferring always to be part of the monetary integration of Europe rather than deal with volatile exchange rates. Their partners in the EMS have preferred to let them devalue rather than make interventions in the foreign exchange markets on their behalf, much less to coordinate their own monetary policies with those of the Iberian countries. Their rates within the EMS track rather closely those of Sweden and the United Kingdom, both of which have stayed out of the EMS

TABLE 7.4
The European Monetary System before EMU: EMS Setup, November 1996

Composition of the ECU since November 25, 1996*			
Currency	per ECU	in the ECU	Share
BFR	39.7191	3.301	8.31 percent Belgian franc
DKR	7.34555	0.1976	2.69 percent Danish krone
DM	1.92573	0.6242	32.41 percent Deutsche mark
FF	6.45863	1.332	20.62 percent French franc
ITL	1906.48	151.8	7.96 percent Italian lira
IRL	0.798709	0.008552	1.07 percent Irish punt
HFL	2.16979	0.2198	10.13 percent Dutch guilder
LFR	39.7191	0.13	0.33 percent Luxembourg franc
UKL	(0.793103)	0.08784	11.08 percent U. K. pound
DR	(295.269)	1.44	0.49 percent Greek drachma
PTA	163.826	6.885	4.20 percent Spanish peseta
ESC	197.398	1.393	0.71 percent Portuguese escudo
ATS	13.5485		Austrian schilling
FMK	5.85424		Finnish markka
SKR	(1.186)		Swedish krone

*Only twelve currencies are included in the ECU, those of the EU12 member states. Only twelve of the fifteen current members participate in the ERM, so the remaining three ECU rates are only notional (shown in parentheses).
Source: Ecustat, 2B April 1997, p. 59.

since 1992. Finland by the end of 1995 was recovering from the shocks to its economy of the early 1990s and formally joined the Exchange Rate Mechanism of the EMS in November 1996, as did Italy. Ireland has the unusual situation of trying to link with the deutsche mark but still subject to much the same market forces that move the exchange rate of the British pound sterling up or down. As the pound was weak relative to the ECU in 1993 through 1995, so was the Irish punt. Although it was only devalued once in February 1993, it was near or at the bottom of the EMS currencies relative to its new central par rate throughout 1994 and 1995. In 1996, however, the pound sterling rose from the middle of the year and with it also the Irish punt. The French franc managed to stay on course for maintaining its link with the deutsche mark since the mishaps of 1992–93 although by the end of 1996 it was the weakest of the ERM currencies. The Danish situation was dominated by the course of the deutsche mark, but like Ireland's punt, the Danish krone was pulled down by the importance of its remaining links with Great Britain and with the other Scandinavian economies until those currencies began to rise in 1996. Next on the graph is the Belgium/ Luxembourg franc, which seems caught between tracing the course of the French franc or the German mark. In the 1990s, the choice has been clear—to follow the mark, much to the satisfaction of the Flemish part of Belgium. What appears as a very thick and ornately marked line at the top of Figure 7.2 is actually the combination of the German mark, the Austrian schilling, and the

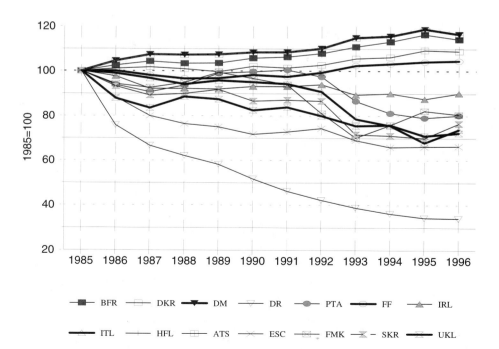

Figure 7.2. Index of ECU exhange rates, EU15, 1985–96.

TABLE 7.5
The European Monetary System before EMU: EMS Setup: November 1996

	100 BFR	100 DKR	100 DM	100 FF	100 IRL	100 HFL	100 PTA	100 ESC	100 ATS	100 FMK	1000 ITL
	European Monetary System—Bilateral Central Rates [November 25, 1996]										
BFR	· · · ·	540.723	2062.55	614.977	49.7289	1830.54	24.2447	20.1214	293.163	678.468	20.8337
DKR	18.4938	· · · ·	381.443	113.732	9.19676	338.537	4.48376	3.72119	54.217	125.474	3.85294
DM	4.84837	26.2162	· · · ·	29.8164	2.41105	88.7526	1.17548	0.975561	14.2136	32.8948	1.01010
FF	16.2608	87.9257	335.386	· · · ·	8.08631	297.661	3.94237	3.27188	47.6706	110.324	3.38773
IRL	2.01090	10.8734	41.4757	12.3666	· · · ·	36.8105	0.487537	0.40462	5.89521	13.6433	0.418944
HFL	5.46286	29.5389	112.673	33.5953	2.71662	· · · ·	1.32445	1.0992	16.0149	37.0636	1.13811
PTA	412.461	2230.27	8507.18	2536.54	205.113	7550.3	· · · ·	82.9927	1209.18	2798.41	85.9311
ESC	496.984	2687.31	10250.5	3056.35	247.145	9097.55	120.493	· · · ·	1456.97	3371.88	103.541
ATS	34.1107	184.444	703.550	209.773	16.9629	624.417	8.27008	6.86356	· · · ·	231.431	7.10655
FMK	14.7391	79.6976	304.0	90.6422	7.3296	269.806	3.57345	2.9657	43.2094	· · · ·	3.07071
ITL	4799.91	25954.2	99000.4	29518.3	2386.95	87864.7	1163.72	965.805	14071.5	32565.9	· · · ·

Source: Ecustat, 2B April 1997, p. 58.

Dutch guilder. The latter two currencies have consistently been pegged over this period with the deutsche mark.

Figure 7.2 is a useful diagnostic device because it shows the recent vicissitudes of the EMU adventure very clearly and also because it reveals starkly the "fault lines" that exist in the monetary structure of the EU. There is clearly a deutsche mark bloc in northern Europe, with the French and the Danes trying to maintain their currencies as part of that bloc and Finland trying to rejoin it. There is a second group of "ins" and "outs" who have let their currencies depreciate through 1995 either as deliberate policy (Britain, Italy, and Sweden) or as the unintended consequence of monetary policy dominated by other goals (Ireland, Spain, and Portugal). Greece is entirely another story, told in Chapter 14. How can a stable monetary structure be built on such a foundation?

The procedure adopted by the European Commission has been to break down the process for obtaining European Monetary Union into separate stages, each with a limited object and a definite time schedule. Any resemblance between this format and the process adopted for achieving completion of the Single Market is more than coincidental. While Stage 2 of the Delors plan was implemented in January 1994, the continued turmoil in the foreign exchange markets and the budget difficulties of all the member states for meeting the Maastricht criteria forced them to recognize that Stage 3 had to be delayed to the last possible date specified in the Maastricht Treaty, January 1, 1999. However, the timetable has been specified that countries must either meet the criteria or show significant progress toward meeting them by the end of 1997. On the basis of monitoring of countries' performance by the Commission and the EMI, decisions will be made as early as possible during 1998 on which countries will join in the common currency. Once the select group has been determined, conversion rates between their national currencies and the euro will be fixed, to take effect on January 1, 1999. This begins Phase B, as termed by the Madrid summit meeting in December 1995. At this time, the European Monetary Institute will cease to exist, becoming the European Central Bank. Its governing body will be a council comprising the central bank governors from the member states who are part of the European Monetary Union. During this period until January 1, 2002, there will be a dual payment system. Corporate bodies and investors will be free, but not obliged, to use the euro in this period. Banks, on the other hand, will be required to use the euro for their accounts with the European Central Bank and with each other. The obvious hope is that all the banking customers will switch to using the euro as quickly and voluntarily as possible. Certainly banks will find it to their advantage to do so, and they will no doubt take appropriate measures to persuade their customers likewise. On January 1, 2002, all payments must be made in euros. Then, on June 30, 2002, euro notes and coins will be introduced at the retail level. The legal problems of determining enforcement of contracts drawn in one currency or the other remain to be worked out.

Why is so much effort being made as such great expense by the citizens of each affected country to achieve a European common currency? The answer given by the European Commission comes in several parts, each designed for a different audience. For the average European citizen, the point is made in terms of the convenience of a medium of exchange. More pointedly, the Commission argues that the success of the Single Market depends in large part on eliminating the transactions costs associated with using different currencies.[19] This was identified by businesses as one of the major costs of dealing across national borders within the EU when the Single Market was being studied. It is clear that there are fixed costs to any currency conversion, and these must bear most heavily on smaller transactions. To make its case to the European public, the Commission uses the example of a tourist (presumably a naive American undergraduate) starting a tour of all the countries in the EU from Britain with £100. Merely changing his or her currency at each stop and doing nothing else, the tourist would end back in Britain with only £14. A more recent study on the costs of transferring small amounts of ECU100 showed, first, that most banks don't bother to give customers written information on costs of cross-border payments, and second, that the average cost was ECU 25.4. These fees are regarded as excessive, of course, and would be eliminated by a common currency.

The second line of argument is directed at the role of money as a standard for deferred payment. Given the credit required to finance long-distance trade and investment, exchange-rate risk has clearly deterred investors from taking full advantage of the Common Financial Market established as part of the Single Market initiative. It is clear that German investment within the European Union has been directed more toward countries with stable exchange rates with the deutsche mark than those with volatile rates. The natural tendency to minimize exchange-rate risk is heightened in the German case by the importance of bank finance and internal funds for business investment in that country. If investment in Spain, say, by a German company is based on funds borrowed from Deutsche Bank in deutsche marks, the German investor will want to keep his or her credit standing with Deutsche Bank by repaying faithfully in deutsche marks. One of the great incentives for Germany's small neighbors to peg their respective currencies to the deutsche mark is precisely so finance of their trade with Germany will not be put at a disadvantage relative to Germany's other possible trading partners.

The third argument relies simply on the unit-of-account role of a legal tender currency. The Commission phrases this in symbolic terms—a common currency is a sign of a truly common European market. Economists should be forgiven for thinking of it in terms of seigniorage, the revenues obtained by a government from its monopoly production of the money supply. Their attention has focused on the problem of competitive seigniorage, the situation where more than one source of money supply is available and they race to increase their respective revenues, creating every higher rates of inflation for everyone. This possibility has been the greatest fear of the Bundesbank from its founding. Every intervention into the foreign exchange markets to support the Italian lira in the early 1980s and the French franc during September 1992 has resulted in large amounts of deutsche marks spent by other central banks making their way back into the German money supply and threatening to raise the German price level. A central European bank, managed as the Bundesbank is with the same goal of maintaining price stability and independent of the pressures from central government to finance budget deficits, would eliminate the problem of competitive seigniorage. It also, of course, would raise the value of the seigniorage remaining in the hands of the central bank. The only remaining issue is how that seigniorage is distributed—in excessive staff and salaries for the bank, in generous rebates to the member central banks, or in payments to the appropriate central government, the EU itself.

These are good arguments and they have been used with good effect by the Commission. However, each point has a rebuttal and it is useful to review some of these to see the nature of the resistance that must be overcome if the common currency is to become both a reality and a success.

Transactions costs in making payments can and have been reduced in other ways than that of relying on a common currency used by a central bank. They are already being eliminated by the increased use of bank cards, either to obtain cash in local currency from one's home bank, typically at a charge of a little more than ECU 1.0, or to debit one's bank account directly to the foreign merchant. True, cross-border transfers of sums from one bank to another often take several weeks, but so do many transfers between different banks within each country. Increased use of computers in some of the European countries has enabled banks to process transfers and clear payments much more rapidly and accurately. The Commission's finding on excessive transactions costs from currency conversions can be taken as an argument either for a common currency and existing bank structures or for existing currencies with improved information technology used by financial intermediaries.

Moreover, the cost savings to individuals and businesses from lower transactions costs requires banks to make major investments and to find alternative ways of recouping lost revenues from commissions on foreign exchange transactions. A survey of European banks by *Euromoney* magazine estimated that the costs of converting to euros between 1999 and 2002 would be ECU 8 to 10 billion or an additional 1 to 2 percent of their operating costs each year for three or four years. For at least three years, banks' information technology must maintain a dual payment system, denominated in two currencies, its national currency and the euro. From the second half of 2002 on for an uncertain period, they must cope with euro and national currency bank notes and coins circulating together. Further the loss of commissions on foreign exchange will be a permanent reduction in their revenue base of 5 to 10 percent.[20] The correspondent banking business across European borders will now be substantially reduced, as any one bank's business can now be consolidated into the largest, most efficient correspondent bank. The article concludes, "In terms of simple return on investment, no sensible banker would actually suggest such a project."[21] This means that the large banks in Germany and the state-owned banks in France will be arguing that they should be compensated with an alternative source of revenue.[22]

Exchange-rate risks are typically hedged effectively for exporters and importers by offsetting contracts with their counterparties, by buying forward contracts in the desired currency, or by selling the current receivable in its currency to a third party. All of these require additional market contacts and do have some fixed expenses. However, the larger the scale of the transactions, typically, the smaller the percentage the fees will be, so for the bulk of foreign trade these commission costs are not a serious impediment. Moreover, the larger and more competitive the market is for forward exchange contracts, the lower the fees will be. It is precisely in the trade off between going to a market-based solution or going to a financial specialist, such as a Continental-style universal bank, that the British and German businesses differ in their assessment. For the French and Germans, the markets are much less competitive than for the British and so they are more concerned to get special deals from their customary banking houses, who do all of their financial business for them, including funding long-term investment projects.

Governments with weak tax bases, such as Greece, Portugal, and Spain not to mention the EU government-in-waiting, necessarily have weak markets for their debt issues as well. How can an investor be confident that a government with uncertain tax receipts and unpredictable demands on its expenditures will pay interest faithfully and redeem the principal when called on? That means they must rely on increases in the money supply they control to cover their expenditures. A counter to the EMU proposal, then, would be to broaden the potential market for the debt issues of governments with weaker tax structures. Indeed, participation in the EMS was a boon for Italian and Irish debt issues, as they continued to pay higher interest rates on their bonds than either the Germans or the French, but had a commitment from the other countries to maintain their exchange rates from depreciating very much. Alternatives, of course, would be to issue debt in the foreign currency of choice for the potential investors. It is not accidental that the first major Euro-bond (debt denominated in dollars by a foreign borrower) issue in the 1960s was to finance construction of the Italian autostrada. But this alternative denies the government in question the possible benefits of seigniorage. Excessive issue of its currency would increase the burden of servicing the debt denominated in foreign currency. Moreover, the government then has to compete with other issuers of bonds to keep its creditworthiness competitive. As the country chapters following will show, no European government has enjoyed doing this.

The existence of different levels and kinds of government debt already issued by the member states, however, raises further problems. Each government will still be required to service its own debt from its own tax base, even though every government's debt is denominated in the same currency—the euro. There is no problem with this: every state in the United States issues its own debt denominated in the common currency of the U.S. dollar. But every state has a balanced budget requirement, so that each new issue of debt has to be backed by a specified source of revenue dedicated to servicing it. This is necessary because no state now has the right to redeem its debt with money that it has created. The problem, however, arose at the outset when the currency union of the United States was formed by adoption of the Constitution in 1789. Alexander Hamilton, the American secretary of the treasury decided to assume the debts that the separate states had issued during the preceding years, including the expensive war years of the American War of Independence. Combining all of their bond issues into one large issue that was backed by the customs revenues and land sales of the new federal government enabled Hamilton to create a broader market for U.S. debt than was possible otherwise. Nothing is foreseen at present for a similar refunding operation in Europe, but the same pressures of differential debt burdens and abilities to service them that prompted Hamilton to do his assumption of state debts will surely emerge in the early stages of the European Monetary Union.

The Commission's counterargument to this scenario is that the sheer volume of euros will create a demand for them in other countries to hold as a reserve currency. Indeed, if demand for a country's currency by others depends on the size of its trade with the rest of the world, it would appear at first sight that the euro will be in greater demand than the U.S. dollar, given the greater importance of the European countries as a group in world trade. If true, then the euro will become the world's favorite currency to hold for reserves by central banks and international businesses. However, it is not true that demand for a reserve currency is determined this way. First, the EU trades mostly with itself, which is why it dominates world trade when intra-EU trade is counted as foreign trade. If we take just the trade of the EU with the non-EU world, it turns out that in the 1990s the United States alone has more trade with the rest of the world than does the EU. Another way to see the point is to realize that the deutsche mark reserves currently held by central banks and businesses in the rest of the EU will no longer be necessary for them, because their own currency, the euro, will be the same as the German currency needed for payments there. Euros will not be foreign reserves for any European bank or firm that is within the EMU, by definition. Only the rest of the world will still need a European currency for financing trade, and it will need dollars more than euros.

This point has been readily recognized. What is less obvious is that the value of the dollar as a reserve currency for central banks and especially for banks and firms around the world engaged at all in foreign transactions rests not so much on the volume of trade flows denominated in dollars as in the volume of capital flows denominated in dollars. It is the liquidity of the U.S. capital market, seen first in the size and ease of transfer among secondary holders of its national debt, and then made truly unmatchable by its broad and deep markets for private equity and bonds, that makes the U.S. dollar, or rather U.S. dollar-denominated financial instruments, so attractive to the rest of the world, including Europe. A study by the Bank for International Settlements concludes that the superior liquidity of U.S. dollar financial instruments explains "why virtually all mean-variance analyses of optimal reserve portfolios find the actual proportion of U. S. dollar holdings to be well above that suggested by efficiency considerations alone."[23] The same study concludes that increased volatility in exchange rates experienced by currency peggers, such as members of the ERM, tended to boost the U. S. dollar share of reserves. If reserves are held to offset volatile changes in a country's, or firm's, balance of payments, then it surely will see the advantage of holding those reserves in the most liquid financial asset available. Again, we come to the conclusion that it is not the common currency that is so important for the success of the Single Market but the additional market for credit that is vital.

Future pressures on the currencies allied closely to the deutsche mark can be alleviated either by moving to a common currency regulated mainly by the leadership of the Bundesbank, or by opting out of the Exchange Rate Mechanism entirely. A two-speed monetary system seems to be the most likely outcome in the future, especially with Austria, Sweden, and Finland in the European Union. Each of them, including even Norway at one point, has pegged their respective currencies to the deutsche mark by reason of the overwhelming importance of German trade to each economy. It will clearly be in their interests to fold their currencies into the common currency regulated by the German monetary authorities via their influence on the European Central Bank. The Netherlands, Belgium, Luxembourg, and Denmark have already made it clear that this is in their interests as well. For Britain, a choice will have to be made, but it has benefited after 1992 from dissociating its economy from the monetary effects of the costs of German reunification. So did Italy, at least until the political decision was taken in late 1996 to rejoin the exchange rate mechanism (ERM). This fixed its exchange rate at a rate that accepted a devaluation of the lira in terms of the deutsche mark of nearly one-third (from 1 DM = 748.22 ITL on September 14, 1992 to 1 DM = 990.00 ITL on November 25, 1996). Other countries, especially Portugal, Greece, and Spain, will find many advantages as well from maintaining separate currencies that can float in value relative to the ECU. There is a compelling economic logic, in short, for a monetary core within the European Union using a common currency, either the ECU or the deutsche mark, and a monetary periphery partly within the European Union and partly associated with it, periodically floating or pegging for varying intervals against the ECU.

Although this is the most likely scenario, it is not clear that a two-speed (or three-speed) system would result in a unified monetary union. Problems could occur from the differences among the closely related countries—after all they are all engaged together in the SEA—and in getting the slower speed countries up to speed in order to join. Barry Eichengreen and Jeffrey Frieden point out that a two-speed system could produce enough destabilization from the outer core to infect the inner core, causing a breakdown of even those countries that are prepared to integrate.[24] Alberto Alesina and Vittorio Grilli attempt to gauge how feasible a multispeed EMU would be to accept new members. They find that once a group of countries forms a restricted union, they might likely never extend the union; this is true even if all the countries would be better off in an initial completely one-speed EMU.[25] This is pessimistic news for both a multispeed union and for new members joining the EU and thereby wishing to be incorporated into a monetary union. What it says to new members is that they cannot expect to be accepted unless they have already aligned themselves with the union. Nevertheless, the variety of market alternatives described above will exist for them as well as for the drop outs and the opt outs.

Endnotes

1. Alexander Italianer, "Mastering Maastricht," in Klaus Gretschmann, ed., *Economic and Monetary Union: Implications for National Policy Makers.* Dordrecht, The Netherlands: Martinus Nijhoff, 1993, p. 52.

2. Robert Mundell, "A theory of optimum currency areas," *American Economic Review* 51, 1961, pp. 637–55.

3. Ronald McKinnon, "Optimum currency areas," *American Economic Review* 53, 1963, pp. 717–25.

4. Paul De Grauwe, "German monetary unification," *European Economic Review* 36, 1992, p. 452.

5. For example, while the United States has a elasticity of the nominal wage with respect to the unemployment rate of -0.61 and Japan has an elasticity of -1.87, Germany and Denmark have values of -0.11 and -0.10, respectively, while the rest of the EU members have elasticities in the -0.2 to 0.4 range. Barry Eichengreen. "Should the Maastricht Treaty be saved?" Princeton Studies in International Finance no. 74, December 1992, p. 21.

6. Expressing intra-community exports as percent of GDP, high-trade countries like Ireland and Belgium have values around 50 percent, while low-trade countries like Greece, the United Kingdom, Italy, and Spain have values at or below 10 percent. See Paul de Grauwe, *The Economics of Monetary Integration,* Oxford: Oxford University Press, 1992, p. 84.

7. See chapter 2.

8. The definitive work on the European Payments Union is Jacob J. Kaplan and Gunter Schleiminger, *The European Payments Union: Financial Diplomacy in the 1950s,* Oxford: Clarendon Press, 1989

9. Charles Kindleberger, *A Financial History of Western Europe,* 2d ed., New York: Oxford University Press, 1993, pp. 443–4.

10. The Group of Ten was formed in the early 1960s as a caucus of the leading members of the IMF to discuss and initiate changes in IMF legislation. It consisted of the G7—United States, Germany, Japan, Britain, France, Italy, Canada—plus the Netherlands, Belgium, and Sweden. Although Switzerland is not a member of the IMF, a representative is often included in the meetings.

11. The history of the snake is given in *European Economy,* no. 12, July 1982.

12. Horst Ungerer, *The European Monetary System: The Experience, 1979–82,* Washington, D.C.: International Monetary Fund, 1983, p. 1.

13. This replaced the European Monetary Unit foreseen by the Werner Report. This was a felicitous change since its acronym in English, EMU, was the name of a bird that couldn't fly, as the English press was quick to point out. The Ecu, on the other hand, was the first gold coin struck in any quantity in medieval France. Ironically, it was introduced in 1337 on the eve of the Hundred Years War with England.

14. If w_i = the weight for country i; u_i = the number of units of its currency in the ECU; and C_i = the central rate of the ECU for country i; then

$$u_i = w_i * C_i$$

As C_i was known from the market rates for the European Unit of Account and w_i was decided in negotiation, the u_i was then determined.

15. Ungerer, note 12, pp. 2–3.
16. "The ERM in 1992," Study No. 5 in *European Economy,* No. 54, December 1993, p. 145.
17. In contrast to the Irish government's technique of distributing brief pamphlets that highlighted the advantages Ireland would enjoy in a single market, the Danish government, at great expense, made widely available complete copies of the full treaty. Even Jacques Delors admitted later that the wording required in EC documents to gain approval of the entire European Council made many parts of them unintelligible.
18. This was done by devaluing the lira 3.5 percent against the ECU and revaluing all the other currencies 3.5 percent against the ECU.
19. Michael Emerson, ed., *One Market, One Money.* A special issue of *European Economy* 44, 1990, makes this argument in detail.
20. *Euromoney,* September 1996, pp. 94–95.
21. Ibid., p. 99.
22. One such source would be preferred access to TARGET, the interbank payments clearing system among banks on the European continent. Already in 1996, the French and German banks have proposed this, with the implicit support of both governments. Needless to say, the British banks have objected mightily and in response have hastened implementation of their more advanced computer technology to facilitate payment clearings with allied banks elsewhere in Europe.
23. Scott Roger, "The management of foreign exchange reserves," Basle: Bank for International Settlements, Economic Papers No. 38, July 1993, p. 68.
24. Eichengreen has dealt with these issues in a variety of places; he and Jeffrey Frieden do a good job of outlining the various reasons for monetary union and run through the various possible outcomes of the EMU process in their "The political economy of European monetary unification: an analytical introduction," *Economics and Politics* 5, no. 2, July 1993, pp. 85–104.
25. Alberto Alesina and Vittorio Grilli. "On the feasibility of European monetary union," *Economics and Politics* 5, no. 2, July 1993, 145–65.

Selected Bibliography

de Grauwe, Paul. *The Economics of Monetary Integration.* Oxford: Oxford University Press, 1992. Good analytical overview of monetary integration with long sections outlining the potential costs and benefits to member states.

de Grauwe, Paul and Lucas Papademos. *The European Monetary System in the 1990s.* London: Longman, 1990. Collection of good articles on the future of the EMU with especially good coverage of Spain, Portugal, and Greece, along with an excellent ariticle by Paul Krugman.

Eichengreen, Barry. "A more perfect union? The logic of economic integration" *Essays in International Finance,* no. 198, June 1996. Excellent integration and analysis of the economic and political aspects of customs unions, common markets, and economic unions.

Eichengreen, Barry. "Should the Maastricht Treaty be saved?" *Princeton Studies in International Finance* no. 74, December 1992. Interesting attempt to evaluate the conditions of the stability of monetary union in Europe.

Gros, Daniel and Niels Thygesen. *European Monetary Integration.* New York: St. Martin's Press, 1992. Good overview of monetary integration with an excellent evaluation of the effects of the EMS on the member states.

Kenen, Peter. *Economic an Monetary Union in Europe: Moving Beyond Maastricht.* Cambridge: Cambridge University Press, 1995. Kenen does a good job of evaluating the stage process of attaining the EMU along with providing a solid theoretical section on the nature of monetary integration. Especially good on the design and process leading up to Stage 2.

CHAPTER 8

External Trade Policies:
The EU and the Rest of the World

The European Community is a very important international player and its relationships with the rest of the world greatly affect the global economy. Although the Community is one of the world's largest trading groups, as we saw in Chapter 3, 80 percent of the Community's trade is within Europe, either intra-EC, with the EFTA, or Eastern Europe. Most of the Community's trade is covered by some trade agreement. Coordination of these arrangements is done by the Commission. By mandate of the Council, the Commission negotiates multilateral and bilateral trade agreements, monitors and applies trade policy, and proposes new legislation.[1]

For most of the EU's history, the arrangements have been closely monitored by the member states with a keen eye to preserve their interests. Insofar as these agreements extend trade concessions, they have been constructed so that they cannot hurt any of the member states. Given the diversity among members, the conditions of any "special treatment" are extremely limited. However, with the reform of the CAP, the EU no longer has the commitment to agricultural protection at any cost, so some of its external arrangements have become less strict. Overall, there has been a general reform and shift in external policy over the past decade. This chapter examines the development of the common commercial policy and how it has been expressed in various regions throughout the world.

THE COMMON COMMERCIAL POLICY

The basis for Community external relations is found under Article 113 of the Treaty of Rome, which states that the Community is to establish a common commercial policy based on a common tariff regime, common trade arrangements with third countries (with some allowances for foreign territories), and a uniform application of trade policy instruments for imports and exports as well as protection in the case of illicit practices, such as dumping or subsidization.

Commercial policy is decided by majority rather than unanimous vote, which has speeded the introduction of new polices controlling trade. The harmonized tariff schedule contains some 9,500 tariff lines with a weighted average of tariff levels at 5.7 percent. (Before the Uruguay Round of the GATT, see below, the average was 6.5 percent.[2]) Safeguards against any member being hurt unduly by external trade have always been a part of the policy, but in the 1980s, with the overall expansion of trade, the EC became even more concerned about foreign commercial practices. In 1984 the Community instituted its New Commercial Policy Instrument, which established new procedures to respond more quickly to illicit trade practices that hurt member states.

Protection not only has been summoned in response to illicit practices; it also has been used as a means to prop up declining industries. The EC has until only recently been very protective about its steel, textile, and shipbuilding industries. As we saw in Chapter 5, the steel industry has gone through dramatic decline, and the EC responded in the late 1970s with dirigistic policies of controlling prices and instituting quotas. None of this was successful, of course, and the EC stopped the attempt to keep the industry from downsizing. The traditional steel industry steadily declined, but new sectors of high-grade small production facilities (so-called minimills) expanded, much as in the United States. In the United Kingdom, the industry was privatized fully, and it has now become one of the most profitable industries in Europe.[3] However, other member states, notably Spain and Germany, have continued to subsidize as national or regional government subsidies were substituted for EC payments, even as the Commission tried to reduce aid and prohibit all subsidization of direct costs and investment. In response to the continued support of the steel industry by European governments, the United States placed countervailing duties on carbon steel in 1993 of up to 110 percent. For the most part, the Commission did not press too hard on member states and tolerated continued support. In the Association agreements with the Eastern European states, however, the Commission has sought to reduce protection in order to allow cheaper steel products to be imported from countries like Poland and the Czech Republic.

Textiles have a long, checkered history. In 1961, the international community tried to coordinate textile quotas through a short-term arrangement, which quickly was revised into a long-term arrangement. In it, countries agreed to increase import quotas and limit the imposition of new quotas. This was the framework until 1974, when the system was ensconced as the Multi-Fibre Arrangement (MFA). The MFA is the framework within which developed countries have been able to protect their domestic textile markets without running afoul of broader international trade agreements. The EC has used the MFA to reduce the import quotas of countries with competitive textile industries, notably Taiwan and Hong Kong, and to provide political concessions to countries that have relatively small production by increasing their quotas. The costs of protecting textile worker employment has been high for Europe. If only quotas were eliminated and tariffs were retained, it is estimated that welfare would increase by U.S. $5.03 trillion.[4] While it is true that many of the poorer countries have relatively large textile sectors, they are disproportionately hurt by increased textile and clothing prices. The insistence by member states to protect their textile industries has severely limited free trade, especially for the developing countries.

The other major aspect of common external policy is the rules under which new members can be accepted into the EU. Article F of the TEU clearly states that member states' governments are founded on the principles of democracy, so any applicant would have to have a democratic structure. Article O states that any European state may make its application to the Council to become a member. To accept it, however, the Council must act unanimously after consulting the Commission and receiving assent from the European Parliament by an absolute majority of its members.

THE GENERAL AGREEMENT ON TARIFFS AND TRADE (GATT)

The international, institutional framework of multilateral trade since the 1950s has been the GATT. This was the basic framework under which the Community conducted its external trade policy until the establishment of the World Trade Organization in 1994. From comprising in 1950 mostly the United States, Canada, and the OEEC countries, GATT membership rose over the years with each round of trade negotiations. From 92 members in 1986, when the Uruguay Round began, GATT membership rose to 114 when negotiations ended in 1993. By the time of the first ministerial meeting of the World Trade Organization in Singapore in December 1996, membership had risen to 126, with another 30 waiting to join. GATT covers four-fifths of all trade. For most of its history the GATT has focused on the trade for manufactures. Agricultural goods were explicitly excluded from its international arrangement until the last set of negotiations (the Uruguay Round).

The GATT rests on two main principles—trade liberalization and nondiscrimination. The GATT has made important strides to eliminate both tariff and nontariff barriers. The nondiscrimination rule is conducted by the most favored nation (MFN) clause, which states that trade concessions granted one member must be granted to all members. It would seem that the Community conducts discriminatory policy, since it has eliminated barriers only among members. However, the GATT allows regional trade arrangements so long as the common tariffs are not higher than the average of its members' tariffs prior to the arrangement (Article 26). Because the Treaty of Rome satisfied these conditions, it was allowed under the GATT. The GATT also provides a Generalized System of Preferences (GSP) for developing countries, whereby developed countries are ensured non-discriminatory trade and the developing nations get concessions on manufactured products. In 1995, the GSP was revised to help support more strongly the industrialization of developing countries, their export diversification, and their realization of higher export earnings. However, because agricultural products have not, until recently, been included, these concessions have done very little for developing nations.

Through the 1960s and 1970s, the GATT was concerned with tariff reductions. For both the Dillon (1961) and the Kennedy (1962) rounds, European integration was a major concern. In both of these rounds and in the Tokyo Round (1975–79), major tariff reductions were established. Only with the most recent round have agriculture and nontariff barriers been fully examined.

- *Dillon Round.* Under the Dillon Round, the EC agreed to reduce the planned common external tariff by 20 percent. With the deepening of the cold war, the United States promoted the integration of Western Europe and supported European nations acting as a unified economic and political force.

- *Kennedy Round.* In 1962 the united strength of Europe made a big impact on the negotiations, which resulted in a reduction of tariffs of an average of 35 percent, and for some industrial goods 50 percent. These reductions were to be carried out by 1972. The United States demanded that some agricultural products be included in the reduced tariffs and the EC did reduce variable levies on some goods.

- *Tokyo Round.* In the Tokyo Round, tariff reductions were on average 33 percent for manufactures, mainly machinery, chemicals, and transport equipment. The conference attacked the widespread use of nontariff barriers (NTBs). Also, the EC demanded that there be some attempt at tariff harmonization on a worldwide basis. The "Swiss Formula" was used— $16T/(16 + T)$—so that a 40-percent tariff became 11.4 percent, while a 20-percent tariff became 8.9 percent.

- *Uruguay Round.* The Uruguay Round was the first international trade round of the post cold war era.[5] This round, the results of which were formally agreed to in 1994, marks a new era for international trade. Agricultural trade was phased into the agreements and a new body, the World Trade Organization (WTO) was created to oversee global trade, as a successor to the GATT, and tariff levels were further reduced. Given the changes due to the SEA, the EC was deeply divided over whether further liberalization would proceed with agriculture. In fact, the EC refused to cut agricultural subsidies by the scheduled deadline of December 1990. However, in May 1992, as we saw in Chapter 6, the EC finally agreed to reform the CAP.

Even though the trade rounds have demonstrated that the Community can form a powerful, unified negotiating block, the diversity of interests across the member states has made trade arrangements very complicated, with individual members demanding special features that suit their own needs. This makes it very difficult for the Community to respond to alternatives offered by its negotiating partners, since any change in position has to meet the approval of all the member states. While there has been a common trade policy, its development has been greatly affected by member state interests.

EUROPEAN FREE TRADE ASSOCIATION

As we saw in Chapter 2, Britain's plans for a wider trade area were not followed after Messina, and plans were begun to create a parallel organization of non-EEC countries to create a free trade area for industrial goods. At the Stockholm Convention of 1960, the European Free Trade Association was created, with members the United Kingdom, Denmark, Portugal, Austria, Sweden, Norway, and Switzerland. Iceland joined in March 1970 and Finland in January 1986, after being an associate member since 1961. Clearly, the trading relationship between the EEC and EFTA would be very important. When the United Kingdom and Denmark joined the EEC in 1973, the Community created bilateral arrangements with the remaining EFTA members. By 1977, all tariffs were removed from mutual industrial goods' trade. In Chapter 3, we briefly discussed free trade arrangements and their need for rules-of-origin regulations, regulating the access of third country imports into the area. Not surprisingly, a dazzling array of rules of origin was instituted, so that non-EEC countries could not get access to the EEC through EFTA countries.

All through the many changes of the EEC, EFTA countries have had to monitor and adapt, making it the obvious enlargement area. For example, most of the EFTA countries voluntarily followed along with the SEA in order not to lose trade with the member states. Although the two areas were closely related, the EC accused EFTA countries of selecting only those parts of EC integration that would clearly help them and ignoring all others. In 1984, with the Luxembourg Declaration, the EC demanded that EFTA countries start to integrate in order to create a real economic space in Western Europe. This signal, directly before the push for the Single European Act, frightened EFTA countries into believing that they might be excluded from a "fortress Europe," and they pushed for increased cooperation.

In response, the European Economic Area agreement was signed in 1992, coming into force in 1994 and being revised in 1995 to extend the four freedoms of the single market (goods, services, capital, and people) to the remaining EFTA countries Iceland, Liechtenstein, and Norway. (Switzerland is an EFTA member but did not sign the EEA.) The agreement also requires adoption of most Community policies on mergers, state aids, consumer protection, labor markets and the environment. Just as in their own original agreements, ETFA countries excluded any measure about agriculture. Although the countries will be consulted about new legislation, Iceland, Liechtenstein, and Norway have no voting rights. With the inclusion of Austria, Finland, and Sweden into the Community in 1995, EFTA trade policy and the EEA have lost their importance.

EASTERN EUROPE

Since the radical collapse of the Council for Economic Mutual Assistance and the Soviet Union, the Community has increased its attention on Central and Eastern Europe countries (CEEC). Over the period 1990–94, the EU allocated

ECU 33.8 billion total aid to this area, which accounted for 45 percent of its total assistance. In 1993 the Community transformed the Europe agreements with Bulgaria, the Czech Republic, Estonia, Hungary, Latvia, Lithuania, Poland, Romania, and Slovakia into association agreements. These agreements are the first stage of accession to membership and mainly control aid and trade arrangements between the Community and the East. The agreements establish reduced tariff levels spread over a ten year transition period with immediate liberalization of certain goods that do not compete directly with those of member states. Associated states are granted some preferences for infant industry-type support, but most trade is restricted in areas in which the East is most competitive, for example, steel, coal, textiles, cement, and agricultural goods. For example, the Central and East European countries have free market access for most live freshwater fish and other fish products; however, given the small fishing sector in the East this lenient provision should have very little impact. We will look more closely at these countries in Chapter 17.

Financial support for the cooperation between the East and the EU is principally carried out by the Poland and Hungary: Aid for Reconstruction of the Economy (PHARE) program. In 1995 its budget was expanded by 15 percent and extended to finance investment support, mainly in large infrastructure projects, environmental controls, and the development of the private sector. As was mentioned in Chapter 5, the Technical Assistance Information Exchange Office (TAIEO) has also been created to speed implementation of PHARE funds and to streamline development procedures.

RUSSIA AND THE NEW INDEPENDENT STATES

The EU accounts for about 40 percent of Russia's foreign trade. The Program for Technical Assistance to the New Independent States and Mongolia (TACIS) is the main vehicle for coordinating EU activity with the transition of these areas to market economies. Projects include restructuring state enterprises, increasing production efficiency, and improving the safety of nuclear power plants. Between 1991 and 1995, TACIS conducted nearly five-hundred projects and spent about ECU 2.3 billion.

Formal Partnership and Cooperation agreements were signed in 1994 and 1995 with Russia, Ukraine, Moldova, Kyrgyzstan, Belarus, Kazakhstan, Georgia, Armenia, and Azerbaijan, but have yet (as of the end of 1996) to be ratified by the respective parliaments of the signing parties.[6] These arrangements have been called halfway houses between no arrangements and the type of arrangements negotiated with eastern European nations. They stress the need to maintain market economies, regional cooperation and at least mention the potential for future trade relationships through the establishment of a free trade area. The signatories agree to MFN status and to liberalize trade in goods other than textiles, coal, and steel; both sides may, though, opt out through a variety of safeguard clauses. Trade with the former Soviet Union is complicated by its weak physical and economic infrastructure. The cooperation agreement had to establish rules allowing for direct EU investment along with the right to repatriate profits, as well as for the liberalization of foreign banks. As in the many other international arrangements, most products are granted access into the EU market except for certain textile and steel products. Pending ratification of the entire agreement, the trade agreements have been in force since February 1996.

MEDITERRANEAN COUNTRIES

With the accession of Portugal, Spain, and Greece, other Mediterranean countries cannot expect to achieve much in terms of trade concessions. Even though the EEC launched a "Global Mediterranean Policy" in 1971 (finally instituted in 1978), the EU has bilateral arrangements with each of the countries. The arrangements are designed to keep trade free for any goods in which the Mediterranean countries do not compete with the EU. For example, most industrial products have free access to the EU, just as they would under the GSP; however, for products such as textiles or refined petroleum (not crude, which the EU hardly produces, but refined, which the EU certainly does) are controlled by quotas. Agricultural policy is just as ungenerous, with most products produced in the EU controlled, or products are seasonally controlled so that out-of-season produce is allowed into the EU. The actual arrangement was set up so that the Mediterranean nonmember countries were given a preferential share of the difference between European demand and supply; however, with the expansion of European production (see the growth of the self-sufficiency ratios given in Chapter 6) these concessions became less and less advantageous. Of course, with the accession of Greece, Portugal, and Spain, the GMP steadily fell into disarray. The nonmember countries had to look for a new relationship with the EU.

In 1995, Algeria, Morocco, Tunisia, Egypt, Israel, Jordan, Lebanon, the Palestinian territories, Syria, Turkey, Cyprus, and Malta met in Barcelona to deepen cooperation. Out of the meeting came the "Partnership Declaration," which establishes the basis for stronger economic and political cooperation between the twelve countries and the EU, increases financial aid, and creates plans for phasing in a free trade zone by 2010.[7]

Turkey, the nonmember state with the longest association with the European Community, reached agreements with the EU at the end of 1995 on a customs union between the two areas, an arrangement originally planned on in 1972. The establishment and operation of the union even now, however, is contingent on the human rights situation within Turkey. This special bilateral agreement would not give Turkey direct rights to any funds, nor does it give Turkey any political power in EU decisionmaking.

AFRICAN, CARIBBEAN, PACIFIC, AND OTHER DEVELOPING COUNTRIES

Overall, cooperation policies are aimed at supporting democracy and fighting poverty. The EU15 and member states provide about ECU 4 billion in aid each year, representing about 45 to 50 percent of all public development aid, compared with about 20 percent from the United States and 18 percent from Japan.[8] As we saw in Chapter 5, development assistance is granted in the form of humanitarian aid, food aid, project cofinancing, and support for community-based cooperation. For humanitarian aid and food aid, the European Office for Emergency Humanitarian Aid (ECHO) has been involved with the many victims of war in the former Yugoslavia, Afghanistan, Armenia, Azerbaijan, and Tadjikistan. The EU has become the second largest provider of food aid after the United States, providing aid worth about ECU 600 million annually.

As discussed in the last chapter, the African, Caribbean and Pacific countries are now seventy countries that receive special treatment under the Lomé agreements. Many of these countries have former colonial relationships with EU members, mainly France and the Netherlands, and current arrangements come out of redefining how former overseas territories would be included in Community policy. In the Treaty of Rome, the colonial areas were included as associate states with the intent of establishing two-way free trade, mainly because they were still attached to member states. However, in the early 1960s, many colonies gained independence and new arrangements had to be found. The first was the Yaoundé Convention of 1963. Yaoundé dropped the notion of establishing an extended free trade area, and countries had bilateral arrangements with the EU. After a revision in 1969, Yaoundé had to be overhauled to accommodate the inclusion of the United Kingdom and all of its former colonial relationships. The first Lomé Convention was signed in 1975 and ran until 1980 with forty-six nations. Lomé II ran from 1980–85 with sixty-three countries, and Lomé III ran from 1985–90 with sixty-six countries.

Under Lomé IV, which will run until 2000, seventy ACP countries receive tariff preferences, and with the serious reform of the CAP since the late 1980s, many agricultural products are now freed. In recent years, 94 percent of total ACP exports were duty free into the EU; under the Fourth Lomé Agreement, 99.5 percent of ACP exports are duty free to the EU. The Community, in turn, gets MFN status and a promise that the ACP states will not discriminate across EU members. Given the relatively high costs of production in ACP countries, the EU ensures nondiscriminatory action at very little cost. The EU also commits aid to the countries, mainly through the European Development Fund, but also through the European Investment Bank. As was explained in Chapter 5, the EU maintains export earning, smoothing funds through Stabex and Sysmin. All of these elaborate relationships, however, must be put into the context of total EU trade. In 1992, the ACP accounted for only about 1.5 percent of total EU trade (fallen from about 4 percent in 1970), reflecting the tragic recent economic history of these countries.

Latin American trade is heavily involved with the EU and accounts for 20 percent of total Latin American external trade. This would seem to suggest that trade arrangements between the two would be important, but only 5 percent of EU external trade is involved with Latin America. For the most part, trade is governed under the GSP, granting the countries only limited benefits. The San José dialogue of 1984 began formal meetings between the EC members and Latin America, mainly on peace and human rights conditions. The "Rio Group" established in 1990 has fostered closer economic and political ties and through it, the EU has signed nonpreferential economic and trade cooperation arrangements with fourteen countries. These mainly consist of lowered tariffs and arrangements on certain goods, like those with the Mediterranean countries. It has, though, increased the European presence in these countries in other ways. For example, over the 1980s and 1990s, European official development aid has rapidly expanded. In 1993, it accounted for 61.5 percent of all aid, exceeding the amounts of the United States and Japan combined.[9]

Traditionally, the ties between Europe and Asia have been weak. With the phenomenal increase in export trade from Asia, however, the EU has begun to focus more attention on it. Since 1980 the Association of South East Asian Nations (ASEAN) has had a cooperative agreement with the EU, as have India and Pakistan. In March 1996 a summit was held in Bangkok with the EU15, the seven members of the ASEAN (Brunei, Indonesia, Malaysia, Philippines, Singapore, Thailand, and Vietnam), China, Japan and Vietnam. Initiatives were begun to create an Asia-European Investment Promotion Plan, an Asia-Europe Business Forum, an Asia-Europe Environmental Technology Center, and an Asia-Europe Foundation for Cultural Exchange. Overall, trade with the area is still low, but the EU has slowly been developing a relationship with this dynamic region. Political disagreements over Indonesia's role in East Timor and Burma's treatment of dissidents, however, have prevented any formal agreements. China, by contrast, has become the EU's fourth largest export market and its fourth largest source for imports. Trade is conducted within the framework of a cooperation agreement signed in 1985 and revised in 1995.

UNITED STATES AND CANADA

As was shown in Chapter 2, the United States was a major force behind the political and economic cooperation of Europe in the aftermath of World War II. While the role of the United States has remained important throughout the history of the European Community, the relations have been strained by trading conflicts as well as by the shift in geopolitical power over the past decade.

EU-Canadian relations have grown since 1980. The EU is now ranked as Canada's second highest foreign investor, accounting for 22.6 percent of the Canadian capital stock—up from 14.1 percent in 1983. Likewise, the EU is Canada's second largest trading partner, after the United States. Trading relationships are governed by the Framework Agreement for Commercial and Economic Cooperation of 1976 and the 1990 Declaration on EU-Canada relations. These arrangements set the timing of meeting between Canadian and EU delegates as well as establish forums for cooperation and negotiation of disputes. The format has not been successful, however, in resolving fishing disputes, which continue to plague relations. Canada should also participate in the New Transatlantic agenda established in Madrid in December 1995.

The United States is the largest foreign investor in Europe and has long, established ties with both European consumers and producers. The United

States has supported European integration, but has been quick to complain about the external impacts of EU policy. Clearly, most of these troubles have relate to the Common Agricultural Policy, since the United States competes in world markets with most of the other European products. From the "chicken war" of the 1960s to the hormone-injected beef ban of the 1980s, the EU and the United States have fought out the implications of either European standards or European dumping. Since the EU has committed to reform of the CAP, tensions have eased in this area. Tensions mounted with the formation of the Single Market in 1992. In the late 1980s, it seemed that the United States would not participate in the deregulation of European markets, especially concerning service industries like banking. Eventually, however, the EU extended concessions to the United States and did not exclude American firms from benefiting from the Single European Act.

In 1995, the EU and United States set about a New Transatlantic Agenda to establish the formal means of cooperation on political, strategic and economic policies, both concerning the signatories and the world. The Agenda establishes a New Transatlantic Marketplace, which is designed to reduce and eventually eliminate barriers hindering the trade of goods and factors between North America and Europe. In addition, it creates the format for regulatory agencies in both areas to communicate and cooperate so that existing nontariff barriers can be eliminated and new ones will not be created. Customs cooperation and mutual assistance programs are also envisioned to further cooperation between the two areas. The Agenda is an extremely ambitious undertaking that will create even stronger ties between the United States and Europe at a time when the Europeans are attempting to extend their own integration into strategic and political realms.

JAPAN AND KOREA

EU–Japanese relations have been rather remote and strained, mainly by the persistently large EU trade deficit with Japan. Like the United States, the EU has appealed to the Japanese to open markets and negotiate trade arrangements to increase EU exports. Member states had used the escape clause in the common commercial policy to establish voluntary export restraints (VERs) with Japan. With the onset of the single market, these various arrangements were consolidated in a uniform policy. A joint declaration was signed in 1991 to establish shared objectives in trade, and a consultation/resolution framework with annual meetings between the presidents of the European Council and the Commission and the Japanese prime minister. Agreements were reached in the sensitive automobile industry, with the EC agreeing to open up the European market after 1999. Until that time, though, the amount of Japanese car exports to Europe is virtually frozen.

Overall trade has been affected as well. In 1992, just after the declaration, EU15 exports were just about 50 percent of Japanese exports to the EU15; by 1995, EU15 exports had expanded so that now they were about 70 percent of

Japanese exports to the EU.[10] Part of the increase in European trade has resulted from the successes of the Trade Assessment Mechanism. This is a system that enables the EU and Japan to get together and compare the status of EU exports in other markets, such as in the United States and Canada, with the Japanese market. If anomalies are discovered, the countries can begin to negotiate on how to intervene. Through mid 1996, there have been sixteen meeting of statistical experts to evaluate over 100 products. Whether the declaration will continue to affect long-run change is yet to be seen, as the short-run is largely still managed by new VERs negotiated not by the member states, but by the EC itself. Japan has embarked on a three-year program, initiated in 1996, to deregulate internal markets so that European firms would have better access. Two years remain to the program. Whether vested interests in Japan will allow meaningful change will have to be seen in the coming years.

Most of Japanese involvement in Europe has been in the United Kingdom and the Netherlands, areas that account for about 61.8 percent of Japanese foreign direct investment in Europe. Still, Japanese presence has been relatively small. From 1951 to 1987 the EC12 received U.S. $20 billion in foreign direct investment from Japan, while over the same period the EC12 received more than U.S. $50 billion from the United States.[11] The EU would like to see more integration of the Japanese foreign direct investment in host countries through subcontracting European firms and establishing R&D centers in Europe. The source of most frustration, though, is in the relatively small amount of EU direct investment in Japan. Given the high fixed costs of investing in Japan and the high tax rates on dividends for foreign firms, European investment has been low in Japan.

Korea agreed to trade and cooperation agreements in 1995 to deepen economic relations between it and the EU and to ensure its entry into the OECD. In 1995, Korea was the EU's tenth biggest export market. Bilateral trade between Korea and the EU is about ECU 15 billion. Because of Korea's growing importance to member states, the Commission began negotiations in mid-1995 to establish the conditions for cooperation between the two areas. On October 28, 1996, Korea and the EU signed the first general accord agreement to arrange the basic provisions on economic cooperation and to strengthen the political dialogue between the two. The signing of the agreement came just three days after Korea joined the OECD and marks a new level of cooperation between Korea and the EU.

CONCLUSION

As the size and ambition of the European Union grows, its relationship with the rest of the world becomes more important. Europe now trades on a global basis, and it has trade and/or development agreements with just about every area of the world. Its relationship with EFTA, the closest of any of its relationships, has been dramatically changed by the accession of three former EFTA members. The European Union has been forced to look beyond Europe and to develop its relationships with other areas of the world. The expansion of the GATT arrangement and the creation of the World Trade Organization has forced the EU to pursue reforms within its own policies, most notably in agriculture. Just as much of the activity within the EU over the past decade has been about opening markets and reducing barriers among its members, its external policies have been to expand and deepen relationships across the globe. While it is true that the EU has not been overly generous in its economic concessions, it has established meaningful links with virtually every geographical area. The formation of the EU and its own political aspirations make the area an extremely important player in geopolitics. The triad of the United States–Japan–EU will be an increasingly important one, especially if the ambitious political union aspect of the TEU is realized.

EVALUATION

From the beginning of the process for economic and political integration of Europe, two advantages have been sought by European policy makers. One is strictly economic: to gain the efficiency that comes from increasing the extent of the market, whether it is achieved by realizing economies of scale in production and distribution or whether it is derived from the competitive forces that speed up technical progress. The other is mostly political, but can be put to economic ends: to gain the advantages that come from exercising greater bargaining power in negotiations with other economic powers. From the figures given in Table 8.1, which are a favorite element of comparison in EU publicity, it is clear that by 1995 the EU had gained the scale in terms of population and gross domestic product to be considered the world's leading economic power. However, in terms of per capita output, measured in purchasing power parity dollars, it is equally clear that fifty years of progress had still left them lagging well behind the other major industrial powers in terms of economic efficiency. Even tiny Luxembourg, which manages to enjoy the highest per capita income within the EU, lags well behind the United States. Apparently, the EU has still not managed to overcome the constraints of national sovereignty and bureaucratic inertia that have kept Europe as a whole from realizing the full possibilities of economies of scale, competitive technical progress, or bargaining power in the economic sphere. It may be an ironic twist of fate that the EU's successes with its political agenda have come at the expense of achieving the long-term goals on its economic agenda, at least in the 1990s. But this may be part of a longer term alternation between political and economic advances, an alternation that has characterized the process of European unification for the past half century.

Figures 8.1 and 8.2 compare the levels of per capita output and gross domestic product for all fifteen current member states with those of the United States, Japan, and Canada from 1960 to 1997. (The figures for 1996 and 1997 are projections made at the end of 1995 and are overoptimistic, especially for the EU.) The levels of both are measured in terms of purchasing power parity

TABLE 8.1
EU15 Compared with United States, Japan and Canada

Area:	Total		
	EU15	3,660,900 km^2	100.0 percent
	USA	9,372,600 km^2	280.9 percent
	Japan	337,800 km^2	10.1 percent
	Canada	9,976,100 km^2	299.0 percent
Population (1/1/1994)			
	EU15	374,963,800	100.0 percent
	USA	260,714,000	69.5 percent
	Japan	124,683,600	33.3 percent
	Canada	28,114,000	7.5 percent
Gross Domestic Product (1994)			
	EU15	$6,323.8 billion	100.0 percent
	USA	$6,419.5 billion	101.5 percent
	Japan	$2,481.9 billion	39.2 percent
	Canada	$564.1 billion	8.9 percent
Per Capita			
	EU15	$17,016	100 percent
	USA	$24,607	145 percent
	Japan	$19,856	117 percent
	Canada	$20,066	118 percent

Source: Eurostat, *Basic Statistics of the European Union,* 32nd ed. (Luxembourg, 1995, with updates from first quarter 1996); U.S. Department of Commerce, *Statistical Abstract of the United States, 1994;* and *OECD Economic Outlook, June 1996.*

dollars at the price levels of 1991, so they avoid the confusion created by the exchange rate volatility among the OECD countries that has existed since 1971, shown in the previous chapter (Figures 7.1a and b). If the economic logic of enlarged markets was at work to increase the efficiency of each economy as it entered the Common Market, then the average level of per capita output should have approached that of the United States over this period. After all, the United States had already exhausted all those gains by 1960, so further increases in per capita output could only come from technical progress or re-allocation of resources to more productive sectors. Given that the countries of the EU15 were well behind the United States in 1960, they should have been able to catch up by making more rapid increases in applied technology or in re-allocation of labor and capital. It is noteworthy that both Japan and Canada were able to do so, at least until 1990. But Europe, for whatever reason, could not and in the 1990s began to drop relative to the United States and Canada. From being less than $6,000 behind the U.S. level in 1960, it had dropped to nearly $8,000 behind in 1995. Japan had surpassed Europe in the early 1980s, and only the prolonged recession of the mid-1990s was pulling Japan back down toward EU15 levels. In terms of total GDP, the EU15 fell even farther behind the

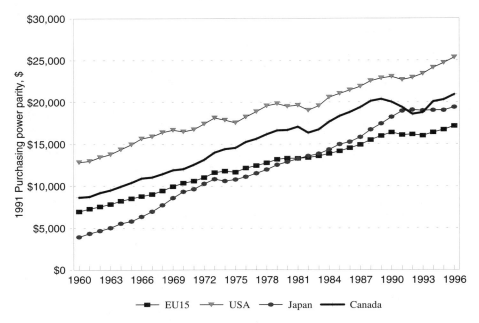

Figure 8.1. Levels of per capita income, 1960–96, EU15, United States, Japan, and Canada.

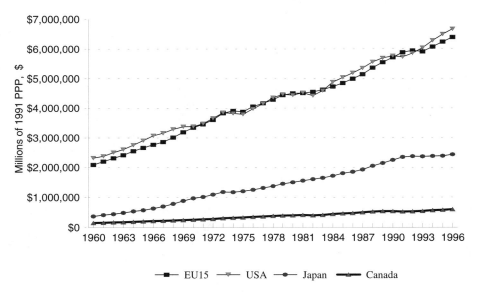

Figure 8.2. GDP levels, 1960–96, EU15, United States, Japan, and Canada.

United States, as the latter added over 82 million people to its population over the period 1960–95, and the EU15 added over 74 million. So much for the dynamic effects of economic unions!

Figures 8.3 and 8.4 compare the average (unweighted) rates of unemployment and inflation, which are the other two major indicators of success for economic policy. Unemployment rates for Europe were much lower and less volatile than in the United States until the early 1980s, when the U.S. rate dropped below the European. By the mid-1990s, unemployment was still falling in the United States, while it remained unpleasantly high among the EU15. Moreover, even with inflation, the United States performed better than the average of the EU15 countries throughout this period. This is certainly contrary to popular impression, but that impression rests upon observing the low inflation experience of Germany and assuming it is characteristic of all Europe. It is not, despite the enviable economic performance of Germany, which might have encouraged more emulation than it has. Evidently, the imitative impulses in the rest of Europe were too weak to be effective or were stifled by constraints imposed by the sovereign nation-states.

Referring back to the GDP levels graphed in Figure 8.2, it is striking that at times the total GDP of the EU15 has caught up with that of the United States, only to fall back again shortly. The first period of catch-up appears to coincide with the decade of the 1970s, actually surpassing the U.S. levels in 1974–77 and 1980–83, and again in 1990–91.

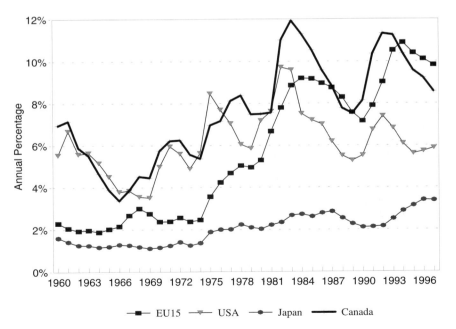

Figure 8.3. Unemployment rates, 1960–96, EU15, United States, Japan, and Canada.

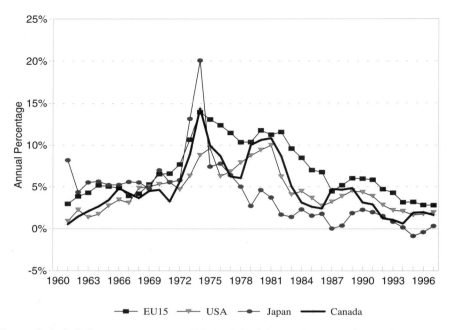

Figure 8.4. Inflation rates, 1961–97, EU15, United States, Japan, and Canada.

What is striking about these dates of overtaking is that they correspond to periods when the political consensus sustaining the institutions of the European Union was weakest. In 1974–77, the turmoil associated with the accession of three new members with quite different expectations about the benefits to be derived from the EU was exacerbated by the diversity of strategies employed by the individual countries to cope with the first oil shock. The second period was one of constant re-alignments in the Exchange Rate Mechanism of the European Monetary System in response to the "Volcker shock." And the period 1990–91 corresponds to the first travail over the collapse of the Soviet bloc and the reunification of East and West Germany. All these shocks were quickly confronted and overcome with renewed efforts at sustaining the forward march to European integration, both politically and economically, by measures agreed on within the context of the European Union decision making structure. Ironically, the political resolution of the European difficulties in each instance led to slackened economic growth, at least relative to growth in the United States. It is also interesting to note that increased political cohesion after each crisis should have increased the bargaining power of the EU relative to the United States, but apparently to little avail in economic terms. The apparent paradox is easily resolved once we understand the differences in political and economic goals that persist among the member countries. This is the objective of the following chapters.

Endnotes

1. Directorates I, IA, and IB share these responsibilities while working with Director-ate III on industrial cooperation and Directorate VIII on Lomé and other develop-ment matters.

2. Commission of the European Communities, (see Bibliography following), "The Eu-ropean Community as world trading partner," p. 193–4.

3. Lynden Moore, "Developments in Trade and Trade Policy," p. 304, in M Artis and N. Lee, eds., *The Economics of the European Union,* Oxford: Oxford University Press, 1994.

4. Carl B. Hamilton, *Textiles Trade and the Developing Countries: Eliminating the Multi-Fibre Arrangement in the 1990s.* Washington, D. C.: World Bank, 1990.

5. This certainly affected U.S. leverage. The threat of Vice President Dan Quayle in 1992 to remove U.S. troops from Europe because of EC unwillingness to cooperate in the Uruguay Round was not the threat it would have been five years earlier. D. Dinan, *Ever Closer Union?* Boulder, Colo.: Lynne Rienner Publishers, 1994, p. 441.

6. Current status of the agreements is updated on the DG1A website at http://euro-pa.eu.int/en/comm/dg1a/nis/pca/pca.htm.

7. The text for the agreement can be found at the DG1B website at http://europa.eu.-int/en/comm/dg1b/en/den-com95495.htm.

8. EUROPA website, address http://europa.eu.int/en/eupol/copad.html.

9. Commission of the EC, "The European Union and Latin America: The present situa-tion and prospects for closer partnership, 1996–2000," available at the DG1B web-site, http://europa.eu.int/en/comm/dg1b/en/den-com95495.htm.

10. Commission of the EC, "Overview of EU-Japan relations," July 1996, available at the DG1 website, http;//europa.eu.int/en/comm/dg01/pol35.htm.

11. Ali El-Agraa. "Japan's reaction to the single internal market," in John Redmond, ed., *The External Relations of the European Community,* New York: St. Martin's Press, 1992, p. 23.

Bibliography

Babarinde, Olufemi A. *The Lomé Conventions and Development: An Empirical Assessment.* Brookfield, Vt.: Avebury, 1994.

Chikeka, Charles Ohiri. *Africa and the European Economic Community, 1957–1992* Lew-iston, N.Y.: E. Mellen Press, 1993.

Coffey, Peter. *The EC and the United States* New York : St. Martin's Press, 1993.

Commission of the European Communities. "The European Community as a world trade partner," in *European Economy* 52, Brussels, 1993. A good overview of the direction, size, and importance of European trade. The report also details European special regional arrangements.

Commission of the EC. *Agreement Amending the Fourth ACP-EC Convention of Lomé signed in Mauritius on 4 November 1995.* Brussels: ACP-EEC Council of Ministers, 1996.

Commission of the EC. *The Community and the Third World.* Luxembourg : Office for Official Publications of the European Communities, 1993.

Commission of the EC. *The European Community and Latin America.* Luxembourg: Office for Official Publications of the European Communities, 1991.

McAleese, Dermot. *Africa and the European Community after 1992.* Washington, D.C.: World Bank, 1993.

Peterson, John. *Europe and America : the prospects for partnership* London; New York: Routledge, 1996. Short description of the growing relationship between the EC and Latin America.

Thomsen, Stephen and Phedon Nicolaides. *The Evolution of Japanese Direct Investment in Europe.* London: Harvester Wheatsheaf, 1991. Details the concentration of Japanese investment.

Worldwide web. See http://europa.eu.int/en/eupol/exrel.html for excellent summaries of EU relations with areas of the world. See also http://europa.eu.int/eu.int/en/comm/dg01/policies.htm for excellent material on recent changes along with detailed reports on external relations policies, updated often.

PART
II
The Economies of Europe

CHAPTER 9

Germany:

From Division to Reunification

Basic Facts		
Area:	356,900 km²	11.0 % of EU
Population (1/1/94):	81,338,100	22.0 % of EU
GDP:	$1,397.8 billion	23.4 % of EU
Per capita:	$17,211	106 % of EU average
Openness (X + M/GDP)	38 %	51 % with EU12

Source: Eurostat, *Basic Statistics of the European Union,* 32nd ed. (Luxembourg, 1995).

INTRODUCTION

Germany's problems and policies are more important than ever for the European Union, because its size and relative weight within the EU have increased sharply and permanently since the reunification of West Germany with East Germany in 1990. And Germany's problems are bigger as well, mostly because of the way reunification has been carried out. By 1995–96, Chancellor Helmut Kohl was making valiant efforts to liberalize the West German economy along lines initiated by the Americans and British and to reduce West German tax rates while liberalizing its labor markets and privatizing some state enterprises.

The German Economic and Monetary Union of July 1990 set the economic terms for reunifying East Germany (German Democratic Republic) with West Germany. The essential feature of German monetary union, which has plagued German policymakers ever since, was to overvalue the East German currency and therefore the money wages of East German workers. It did this by setting the exchange rate of the deutsche mark, the West German currency, with the ostmark, the East German currency, at close to 1:1, so that on average only 1.2

ostmarks were required to purchase one deutsche mark. Any realistic exchange rate would have required at least six ostmarks and perhaps as many as twelve to purchase one deutsche mark. The political consequences of this decision were dramatic: the East German voters, recognizing how advantageous these economic terms were, voted in a referendum held in April 1990 to abolish the East German state and to join West Germany on the terms provided in the Basic Law of the Federal Republic of Germany. The Basic Law has always specifically allowed new states, or *Länder,* to be added. The five new states that comprised the former East Germany were then formally added to the Federal Republic of Germany in October 1990. With this reunification of Germany, a formal peace treaty was signed with the Federal Republic of Germany by the Allied Powers of France, Great Britain, the Soviet Union, and the United States. Germany became once again a fully sovereign nation-state.

The economic price for this long-sought political prize has proven to be much higher than anticipated. Part of the reason is the hubris of West German policymakers in 1989, who, knowing that the East German economy was at most 10 percent the size of the West German economy, felt that absorbing the most advanced and competitive economy of the Eastern bloc would be well within the capability of the most advanced and competitive economy of Western Europe. But the major part of the increased price has been the realization of just how backward and uncompetitive were the infrastructure, technology, and machinery of East Germany compared with Western standards. This meant that East German wages and prices, now set in West German deutsche marks, were too high to be competitive in the West German market. Unemployment rose sharply in East Germany, whose workers were now entitled to unemployment benefits on the generous West German standards. These payments added to the financing burden of West Germany. East German backwardness also meant, however, that the costs of reunification now included the costs of rebuilding the entire infrastructure of East Germany. Everything—roads, electric power generation and transmission facilities, railroads, airports, telephone systems, water and sewage treatment and distribution plants—had to be rebuilt to bring it up to West German standards.

These costs are being met almost entirely by West Germans. A special "reunification tax" has been levied on West Germans and higher VAT rates imposed on all consumption goods. The European Union, as explained in previous chapters, is not capable of contributing adequate resources to meet this kind of shock. Moreover, it has objected to making the East German states eligible for structural funds designated for backward regions or even for counting East German farm production under the provisions of the Common Agricultural Policy, given its limited budget. The possibility of foreign investment in the privatized enterprises of East Germany was sought by the Treuhandanstalt, a temporary agency set up by West Germany to dispose of the state enterprises of former East Germany. But the problems of high wages, obsolete plant and equipment, and deficient infrastructure were especially discouraging to foreign investors who lacked the cultural and family ties with East Germany that many West German firms possessed.

The problems of mobilizing sufficient resources to bring East Germany up to the economic level of West Germany have been made worse by the restrictive monetary policy of the Bundesbank. The central bank of unified Germany momentarily lost control in 1990 of the German money supply when East German ostmarks were converted into deutsche marks at fixed conversion rates. But between the fall of the Berlin Wall in November 1989 and the establishment of German Economic and Monetary Union in July 1990, the East German government produced many more ostmarks. The result when they were converted into deutsche marks was an unusually sharp rise (by West German standards) in the price level. The Bundesbank responded by curtailing the growth of the future money supply. This strengthened the deutsche mark on the foreign exchanges, which was good for paying for the imports required to rebuild East Germany, but bad for the traditional export-based industry of West Germany.

The strengthening of the deutsche mark as a result of the Bundesbank's response to the currency union with East Germany also meant that EC members of the European Monetary System saw their currencies strengthen and their exports other than to Germany and each other fall off. The result was a marked slowing in real output, a rise in already high unemployment rates, and an actual decline in real output per capita throughout the European Union starting in 1990. In this sense, Germany's EMS partners are paying a price as well for Germany's reunification, but as their lower incomes reduce their demand for German exports, their economic slowdown makes it even more difficult for West Germany to bear the costs of reunification. West Germany's unfortunate experience with the costs of reconstructing East Germany, the most advanced of the Eastern bloc nations, has also cast a pall over the European Union's enthusiasm for extending aid to the transition economies of Central and East Europe.

MACROECONOMIC POLICY INDICATORS: 1960–97

Figure 9.1 traces out the growth rates, inflation rates, and unemployment rates of West Germany from 1960 through 1990, and of unified Germany from 1990 on. The growth rate of real GDP[1] shows clearly that the economic miracle of the 1950s was slowing down in the 1960s. The underlying causes were mainly a slowdown in the rate of population growth, mostly due to falling birth rates and partly due to the Berlin Wall cutting off the refugee flow from East Germany. To the extent that this was offset by importing larger numbers of guest workers, technical progress in German industry was discouraged. Despite the signs of longer term problems, unemployment rates remained very low and inflation was kept low, so that the West German economy was still the marvel of Europe.

The first oil shock of 1974 raised unemployment rates (permanently, as it turned out), and initially reduced growth rates to an absolute decline in 1975. These recovered dramatically, however, in comparison with those of the rest of Europe, until the second oil shock in 1979. Perhaps the reason for both phe-

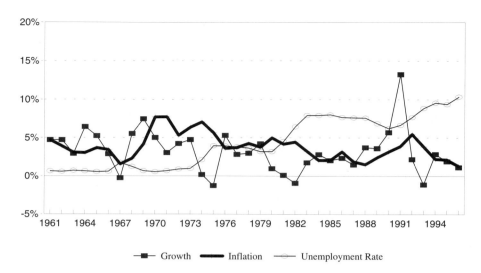

Figure 9.1. Macroeconomic policy indicators, Germany, 1961–96.

nomena was the striking control over inflation rates that was maintained by the Bundesbank in a period when inflation in the rest of the industrialized countries typically exceeded 10 percent. In the post-Bretton Woods period of floating exchange rates, the relatively low rate of inflation in Germany compared with its major trading partners meant a substantial strengthening of the deutsche mark in the foreign exchanges. Because oil was priced in dollars, each strengthened deutsche mark could purchase more dollars, and therefore more oil. While Germany's exports were hurt by the stronger deutsche mark, which raised their price to foreign customers, the costs of producing these goods were reduced in that the costs of imported raw materials and fuel were reduced.

Germany's success in weathering the first oil shock with this strong currency strategy encouraged its closest economic partners in the European Community to imitate the strategy. The central banks of Italy and France, unlike the Bundesbank, were completely under the control of their respective central governments. So they had first to get the agreement of their governments to restrict the growth of their money supply. This they accomplished by establishing the European Monetary System in 1978, described in Chapter 5, which required them and the Benelux countries, Denmark, and Ireland to maintain exchange rate stability with the deutsche mark and each other's currencies. To do this, of course, required them to restrict the growth of their respective money supplies to the rate established by the Bundesbank for the Germany money supply. The second oil shock in 1979–80, however, disrupted the exchange rates agreed on and cast some doubt on the wisdom of Germany's restrictive monetary policy as well. While inflation remained under control, Germany's unemployment rate was notched up permanently another few percentage points and its growth rate fell to the lowest levels since World War II.

A change of government from the Social Democratic party led by Helmut

Schmidt to the Christian Democratic party led by Helmut Kohl occurred in summer 1982. Chancellor Kohl has led West Germany ever since. Initially, Kohl chose to challenge the strength of German unions, whose continued wage demands despite low inflation, one could argue, had kept Germany from increasing exports at a time when the deutsche mark was relatively weak compared with the U. S. dollar. But the strong dollar did not increase imports from Europe; rather it led to increased imports from Asia and Latin America. Moreover, the British economy was then showing renewed vitality (Chapter 11) under Prime Minister Margaret Thatcher's vigorous liberalization policies. But German economic performance did not improve under Kohl until the Single Market initiative began to take effect and Spain and Portugal entered the European Community—their combined effect showed up after 1987. In common with the rest of oil-importing Europe, Germany also benefited from the collapse of oil prices in 1986, the third oil shock.

German exports boomed to the rest of the now expanded European Community in anticipation of the growth potential of the Single Market to be achieved by the end of 1992. Growth rates rose to near the levels of the wonderful 1960s; unemployment, while still high, began to decline noticeably. Only inflation seemed troublesome as it began to rise to levels high enough by 1990 to make the Bundesbank nervous. We shall never know how long this renewed growth would have lasted under the scenario envisioned by the European Community, which was to incorporate the rest of Western Europe into the customs union after the completion of the Single Market. As the member states of the European Free Trade Area were all trading partners principally with West Germany, the free trade area for German exporters would have expanded and German economic policy would have been focused on exploiting these trade opportunities. So the growth spurt could have continued for at least a few more years.

History, with the helping hand of Helmut Kohl, changed course in 1990 with the reunification of Germany. East Germany, larger in population than any of the EFTA member states whose applications for membership were being delayed until after completion of the Single Market, was immediately absorbed into West Germany—and into the European Community as well. The consequence is that an entirely new set of challenges and possibilities for the German economy have been created, quite independently of the internal dynamic of European unification embodied in the institutional framework of the European Union. As Figure 9.1 shows, however, the German policymakers have largely responded to date by maintaining the courses of action that have sustained them since the end of World War II. The initial inflationary impulse of reunification, caused by the conversion of many more ostmarks than anticipated into deutsche marks, has been rapidly brought under control by the Bundesbank. The cost has been to increase unemployment to yet higher levels, concentrated in the East, but still higher than before reunification in the West. And growth, initially projected to regain its pre-1990 rates, has stagnated at the levels of the early 1980s. But a few years of adversity in the face of an enormous challenge are not going to undo all at once the policy framework that had proven so successful for Germany for forty years.

WIRTSCHAFTSWUNDERZEIT: 1945–57

It was up to the four Allied Powers—the United States, the Soviet Union, the United Kingdom, and France—to decide what to do with Germany after its complete defeat and unconditional surrender on May 8, 1945. Agreement had already been reached at the Yalta Conference in February 1945, which included only Roosevelt, Stalin, and Churchill, that postwar Germany would be divided up among them and administered jointly from Berlin. Basically, the Soviet Union took the eastern third including Berlin, Britain the northern third including the great ports of Hamburg and Bremen and the industrial heartland of the Ruhr, and the United States assumed responsibility for the southern third. France was included for one of the occupation zones, but the Rheinland-Pfalz and Saarland Länder and the southern halves of the Baden and Württemberg Länder had to be carved out of the American zone to constitute it. These arrangements were confirmed and clarified at the Potsdam Conference in July 1945 attended this time by Truman (Roosevelt had died in office in April), Stalin, and Churchill/Attlee (Attlee replaced Churchill during the conference due to the British elections). France objected to the terms immediately, as it had not been represented at either Yalta or Potsdam. Both France and Russia wanted reparations in kind and as soon as possible. The British resisted the idea of reparations in principle, while the Americans maintained ambivalence, most charitably explained by a desire to hold the wartime alliance together as long as possible. Due to differences in objectives among the Allies and to changed leadership in the United States and the United Kingdom, conflicts arose immediately among the Allies over the implementation of the Potsdam Agreements.

The French occupation zone included the coal resources of the Saarland, which provided the most economical way of smelting and refining the iron ore of Lorraine. French hopes were that continued occupation would lead eventually to incorporating the Saarland into France, much as Alsace-Lorraine had been incorporated into Germany from 1871 to 1914 and again from 1940 to 1944. But even these coal resources were deemed inadequate for French purposes of reconstruction, so French policy became focused on gaining access to the coal and iron facilities of the Ruhr Basin, which had been assigned to the British. Like the French, the Russians wanted to dismantle the factories of Germany to eliminate the threat of renewed armament or, perhaps, to replace their own factories that had been destroyed during the war. While they had access to the industrial plants of Silesia (now considered part of Poland), Upper Saxony, and Brandenberg, the bulk of the factories lay in the Ruhr, which was in the British zone. They repeatedly proposed placing the Ruhr under international supervision so that a large part of its output could be directed to rebuilding efforts outside Germany. The Americans were left with responsibility for maintaining order among a growing population of refugees with a large occupation army, both of which could only be supplied through the British zone.

As these conflicting objectives for access to the British zone were played out, the British found the expenses of maintaining a large standing army and caring for a large refugee population in their area of Germany, the one most flattened by Allied bombing, to be simply overwhelming. Their policy, born out of immediate expense and remembrance of reparations failures after World War I, quickly came to be reconstructing German industry and rebuilding housing in their zone. American official policy was presumed to be given by the infamous Morgenthau Plan, in which the American Secretary of the Treasury proposed to dismember Germany politically, dismantle its factories, and maintain per capita income in Germany at the lowest level in Europe. This would ensure an end to the German problem, which had caused three major wars in Europe in less than a century. American military forces occupying the American zone, however, found that they had the expense of housing and clothing millions of refugees from the East, and this had to be done to maintain any kind of order. So they never implemented the Morgenthau Plan in practice, save for continuing the dismemberment of Germany politically for awhile. By September 1946, American policy was converging to the British policy in practice. It was mutually convenient for both to combine operation of their zones from January 1947 on as Bizonia. This became the basis for the formation of the Federal Republic of Germany established as a separate, independent (but not yet sovereign) state in May 1949, which now included the French zone as well. This was the final result of four years of experimentation and conflict among the victorious Allies of how to deal with defeated Germany. The new state of West Germany was clearly committed to cooperation with the Allies in the rebuilding of Western Europe. We'll discuss in following chapters how committed were other Europeans to the restoration of German economic might, but clearly both the Americans and British were. Their consensus provided the political framework within which Germany's economic miracle occurred.

Economic historians in recent years have revised considerably our view of how miraculous was the economic recovery of Germany from World War II. Certainly to observers at the time, the devastation wrought by the Allied round-the-clock bombing for two years and the complete overrunning of German territory by the methodical advances of the Russian and American armies seemed total and as unconditional as the surrender extracted from Admiral Dönitz in May 1945. The reemergence of West Germany as the strongest economy in Europe by the mid-1950s seemed an incredible tribute to the combination of German work ethic and American generosity. Scholars sifting through the archival materials that have become increasingly available in the past twenty years, however, have identified more mundane factors that help explain both the miracle of recovery and the role that Germany played in the economic integration of Western Europe.[2]

The first revision to come was the reassessment of the loss of capital stock to the German economy caused both by the brutal combination of Allied bombing, artillery barrages in the ground advance, and the "scorched earth" defensive strategy of retreating German forces. Allied bombing, it turned out, flattened buildings and disrupted transportation links, especially at harbors and railyards, but left machines largely intact. German factory managers were explicitly ordered by Albert Speer, the minister in charge of armaments production, to not destroy the machinery but rather disable the abandoned plants so they could be restarted quickly in recovery from defeat. In fact, the capital stock of just the West German economy was larger at the end of the war than at the beginning, thanks to the large investments made during the war. Moreover, it was readily convertible to production of civilian goods, unlike much of the British and American manufacturing plant that used specialized machinery for mass production of military items. So the German economic miracle began with excess capacity in its relatively modern and up-to-date manufacturing capital stock.

The second revision came in reassessing the refugee and displaced person problem. Approximately 11 million individuals poured into the Western occupation zones of Germany in the ten years after the war. Nearly the same number left Germany—inmates of concentration camps, prisoners of war, and foreign workers—but the total population of postwar Germany, including the Soviet zone and Berlin, had actually grown over 10 percent from May 1939 to October 1946. Importantly, it had shifted location considerably, out of the great cities such as Berlin and Hamburg and into more rural areas of Schleswig-Holstein, Lower Saxony, and Bavaria. Internal as well as international migration was the dominating characteristic of the German population.[3] Moreover, the new population was German speaking, and after 1950, when 3.6 million refugees fled the Soviet zone to come to West Germany, it was well educated and at prime working ages. Perhaps most important, all 11 million immigrants as well as the larger number of internal migrants were highly motivated to work hard and save stringently to restore their material situation as quickly as possible. Hence, the excess capacity of West German manufacturing plant could be staffed immediately by new workers eager for employment and easily trained. Ironically, the Russian policy of pushing Germans out of Eastern Europe and encouraging them to leave even East Germany provided more aid to the recovery of the West German economy than all of the American aid.

Marshall Plan aid did not materialize until early 1948, by which time the forces described above had already served to begin economic recovery at a rapid rate. Moreover, the total aid given to Germany was substantially less than that given to Britain and France and even less than that provided Italy. (American aid of $1.62 billion given under the GARIOA (Government and Relief in Occupied Areas) program until mid-1950, however, slightly exceeded the $1.56 billion given under the Marshall Plan.[4] Even as a share of total capital formation, German Marshall Plan aid was small, save in the first year. Nevertheless, Alan Kramer argues that even the aid to Britain and France was important for Germany's recovery, for two reasons. First, American aid to its Western Allies removed their claim on Germany's industrial plant for reparations, which removed much of the uncertainty over final ownership of Germany's excess capacity and allowed German entrepreneurs to resume restoring and converting their capital stock to civilian production. Second, the Marshall Plan aid was directed into sectors such as cement, coal, and electricity where price controls were maintained, which discouraged private investment in these vital sectors.

The currency reform of June 1948 marked a sudden resurgence of the German recovery, which seemed to have stalled out in the months preceding. Part of the reason for the temporary slump was the severe winter, following the very severe winter of 1946–47, but most of it probably stemmed from the withholding of goods from the market until the new currency, the deutsche mark, was actually introduced into circulation. A large informal, quasi-barter economy had arisen in the meantime awaiting currency reform. The occupation currency introduced by the Allies quickly depreciated, since there was no central control of the amount issued. So the easiest way to pay occupation expenses (and extract reparations in kind for the French and Russians) was to issue more of the currency—a case of competitive seigniorage. Germans in the Western zones avoided the price and wage uncertainty created by the depreciation of the occupation currency by substituting other universally recognized standards of value, namely American cigarettes and chewing gum.

The new currency was issued just for the combined American and British zones (Bizonia), and the issue was strictly controlled by the incipient central bank, the Bank Deutscher Länder. The Russians responded by creating their own currency for their occupation zone and imposing the blockade on Berlin. The French responded by combining their occupation zone, which had been carved out of the American zone in the first place, with Bizonia, thereby creating, briefly, Trizonia. The terms of the currency reform are interesting in light of the similar transition problems faced in the early 1990s by the former Communist countries, and especially by the soaking up of the East German currency that occurred in July 1990. The deutsche mark was exchanged one to one for the first forty old Reichsmarks in June 1948. In two months another 20 deutsche mark could be obtained again at the one to one rate. But all other financial assets, checking and savings accounts to mortgages and insurance policies, were cashed in at the rate of 1 deutsche mark per 10 RM. In other words, the money supply in one fell swoop was reduced by nearly 90 percent. Holders of physical assets such as inventories of merchandise, factories, land, or houses benefited greatly. Savers in financial assets were again, as after World War I, wiped out. The incentives to the West German population were clear: to obtain more than 60 DM of the new money they had to be willing to put either their real assets or their labor skills on the market.

Contrary to the advice of the Allied economists, Ludwig Erhard, a free market economist appointed by the Allies to be finance minister of the new West German government, removed most price controls. This temporarily boosted prices of consumer goods, encouraging dishoarding by merchants and also generating increased tax revenues for the government via their turnover taxes, excise duties, and customs revenues. Erhard's gamble may have been driven mostly by his laissez-faire ideology, but his confidence must have been boosted by observing the Italian success in the previous year with lifting price controls rapidly. Moreover, he maintained rent controls and rationing for some basic foods, as well as price controls on utilities and basic coal and steel supplies for industry. This meant that both supply and demand could expand for manufactured consumer goods without quickly running into constraints of rising prices for inputs on the supply side or of consumer essentials on the demand side. It also meant that workers could accept continued low wages, knowing they would be adequate to provide at least housing and basic food. Further work effort was stimulated by exempting overtime wages from income tax. Whatever the innate propensity of Germans to work hard, they were certainly given the appropriate incentives by Erhard!

While the economic demands of the uprooted and impoverished Germans were strongest for scarce consumer goods, the productive capacity of the West German manufacturing sector was best suited for producer goods. These were precisely what was needed in the rest of war-torn Europe, however, so the resurgent German economy was export oriented from the beginning of the recovery process. Further expansion of Germany's productive capacity in these sectors was encouraged by accelerated depreciation allowances on investment for the tax liabilities of business firms. The tight money policy followed by the Bank Deutscher Länder tended even then to raise the value of the deutsche mark relative to the currencies of its trading partners, which would have hurt exports had there been any major competition. In September 1949, however, in common with the other European countries, the deutsche mark was devalued by one-third. Even so, future European demand for German machine tools, equipment, and vehicles might very well have been limited had it not been for the creation of the European Payments Union in 1950 and the fillip to export demand for the Europeans that was created by American financing of the Korean War. But with that, the West German economy was firmly on its course of export-led growth, which continued until, ironically, the creation of the Common Market in 1958. To reprise, the key elements in the German economic miracle of the period 1948–58 were excess capacity for the production of producers goods, an elastic supply of well-educated, highly motivated workers, and an incentive structure that permitted rising standards of living for moderately paid German workers thanks to an appreciating deutsche mark. These were exceptional conditions, which help in large part to explain why the German growth experience in this period was also exceptional.

SLOWING DOWN: 1958–73

While 1958 was marked by a brief slowdown in the rate of expansion of the Germany economy, in common with the rest of Western Europe, the turning point in its miracle period has to be 1961. In this year the Berlin Wall was erected to complete the closure of the border between East and West Germany in order to stop the flow of refugees, which it did. The free movement of labor within the Common Market, mandated by the Treaty of Rome, might have been expected to induce an influx of Italian workers into Germany to make up the shortfall of labor required to staff the still rapidly expanding capital stock of Germany. In fact, the Common Market increased the export opportunities for Italian manufacturers and their demand for labor rose, reducing the supply of Italian laborers to the rest of Europe. Accustomed to docile labor recruited from the underemployed population of the German countryside or from the exploited population of East Germany, German industry responded by initiating the Gastarbeiter (guest worker) program.

The Gastarbeiter program succeeded wildly. Meanwhile, German capital stock continued to grow as it became the favorite destination for direct investment by British and American firms. Firms that had been exporting to Germany with its growing demand for consumer goods and low tariff barriers now were partly concerned that their German market might be lost thanks to a high common external tariff but were mostly eager to have a European base from which to export to the rest of the Common Market, where high tariffs and quantity restrictions had kept them out previously. It was natural for British firms to locate in the British occupation zone and for American firms to locate in the American zone, comprising the southern Länder of Hessia, Baden-Württemberg, and Bavaria. These became the growth poles of German expansion in the 1960s, and the destination of choice for the guest workers. These were recruited from various countries, originally Spain, then Yugoslavia, and finally Turkey. Turkey, with its large, growing population and rapid structural change as a result of being an American military client state, proved capable of supplying all the workers German industry could desire. German workers did not mind as much as one might think from later developments because their superior education and prior training kept them in superior jobs, whereas the temporary foreign workers took the lowest paying, least skilled positions available. By 1971, Germany's export-led economic expansion had raised its share of world trade to 10 percent, nearly the same share enjoyed by the German Empire in 1913 (12.1 percent).[5]

German firms could continue to be competitive in their export markets by lowering their average unit costs thanks to the low-paid guest worker taking the least skilled positions. But the rate of investment also slowed down, because German export markets had also slowed their growth and German firms were barely able to keep their market shares built up over the past decade. Investment that did occur was designed to make maximum use of the elastic supply of low paid, unskilled foreigners. This meant it was not as technologically advanced as capital invested by competitors not so favorably supplied with cheap labor, such as the United States.

The use of guest workers for low-skill jobs also meant that these entry level jobs were not available for on-the-job training for young Germans or for German women. German youth remained committed to the apprenticeship program funded jointly by the government and by business. This was and still is a model program for providing access to human capital for the native population of a country. But it is inflexible in the numbers trained for each skill and occupation. So slow growing sectors will have a backlog of potential entrants, who are forced into unemployment while waiting for a job appropriate to their training to open, while rapidly expanding sectors will have unfilled positions. The option of guest workers enabled export-oriented firms to meet their labor requirements without urging changes in the composition of apprentices in their favor. Moreover, it discouraged German women from entering the labor force in greater numbers, so that their participation rate in the labor force failed to rise any further during the 1960s. It is true that women's education levels rose substantially as Germany expanded greatly its institutions of higher learning and filled them up largely by admitting women.

To sum up, the reliance on foreign workers for continued growth of labor inputs until 1973 enabled Germany's Golden Age to continue, albeit at gradually reduced rates of growth and of investment. But it stored up future problems in that capital equipment installed was not at the cutting edge of modern technology, exports remained concentrated in product lines whose markets were not expanding as rapidly as before, and the stock of human capital in the manufacturing sector was no longer growing as rapidly as in the 1950s.

THE THREE OIL SHOCKS: 1974–85

If the shock of the Berlin Wall was insufficient to change the growth strategy of West Germany, one might wonder whether the oil shocks beginning in October 1973 might not do the trick. Actually, the German strategy for confronting the oil shocks had already been established in the way it dealt with the earlier shock of the collapse of the Bretton Woods system in August 1971. The Bundesbank, the successor to the Bank Deutscher Länder in 1957, was committed to maintaining price stability within Germany. In a world of rising prices, led by a rapidly growing supply of U.S. dollars in the international economy, this meant a steady appreciation of the deutsche mark. In the era of fixed nominal exchange rates, lasting from 1949 to 1971, the deutsche mark would depreciate if West Germany kept a lower rate of domestic inflation than existed in its trading partners. The Bundesbank was committed to this strategy by law, in order to prevent any risk that the financial assets of small savers might be dissipated by inflation, as had happened after both World War I and World War II. Part of the reason German industry could keep nominal wage increases low was that German workers were assured that their pensions would maintain their real purchasing power after retirement, thanks to the antiinflation commitment of the Bundesbank.

When exchange rates became flexible in 1971, the nominal exchange rate of the deutsche mark rose sharply relative to most of its trading partners, including the United States. This raised the price of German export goods to its customers, unless German producers either lowered their prices in terms of deutsche marks or raised the quality of the product to the foreign importers. In fact, they did both, but either strategy decreased profit rates and led to lower rates of investment in Germany. On the benefit side, the cost of imports was reduced. This kept down wage demands insofar as German consumers could benefit from lower prices of imported consumer goods, and it reduced the costs to German industry of a wide range of raw materials and intermediate goods, including imported petroleum.

One of the ways German exporters had raised the quality of their products to foreign buyers was to move beyond producing a variety of specialized machinery to setting up entire "turnkey" factories, especially in developing world countries trying to build up a modern manufacturing sector from scratch. The idea was that at final delivery, the buyer would simply turn the key on and the factory would be ready to produce at full capacity immediately. Payment for such factories was arranged through long-term contracts in which the customer would deliver intermediate products to the German exporter for a number of years at fixed, below market, prices. A wide range of such deals were quickly completed with Iran, for example, at the outset of the first oil shock in October 1973. These arrangements, actually initiated with the Shah of Iran's father by Hjalmar Schacht in the 1930s, continued to provide strong trading relationships between Germany and Iran through the overthrow of the Shah in 1978 and into the 1990s. The combination of such fixed price contracts for the long-term delivery of oil and the continued appreciation of the deutsche mark relative to the dollar helped Germany weather the effects of the first oil shock much better than, say, Italy or France.

Nevertheless, the oil shock caused sharp reductions in demand throughout Europe, Germany's primary export market, and the German output fell as well with a noticeable rise in unemployment rates. Attention turned to the presence of the guest workers, who, it was felt, should be returned promptly to their home countries, preserving their jobs for Germans. Unfortunately for this strategy, which had great appeal politically, German employers had concentrated their employment of guest workers at only one or two stages of the production process. Eliminating all of them in any one firm, therefore, meant closing down the entire production process until new workers could be found to replace them. And the new workers would have to be willing to accept the low wages and status that went with that part of the production line. It turned out not to be feasible to solve the unemployment problem by simply eliminating the foreign workers. Moreover, a surprisingly large number of such workers had proven so valuable for their employers that they had been in the country for as long as ten years. That meant they could apply for German citizenship, and in any case they were eligible for unemployment relief, as long as they stayed in the Federal Republic. To discourage this, the government tried at first to bribe them to return to their home country, usually Turkey. But the amounts required to get any response turned out to be higher than the government felt it could afford. The next alternative attempted was to eliminate children's allowances for any German employee whose children were not physically present in Germany. This led to an influx of fresh foreign immigrants, comprising primarily of children and their mothers, grandparents, and aunts to take care of them. The problem of the Turkish population for German social stress was only alleviated when employment opportunities increased in Turkey itself for a period of time in the mid to late 1980s.

The social stresses within the Federal Republic were heightened by the second oil shock of 1978–79. Unemployment rose again and the economic miracle seemed definitely at an end. It didn't help that after the OPEC oil ministers doubled the price of oil again in dollars in 1979 that the U.S. dollar began to strengthen relative to the European currencies, including the deutsche mark, in 1980. This exacerbated the effects of the second oil shock for all of Europe including Germany. The underlying institutional arrangements that had propelled Germany back to the preeminent economy of Europe came under renewed scrutiny. Wendy Carlin identifies three key institutions that differentiated Germany from much of southern Europe and certainly from the United States and the United Kingdom. These are: (1) the co-determination principle of corporate governance, which requires each German corporation to have on its board of directors representatives of its labor force and of the general public; (2) an elaborate system of apprentice training jointly administered by federal, state and local governments as well as private businesses; and (3) universal banking practiced in the financial sector, so that banks lending to business could also own part of the borrowing firms.[6]

Co-determination had the initial benefit of satisfying German workers that if the profits of the firms employing them went up as a result of their moderate wage demands, these profits in turn would be used to expand capacity and create more jobs. The presence of union leaders on the board of directors meant that business managers, in turn, could be confident that wage demands would be kept down long enough to allow new investments to become profitable. This device for coordinating the decision-making process of management (to invest or not to invest) and labor (to strike or not to strike) may have been instrumental in moderating German labor union demands for wages, maintaining high rates of investment by German business, and keeping unemployment rates low until the oil shocks of the 1970s. Of course, an elastic supply of labor, first from Eastern Europe under Soviet domination, then from East Germany, and finally from Yugoslavia and Turkey, helped do the same things.

When the effects of the second oil shock kept persisting into the early 1980s, however, the negative aspects of co-determination received more attention. If labor shedding, downsizing, or purging the work force became necessary to maintain competitiveness in an industry, then labor and consumer interests represented on boards of directors were sure to resist. In short, the institutional device was useful for its initial purpose—to establish the legitimacy of the new capitalist economic system in a country imbued with a corporatist tradition—but dysfunctional for making rapid adjustments to changed economic conditions.

The second institution, an active apprentice program in industry available to all German school leavers on a competitive basis, kept up the level of human capital in the German economy. By its design, it combined generally useful skills of literacy and numeracy through the formal education system with specifically targeted skills in particular trades through the apprenticeship service. Apprentices completing their term of service found employment readily with the company they had served. German industry could underpay entry level workers while they were apprentices and part-time students and after prescreening and training them hire them in as fully productive members of the production team. This avoided the free-rider problem caused when firms might lose young workers to competitors after having invested time and money in training them to be productive in their own system. The benefits of this system were clear with a stable structure of occupations in the economy, which was the case through the 1950s and the 1960s. But faced with the structural changes required to meet the challenges of the successive oil shocks in the 1970s, the system was inflexible. Occupations with stagnating employment opportunities continued to be supplied with trained apprentices, who waited longer and longer for appropriate jobs to open up that would reward them for the skills acquired. Meanwhile, sectors where demand was rising rapidly found it difficult to recruit new workers, the most promising of whom were already committed to prior apprentice programs.

The third institution, the close relationship between German banks and business firms, has been much admired in the rest of Europe and indeed in many developing countries. The theoretical advantages of banks taking equity in the companies borrowing from them have been spelled out clearly. Being privy to management decisions made by a business customer helps remove what economists call asymmetric information. This means that borrowers are much better informed about what they intend to do with the proceeds of a loan and how well their project is paying off than are their creditors. This is especially the case with stock or bond holders in the American or British financial systems, who typically only observe how the capital markets evaluate their financial assets and know little about the operations of the companies issuing their stocks and bonds. The down side of such close relationships is becoming clearer to the Germans, especially in the 1990s, but has long been appreciated in economic theory (as well as in Anglo-American banking practice). This is that the bank itself can become hostage to bad business decisions in which it may have participated or approved initially. Moreover, knowing the intentions and probity of an individual business person is no guarantee that his or her product will sell profitably in a rapidly changing and competitive marketplace.

To sum up, the vaunted institutions of West Germany, all of which certainly helped maintain its exceptional growth record in the golden age of 1950–73, proved increasingly incapable of meeting the challenges of the 1980s and 1990s. Expanding exports continued to be the key to general economic success in the Germany that had emerged after World War II, and increasingly the best way to expand exports was to expand the market it had come to dominate, the European Economic Community. This was the fourth, and perhaps most important, institution maintaining Germany's economic success. This explains the eagerness of Germany to expand the membership of the EEC, bringing in Britain, Ireland, and Denmark in the first expansion of 1973, then the premature accession of Greece in 1981, and finally the inclusion of Spain and Portugal in 1986.

FROM SINGLE MARKET TO UNITED GERMANY: 1986–96

A number of positive events occurred in 1986 to reinvigorate the German economy and rouse it from the prolonged stagnation that had followed the recession of 1980–81. The expansion of the European Economic Community to include Spain and Portugal stimulated a surge of foreign investment in those two low-wage countries. Whether the new production and distribution facilities were financed by American, Japanese, or European firms they required construction equipment and machines, both of which were Germany's most competitive exports. The imminent passage of the Single European Act stimulated renewed business investment throughout the European Community, including Germany. The third oil shock rapidly lowered the price of imported oil. Moreover, the American commitment to weakening the dollar in order to stimulate U.S. exports further reduced the cost of imported oil to Germany. Finally, the third oil shock removed pressures on the currencies of the participants in the Exchange Rate Mechanism of the EMS, so they were all allowed to appreciate lockstep with the deutsche mark. The strengthening of the EMS as a result led to increased momentum for completing the single market in 1992 as well as for formulating the outlines of the Maastricht Treaty discussed in Chapter 4. But it also helped maintain Germany's access to its primary export market, the rest of the European Economic Community.

The expansion did have one blemish: it failed to make much of a dent in the historically high rate of unemployment that arose during the second oil shock. This led to the formulation of the hysteresis hypothesis for European unemployment, a hypothesis that obtains a great deal of credibility for the rest of the European Union countries as well. Briefly, the idea is that employers are selective in the workers they lay off during a recession. They focus on the workers whose productivity is lowest relative to their wage, which means those who are older, less skilled, less educated, less healthy—in short, less capable of increasing their productivity relative to their wages. And they are less likely to hire these disadvantaged workers back during an expansion. Such workers could, in theory, offer their services for lower wages, but union rules of wage determination by acquired skill and seniority restrict employers from accepting such offers. Further, generous unemployment benefits, 63 to 68 percent of the last net wage for up to two years and 56 to 58 percent thereafter, limit the extent to which long-term unemployed workers would be willing to work for lower wages in the first place. The result is a growing proportion of long-term unemployed in the ranks of the unemployed. These outsiders become less and less attractive to potential employers, the longer they remain unemployed and their skills stagnate or become obsolete.

The other blemish became increasingly evident as negotiations proceeded both on how to lower non-tariff barriers within the European Community as the Single European Act was implemented and on how to lower non-tariff barriers with the rest of the world as GATT negotiations continued in the Uruguay Round. This was the extent to which parts of the German economy had become dependent for their success on nontariff barriers that had risen as rapidly, or more rapidly in some cases, than tariff barriers had fallen. Under GATT rules, import quotas could be imposed against certain countries on specific products if it was found they were selling at less than cost of production. These could be held off if the offending country, usually Japan, agreed to a voluntary export restraint (VER). Germany, in common with the other countries in Europe, resorted to these with increasing frequency in the late 1970s and early 1980s. They continued to employ them even with the expansion of the late 1980s. These specific quotas and VERs were administered at the national level, not at the Community level.

True, Germany was not the worst offender in the Community in the use of these forms of nontariff barriers. (France and Italy are discussed in the following two chapters.) But it had also compounded the effect of these by providing subsidies to certain declining, or "sundown," sectors. Perhaps the most egregious example was coal, which was produced at $100 a ton to maintain employment for coal miners and electric power plants and steel mills were subsidized for using it rather than being able to buy American coal for $10 a ton. Agriculture was another example, of course. Given the declining numbers employed in these sectors and their diminished political influence within West Germany, more and more opposition arose to the continuation of nontariff barriers, which took the form of nationally tailored subsidies.

Both the bloom of the expansion and the concern about the blemishes were put aside in the throes of the political shock of reunification with East Germany. The first manifestation of the shock was the huge influx of young, prime working age East Germans into West Berlin and into West Germany via Hungary and Austria. Some economists saw in this collapse of the Berlin Wall and the physical reconnection with East Germany the possibility of a reprise of the postwar economic miracle. This had been prolonged by the continued infusion of eager, skilled refugees from East Germany until the Berlin Wall was built in 1961. Now that it was torn down, the current expansion under way in the late 1980s could also be prolonged. This scenario, however, had been upstaged for fifteen years by another drama—what to do with unwanted guest workers. Now that the Turkish problem was on its way to solution (see Chapter 16), the West Germans did not care to see that drama repeated. The key to solving the Turkish dilemma had been to invest in Turkey itself, providing employment opportunities there in the production of goods for the German market. This seemed the obvious thing to do with East Germany.

As explained previously, this strategy was carried out by the German Economic and Monetary Union of July 1990. The essential element of this was to convert the East German currency into the deutsche mark at a rate of one to one for the equivalent of two months wages and at 2 ostmark for 1 deutsche mark above that amount. Meanwhile, basic foods, utilities, and rental prices would be maintained under control. In short, East Germans were being paid very well not only to vote for reunification on West German terms but also to stay put in their subsidized housing and buy Western-made consumer goods with their deutsche marks. So West German firms were denied the possibility of an influx of cheap, easily trained, and highly motivated workers. The vaunted institutions of co-determination and specially tailored apprenticeship programs for training workers served as serious institutional obstacles to exploiting the positive possibilities of reunification.

But West German firms had an increased market in East Germany for their goods, so initially they could make higher profits from the increase in domestic demand. As the unrealistically high exchange rate for the East German currency also put the contractual wages of East German workers well above their productivity level, however, unemployment rose. Not only did this increase the subsidies in the form of unemployment benefits that now had to be paid by

West Germany to East Germany, it also decreased the attractiveness of East German enterprises to foreign investors. Only West German firms and entrepreneurs could be induced to invest in the state enterprises being privatized in East Germany. The highly prized German social safety net for its citizens meant both that the price of reunifiying with East Germany was raised and that it would have to be paid mainly by West Germany.

The West German financial system was also imposed on East Germany, while the financial system of East Germany was rendered immediately bankrupt by the terms of the currency conversion. For all East German financial intermediaries, it took at least 2 ostmarks of their assets to get 1 deutsche mark, while most of their liabilities were charged against them at the rate of 1 ostmark per 1 deutsche mark. Given the importance of bank finance for business investment in the West German system and the importance of close relations between bank lenders and business borrowers in that system, this meant that while only East German firms and entrepreneurs knew the local profit opportunities, it was only West German firms and entrepreneurs who could get financing to exploit them. So the last of the unique West German institutions associated with the postwar economic miracle, the system of universal banking, turned out to be an obstacle rather than an asset in meeting the challenge of refurbishing the East German economy.

The measure of these failures was the turnaround of the German trade account from healthy surpluses in the late 1980s to deficits in the early 1990s. As unemployment rose in East Germany, unemployment actually began to rise in West Germany as well. Some signs of turnaround seemed to appear by 1994 and especially in 1995 as an export surplus began to emerge once again. By mid-1996, however, this was petering out, and on reflection it seems that the exports, as usual concentrated in machinery and equipment, were going in an important part to equip German factories being relocated outside of Germany and indeed outside of Western Europe. (See chapter 17 on the transition economies of Central and East Europe.) The export surplus in goods and services in this case was corresponding to decreased employment opportunities in Germany instead of expanding them.

CONCLUSION

West Germany must respond to the challenge of reunification with East Germany in the 1990s in its own way, which must be different from the approach it developed toward the partition of East Germany in the 1950s. The postwar arrangements were induced by the various initiatives of the Allies, to which the Christian Democratic government of Konrad Adenauer responded eagerly, albeit on the basis of institutions that were tried and true from the preNazi era—universal banks, an independent central bank, strong municipal governments, highly organized trade associations, and a commitment to honor social obligations such as health insurance, education, and pensions. The success of the German institutions within the structure provided by Allied postwar arrangements has encouraged the rest of Europe to try to imitate them to the extent their own cultures and political constraints permit. Moreover, the German governments have, by and large, worked faithfully to expand and strengthen the international arrangements that provided a felicitous environment for their own institutions. This has meant a strong commitment to the military alliance of NATO, the economic market of the European Union, and all of the specialized groups for European cooperation that have arisen since World War II.

This commitment manifested itself quickly after German reunification as Chancellor Kohl pushed for the European Community to move quickly beyond the Single Market to the Treaty of European Union, which led to the prompt signing of the Maastricht Treaty and its eventual ratification in 1993. But even though support for backward agriculture and depressed regions has become the focus of the EU's budget over the past twenty years, very little aid has been forthcoming from the EU to help West Germany resuscitate the economy of East Germany. Consequently, the expenses of reunification have been borne almost exclusively by West Germany. Given the enormity of this project, it is perhaps not surprising to learn that despite German leadership in promoting and passing the Single European Act and the subsequent Treaty of European Union, Germany in 1995 was one of the three most laggard member states in implementing the directives of the Single Market into national legislation. Moreover, public opinion polls consistently show a majority of the German citizens opposed to a common currency for Europe that would replace the deutsche mark. (European Union officials console themselves by noting that Germans also believe that the common currency will come to pass despite their objections!)

Can the West Germans adapt their own domestic institutions to meet the challenge of reunification successfully and swiftly? Can they modify the economic and political institutions of the European Union to support them both in this effort and in the effort to encompass the transition economies of Central and Eastern Europe? These are the questions that concern the German citizens and government in the 1990s. They should concern everybody else in Europe as well.

Endnotes

1. Due to the volatility of foreign exchange rates, all international economic comparisons are now made in purchasing power parity exchange rates (PPP), which adjust for the different price levels within each country. In the early 1980s, the U.S. dollar was overvalued in the markets compared with its domestic purchasing power, while in the early 1990s it was undervalued. Using the market exchange rates to compare the United States with Europe, it appears that the U.S. economy has slowed down markedly compared with that of the EU. Adjusting for the large swings in the exchange rates that are not passed on to domestic price levels, however, shows that the U.S. economy has grown faster than the EU economies over the past decade. The PPP exchange rates used in this book are the 1991 U.S. dollar equivalents as calculated by the Organization for Economic Cooperation and Development in Paris.

2. The best single source for reviewing these revisions is Werner Abelshauser, *Wirtschaftsgeschichte der Bundesrepublik Deutschland 1945–1980*. Frankfurt: Suhrkamp, 1983. Both Carlin (note 6) and Kramer (note 3) summarize his findings, while still finding an important role for both Marshall Plan aid and the currency reform of 1948.

3. Alan Kramer, *The West German Economy, 1945–1955*. New York: Berg German Studies Series, 1991, p. 12.

4. Ibid., p. 149.

5. Karl Hardach, *The Political Economy of Germany in the Twentieth* Century, Berkeley, Calif.: University of California Press, 1980, p. 228.

6. Wendy Carlin, "West German growth and institutions, 1945–90," in Nicholas Crafts and Gianni Toniolo, eds., *Economic Growth in Europe since 1945,* Cambridge: Cambridge University Press, 1996.

Bibliography

Abelshauser, Werner. *Wirtschaftsgeschichte der Bundesrepublik Deutschland 1945–1980*. Frankfurt: Suhrkamp, 1983.

Berger, Helga and Albrecht Ritschl. "Germany and the political economy of the Marshall Plan, 1947–52: a rerevisionist's view," in Barry Eichengreen, ed. *Europe's Post-War Recovery*. Cambridge: Cambridge University Press, 1995.

Carlin, Wendy. "West German growth and institutions, 1945–90," in Nicholas Crafts and Gianni Toniolo, eds. *Economic Growth in Europe since 1945*. Cambridge: Cambridge University Press, 1996.

Economist Intelligence Unit. *Country Report, Germany*. London: Economist Intelligence Unit, 2nd quarter, 1996.

Giersch, Herbert, Karl-Heinz Paqué, and Holger Schmieding, eds. *The Fading Miracle: Four decades of market economy in Germany*. Cambridge: Cambridge University Press, 1992.

Hardach, Karl. *The Political Economy of Germany in the Twentieth Century*. Berkeley, Calif.: University of California Press, 1980.

Kramer, Alan. *The West German Economy, 1945–1955*. New York: Berg German Studies Series, 1991.

Lipschitz, Leslie and Donogh McDonald, eds. *German Unification: Economic Issues*. Occasional Paper No. 75. Washington, D.C.: International Monetary Fund, December 1990.

Ritschl, Albrecht O. "An exercise in futility: East German economic growth and decline, 1945–89," in Nicholas Crafts and Gianni Toniolo, eds. *Economic Growth in Europe since 1945*. Cambridge: Cambridge University Press, 1996.

Wallich, Henry C. *The Mainsprings of the German Revival*. New Haven, Conn.: Yale University Press, 1955.

CHAPTER 1 0

France:

The Germans, the Colonies, the Provinces

Basic Facts (1993)		
Area:	544,000 km^2	16.8 % of EU15
Population (1/1/94):	57,779,300	15.6 % of EU15
GDP:	$1,045.8 billion	17.5% of EU15
Per capita:	$18,138	112% of EU15 average
Openness (X + M)/GDP	35 %	63 % with EU12

Source: Eurostat, *Basic Statistics of the European Union,* 32nd ed. (Luxembourg, 1995).

France has made substantial economic commitments to maintain the political momentum of the "deepening" process for the European Union, which will ensure that an enlarged, reunited Germany is enmeshed entirely in a democratic rule of law for Europe. These efforts all derive from the *franc fort* policy, namely, to keep the French franc as strong as the deutsche mark, whatever the cost. (As the European Central Bank will be located in Frankfurt, Germany, there is an ironic pun intended as well.) With the strengthening of the deutsche mark after 1990, maintaining an equally strong French franc has required restrictive monetary policy, which has led to higher unemployment and slower growth. As French government deficits must be reduced to meet the Maastricht criteria, the only policy option available to French authorities has been to liberalize the labor market, making it easier to for employers to hire or fire workers. This, in turn, has provoked a series of strikes.

France, geographically fated to be always the heart of Europe, has dealt throughout its history with challenges to its integrity from each of the six sides of its roughly hexagonal shape. The Romans from Italy, the Moors from Spain, the English from the Atlantic and the Channel, the Habsburgs from all directions, and in modern industrial times the Germans from either the east or the northeast, have threatened its integrity. Under Charlemagne and Napoleon I, France in turn attempted to unify Christian Europe under its enlightened rule. Either defeated or badly bloodied by German forces repeatedly from the Battle of Waterloo in June 1815 until D-Day in June 1944, French strategy has been militarily defensive and politically offensive, attempting to coordinate through diplomatic relations a system of alliances that could thwart German expansionism while maintaining a credibly strong military defense. From the end of World War II until the present day, the relationship between France and Germany has determined the political architecture of Europe, from which economic policy has been derived.

The reunification of Germany in 1990 was accepted by France in return for the German commitment to deepen the political structure of the European Union, which led to the signing of the Treaty of European Union in 1992 (the Maastricht Treaty) and its ratification by all twelve member states of the European Union by November 1993. A key provision was to revise the treaty to clarify both the internal political structure of the EU and the external political role of the EU. Further, this had to be done before European monetary union took effect in 1997 or 1999. This need to clarify the political environment for the planned monetary union is the basis for the Inter-Governmental Conference that began in March 1996 and is to complete its report on changing the political structure of the European Union by June 1997. The key issue is how to make the European Union function effectively with a steadily increasing number (potentially twenty-seven) of member states with much greater diversity in size, structure, and objectives than ever before. Enlargement in the first round after completion of the Single Market enclosed Germany on the south (Austria) and the north (Sweden and Finland) but gave potentially much greater voting power to German interests. This will only partially be offset by the inclusion of Malta and Cyprus, as representatives of France's Mediterranean interests. So it is in the interests of both France and Germany to ensure a smooth accession of Poland, Czech Republic, and Hungary as soon as possible after 2002, when it is foreseen that the European Monetary Union will be fully operational.

MACROECONOMIC POLICY INDICATORS: 1960–97

Figure 10.1 traces out France's economic success after joining the European Economic Community in 1958. Almost immediately, French economic growth rates began to catch up with, and then surpass, those of West Germany, averaging over 5 percent annual growth of GDP until the first oil shock in 1974. Part of the reason for France's participation in the economic growth miracles of Western Europe in the 1960s was the beneficial effect of the Common Market, as explained in Chapter 3. But a larger part was probably played by the decolonization carried out by General Charles DeGaulle. DeGaulle became president of France under a new constitution that formed the Fifth French Republic in 1958. Withdrawing from Algeria eliminated much of the fiscal drain on the

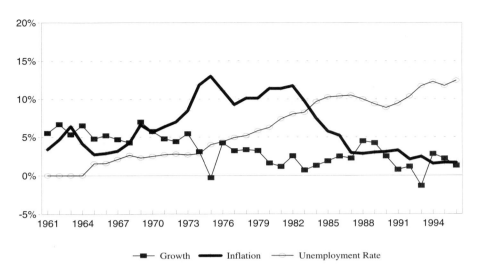

Figure 10.1. Macroeconomic policy indicators, France, 1961–96.

French government caused by the futile attempts to regain control of their pre-war colonies in Vietnam and Algeria. The former colonists returned to France with their labor, skills, and capital in large numbers thereafter, which helped stimulate growth in the domestic economy. DeGaulle's economists also carried out a monetary reform, creating a *nouveau franc* equal to 100 *anciens francs* while devaluing the *nouveau franc* relative to the U.S. dollar and the rest of the European currencies at the same time.

DeGaulle's reforms and the export opportunities provided by the Common Market brought the rate of French economic growth up to and then beyond the levels of Germany and Italy. But the massive structural changes created by rapid growth led to rising social tensions. These exploded in the events of May 1968. Then university students incited what became a nationwide strike to protest President DeGaulle's economic policies, as well as his educational policies. Calm was restored only by the Grenelle Agreements of 1968, which basically granted the demands of the workers and students. This exacerbated French inflation relative to the continued low inflation rate of Germany. So at the end of 1969, the Franco-German exchange rate was adjusted by first a devaluation of the French franc and then a revaluation of the German deutsche mark.

In the subsequent shocks to the European financial system, however, France continued its loose monetary policy and let inflation rates rise ever higher. The first shock was the collapse of the Bretton Woods system in August 1971, which meant that the dollar floated against all other currencies for the first time since World War II. The dollar float caused all intra-European exchange rates to become unstuck as well, as each set its own course against the dollar. Initially, the French franc appreciated against the dollar as French authorities tried to keep the franc rate with the deutsche mark steady. However, the first oil shock, coming in October 1973, caused the French government to respond with an expansionary monetary and fiscal policy. This led to a rapid depreciation of the franc against the dollar and especially against the deutsche mark, which continued to appreciate against the dollar. But depreciation of the franc did nothing to abate the continued rise in unemployment, and the growth rates of GDP continued to fall, albeit not as badly as in other OECD countries hit by the first oil shock.

The dramatic socialist policies that François Mitterrand imposed in the early 1980s proved disastrously unsuited for coping with the second oil shock of 1979. Mitterrand held out the promise of renewed technological advance, financed by the central government, which enlarged its capacity enormously by nationalizing banks and basic industries. While this strategy might have promoted growth in the long run, in the short run it provoked massive capital flight. Moreover, the fixed exchange rates with Germany agreed to under the European Monetary System facilitated the flight of capital from France, even though France tried to tighten its controls on capital movements and devalued the franc repeatedly within the framework of the EMS.

In contrast to the growing success of Margaret Thatcher in Great Britain, who was pursuing a counterstrategy of privatization, Mitterrand had to reverse his economic strategy by 1983 and begin to denationalize many of the firms he had hastily nationalized. Since 1985, the French franc has been stable against the deutsche mark as well, putting aside the attacks on the franc in 1992 and 1993. The results were to decrease inflation sharply and, with a lag, to improve growth rates gradually, which almost reached 5 percent again in 1988. By the late 1980s, unemployment rates had started to decline slightly as well. The Single Market initiative was proving its worth for the French economy as well as for the German economy. But having tied its economic policy so closely to that of Germany, when the German economy was setting the standards of performance for all of Europe, France now had to cope with the same economic consequences as Germany confronted with the reunification shock of 1990.

Like Germany, France weathered the reunification shock with little change in inflation, a sharp contrast with its performance during the oil shocks. Also like Germany, France suffered a drop in growth rates, especially in 1993, when the franc was attacked on the foreign exchanges by speculators who believed it would have to devalue in view of the continued loss of reserves. Even without having to deal with forcibly unemployed East Germans, France managed to increase its unemployment rate to well above 10 percent! By linking its economic policy—tight money, balanced budgets, and gradual liberalization and privatization—to that of Germany, France managed to share in the economic costs of Germany's reunification, even though it contributed very little toward the actual financing of reunification. If misery loves company, however, the shared economic travail of the two largest economies in Europe has strengthened their political commitment to expand and deepen the institutional framework of the European Union.

THE TRAVAILS OF THE FOURTH FRENCH REPUBLIC: 1945–57

Occupied by Nazi Germany from May 1940 until the liberation of Paris in August 1944, and omitted from the postwar planning conferences carried on mainly between the Americans and British but including on key occasions the Russians, France emerged from World War II politically isolated, internally divided, and economically devastated. Unlike Germany, France had stagnated throughout the 1930s, shifting from one misguided policy to another so that national income in 1939 was no higher than it had been in 1929. Quickly defeated by the German invasion of May 1940, France was ruthlessly taxed by the occupation forces for the remainder of the war. French industry was directed toward supplying consumer goods for the German market, where industry was diverted entirely to producing military goods. The French capital stock, far from being expanded and updated as in Germany, was simply allowed to wear out, while skilled French workers were deported to work in the factories seized by the Nazi forces in Central and Eastern Europe. Caught in the fierce advance of the Russian forces, most of these French workers never returned.

Under the political leadership of General Charles DeGaulle, who had been installed in London during the war as leader of the Free French, the Fourth French Republic was established in 1945 as a parliamentary democracy, revenge against Nazi collaborators was quickly carried out, and Jean Monnet, known today as the Father of Europe, proposed his *Plan de Modernisation et d'Équipement.* The Monnet Plan was officially adopted as a four-year plan in 1946 and was extended later for two years to coincide with the funding of the Marshall Plan. Monnet's vision was to focus on building up the basic sectors in France that had been the key to German economic and military superiority. These were coal, steel, cement, electricity, transport, and agricultural machinery. As many of the large firms in precisely these sectors had been nationalized immediately following the war, all that seemed necessary to implement the Plan was to indicate to the respective managers what was needed as inputs in each sector to achieve its goals for increased output by the end of the plan. The key French agency, the *Commisariat du Plan,* had no direct power to allocate resources, but concerned itself instead with acquiring information on the input-output structure of the economy and disseminating this information to the leaders of each sector. Hence the phrase "indicative planning" is used to describe the French method.

If financial constraints seemed to inhibit certain sectors from expanding as rapidly as desired, recourse could be had to loans from any of the four largest banks, all of which had been nationalized, or to government subsidies directly upon approval by the Treasury, which had unlimited recourse to loans from the Banque de France. All three sources of finance—nationalized commercial banks, the Treasury, and the Banque de France—were under the supervision of the Minister of Finance. Unfortunately for the success of Monnet's plan, however, the banks were concerned more about regaining their financial health than in fulfilling his vision by making large loans to nationalized enterprises that had no track record of repaying their debts. Moreover, the government was limited in its ability to subsidize investment due to chronic budget deficits. No firm tax base had yet been established, but wage demands of workers in the nationalized industries and in the government had to be met in order to establish postwar legitimacy of the new government. Consequently, inflation became a chronic problem, which further inhibited banks from providing the requisite financing for long-term projects. By the end of 1947, little progress had been made while the French franc encountered the first of many balance-of-payments crises that were to afflict it over the coming years.

While France was one of the initial members of the International Monetary Fund, the 44 percent devaluation of the franc at the beginning of 1948 was well above the 10 percent limit beyond which members of the IMF had to agree they would not devalue without prior approval from the Fund. France's unwillingness to cede its tenuous sovereignty to a new, untried international agency at this moment seriously undercut its ability to attract foreign loans from private sources. The Fund had been unwilling to accept the French devaluation because France had proposed at the same time to produce a two-tier exchange rate. For capital account transactions, in which it was to French advantage to have an overvalued franc, the new rate would be fixed and applied to all transactions approved under the French system of tight capital controls. For obtaining scarce dollars, however, exports and imports of goods and services would be at a floating rate, most likely well below the fixed rate for capital transactions. Faced with the refusal of the Fund to approve what could have become the first of multiple exchange rates for the franc, the French went ahead and devalued anyway. The reluctance of its major trading partners, Italy and Belgium, to trade with it on terms that could be rendered so disadvantageous suddenly and without consultation forced France into making bilateral barter agreements with each. Constrained in its ability to earn foreign exchange from exporting, France limited imports of consumption goods to 3 percent of French consumption of the particular item. Such bilateral agreements and quota restrictions confined the possible expansion of French trade and damaged the long-run possibility of attracting foreign investment.

Smaller devaluations were carried out in 1948 and 1949 but now in consultation with the Fund. But the saving grace for finance of the Monnet Plan clearly came from the funds provided France under the Marshall Plan. More than any other recipient, France directed its American aid into purchases of the construction materials and machinery required to expand the output of its targeted six sectors. Even so, it found its output targets continually frustrated in coal and steel, where inputs from the coal fields of Belgium, the Saarland, and the Ruhr basin were essential. Costs of transport and the much larger amounts of coal than iron ore needed in the smelting and refining of steel meant that it was only rational to send French iron ore to German coal and bring back the finished steel products for use in France. Toward this end, initial French policy was to try to incorporate its occupation zone of the Saarland into the adjacent French province of Lorraine with its rich iron ore mines and to press for international control of the Ruhr basin, where it could have a decisive voice in determining the allocation of coal between German domestic use and export to Belgium and

France. The French finally accomplished a diluted version of their goals when the International Control Authority for the Ruhr was established in March 1948, with the United States, Britain, France, West Germany, and the Benelux countries all having a voice. To placate the West Germans and to ensure the success of the Monnet Plan, the French prime minister, Robert Schuman, proposed his plan for a European Coal and Steel Community. (See Chapter 2 for discussion of the ECSC.)

The Schuman Plan and the consequent expansion of the European coal and steel capacity did save the Monnet Plan, which perhaps was unfortunate for France. The attempt at unbalanced growth within an economy that was trying to be as self-sufficient as possible while restoring authority over distant colonies that had been lost during World War II proved ineffective for increasing the growth rate of the whole economy. True, the output of the six key sectors increased, but shortages of consumer goods led to increased wage demands by workers and chronic balance of payments problems. While growth of GDP was certainly higher than during the 1920s and 1930s, in retrospect this was due to a prolonged "catching up" effect. This was especially powerful for France given how backward it was in 1945 relative to Germany and especially the United States. But unlike Italy and Germany, where the catching up effect was reinforced by rapid productivity advances in the export sectors, France had no leading sector to provide the kind of productivity advances that could have raised French real wages without causing inflation and balance-of-payments difficulties. Moreover, the expenses of trying to regain control of Vietnam, lost to the Japanese during World War II and finally lost to indigenous Communist forces in 1954; and to maintain control of Algeria; and to take its place as a full-fledged occupying power with the British, Americans, and Russians in defeated Germany was a constant drain on government finances and French savings.

The loss of Vietnam in 1954 and the humiliation of defeat in the Suez Crisis of 1956 led to increased vigor in the Algerian fight for independence and decreased political will in France, where parliamentary divisions led to frequent change of ineffectual governments. After Suez, both Britain and France suffered speculative outflows of their already reduced holdings of gold and dollars. For France, there were increased drains as well on the government's budget to finance the intensified war in Algeria. These financial pressures led to closer cooperation with the International Monetary Fund and World Bank, something the French had resisted until then, seeing these twin pillars of the Bretton Woods system more as instruments of American hegemony than as precursors of a truly international monetary system. They also saw a need to intensify their cooperation with Germany and the Benelux countries, which were enjoying continued economic growth and rising prosperity. This stimulated their accession to the Treaty of Rome in 1957 to set up the European Economic Community as an overdue complement to the European Coal and Steel Community. The change in French economic policy, forced upon it by the costly losses in Vietnam, Suez, and now in Algeria, was made permanent by a signal domestic political event as well. In 1958, General Charles DeGaulle, leader of the Free French during World War II from London, who had stepped down from power in January 1946 in disgust at the political gridlock of the Fourth French Republic, was called back to be premier of France. He proposed a referendum on a new constitution to form the Fifth French Republic, saw it pass approval for a stronger residential form of government, and was elected the first such president.

THE TRIUMPH OF THE FIFTH FRENCH REPUBLIC: 1958–68

DeGaulle's decade of rule really started in 1958 when he became premier with nearly dictatorial, if temporary, powers and ended in 1968, when his party forced him to make political concessions after the general strike of May 1968. Formally, he was president from January 1, 1959, until April 1969 when he resigned after a second referendum on constitutional reform failed to pass. De-Gaulle's initial political reforms that created the Fifth French Republic were quickly complemented by economic reforms, starting with a currency reform. This replaced the ancien franc, as it became called, with the nouveau franc. The new currency was exchanged for the old at a rate of 1 nouveau franc to 100 anciens francs, so immediately two zeroes were lopped off all prices and wages. This made it seem much stronger, but at the same time, the exchange rate with the dollar was devalued.[1]

The currency reform was part of the Rueff Plan devised by Jacques Rueff, DeGaulle's first finance minister. He also attempted to bring inflation under control in order to maintain the competitive advantage of the devalued franc as long as possible. To do this, Rueff abolished cross indexation between agriculture and industry, which had kept up the level of subsidies to French farmers as industrial prices rose in response to liberalization. He also cut public subsidies for food and nationalized industries, which led to a rise in their prices. Cuts in social transfers, family allowances, repayments of medical charges, and exservicemen's pensions were also made to reduce government spending. Revenues were raised by increasing corporate taxation. All in all, the Rueff Plan prepared France well for the competition with Germany. This had been opened by the Treaty of Rome, which came at the same time that the European currencies became mutually convertible for transactions on current account. The two events in combination meant that 90 percent of French trade was now open to price competition, primarily from Germany. The effects of competition were temporarily forestalled, however, by maintaining very high tariffs. In 1958, tariffs averaged 17 percent compared with 6.4 percent in Germany.[2] Only after 1966, when the common external tariff had been progressively reduced by the Dillon and Kennedy rounds of negotiations under the General Agreement on Tariffs and Trade, did French industry truly feel the effects of international competition. By that time, high levels of investment had made some firms competitive in European markets, at least.

The pattern of French trade continued to change over the next ten years. The EEC countries kept replacing the franc zone countries (existing and former colonies of France) in both exports and imports, but at a more rapid pace than before the customs union was formed (Table 10.1). Oddly, the commodity struc-

TABLE 10.1
Destination of French exports, 1952–84 (percent of total)

	Former French Colonies	Non-EEC OECD	Original EEC
1952	42.2	27.3	15.9
1958	37.5	24.4	22.2
1962	20.8	27.9	36.8
1968	13.5	27.0	43.0
1973	9.2	27.5	48.6
1984	9.3	30.7	37.3

Source: William J. Adams, *Restructuring the French Economy* (Washington, D.C.: Brookings Institution, 1989), table 22, p. 178.

ture of France's foreign trade did not change much in terms of the relative importance of agriculture and manufacturing within both exports and imports. Agriculture remained between 13 and 16 percent of exports, while manufacturing stayed between 50 and 55 percent of exports. However, within manufacturing there was a reversal in the relative importance of semimanufactures, which fell from one-third of exports to one-fifth, and machinery and transport equipment, which rose correspondingly.[3]

Despite the improved growth performance that resulted from the combined effect of DeGaulle's reforms and the steadying management of aggregate demand by his economists, unemployment rates rose gradually until 1968. Moreover, the Rueff reforms had shifted the distribution of income in favor of capital, away from labor, and real wages had fallen as prices rose more rapidly than nominal wages. The gradual culmination of these processes helped to provoke the events of May 1968. At that time, university students incited what became a nationwide strike to protest President DeGaulle's economic policies, as well as his educational policies. But unemployment rates were still very low, especially by comparison with the years since, and inflation rates seemed livable, especially by comparison with the immediate postwar years. Nevertheless, France's inflation rates were significantly higher than those in Germany throughout the 1960s. By the end of 1968 it was clear that the exchange rate fixed by DeGaulle's finance experts when he came to power in 1958 was no longer sustainable. Finally, in August 1969 the franc was devalued, this time by 10 percent against the U.S. dollar. Then, at DeGaulle's insistence, the deutsche mark floated in September and was revalued in October 1969 by the same percentage as the franc had devalued. But by this time, DeGaulle had resigned in dismay at the concessions extracted by the unions from Parliament despite his powers as president. His successor, Georges Pompidou, proved more facile in dealing with political pressures, but the Gaullist political movement would be divided from then on.

The DeGaulle era was marked at both the start and the end with dramatic political events that brought major changes in the French political system. Economic historians, however, have been surprised at how smoothly the French economy seemed to grow relative to the rest of Europe, despite France having more serious political disruptions than its neighbors. It seemed that high, smooth rates of growth were necessary to maintain a tentative social consensus in a society that was being torn apart by the stresses of adjusting to the modern economy. In just the period 1948–62, for example, nearly two million people moved out of agriculture, reducing the absolute size of the rural population by one-third. The southern, mountainous region called the Midi was in danger of depopulation, while all the outlying regions lost population to the magnetic attractions of the Paris basin. Manufacturing absorbed only 170,000 of the rural migrants, construction another 550,000 and the rest, over one million strong, went into the service sector. Moreover, despite the obvious attractions of high growth sectors in manufacturing for new labor, the wage gap between manufacturing and agriculture remained relatively constant. Even the skill differentials within manufacturing did not change over time. In other words, the tremendous quantity adjustments that were made at great personal cost to literally millions of French citizens did not have the desired or expected impact on relative incomes by sector, gender, or qualification.

The smoothness of aggregate French growth may be held accountable in part for this odd pattern of structural adjustment, made apparently not so much in response to price signals emitted by the market but rather to "indications" provided by the planners. In fact, it has been accepted that French demand management was able to sustain the confidence of capitalists, so they continued to maintain high rates of investment, financed mainly out of retained earnings by the firms. This was the *auto-financement* of French business, or self-financing without recourse to outside debt or equity in the capital markets or even very much to credit from the banking sector. Closer examination of each successive five-year plan and the specific goals announced by each at the beginning, however, shows that the latent tensions in the French economic fabric were very much at work. While most plans came very close to their announced goals by the end of each five-year period, the usual pattern was to note serious shortfalls emerging after two to three years into the plan, divert substantial government resources to making up the shortfall in the last two or three years, and then announce success once again at the conclusion of the plan period. Meanwhile, the next plan would be devised to cover over weaknesses or unplug bottlenecks that had emerged during the course of the previous plan. As long as this held, the private sector could avoid fulfilling its presumed obligations in each plan and focus on exploiting the opportunities that would emerge from expanded activity by the public enterprises. Few countries had the central government capacity to mobilize resources so quickly for specific objectives without further political debate and decision making. Attempts in other countries to imitate the French success with indicative planning usually faltered by stimulating effective resistance to a plan's objectives by interest groups who felt they would be losers in the process.

As French economic success became apparent in the early 1960s and the course of the Common Market appeared increasingly attractive to other countries in Europe, Great Britain changed its mind and decided to apply for membership in 1963. DeGaulle objected and single-handedly vetoed British membership, arguing that the Common Market was not ready for new members. Britain applied again in 1967, just as the elimination of internal tariff barriers was about to be achieved and the EEC was clearly a solid success as a customs union. This time DeGaulle objected on grounds that Britain was not ready for membership! It is clear in retrospect (and was obvious at the time to many) that DeGaulle's resentment of his treatment by the British and Americans while leader of the Free French in exile in London during World War II had turned him into an Anglophobe, if he hadn't been one before. This helps account as well for his removal of France from NATO and the ouster of American forces from France. But it seems also clear that his views were shared by many French, and his sense of history was surely acute in recognizing that France geographically is at the heart of Europe, but could not play the central role necessary for its long-run survival without achieving greater economic success (and military power). Toward this end, he committed France to the Common Market and ever closer economic and political relations with Germany, but with France in control of the speed and pace of European integration.

THE SUCCESSIVE SHOCKS OF DEVALUATION, OIL, MITTERRAND: 1969–85

France confronted the end of the Bretton Woods system in August 1971 and the first oil shock of October 1973 while still adjusting to the end of the DeGaulle era. French policy was still in the Gaullist mode, so the collapse of the U.S. dollar as the key currency of the Bretton Woods system was welcomed. It seemed to give France a fresh opportunity to play a major role in shaping the international economy. The favorite French prescriptions for reform were either to devalue the dollar against gold or to substitute some other commodity standard, such as oil, for gold. The first proposal, which was the official French position for a long time, would have had the effect of greatly enlarging the value of the foreign reserves of the Banque de France relative to those of the Bundesbank. The Banque de France consciously tried to maintain a higher proportion of gold and dollars in its reserves, while the Bundesbank built up large reserves of dollars. Neither the Americans nor the Germans could see much advantage in giving such a windfall simultaneously to the French, the Russians, and the South Africans, so the French proposal was never seriously considered. Moreover, French domestic monetary policy made it an increasingly weak negotiating partner in the deliberations that followed the breakup of Bretton Woods.

At this time, the policy changes that had been made in 1968 and 1969 to placate the discontented French workers came to bear on French inflation rates. The minimum wage had been increased 35 percent in June 1968, with other wages raised 10 to 15 percent and the length of the work week had been cut. But most dangerously, in light of the inflationary oil shock of 1973–74, wages had been indexed formally to prices, which provided a wage-price spiral that could not end once one or the other had started to rise. The social peace that had been gained by the Grenelle Agreements in 1968 was not to be easily forsaken. French real incomes would not be allowed to fall despite the rise in oil prices, the adverse balance of payments, and the claims of the OPEC oil producers upon French national income. The result of this determination to maintain French real incomes was an increase in inflation and a sustained rise in unemployment—the combination that came to be termed stagflation. France was not alone in this experience, and in fact, its economic performance in terms of both inflation and unemployment appears to be roughly the European average, while its growth of output held up well compared with that of the rest of Europe, dropping only by half from the average rate enjoyed in the "golden age" of growth.

Unfortunately for the Gaullist vision of France's role in Europe, the German response to the end of Bretton Woods and the first oil shock was quite different. As described in Chapter 9, Germany chose to maintain low inflation rates throughout. The predictable result was a further depreciation of the French franc relative to the deutsche mark. France joined the European "snake" in April 1972 to demonstrate European solidarity in face of the depreciating dollar and to maintain the feasibility of financing the Common Agricultural Policy, as explained in Chapter 6. But the difference in inflation rates between France and Germany, which came to dominate the snake, forced France out with the first oil shock. It tried again to reenter in July 1975, only to be forced out once again in March 1976. This was when the antiinflationary measures devised by Raymond Barre seemed the best political alternative.

In the meantime, the French government of Georges Pompidou, DeGaulle's successor as president of France in 1969, welcomed the third overture of Great Britain to join the Common Market. Edward Heath's Conservative government made the final push with negotiations carried out in 1971–72 in common with Ireland, Denmark, and Norway. Part of the French motivation at this time was probably to bring in a counterweight to the increasing stature of Germany within the affairs of the EEC, and part was probably to gain access to the markets of the sterling area. But most of the initiative came from the British side, which successively adopted a value added tax, changed its agricultural policy to the price support system of the Common Agricultural Policy, accepted the common external tariff against the sterling area countries, decimalized its currency, and floated the pound from the middle of 1972, while the EEC countries tried to maintain for a while longer their new par rates with the dollar. Faced with this overwhelming turnabout in British attitudes and practices, France had to accede to its entry.

With Britain entering, Ireland and Denmark had little choice but to join as well, and both looked forward to taking advantage of the Common Agricultural Policy. Norway, meanwhile, put the matter to a popular referendum, where it was defeated, as it was again in 1994. When the Greek colonels' regime of some six years was replaced by a democratic government led by a conservative politician, Karamanlis, in 1974, France also pushed for Greece's rapid entry, in order to solidify the legitimacy of the new democracy. It was less forthcoming, however, on the possibility of entry of Portugal and Spain. Both of these countries had emerged from authoritarian rule only a year later than Greece, but the authoritarian regime in each had a much longer history to overcome. France was at the center of a nine-member European Economic Community from 1973 onward and a ten-member EEC from 1980. During the oil shocks, the deepening process of the European Community was put on hold, while the first major steps at widening the EC were made. French national interests were very much in evidence in this shift of direction in the process of European integration.

At the same time, France under the presidency of Valery Giscard d'Estaing (1974–81) opened up other initiatives for international cooperation outside the European Community. His director of the Treasury, Jacques de Larosière (later to become managing director of the IMF) was instructed to work out a mode of cooperation with the United States within the framework of the International Monetary Fund. These meetings culminated in the world's first economic summit at the Chateau de Rambouillet in France. The heads of government of the six leading industrial economies—the United States, Japan, Germany, France, Italy, and Great Britain—met in an informal "house party" at the eighteenth-century chateau with their foreign and finance ministers in attendance. This was the forerunner of the now annual G7 meetings, where current economic problems are discussed and common policy positions are announced. It was also the stimulus for the now semiannual meetings of the European Council, the meeting of the heads of government of all the member states of the European Union. This meeting, at first as informal a method of policy coordination as the G7 meetings, has now been formalized as part of the European Union's set of institutions. The Rambouillet summit led directly to the second amendment of the Articles of the IMF, which acknowledged the changed role of exchange rates in the world. No longer would the IMF uphold fixed exchange rates, but instead would "assure orderly exchange arrangements and promote a stable system of exchange rates."[4] Cooperative interventions in the foreign exchange markets could occur by mutual agreement, but the object was to keep the system stable, not the exchange rates as such.

By 1976, when the Barre Plan was introduced in France, extreme antiinflationary measures seemed called for. Rather than continue to devalue the franc, the Barre Plan tried to control the government budget by cutting subsidies and raising taxes. The intent was to eliminate the need for the Bank of France to increase the money supply by covering the increasing government deficit and thereby fueling further inflation. However, the Bank of France continued to increase the money supply by making exceptions for exports, for investment in energy-saving equipment, and for housing construction. The government also had to help finance investment in the six new strategic industries it targeted for expansion. Reflecting the technological changes that had occurred in the thirty years since the Monnet Plan, the strategic industries in the Barre Plan were offshore technology, office information systems, electronics, robots, bioindustries, and energy-saving equipment. Again, any investment in these was facilitated by government finance, so France's inflationary spiral, begun by the wage increases of 1968 and continued by the practice of wage indexation, was exacerbated by the first oil shock.

To rein in these pressures on the Banque de France, Barre promoted the entry of France into the European Monetary System. By committing the French government to maintaining a stable central par rate with the other members of the EMS, which meant primarily with Germany and the Benelux countries with their perennially strong currencies, Barre hoped to force it into allowing the Banque de France to pursue an equally tight money policy instead of acceding to the demands of France's numerous pressure groups. The Barre Plan was effective in reducing the rate of inflation, just in time for the second oil shock. This sent unemployment soaring again, and with no short-term solution available to French policymakers to cope with labor unrest, the conservative government fell in the presidential elections of 1981. François Mitterrand became the new president and immediately began to carry out a set of socialist economic reforms.

He began by nationalizing more industries, especially the largest remaining private banks, imposing price controls, raising wages, and installing worker councils in the major firms. It was definitely a counterstrategy to the tight money policy of Germany and Benelux and to the privatization and deregulation initiatives under way at the same time in the United States and Great Britain. There was certainly no thought initially of devising a common European strategy to cope with what, after all, had been a series of common shocks to all of the member states. These had been the collapse of the Bretton Woods system of fixed exchange rates, with dollar deficits fueling the rise of international reserves and prices; the two oil shocks in 1973 and 1979; and the "Volcker shock" of 1980–81. The latter shock was the result of the U.S. Federal Reserve System changing its policy from stabilizing the interest rate on U.S. government debt to stabilizing at a much reduced rate the growth rate of the U.S. money supply. But all of these shocks had affected every European country in much the same way. It is a mark of the failure of the European ideal articulated by Jean Monnet that this decade-long string of common threats to the economic security of Europe should have seen such a variety of individual national initiatives seeking to meet them separately with no thought of the consequences of their actions for the rest of Europe.

As it turned out, Mitterrand's "socialism in one country" strategy proved disastrous. With the French franc holding its strength relative to the other European currencies in the EMS and the property rights of business firms threatened throughout France, capital flight began in earnest. With the U.S. dollar becoming stronger all the time as the Volcker strategy took hold, much of the flight capital even went to the United States, in addition to the traditional safety perch of Switzerland. An example of the strength of incentives for capital flight created by Mitterrand's initial policy was that the French Rothschild's actually set up a U.S. branch, the first time this storied international banking firm had dealt directly in the United States. Within the EMS, France had to devalue repeatedly against the other currencies. And this time the devaluations had no effect in maintaining French exports. Instead, they simply raised the price of oil further and accelerated the pace of capital flight.

By 1983, Mitterrand (and the French electorate) realized the error of his economic policy and began to reverse it. The key actor in effecting this turnaround was his finance minister, Jacques Delors, later to become famous as the architect of the European Monetary Union. The first steps were to halt nationalization and firm up the commitment to the European Monetary System in order to avoid further devaluations. In fact, this proved successful in stabilizing the franc and halting further capital flight. It did nothing, of course, to reduce the rate of unemployment, which remained uncomfortably high. And it did nothing to restore the high rates of growth that had kept domestic peace during much of the 1950s and 1960s. At the center of an enlarged European Community, France by the mid-1980s was also at the heart of the economic stagnation afflicting most of Europe. The situation was aptly dubbed Eurosclerosis. But the initiative out of this predicament came again from France. Jacques Delors, passed over at the direction of François Mitterrand for the office of prime minister in the Socialist government in the elections of 1984, resigned as finance minister to become president of the European Commission. Over the next ten years, his initiatives in promoting the establishment of the Single Market and then of European Monetary Union led to at least a modest resumption of growth and a resurgence of hope.

FROM ECU TO FRANC FORT: 1986–96

The Single Market initiative emanated directly from the European Commission under the leadership of Jacques Delors. Yet it fell on fertile soil. Big businesses throughout Europe were upset at the continued restrictions of trade across national boundaries and envious of the rapid economic recovery under way in the United States where de-regulation seemed to be stimulating a flurry of investment activity. Even the United Kingdom, with the privatization initiatives of Prime Minister Margaret Thatcher, was growing more rapidly than the traditional leaders of Europe's growth league. A conservative majority in the French parliament in 1986 forced Mitterrand into a policy of "cohabitation" with the conservative prime minister, Jacques Chirac. Blocked by political circumstances from domestic innovations in economic policy, Mitterrand supported the efforts of Delors at increasing the vitality of European integration. When it seemed that the dispute over harmonization of VAT rates would prove insoluble, for example, it was France that broke the logjam by changing the structure of its own rates first. The resurgence of investment and the rise in the rate of economic growth that anticipated passage of the Single European Act in 1987 helped Mitterrand win reelection as president in 1988.

This success solidified his commitment to the European Monetary System. After 1985, there have been no further changes in the central par rate between the French franc and the deutsche mark. Later, to facilitate accomplishment of the European Monetary Union, France passed legislation to make the Banque de France legally independent from the credit demands of the government, the first time this had been considered since its founding in 1801. The commitment of France to a stable currency and a fixed exchange rate with the deutsche mark and the deutsche mark bloc encouraged other countries to join in the

EMS as well. By April 1991, every member state had joined except for Greece, and the future of the system seemed assured.

This was when the pressures of German reunification began to be felt. Thanks to the artificially maintained system of fixed exchange rates within the European Community at the time, these pressures were transmitted to the rest of the member states. As the deutsche mark rose in value relative to other currencies in the world, especially the U.S. dollar, exports were hurt and imports encouraged. This was fine for directing resources toward the reconstruction of the German economy, but it was not in the economic interests of the other member states to cut short the economic expansion that had barely begun in response to the Single Market initiative. Now for strictly political reasons that had much more to do with the future architecture of Europe and Mitterrand's place in world history than with domestic elections, much less the domestic economy, France remained committed to the EMS. The Maastricht Treaty that embodied this commitment was barely passed in a referendum in France in 1992. The narrowness of this vote surely played a major role in provoking the crisis for the Italian lira and the British pound sterling that followed shortly afterward.

The power of the conservative party was clear in Parliament, which saw the continued high rates of unemployment as an opportunity to restrain the role of unions and to liberalize the operation of the labor market. An ailing Mitterrand did nothing to aid the Socialist party in the elections of 1994, although the continued high unemployment rates did lead to the defeat of the presidential ambitions of the prime minister, Edouard Balladur. But instead of a Socialist president, it was the other conservative candidate, Jacques Chirac, who won the presidency by promising to attack the problem of unemployment first of all. In office, however, Chirac has retained the commitment of France to partnership with Germany and defines that as joining with Germany in a common currency. Chirac even conceded to rename the common currency from "ecu," which had distinct francophone overtones, to "euro," which sounds completely different when spoken by a German.

Rather than pressure Germany explicitly to change the way it is handling the shock of reunification with East Germany, France has chosen to undergo a sympathetic travail of sluggish growth, rising unemployment, but stable prices. And this will simply help to make its German partner larger and stronger relative to it. By the mid-1990s, it appears that rather than directing the course of European integration toward its own national self-interest, which had been the logic of French policy through the resignation of President DeGaulle in 1969, France has now found itself in the position of letting the course of European integration as determined by the German initiatives direct its national economic policy.

CONCLUSION

As France confronts the domestic problems of increasing numbers of strikes and ever-rising rates of unemployment under the administration of President

Jacques Chirac, it seems determined to see the terms of the Maastricht Treaty completed. They, after all, were set by a former finance minister of France, who had very much the long-term national interests of France in mind. Both Chirac and Alain Juppé, his prime minister, have consistently affirmed that France will do its part to achieve both the European Monetary Union by January 1, 1999, when the exchange rate between the French franc and the German deutsche mark will be permanently fixed, and the common currency of the Euro by January 1, 2002. To do this requires continued reduction in the French budget deficit in order to meet the criterion of less than 3 percent of gross domestic product by January 1, 1998. There is some leeway provided in the Maastricht Treaty on this score, but not enough to allow a French government to use the traditional French policy of satisfying demands for higher wages by expanding government spending and the money supply. By the autumn of 1996, French unemployment was at a record high, well over 12 percent of the labor force, but the determination of the government to reduce the deficit appeared unshakable. Chirac's surprising call for new parliamentary elections to be held in June 1997 simply reinforced his commitment.

In terms of the ongoing Inter-Governmental Conference, the French position again seemed clear and most likely would be effective. At the heart of all issues about the institutional design of an enlarged European Union is the need to maintain the Franco-German partnership, according to both French and German government leaders. This means that both wish to see the powers of the European Council, reflecting the wishes of heads of member state governments, enlarged and made more effective. Especially important to France is the role of the Council for projecting a common foreign and security policy (CFSP) in order to strengthen the third pillar of the European Union. This will be done by reducing the number of Commissioners, switching some of the staff of the Commission to an enlarged secretariat for the Council. Then, increasingly, the initiative for EU legislation will come from the European Council rather than from the Commission.

To ensure that such legislation is effective, the French emphasize the importance of keeping national parliaments informed of the course of legislation. The intent would be that national parliaments could influence the direction of European-wide legislation by anticipating it with domestic legislation or objecting to it early on. The cooperation between national parliaments and the European Parliament then could also be enhanced by making the EP more reflective of the relative weight of the member states. In other words, the two largest countries in the EU, France and Germany, are not willing to continue the past practice of grossly overweighting the influence of the smaller countries. This change of strategy would also be reflected in the composition of the Commission and in the increased use of qualified majority voting in the Council of Ministers.

Finally, the French position has been clear through successive administrations that the objections of some countries to deepening the European Union should not hold back France and Germany from making these changes in the political architecture of Europe. Of course, they have Great Britain in mind, with its opt out on the European social policy and its resistance toward reentering the European Monetary System, much less toward joining the common currency. Great Britain and other countries that hesitate to commit immediately to the new institutional arrangements, especially to EMU, however, should be encouraged to enter into the new arrangements as soon as possible. It remains a matter of continued discussion and decision to what extent the "encouragement" should be positive, by making concessions to specific national concerns, or negative, by imposing penalties on outsiders or shirkers.

Economic historians can see the dilemma facing France as clearly, no doubt, as French politicians and voters see it. On the one hand, the European Union and its predecessors in economic integration have maintained peace in Europe between France and Germany for over fifty years—which marks a new record of peace duration for Europe since the beginning of the military revolution in the sixteenth century. So it seems vital to the national security of France to strengthen as much as feasible the institutional arrangements that have provided this opportunity for continued economic growth and prosperity. On the other hand, these same fifty years have been marked by periodic social turmoil within France, episodes that have led to major changes of economic policy and political governance. It may be time for such an episode to occur again.

Endnotes

1. The French franc was originally set at a par value of 119.107 francs to the U.S. dollar on December 18, 1946, when France finally decided to join the International Monetary Fund. It insisted on not having a par value with the IMF from January 26, 1948, to December 28, 1958. In the meantime, however, its market value was kept at 350 francs per U.S. dollar from the devaluations of September 1949 until November 1957. Then, under the pressure of domestic inflation and speculative attacks on both the French franc and the British pound after the fiasco of their joint effort in 1956 to regain control of the Suez Canal in Egypt, the franc fell to 420 francs per U.S. dollar, a 20 percent decline. DeGaulle's economists carried out further devaluation to 490 francs per U.S. dollar in December, 1958. They also set the par value of the French franc with the IMF at 493.706 to the U.S. dollar at the end of 1958. Then, on January 1, 1960, they introduced the *nouveau franc*, with a par value of 4.93706 NF to the U.S. dollar. Ultimately, this was a 40 percent devaluation from the beginning of the Vietnam War until the conclusion of peace terms with independent Algeria. From the end of World War II, this was a 315 percent rise in the value of the dollar relative to the French currency!

2. Stephen A. Resnick and Edwin M. Truman, "An empirical examination of bilateral trade flows in Western Europe," in Bela Belassa, ed., *European Economic Integration*. Amsterdam: North-Holland, 1975, p. 63.

3. Christian Sautter, "France," in Andrea Boltho, ed. *The European Economy: Growth and Crisis*, Oxford: Oxford University Press, 1982, p. 454.

4. Harold James, *International Monetary Cooperation since Bretton Woods*, Washington, D. C.: International Monetary Fund and New York: Oxford University Press, 1996, p. 271.

Bibliography

Adams, William J. *Restructuring the French Economy,* Washington, D.C.: Brookings Institution, 1989.

Carré, Jean-Jacques, Paul Dubois, and Edmond Malinvaud. *La croissance française: un essai d'analyse économique causale de l'après-guerre.* Paris: Le Seuil, 1972.

Divisia, François, René Pupin, and René Roy. *À la recherche du franc perdu.* Paris: Société d'Éditions Hommes et Mondes, 1995.

Economist Intelligence Unit. *Country Report, France,* London: Economist Intelligence Unit, 2nd quarter, 1996.

James, Harold. *International Monetary Cooperation since Bretton Woods.* Washington, D.C.: International Monetary Fund and New York: Oxford University Press, 1996.

Machin, Howard and Vincent Wright, eds. *Economic Policy & Policy-Making under the Mitterrand Presidency, 1981–84.* New York: St. Martin's Press, 1985.

Resnick, Stephen A. and Edwin M. Truman. "An empirical examination of bilateral trade flows in Western Europe," in Bela Balassa, ed. *European Economic Integration.* Amsterdam: North-Holland, 1975.

Saint-Paul, Gilles. "France: real and monetary aspects of French exchange rate policy under the Fourth Republic," in Barry Eichengreen, ed. *Europe's Post-War Recovery.* Cambridge: Cambridge University Press, 1995.

Saint-Paul, Gilles. "Economic reconstruction in France: 1945–1958," in R. Dornbusch, R. Layard, and W. Nolling, eds. *Post-war Economic Reconstruction : Possible Lessons for Eastern Europe.* Cambridge, Mass.: MIT Press, 1993.

Sautter, Christian. "France," in Andrea Boltho, ed. *The European Economy: Growth and Crisis.* Oxford: Oxford University Press, 1982.

Sicsic, Pierre, and Charles Wyplosz. "France, 1945–92," in Nicholas Crafts and Gianni Toniolo, eds. *Economic Growth in Europe since 1945.* Cambridge: Cambridge University Press, 1996.

CHAPTER 11

Italy:

The Mezzogiorno, the Northern League, Scala Mobile, and La Dolce Vita

Basic Facts (1993)		
Area:	301,300 km^2	9.3 % of EU15
Population:	57,138,500	15.4 % of EU15
GDP:	$989.4 billion	16.5 % of EU15
Per capita:	$17,345	107 % of EU15 average
Openness (X + M)/GDP	32 %	54 % with EU12

Source: Eurostat, *Basic Statistics of the European Union*, **32nd ed. (Luxembourg, 1995).**

In the 1990s, Italy was more concerned about changes in its political system than in maintaining its leading role in the development of the European Union. As a result, when the lira was attacked by foreign exchange speculation in September 1992, Italy withdrew from the European Monetary System and allowed the lira to float. The substantial devaluation that resulted helped renew Italy's exports, especially to its trading partners in the EU. As a result, the economic performance of Italy, especially in the industrial north, has been much more satisfactory than in Germany and France. The main economic problem facing Italy is the cost of servicing its huge public debt, which reached 122.7 percent of its gross domestic product by the end of 1994. While running substantial surpluses in its primary government budget since 1992, the high interest charges on the existing stock of debt mean that Italy continues to have substantial budget deficits, well over the 3 percent guideline set by the Maastricht Treaty. Political difficulties have, to date, thwarted various initiatives designed to reduce the government deficit. In the fall of 1996, however, Prime Minister Prodi introduced a stringent budget designed to bring the Italian deficit under 3 percent by January 1, 1998. He also proclaimed his intention to bring Italy into the European monetary union with the first group of entrants in 1999. Toward this end, he managed to put the Italian lire back into the exchange rate mechanism of the European monetary system at a very favorable exchamge rate compared to the level in 1992 (see Chapter 7).

Italy, for all its ancient ruins and vestiges of Roman glory, is one of the newest nation-states in Europe. Unification of the entire peninsula under one democratic government was not achieved until 1861. The longest ruling government since then was the Fascist regime of Benito Mussolini, lasting from 1922 until his overthrow and execution in 1944. Much of the fascist economic legacy remains in Italy in the form of the massive state holding companies. The largest is the Istituto per la Ricostruzione Industriale (IRI), which includes as its subsidiaries not only manufacturing companies in the basic industries but also the national shipping company (Finmare), the national airline (Alitalia), the telephone company (Telecom Italia), the toll roads, and major banks. Comparable in influence is the Ente Nazionale Idrocarburi (ENI), which in addition to holding the monopoly on petroleum has extended its operations into petrochemicals and electricity. It is obviously imperative to break up and privatize these holding companies, first, to improve their competitiveness and efficiency, and second, to reduce the drain on state finances required to subsidize them as well as to give the government one-time reductions in its stock of debt. Over time, the state holding companies have gradually stagnated, becoming overstaffed and uncompetitive as political pressures forced them to provide opportunities for political patronage while they were largely protected from economic pressures to perform efficiently.

Despite this drawback, Italy was one of the first European economies to experience export-led growth after World War II. Its medium-sized manufacturing firms, predominantly located in the north, have maintained export competitiveness in consumer goods. Its high fashion goods for both men and women are well known, but its exports also include furniture, kitchen appliances, and upmarket linens. Its success gradually transformed Italy from a source of migrant labor for the rest of Europe in the 1950s to a net immigration country by the end of the 1970s. Despite being heavily dependent on imports for fuel and most raw materials, Italy has managed to have a net current account surplus for most of its postwar history. This has been achieved by varying combinations of expanding exports, emigrants' remittances, and tourist expenditures.

The export success of Italy is even more remarkable for the generally inflationary environment created by its loose monetary policy since the 1960s. Recurrent bouts of inflation occurred as the deficit spending of the central government had to be accommodated by the Banca d'Italia, which until the 1990s was under the formal control of the Minister of Finance. It has to be said, however, that the recurring deficits did manage to maintain the Christian Democratic party as the majority partner in most of the coalition governments formed until 1993. Despite the frequent changes of coalitions, Italy's underlying power structure was remarkably stable until the early 1990s. Then, evidence of pervasive corruption produced by crusading prosecutors determined to uproot the control of the Mafia in the south of Italy led to widespread consensus that political reform was required. A series of reform governments has ensued, dominated by central bankers (Carlo Ciampi, the governor of the Banca d'Italia, was chosen as the first caretaker prime minister, and Lamberto Dini, his successor, also became a caretaker prime minister), a successful businessman (Silvio Berlusconi, owner of several television networks and the leading soccer team in Italy), and even an economics professor (Romano Prodi). The prevalence of economically knowledgeable men as political leaders in the 1990s is striking, and indicates the high priority now being placed on economic reform.

A striking feature of Italy's postwar economic arrangements has been the persistent efforts to improve the economic level of the south of Italy, the Mezzogiorno, as the region south of Rome is called. Since 1951, the Cassa per il Mezzogiorno has spent an average of 0.7 percent of Italy's measured GDP on a variety of development projects intended to raise the standard of living of the southern Italians closer to that of the northern Italians. By the end of the 1980s, while per capita income had risen substantially in the south, it was still only 55 percent of the northern level—exactly as it had been in 1950 when the Cassa was formed. Moreover, it was clear that the financing of this effort came basically from the more prosperous north in the form of higher tax revenues and increased issues of government debt, which were held mainly in the north. Finally, it appeared that the south had become structurally dependent on state transfers, which were used to reinforce the patron-client relations that formed the basis of the Mafia's power. The two endemic problems of the Italian economy—the rising indebtedness of the central government and the persistent backwardness of the Mezzogiorno—were mutually aggravating.

That this situation could persist until the political reforms begun in 1992 cannot be explained solely by political intransigence. A favorite explanation provided by economists is the rise and pervasiveness of the informal economy in Italy. Tax avoidance, evasion, and outright corruption are seen as part of the Italian national genius. Estimates of the importance of the informal, or unregistered and therefore unmeasured, economy range as high as 25 to 30 percent of the measured gross domestic product—a ratio far higher than in any of the northern EU economies. The economic incentives are clear for both northerners and southerners. The northerners wish to avoid paying taxes for which they see no comparable benefit in public services; the southerners wish to avoid appearing more prosperous and losing their entitlements to government transfers. Ironically, if the informal economy is included in measures of Italy's GDP, the government deficit is reduced considerably, and so Italian economists have argued they are close to meeting the Maastricht criterion of a deficit under 3 percent of GDP!

The importance of the informal economy also, however, helps explain the political acceptance of reform of the *scala mobile* in August 1992. The *scala mobile* indexed wages to the rise in the cost of living. As rising wages were a major cause of future rises in the cost of living, this system locked Italy into an inflationary process that was incompatible with maintaining a fixed exchange rate with the deutsche mark. So the rate was first frozen and then amended to rise less than the cost of living by the amount that labor productivity increased.

By 1996, this had worked well to keep wage inflation down, but workers were becoming upset that actual inflation kept outstripping the estimated inflation rates used to calculate wage adjustments.

Moreover, years of political patronage for government employees and employees of the state holding companies had resulted in huge pension obligations. Not only did these imply further increases in the government's budget problems if they were not refinanced somehow, they also impeded privatization of the state enterprises, whose pension obligations presumably would be sold with them if the state was to get any advantage at all. The pension problem for Italy, in common with all advanced industrial countries, is bound to become worse as the population ages. Beginning in the 1990s, Italy's rate of natural increase turned negative, with more people dying each year than were born.

In view of all these problems, Italy's main concern with EU policy is to maintain preferred access to the internal market and to use the external pressures of EU directives on conditions for monetary union, competitiveness, and agricultural reform to push through much needed economic reforms against domestic political resistance.

MACROECONOMIC POLICY INDICATORS: 1960–97

Figure 11.1 shows the performance of the Italian economy since 1960 in terms of growth rates of GDP, inflation rates, and unemployment rates. Until 1971, Italy was one of the star performers in the high growth league of continental Europe. Unemployment rates, while high by French and German standards, were stable and concentrated in the Mezzogiorno, which was seen as economically backward. Beginning in the late 1960s, however, wage pressures built up in northern Italy, leading to serious strikes and to wage inflation, which was accommodated by the Banca d'Italia. Hit heavily by the two oil shocks in the 1970s, Italy managed reasonable rates of growth only at the expense of very high inflation rates. Even these, however, failed to protect it from the decline in growth rate and rise in unemployment that occurred with the second oil shock of 1979–80.

The course of the 1980s until the present has been to reduce inflation rates and raise unemployment rates while stabilizing the rate of growth at reasonable levels. The downward course in inflation rates was interrupted by the German reunification shock of 1990 for a couple of years. Part of this was due to a surge of capital imports beginning early in 1990 when Italy tightened its commitment to the EMS by narrowing its exchange rate band to ± 2.25 percent from the previous ± 6 percent it had pledged since 1978. Removing this amount of exchange rate risk while still paying high interest rates on its large stock of government debt made Italian portfolio investments very attractive to other Europeans, including wealthy Italians who had been investing their export profits abroad for years (part of their tax evasion genius). Nevertheless, Italian growth kept declining as import demand from its EU customers fell off in response to the German reunification shock.

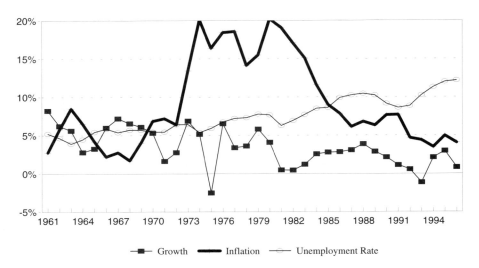

Figure 11.1. Macroeconomic policy indicators, Italy, 1960–96

The crisis for Italy culminated in September 1992 when its efforts to maintain its central par rate with the strong franc and deutsche mark exhausted its reserves of foreign exchange. Jointly with Britain, Italy abandoned the EMS and let the lira float to its equilibrium level in the foreign exchange markets. The financial uncertainty, combined with the political uncertainty as more and more Italian politicians were indicted on charges of corruption, actually reduced GDP in 1993. But from then on, the competitive advantages regained by Italian manufacturers as a result of the devalued lira led to sustained growth rates of GDP. While nowhere close to the economic miracle levels of the 1960s, they were enviably higher than the levels achieved by Germany and France. Nevertheless, unemployment rates remain high as expanding firms find it much safer to hire additional labor in the informal market than to incur the heavy liabilities of fixed wages, heavy Social Security contributions, and restrictions on dismissal for labor hired in the formal market.

Because France and Germany are Italy's biggest customers, there is a natural tendency for Italy to associate itself with any initiative the two major powers agree upon for the future course of the EU. But the contrast between the interests of the poor countries on the periphery of the EU (who are benefiting increasingly from the diversion of cohesion and structural funds toward them) and the interests of the rich countries in the heart of the EU (who are willing to pay these transfers for the benefit of access to an enlarged single market) are epitomized in Italy. If the Northern League political party, which wishes to undo the 1861 unification of Italy, were to succeed in dividing Italy into two countries, for example, the rich north would have 122 percent of the average per capita income of the EU and would be by far the wealthiest country in the EU. By contrast, the poor south would have less than 70 percent of the average per capita income and would be as poor as Ireland, Greece, Portugal, and Spain on average—and would be entitled to at least a fourth of the cohesion funds. If the rest of the EU were to take the lessons of Italy's history to heart, however, they would seek to limit as quickly and firmly as possible the use of cohesion funds as an instrument of political assimilation, much less as a means of economic development.

FROM BILATERALISM TO MULTILATERALISM: 1945–63

Italy emerged from World War II in much the same condition as Germany in that its distribution network and consumer production facilities were devastated by wartime destruction and overburdened by the return of refugees and demobilized soldiers. As a result, its per capita income was perhaps half that before the war and some estimates put it as low as the 1900 level. Also like Germany, its producer goods facilities, especially in engineering products and transport equipment, had been greatly expanded during the war by the Fascist regime. Even with the destruction imposed by bombing and demolition by the warring armies, the total capital stock available was probably only 8 percent less than in 1938, while in the engineering sector it may have been as much as 50 percent greater, even allowing for wartime losses.[1] The basis for postwar industrial expansion was thus similar to Germany's—a modern industrial plant available for conversion to consumer goods once it could be staffed and provisioned and markets were opened up. Unlike Germany, however, it was not permanently divided by the Allied powers, although the country had been physically divided during the last two years of the war. The reunification of the country took place immediately rather than forty-five years later, as it did in Germany. This required immediate attention to "making both ends meet," in the felicitous phrase of Ferruccio Parri, the prime minister in 1945. In retrospect, it may have been better for Italian long-run growth to delay dealing with the backward part of the country, as in the German case.

Another major difference from Germany is that there was no currency reform in Italy. The currency continued to be the prewar lira, and Italy joined the International Monetary Fund with its exchange rate pegged at 100 lira to the dollar. This was a substantial devaluation from its prewar value of 19 to the dollar, but it still didn't take sufficient account of the tremendous increase of currency issued during the war. Not only the Fascist government of Mussolini during the active participation of Italy in the war, but also the revolutionary government during the civil war that followed his fall from power relied primarily on seigniorage, the creation of new money, to finance their military expenditures. This practice continued after the war as the peacetime governments were confronted with the need to reestablish national unity and create legitimacy for the new republic. One estimate suggests that the Italian money supply had increased fifteen-fold in the seven years from 1938 to 1945. Most of this increase came in the form of notes, which rose from 57 percent of the total to over 70 percent.[2] In the next two years, the money supply was increased at even faster rates as prices were liberalized and commercial banks began to expand their loan operations, which leveraged up the increase in note issue into even larger increases in deposits. The official rate of the lira was raised from 100 to 225 to the dollar at the end of 1946, reflecting the rapid inflation that had taken place.

In May 1947, a new government headed by the Christian Democrat, Alcide de Gaspari, came to power. De Gaspari immediately made the governor of the Banca d'Italia, Luigi Einaudi, his deputy prime minister and budget minister. In this position, Einaudi was able to enact legislation that permitted the central bank to exercise control both over the emission of new money and the banking sector's ability to expand deposits. The key was to impose effective reserve requirements on the banks for the first time. By September 1947, Einaudi had increased these to 25 percent of deposits. Henceforth, the government could continue to run deficits (which it did relentlessly), but instead of financing them by issuing notes it could now finance them by issuing short-term debt. Banks could count this as part of their reserves, and typically preferred holding government debt to notes because the debt earned them interest, usually at high rates. So most of the government's new debt was sold to banks rather than to the general public. Banks continued to expand their loans on the basis of this increase in reserves, but now at a much reduced rate, because 25 percent of any deposits created had to be backed by legal reserves in addition to the cash reserves they kept on hand to meet fluctuations in withdrawals. This "Italian monetary arithmetic" allowed the government to continue deficit spending and both the central bank and the banking sector to expand the money supply while keeping inflation at modest levels and stabilizing the exchange rate of the lira. This had been devalued by Einaudi in August 1947 to 350 lira to the dollar. In September 1949, when a general devaluation of European currencies occurred, he devalued the lira again to 625 to the dollar. There it remained until the problems of the 1960s.

In trade developments, Italy quickly found it had a comparative advantage with the rest of Europe in engineering products and transport equipment, as well as chemicals and clothing. By 1961, production of these had all expanded dramatically, creating an export-led growth miracle for Italy. This was directed mainly toward Western Europe (60%) and especially toward its partners in the EEC after 1958 (30%). Export earnings helped finance the growth of imports as well, composed mainly of food and raw materials at first, and then fuel in increasing importance over the 1960s. Despite clear evidence of export-led growth, however, Italy typically ran a deficit on trade in goods and services. This was more than covered, typically, by growing tourism expenditures and, especially, emigrants' remittances. For the rest of Europe in these early years, Italy's true comparative advantage was in tourist sites and migrant labor. The returns from these "invisibles" on current account led to a remarkable increase in Italy's foreign reserves. From barely $26 million at the end of 1947, when Einaudi's reforms began to take hold, they had expanded to $4.6 billion at the end of 1961.[3]

The Marshall Plan played an important role in focusing Italian policymakers' attention on critical investment programs and in strengthening the economic liberalism of the early Italian governments. De Gaspari had been disappointed in early 1947 when he went to the United States in person to seek aid specifically for Italy. It was on his return in May that he shook up his cabinet by replacing left-wing ministers with more conservative types, bringing in Einaudi as budget minister and deputy premier among others. Marshall's speech came the next month, and Italy was an eager participant in the resulting European Recovery Plan. In response to the American request for specific plans for using the grants, the Saraceno Plan was devised between the summers of 1947 and 1948. It focused on productive investment in heavy industry and infrastructure, much like the Monnet Plan in France. The intent was to position Italy for competing effectively in the forthcoming liberalization of European markets. It specifically anticipated restricting the growth of consumption. While the plan had even less force behind it than the Monnet Plan in France, a comparison of its projections to 1952 and the results actually achieved by the end of the Marshall Plan indicates that its goals were realized to a surprising extent. The only major shortfall was in the amount of rail freight, but this was due to the unexpectedly large increase in freight transport by road.[4] Much of the Marshall Plan aid went directly to finance the capital projects of Italy's huge state holding companies, the IRI for iron and steel production as well as a huge range of machinery from household appliances to heavy equipment, and ENI for hydroelectric power plants and oil refineries. Both were viewed with suspicion by American advisors at the time, but each became a huge, vertically integrated, conglomerate. Only in the 1990s have steps begun to privatize parts of each.

The comparative advantage of Italy in providing migrant labor for the rest of Europe was corroborated by large unemployment, especially in the south. This became an increasing concern first of American advisors, who encouraged public works projects along lines of the Tennessee Valley Authority for creating jobs. Moreover, a series of peasant revolts broke out due to the excess labor force in agriculture. Over 40 percent of the total labor force of Italy at the time was in the agricultural sector. The peasant revolts aimed first at land reform, the breaking up of the large estates that prevailed especially in southern Italy. Their demands were met by setting up "reform zones" within which the least utilized land might be confiscated for redistribution to peasants. Most such redistributions occurred in the south, and despite the unattractive nature of the confiscated land, they did lead to an increase in the area farmed by peasant-owners. The other solution to underemployment in rural and southern Italy, of course, was migration to the cities in northern Italy, especially in the triangle formed by Genoa, Turin, and Milan. However, despite the rise of manufacturing output in the export booming sectors, very few new jobs were created in the manufacturing sector. Part of the explanation was the capital-intensive nature of the most successful firms. Part was the growing strength of labor unions in the North, who prevented easy access to their high-paying, skilled-labor jobs. And the remaining part was due to the restrictions on labor mobility that had been imposed by the Fascist regime before the war. The last such act, passed in 1939, forbade anyone of working age to move from his or her locality to another within Italy without a written employment contract from the new location. It was not repealed until 1961, although it had been ignored increasingly over the postwar years.[5]

The resolution of the unemployment–land distribution dilemma was confided to the Cassa per il Mezzogiorno, founded in August 1950. From the beginning, its efforts to close the gap in per capita incomes between the south and north of Italy were failures. But each failure led to more funding, either on grounds that the initial projects had not been large enough to generate self-sustaining development, or that they had been mis-directed and different projects were required. The first projects focused on improvements to the worthless land being redistributed to discontented peasants. This meant irrigation projects and roads and lucrative contracts for manufacturing and construction firms in the north. Reevaluating the lack of progress in closing the income differential, the Cassa shifted its priorities toward large-scale industrial projects. Again, these had an immediate effect on stimulating expansion in the manufacturing sector for capital goods in the already dynamic north. The end result was to encourage continued out-migration from the south, both abroad and to the north. In this way, the unemployment problem was gradually eliminated. In 1963, the unemployment rate dropped to its lowest level in the twentieth century (see Figure 11.1), a level it seems unlikely to reach again before the end of the century.

In sum, the first sixteen years of the Italian miracle (1947–63) can be explained by an unusually favorable set of circumstances that happened to combine at this time. First and foremost was the political commitment of the Italian government toward export promotion and a firm attachment to the rest of Western Europe. Under de Gasperi and then Einaudi, the Italian government embraced Marshall Plan aid and joined the International Monetary Fund in 1947, while taking steps to stabilize the exchange rate of the lira and to make it fully convertible for foreign trade within the confines of the European Payment Union. Italy also was an original member of the North Atlantic Treaty Organization, despite being nowhere close to the Atlantic, and quickly joined the European Coal and Steel Community in 1953, despite being left out of the original negotiations that determined its institutional design. These commitments culminated with the Treaty of Rome signed in 1957 to set up the European Economic Community.

The second favorable circumstance was the enormous supply of labor in rural Italy, which helped provide cheap, productive labor to the construction and manufacturing sectors in Italy, as well as to much of the rest of Europe, especially France and Germany. The third factor was the ready supply of financing available to Italian industry from the plowback of profits or from the government-directed banking sector. The high rates of investment by both private and public firms were matched by high rates of saving. These were motivated, as in the rest of war-torn Europe, by the desire of individuals to rebuild as quickly as possible a secure stock of assets to replace what had been lost during the depression, the war, the disruption of the postwar settlements, or in the process of migrating. A liberal economic environment, an elastic labor supply, and high rates of saving and investment combined to allow Italy to catch up quickly with the levels of technical advance available in the United States and the more advanced industrial countries in Europe.

FROM EMIGRATION TO IMMIGRATION: 1963–73

The policy variables traced out in Figure 11.1 do not show any particular break in pattern after 1963. But in the political sphere some important changes did occur, which were to lay the basis for increasing problems in the future. The center-right coalition that had guided Italy out of postwar depression into the "golden age" of economic growth was replaced by a center-left coalition that was more responsive to the social needs of transplanted workers and the aging population. The new Republic of Italy formed after the war had deliberately built in numerous checks on the power of government bureaucracy to control the economy and the society to avoid the recurrence of Fascism. But the governing politicians quickly found they had to establish legitimacy the "old-fashioned way," namely by granting favors to constituents and building up a base of patronage. As labor became scarce for Italy's expanding economy, labor unions were able to exercise more influence over wages and working conditions. Firms responded by investing more in labor-saving capital and reducing the rate of increase in employment. Government responded by investing more in public works projects designed to increase employment. Growth continued as a result, but inflation began to rise, and under the surface, tensions were increasing as southern migrants tried to assimilate in the north and returning migrants from abroad tried to reestablish themselves.

Tensions led to the "hot autumn" of 1969, the delayed counterpart of the "events of May" that had disrupted the economy and political system of France the year before. Strikes that had been increasing in number and severity over the course of the 1960s now became general and essentially closed down the Italian economy for awhile. The government responded by strengthening the role of unions in industry and the public sector even further. An essential part was indexing wages to the cost of living index more closely and more widely than before. The *scala mobile* thus amended was a key factor in accelerating inflation when the first oil shock hit the Italian economy at the end of 1973. The pension schemes were also altered to widen their coverage and to index their outpayments less to the previous earnings of the retiree and more to the general rise in the cost of living and in the average wage level. This was to prove an increasing burden on the financial resources of the state. As in the case of France, a general rise in wages was agreed on, and labor unions were given more power over work rules. Finally, the level of unemployment benefits was increased to 100 percent of the worker's previous earnings and the duration of eligibility was increased.

This latter concession opened a Pandora's box. Not only were laid-off workers now less likely to search hard for new jobs, since they could maintain their standard of living without the nuisance of actually working for an income, but unions could press for higher wages knowing that the resulting layoffs would make their members no worse off. Firms then were willing to accede to demands for higher wages, knowing they could lay off more workers without facing union resistance. Faced with the duty of paying higher contributions to unemployment insurance and eventually faced with restrictions imposed by the government on firing workers, however, the firms became increasingly reluctant to hire new workers. So both firms and unions conspired to make the government pay higher levels of unemployment benefits to ever larger numbers of unemployed.

The rise of the informal economy in this period led to the de facto division of Italy into three major regions—the north, the south, and the center. Each began to identify itself separately from the rest of Italy, much as Italians traditionally had identified first with their family, then with their village, and then with the rest of the world, quite overlooking the role of the Italian nation-state in their lives. The ruling political coalitions in the government, despite the rapid change of cabinets that began in this period, were remarkably stable in their composition. They always consisted of the Christian Democratic party and its current leader at the heart of the coalition, with temporary, uneasy alliances made with just enough parties in Parliament to reach a bare majority. This meant that any small party could defect and create another change in cabinet if it thought it would benefit some way. The upshot of this system of proportional representation in Parliament meant that even the political parties found it in their interests to conspire against the nation-state!

The overall stability in the leadership of the government that resulted, however, meant that no new political initiatives were forthcoming to deal with Italy's changed role in the world and its changed economic structure. Such changes as occurred merely strengthened the existing organizations—the labor unions, the huge public sector combines, the Cassa per il Mezzogiorno, and even the Mafia. The result was an increasingly rigid structure unable to withstand the shocks that faced all of Europe in the 1970s.

FINANCING THE OIL SHOCKS: 1974–85

The weaknesses of the government that had been built deliberately into the constitution of the Italian republic prevented it from defending itself from the combined assault on its resources by workers, firms, and politicians. The consequence was ever larger government deficits and a mounting stock of debt to be serviced. Figure 11.2 shows clearly what happened. The first oil shock shifted this inflationary mechanism that had been constructed in 1969 into high gear. Italy suffered the highest and most persistent rates of inflation of any West European country through the two oil shocks of the 1970s. The depressed economies of the rest of Europe meant rising unemployment there as well, so more Italian workers returned home. Italy, like France, was faced with "stagflation," which it had managed to create for itself by its own policies. The stock of government debt, which had already been high at 30 percent of GDP in 1961, had

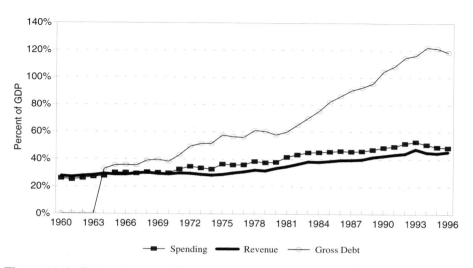

Figure 11.2. Government spending, revenue, and debt, Italy, 1960–96.

risen to over 50 percent by 1982. Individuals responded by moving into the "informal economy," which meant that not only did they avoid paying income taxes, a time-honored Italian tradition made possible by weak government, but they also avoided reporting their employment, so they could continue to draw unemployment benefits, pensions, and disability pay. Moreover, the small and medium-sized firms hiring them could avoid paying social security contributions, which added at least 40 percent to the cost of formal labor, and actually offer the workers higher direct wages as a result. Now both workers and employers found it beneficial to conspire against the state to enlarge the informal, unrecorded part of the Italian economy.

In the midst of this increasing dysfunctionality of the state, one step was taken that held out the promise of eventual recuperation. This was the determination of the Banca d'Italia to join the European Monetary System and commit Italy to maintaining a fixed exchange rate with respect to the strong, stable currencies among its primary trading partners. In one sense, the Banca d'Italia was joining the general conspiracy against the weak government, allying itself with the powerful and independent Bundesbank to resist the pressure placed on it by national politicians to increase the money supply and ease the controls on domestic credit. But in a more important sense it was reaffirming the original commitment of Italy to European integration. Even though it had the highest margins of fluctuation for its central par rate with the ECU, 6 percent in place of the normal 2.25 percent, Italy was now on track to restoring the stable lira that had characterized the years of economic miracle. Moreover, it was assuring its primary trading partners that it would not be engaged in competitive, advantage-seeking devaluations. The evident success of Germany in weathering the first oil shock by appreciating its currency against the dollar was an incentive for initiating a strong currency policy, but an even stronger incentive was the unwillingness of the Bundesbank to continue supporting the lira without such a commitment by the Banca d'Italia and the Italian government. Previous loans to Italy to help it meet payments for imported oil had led to a return flood of the deutsche marks to business accounts in Germany, making the Bundesbank uneasy about this temporary loss of control over the German money supply. Still, the Italian commitment to the EMS was a major step to take.

More than any other European country, Italy was dependent on imported oil as the primary source of energy for its now industrial economy. In common with the bilateral deals that Germany was striking with Iran and France with Iraq and Algeria, Italy turned to Libya as a prime source for assured supplies of vital fuel. It made overtures to the Soviet Union for tapping into those vast reservoirs of natural gas and petroleum and attempted a series of countertrade arrangements—Fiat factories for fuel at fixed prices. Threatened by renewed rural unrest, Italy was reluctant to see Greece, much less Spain and Portugal, enter into the Common Agricultural Policy and compete with its farmers in the south. Having seen employment opportunities in the rest of the Common Market taken up by foreign guest workers imported into Germany from Turkey and Yugoslavia and into France from Portugal and Spain, Italy could no longer rely on its EC partners to absorb its labor surplus. In view of all these forces tending to reduce Italy's reliance on mutual support from the other member states of the EEC, its commitment to enter the European Monetary System when it began operation in 1979 is all the more striking.

Of course, this made Italy, like France, all the less capable of meeting the second oil shock in 1979 and the subsequent Volcker shock (see Chapter 10), except by further government spending and enlarged deficits. From an already high ratio of government debt to GDP of over 50 percent in 1982, the ratio quickly rose to over 100 percent by the end of the 1980s. Unemployment nevertheless rose even more sharply as the rate of inflation was brought down close to Community levels. With rising unemployment and increased rates of retirement came permanent demands on central government spending for unemployment benefits and pensions. The early 1980s saw Italy's growth rates of GDP staggering at their lowest levels since 1947. Small wonder that it was responsive to the Single Market initiative and the promise of expanded markets for Italian goods that had proven their attractiveness to the rest of the world in previous decades.

IN AND OUT OF THE EMS: 1986–96

In common with the rest of the EC, Italy enjoyed renewed rates of growth in the mid 1980s and was able to continue bringing down the rate of inflation. Only a couple of devaluations were necessary for the lira within the EMS. As all of the European currencies devalued against the U.S. dollar in the early 1980s, Italy was able to increase its exports outside of Europe. Moreover, the collapse in the price of oil after 1985 helped Italy more than the rest of Europe due to its greater dependence on imported oil. Unemployment, however, remained high and even began increasing again by 1986. The government's deficits continued. However, thanks to its commitment to the European Monetary System, it found that the market for its debt had been greatly enlarged. Now that Italian bonds with their high rates of interest paid in lira could be expected to pay these rates as well in francs or deutsche marks, they became an attractive asset for investors in the rest of Europe. Italian monetary arithmetic, first discovered with the financial repression imposed on Italian banks by Luigi Einaudi in 1947 and then amplified by the appeal of high-yield, very liquid financial assets to the Italian public, now received another boost from entry into a fixed exchange rate regime with its wealthier trading partners in Europe.

The access to a wider market for Italian financial assets was taken advantage of by Italian support for the removal of capital controls as an extension of the Single Market. One of the four freedoms was the movement of capital. Initially, this led to a boom in the Milan stock market. Italian banks were forced to compete with foreign banks and with mutual funds for their deposits for the first time in history. Mutual funds sprang up to direct household savings into Italian equities, and foreign banks and investment firms set up shop in Milan to gain access to these high-yielding, exchange rate riskless assets for their customers. Italy helped the process by renouncing the 6 percent fluctuation bands in 1989, reducing them to the 2.25 percent used by everyone else. Immediately, an influx of fresh capital occurred, pasting the lira against the upper intervention band. This success, as much as anything, helped persuade first Spain and then even Great Britain to join the EMS in 1990. Unfortunately, it also encouraged the Italian government to continue its deficits and the building up of its mountain of overhanging debt.

As a result, Italy, now committed to close parity with the deutsche mark in foreign exchange markets and stripped of its previous defenses that relied on capital controls and limited competition within the financial sector, was more vulnerable than any other European country to the German reunification shock that occurred in late 1990. (See Chapter 9.) Foreign capital that had found the high interest rates of Italian bonds attractive, now found the rising interest rates in Germany even more attractive. Moreover, excess savings available for investment in Italian bonds by the rest of Europe were now diminished. Foreign capital that had flowed in quickly began to flow out just as rapidly. The mounting pressure on Italian foreign reserves culminated in September 1992, when Italy was forced to withdraw from the European Monetary System and let the lira float. It promptly fell sharply and has only slowly begun to rise back toward its previous levels in the years since.

As Figure 11.1 shows, the devalued lira allowed Italian growth rates to rise again, led by increased exports. The rate of inflation continued to be low, while unemployment began to fall again after an initial increase. The favorable experience of Italy on withdrawal from the EMS, in common with that of Great Britain (Chapter 12), which withdrew or was ejected at the same time, should have shaken Italian confidence in the continued value of following the lead of France and Germany toward deeper and deeper modes of economic integration. In the end, it did not, primarily because Italy was more preoccupied with reforming at long last the weak, corrupt, and now dysfunctional political system it had created at the end of World War II. The determination of independent prosecutors to root out the influence of the Mafia in the south led to revelations of political corruption in the north as well and eventually to a revulsion against the entire political establishment.

Referendums were held in 1991 and again in April 1993, in which the Italian electorate overwhelmingly expressed their desire for a new electoral system that would give clearer results and allow strong governments to be formed by the winning parties. On this basis, the prime minister at the time, Giuliano Amato, leader of the reformed Communist Party which now called itself the Democratic Party of the Left, resigned to permit the transition toward a Second Republic of Italy to begin. Under the leadership of Carlo Ciampi, the former governor of the Banca d'Italia, constitutional reform proposals were approved. These combined "first past the post" election rules for some seats in Parliament with the traditional "proportional representation" rules of the past. Elections to constitute the new Parliament based on these new rules were held in March 1994. As a result, an entirely new coalition of right-wing parties led by Silvio Berlusconi's new Forza Italia party came to power. However, by refusing to give up his extensive business interests and even promoting legislation that would increase the profitability of his television empire, Berlusconi quickly managed to lose support of his allies and had to resign in December 1994. A caretaker government led by yet another former head of the Banca d'Italia, Lamberto Dini, was formed.

Dini tried to reduce the budget deficit by continuing privatization of parts of the state holding companies, IRI and ENI (see above), and reforming the state pension system to reduce the future liability of the state to manageable dimensions. Only by agreeing to step down at the end of 1995 was he able to stay in power long enough to enact the beginning of these reforms. In the new elections held in April 1996, yet another untried coalition of new parties came to power. This was the center-left Olive Tree coalition led by a moderate economics professor, Romano Prodi. While he enjoyed an absolute majority in the upper house, he had to form a coalition with smaller parties in the lower house to maintain the premiership. Nevertheless, he was able to accomplish this while maintaining the commitment for privatization and pension reform made by the previous Dini government and insisting on further measures to reduce the deficit. By the fall of 1996, Prodi was able to announce the determination of Italy to rejoin the EMS by the end of 1997, in time to be an initial participant in the European Monetary Union, scheduled to begin Stage 3 January 1, 1999. In fact, he negotiated Italy's reentry to the exchange rate mechanism of the EMS effective November 25, 1996.

The primary budget of Italy, that is, the part that excludes payment of interest on the outstanding stock of accumulated debt, continues to be in surplus. Meanwhile, the continued low rates of inflation and reductions in budget deficits have led to a fall in the interest rates on the government debt. Any fall in interest rates, in turn, reduces significantly the amount of spending on debt service that is required, as older debt issues with high interest rates can be paid off by issuing new debt with the lower interest rates. Prodi was confident that if the foreign exchange markets gave increasing credibility to the Italian commitment to the European Monetary Union, interest rates would continue to fall. The combined effects of falling debt service and a primary budget surplus could lead quickly to an overall surplus. That would begin a downward trend in the stock of government debt, which could satisfy the Maastricht criterion that satisfactory progress should be under way to reduce the proportion of debt to gross domestic product to under 60 percent.

Another factor that should accelerate the fall in the deficit and debt ratio is the continued rise in the measured level of Italian GDP. This results from two factors. First, and initially most important, is an attempt to include in the official statistics some estimate of the size of the informal sector, which is presumed to be larger than in any other member country in the EU. Second, as tax reforms are made and regulations on hiring and firing practices of firms are rationalized, more economic activity should become evident in the formal sector. But all this depends on the continued commitment of Italian governments to economic reform along the lines shown to be effective in the American and British cases during the 1980s.

CONCLUSION

Italy's commitment to the development of a Europe integrated economically and cooperating peacefully politically remains undiminished despite the travails, both economic and political, that it has undergone in the past decade. Despite opting out of the European Monetary System in 1992 and remaining out at least until 1996 it has affirmed its desire to remain on the "fast track" of European integration by being in the first wave of entrants to the European Monetary Union being promoted by France and Germany. In common with the core countries of the European Union, Italy wishes to enact the Schengen Accord, which would oblige it to enforce at its borders the same controls on immigration from Central and Eastern Europe that Germany imposes and on immigration from North Africa that France imposes. This would be consistent with its desire to limit the influx of refugees from Albania and the former Yugoslavia as well.

In terms of the institutional reforms of the European Union being considered by the Inter-Governmental Conference of 1996–97, the Italian position is quite consistent with that of both France and Germany. It wants to see a more effective structure of decision making at the European Union level put into place. This requires more decisions to be made by majority voting within the Council of Ministers, fewer commissioners, a stronger presidency of the Commission, and a stronger role for the European Parliament, provided its composition reflects the relative weight of the member states more accurately than at present. The majority voting in the Council, however, should be a double majority. That is, there should be both a majority of the member states and of the population of the entire European Union in support of a particular piece of legislation before it can be enacted. In a potential compromise between the large countries and the small countries over the issue of representation on the European Commission, Italian leaders have suggested just one Commissioner for each country, but possibly a deputy commissioner for the larger countries as well. On the issue of the relationship between national parliaments and the European Parliament, Italy simply asks for closer consultation between the two with respect for the principle of subsidiarity setting the terms of consultation. Again, in a spirit of compromise, Italy rejects the idea of codifying what constitutes subsidiarity or of specifying the lines of authority between national parliaments and the legislative authority of the European Union.

On the issue of a common security and foreign policy, Italy supports the common position of France and Germany to try to project a common European Union position in this dimension. One thought, again in the spirit of Italian compromise, is to continue the current role of rotating presidencies among the member countries, but to appoint a separate secretary-general, who would have a three- to five-year term and be responsible for representing the EU on foreign policy issues. Eventually, the goal would be to place the EU on the Security Council of the United Nations, counter to the long-standing American objective of placing both Germany and Japan as permanent members of the Security Council.

Finally, the West European Union is seen as the eventual military arm of the EU, projecting the necessary force to make credible its common security and foreign policy. Nevertheless, Italy continues to pledge its adherence to the North Atlantic Treaty Organization and to support the continued close relationship of Europe and the United States as both political and military allies. The entry of new members into the EU is seen as a completely separate issue from their joining NATO. But while the entry of the Central and Eastern European states should be encouraged, the role of Mediterranean states should not be overlooked, which implies support for the prompt entry of both Malta and Cyprus. Even Slovenia, despite its territorial disputes with Italy, which have reopened the discussions over the role of Trieste and its hinterland, would be viewed favorably for membership in this context (see Chapter 17). Moreover, all the potential new members have to be helped to implement legislation that is conformable to EU standards already in place. The Common Agricultural Policy may have to be revised in any event, but whatever changes are decided on, the new member states will have to play by the rules that have been decided on previously.

From this brief overview of the initial bargaining position of Italy in the Inter-Governmental Conference that will decide the political structure of the EU going into the twenty-first century, it can be seen that Italy has a split personality in its European identity, just as it has a deep split between the north and south internally in its national identity. While the major powers of Germany and France insist on projecting forward into the next century their common vision of Europe that was formed in the 1950s, while Great Britain remains on the sideline as diffident and dubious now as it was about this vision in the 1950s, Italy may play the decisive role in determining Europe's future. After all, it is in the midst of a serious reexamination of its own constitutional structure and is experimenting with alternative forms of governance on an ongoing basis. Out of the lessons learned from its inner travail, Italy may well propose the realistic procedures needed for Europe to achieve the next stages of integration.

Endnotes

1. Vera Zamagni, *The Economic History of Italy, 1860–1990. Recovery after Decline,* Oxford: Clarendon Press, 1993, p. 321.
2. George Hildebrand, *Growth and Structure in the Economy of Modern Italy,* Cambridge, Mass.: Harvard University Press, 1965, pp. 16–17.
3. Hildebrand, note 2, p. 79.
4. Zamagni, note 1, p. 328.
5. Ibid., p. 312, fn. 27.

Bibliography

Böhm, Bernhard and Lionello F. Punzo, eds. *Economic Performance, A Look at Austria and Italy.* Heidelberg: Physica-Verlag, 1994.

Donata, Pierpaolo. "Social welfare and social service in Italy since 1950," in Roger Girod, Patrick de Laubier and Alan Gladstone, eds. *Social Policy in Western Europe and the USA, 1950–1980. An Assessment.* New York: St. Martin's Press, 1985.

Economist Intelligence Unit. *Country Report, Italy.* London: Economist Intelligence Unit, 2nd quarter, 1996.

Hildebrand, George. *Growth and Structure in the Economy of Modern Italy.* Cambridge, Mass.: Harvard University Press, 1965.

Kostoris, Fiorella Padoa Schioppa. *Italy, the Sheltered Economy.* Oxford: Clarendon Press, 1993.

Podbielski, Gisele. *Italy. Development and Crisis in the Post-War Economy.* London: Oxford University Press, 1974.

Rey, Guido. "Italy," in Andrea Boltho, ed. *The European Economy, Growth and Crisis,* Oxford: Oxford University Press, 1982.

Rossi, Nicola, and Gianni Toniolo. "Italy," in Nicholas Crafts and Gianni Toniolo, eds. *Economic Growth in Europe since 1945.* Cambridge: Cambridge University Press, 1996.

Zamagni, Vera. *The Economic History of Italy, 1860–1990. Recovery after Decline.* Oxford: Clarendon Press, 1993.

Great Britain:

Decolonization, Declining Regions, and the Thatcher Legacy

Basic Facts (1993)		
Area:	244,100 km²	7.5 % of EU15
Population:	58,276,000	15.7 % of EU15
GDP:	$949.7 billion	15.9 % of EU15
Per Capita:	$16,367	101 % of EU15 average
Openness (X + M)/GDP	41 %	51 % with EU12

Source: Eurostat, *Basic Statistics of the European Union,* 32nd ed. (Luxembourg, 1995).

Like Italy, Britain has had a positive turn of economic fortunes after leaving the European Monetary System and allowing the pound sterling to depreciate against the currencies of its main trading partners on the Continent. Growth rates have risen, unemployment continues to drop, and inflation has been moderate. With its language, legal system, and market regulations familiar and congenial to non-European firms, Britain has become a favorite destination for foreign direct investment in the 1990s. Despite these short-term advantages of remaining apart from the Franco-German enterprise, however, Britain's long-term destiny seems bound more and more with that of Europe. Failure to participate fully in the decision-making process of the European Union may mean losing out on the long-term benefits of the Single Market and a common currency.

To be in or not to be in? This question about their relations with Europe has plagued British policymakers since the end of World War II. As the one country in Europe that avoided domination by the Nazi war machine during World War II, Britain served both as the supply depot for American material support and as the launching pad for American military force against the Nazi-occupied Europe. In this critical position, British leaders managed to play an equal role with their American counterparts in formulating Allied policies, from high politics (Churchill and Roosevelt) to military strategy (Montgomery and Eisenhower) to international finance (Keynes and Morgenthau). Following the war, however, Britain was in no position to play on equal terms with its super-power partner across the Atlantic. Two economic factors, one external and one internal, were to plague Britain for the next three decades.

Externally, British war finance created enormous debts, denominated in pounds sterling, that Britain owed to its sterling area trading partners in order to maintain British forces around the world and to supply vital materials to the war effort in Europe. Offsets to the debts were arranged with Canada, Australia, and South Africa; U.S. aid came under the provisions of the Lend-Lease Agreement; but India and Egypt held large sums on account. Against total liabilities of over £3 billion (£1.7 billion to India, Burma, and the Middle East) at the end of 1945, Britain had available less than £0.5 billion in gold and dollar reserves.[1] These reserves would have been lost immediately to Britain's creditors if the sterling balances could have been converted into gold or dollars at the exchange rate agreed on at Bretton Woods with the Americans (and the independent countries in the sterling area). Indeed, an American loan of $3.75 billion granted in 1946 on condition that the pound resume convertibility just on current account transactions was exhausted by mid-1947, within weeks after convertibility was allowed. Britain now needed more imports from the dollar area than from the sterling area, while the sterling area needed more imports from the United States than from Britain. So the result was that exporters throughout the sterling area turned in their sterling proceeds for dollars to pay for imports from the United States. Scarred by this episode, British authorities became obsessed about exchange rate policy and available foreign reserves. They continued to block the sterling balances from being converted into dollars or gold, which meant keeping trade within the sterling area from becoming fully integrated within the multilateral trading system desired by the United States. Indeed, the blocked sterling balances were not fully eliminated until 1979, as part of the conditions for an IMF loan to Britain.

The internal problem stemmed from the promise of the wartime government that British labor would be paid for its wartime sacrifices by payments deferred until the war was over. This created a monetary overhang domestically as well. Eliminating it in the French fashion by allowing rapid inflation would have caused a rapid devaluation of the pound on current account. This would have increased immediately the burden of the sterling balances, which had been pegged to the dollar and gold. Eliminating it in the Italian fashion by financial repression on the financial sector would have reduced its foreign exchange earnings, which were important for covering Britain's traditional deficit on trade. As a result, wartime measures of price controls and rationing had to be continued until the early 1950s, with some lasting until 1954. These were the domestic counterpart of blocked sterling balances to overseas creditors.

To ensure the end of a war economy, British voters elected a Labour party government in the first postwar election. Labour immediately implemented its program of the modern welfare state, characterized as "cradle to grave" insurance, and nationalized basic industries to ensure that workers continued to be employed and not laid off in massive numbers as had been the case after World War I. Only after Margaret Thatcher was elected prime minister in 1979 was any attempt made to undo nationalization or to limit the power of labor unions. Nationalization reduced the government's tax base while its commitment to extensive entitlements increased its peacetime expenditures. Labour's social policy therefore made British governments very aware of fiscal policy and its uses, while the use of price controls and rationing effectively ruled out paying much attention to monetary policy.

At first, Britain took the lead in organizing the European response to the American initiative of the Marshall Plan and benefited correspondingly as the largest single recipient of Marshall Plan aid. But under the European Payments Union, the bulk of British trade proved to be with its former trading partners in the sterling area and with the United States, rather than with the other European members. This may help explain why it had no part in the Schuman Plan, much less the European Coal and Steel Community, which were entirely continental enterprises. When the idea of forming the European Economic Community and Euratom arose, Britain continued to opt out, preferring to rely on its special relationship with the United States. These decisions must be seen in retrospect as stemming from British preoccupation with the perils of decolonization, which in the case of India and Egypt were complicated by settlement of the wartime sterling accounts, as well as reflecting the non-European orientation of British trade. While West Germany and Italy were recovering rapidly in the 1950s, France and Belgium were lagging, so it was not yet clear that British economic strategy was inferior to the European.

This did become clear during the 1960s, however, as the original six members of the EEC enjoyed continued high and smooth rates of economic growth, while Britain's growth rate continued to lag. Perhaps it was the low savings rate of Britain that kept down its rate of investment and therefore of modernization of its industry. Perhaps it was the exceptional openness of the British economy, which meant that any expansion of exports from devaluation was quickly offset by an increase in the price of imports and the cost of living; this led to increased wages and a loss of the devaluation effect in the price of exports. Perhaps it was the aggressive, undisciplined behavior of British labor unions, which called out strikes at the least provocation to any craft in any plant, regardless of the broader interests of a national or industrial union such as maintained labor peace on the continent.

Whatever the diagnosis, it appeared that it would be better for Britain to have improved access to the European trade area. Even though the common external tariff against British exports was being reduced by the Dillon and Kennedy rounds, there would always be a price wedge between European and British goods and border controls that would disadvantage British manufacturers. So Britain made a belated application to join the EEC in 1963, only to be rejected because of DeGaulle's hostility to the British (and American) vision of Europe's future. Even when a Labour government reapplied in 1967, France rejected its application. It was not until President DeGaulle was replaced by Georges Pompidou in 1969 that British membership could be accepted. And then it took a Conservative government led by Edward Heath to renew the British application. By the early 1970s, American preoccupation with the Vietnam War and then its unilateral abrogation of the Bretton Woods system in 1971 ended the special financial relationship with Britain that the Bretton Woods Treaty had codified. This had the effect of making the Europeans much more receptive than previously to Britain's membership. In 1973, it joined the EEC along with two of its closest European trading partners, Ireland and Denmark.

Ironically, by the end of its first year in the European Community, the first oil shock occurred (the OPEC oil embargo of October 1973) and the fundamental differences in economic strategy between Britain and its European trading partners were again brought to the fore. While each European country formulated it own, specifically national, response to the quadrupled price of imported oil, only Britain and Norway had access to the one potential source of crude petroleum in Western Europe—North Sea oil. For Norway, having opted out of the British initiative to join the EEC in 1973 (although coming very close, as again in 1995), the strategy was clear. This was to invest heavily in offshore drilling platforms to tap the North Sea oil fields and to do everything to keep the price of oil high in the meantime, to ensure that the costs of developing the production facilities over several years could eventually be repaid. It did not take long for this to become the announced British strategy as well. Both countries benefited more than they lost, therefore, from the second oil shock in 1979 when OPEC doubled the price of oil.

But until the second oil shock, Britain's investment in North Sea oil created more problems because it had to finance the outlays while paying extraordinarily high prices for necessary imports of fuel. The pound weakened against the dollar in 1976, raising the cost of imported oil further. A loan from the IMF was made conditional on unblocking the last of the sterling balances left from World War II. Inflation rose even more than in the Italian case and unemployment soared also. Despite the improvement in British external accounts in 1977 and 1978, the winter of 1978–79 brought general discontent by the rest of the country. In May 1979, Margaret Thatcher became prime minister and launched the Thatcher revolution just as the second oil shock hit the industrialized world.

Thatcher was determined to limit the power of the unions, to privatize the basic industries that had been nationalized, to reassert British military power, and, in general, to undo the democratic socialist experiment that had begun in Britain after World War II. In her view, it had been given a fair test and had failed miserably. One element of this grand strategy was to win back concessions from the European Community, which had become an increasing, if still relatively minor, drain on British finances. Britain had always recognized that adoption of the EC's Common Agricultural Policy, which relied on price supports instead of income payments, would impose a net drain on the British economy. Britain imported most of its food supply from abroad, although like the rest of postwar Europe it was less reliant on imports than before the war.

Nevertheless, it would now have to impose the high variable levies of the EC instead of finding the cheapest source of supply, say from Canada or New Zealand. To compensate for this, British negotiators insisted on expanding EC expenditures on regional development projects for backward regions, including those affected by a declining industrial base (northwest England and south Wales, for example). The two oil shocks that followed British entry into the EC, however, also raised agricultural prices worldwide in addition to creating an industrial slump. This made the agricultural shortfall worse and exacerbated the problems of Britain's declining regions, so the compensation scheme did not begin to work as hoped.

It proved impossible to change the CAP to British tastes, especially as both Ireland and Denmark benefited enormously from it. Thatcher insisted on obtaining an explicit rebate on Britain's excessive net contribution to the EC's budget. This caused much antagonism toward Britain and prevented the British government from taking an effective role in setting the rest of Community policy. Finally, in 1984 a permanent rule was agreed on for determining the size of the British rebate. This may have helped increase British influence in the EC initiatives that followed: first was the enlargement to include Spain and Portugal (against the reluctance of France, Italy, and Greece); second, and most important, was the Single Market initiative in 1985. British support for the Single European Act created a momentum that surprised even the Eurocrats and the British, leading as it did to the Treaty of European Union in 1992. British cooperation with EC strategy culminated with the entry of Britain into the European Monetary System in October 1990, although this was motivated less by a burst of Euro-idealism than an effort to get the recurring problem of inflation under control by constraining the flexibility of the exchange rate. Ironically, entry into the EMS occurred just one month before Thatcher was eased out of office by her own party and replaced by her Chancellor of the Exchequer, John Major.

Under Major's leadership, Britain urged rapid completion of the Single Market and expansion to include the states of Central and East Europe as quickly as possible to solidify their newly elected, democratic governments. In this it made common cause with Germany. However, it drew back on the Maastricht Treaty, withdrew from the European Monetary System in September 1992, and has fought a series of battles over EU initiatives. These have ranged from the terms of qualified majority voting with expansion of the Council of Ministers to include Austria, Finland, and Sweden to objections to the terms imposed by the EU for assisting Britain in dealing with the mad cow disease. In each instance, Britain has ultimately lost its case and diminished its influence in setting the course of EU policy for the future.

MACROECONOMIC POLICY INDICATORS: 1960–97

Figure 12.1 shows the course of growth rates, inflation, and unemployment for Britain from 1960 to 1997. The growth rates of the 1960s were smooth and high by historical standards for Great Britain, but well behind those generally

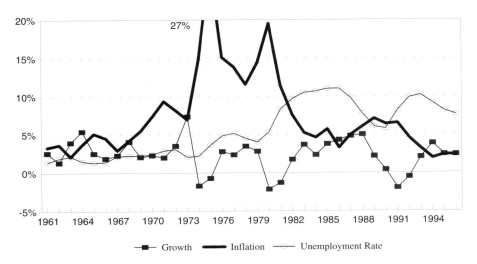

Figure 12.1. Macroeconomic policy indicators, Great Britain, 1960–96.

experienced on the European continent. Unemployment rates likewise were low by historical standards but still above those in the economic miracle leaders in the EEC. Moreover, inflation was definitely more of a struggle for British policymakers than for Germany or France, approaching double digits even before the first oil shock in 1974. This clearly hit Britain harder than any of the other large countries in Europe. Unemployment rates doubled, growth rates of GDP turned negative for two years running, and the inflation rate peaked at a record 27 percent in 1976. Small wonder Britain was a supplicant to the International Monetary Fund and had to meet stringent terms imposed at the insistence of both the United States and Germany.

It is interesting that the economic indicators were all improving in 1977 and 1978, despite the worsening political situation for the ruling Labour party. If the beginning of the Thatcher revolution was, in fact, the prime mover for these macroeconomic indicators in the years 1979–81, one would have to infer it was a disaster. Inflation shot up again close to 20 percent, unemployment rates jumped, never returning to their pre-Thatcher levels, and growth rates turned negative once again. Of course, the full panoply of Thatcher economic reforms was not yet in place or even begun as far as privatization or monetary policy was concerned. The second oil shock in 1979 and then the "Volcker shock" of 1980–81[2] were the dominant forces acting on the British economy, as they were on the rest of the European economies. The second oil shock, which doubled the price of oil, didn't affect Britain directly, since it exported as much oil by then as it imported. However, it certainly reduced worldwide demand in general and demand for British exports in particular. Worse, the British suffered even more than the EMS countries because in 1980, when the EMS currencies and most of the rest of the world's currencies began to fall against the dollar, the pound kept on rising. This further reduced Britain's export competitiveness.

The recovery of the British economy from the double shocks inflicted by OPEC and the United States was more rapid and more effective than that of its European trading partners. Even so, it took time and it seems doubtful, given the extra pain that the British had endured in Thatcher's first years of office, that the reforms Thatcher initiated would have been allowed to continue if she had not won reelection in 1983. That, in turn, was due to her ability, under the British system, to call for an election when popular opinion was favorable due to the British victory in the war over the Falklands/Malvinas islands off Argentina. Under Thatcher's continued leadership, inflation rates fell sharply and leveled off close to their 1960s levels while growth rates rose well above the 1960s levels by the late 1980s. Eventually, even the double-digit unemployment rates began to decline, in contrast to the continental experience, where they remained high. Confidence in the validity of the new policy regime rose even further as Britain seemed to be gaining more than the other large economies from the implementation of the Single Market program. The one, continuing, problem was the tendency for inflation to pick up with recovery in the economy. This has been the perennial problem facing British economic policymakers since the end of World War II, but it was especially frustrating that a determined policy to limit the growth of the money supply could not solve it. Thatcher finally relented under pressure from successive Chancellors of the Exchequer to try controlling inflation the way the French and Italians had—by joining the European Monetary System. Britain finally joined in October 1990.

This decision, coming at the same time Germany completed its reunification, enabled the British economy to share fully the economic shocks of German reunification. Growth rates fell and unemployment rose, but inflation rates did fall as hoped. Only by withdrawing from the European Monetary System in September 1992 was Britain able to restore some measure of the healthy growth it experienced at the height of the Thatcher era. And unemployment rates again began to edge down. Small wonder that doubts and fears about the economic wisdom of joining in the European march to a common currency by 1999 were felt most strongly and voiced most loudly in Great Britain, and within the ruling Conservative party at that.

FROM GREAT POWER TO WITHDRAWAL FROM EAST OF SUEZ: 1945–57

While free from actual invasion during World War II and firmly allied with the United States in the final victory, Great Britain found the price of winning to be very high indeed. If it were to maintain its wartime equality with the United States in determining global strategy, it had to sustain a large military force in peacetime. Of course, Britain had to maintain equal standing with the United States in the occupation and control of defeated Germany. In addition, however, vital British interests ranged from Hong Kong in the Far East to Newfoundland in the North Atlantic, with especial focus on India and the sea routes between Britain and India. Of special concern to a naval power with no domestic petroleum sources was continued access to the oil reserves of the Middle East. Attempts to regain control, however, were resisted everywhere by nationalist independence movements that had gained momentum throughout the interwar period and now seemed to be erupting everywhere. Consequently, military expenditures remained extremely high despite the election in 1945 of a Labour government committed to improvement of domestic living standards.

Part of the response of Britain was to persuade the United States to take a bigger role in protection of the Mediterranean sea lanes by coming to the support of anticommunist movements in Greece. In addition, the United States recognized the importance of maintaining rights of exploitation to the Iranian oil fields, rights that seemed to be jeopardized by Russian troop advances to the north of Iran. But the major response had to be coming to terms with the independence movement in India, the crown jewel of the British Empire since the middle of the eighteenth century and the source of the majority of Britain's land forces. Trade with India was considered, rightly, as the primary economic asset to Britain of the sterling area. Not only did imperial preference provide British exports of manufactured goods preferred access to the huge Indian market, but the earnings from providing the necessary shipping, insurance, brokerage, and financing services to sustain the trade were a valuable source of foreign exchange earnings. Britain's overall surplus on current account with India was hoped to offset its deficit with the United States and continental Europe, much as it had before World War I and again during the 1930s.

Providing political independence to Indian nationalists while maintaining the economic ties that had grown over two centuries meant reducing the drain on military resources required to reassert colonial control over a vast country while increasing the chances of restoring Britain's surplus on foreign account. Key to the success of this strategy was to maintain inconvertibility of the sterling balances that the colonial administration of India had built up during the war. A gradual reduction of these debts would then be possible by means of resuming an export surplus with not only India but the entire sterling area, which included Australia and New Zealand as well as South Africa, Malaysia, Egypt, and the remaining British colonies scattered around the globe. But to make this strategy work required limiting access of these traditional British customers to the now much preferred American market. The most effective way of doing this was to make the sterling balances inconvertible save against specified transactions with Britain.

In fact, this strategy worked well for its immediate purpose. Britain quickly removed its import deficit, which had continued for a couple of years after the war due to the need to restock its industrial and distribution system for civilian goods, but it did so mainly by increasing exports to the sterling area in the late 1940s. The export surplus with the sterling area, however, only partially reduced the overhand of sterling balances accumulated during the war and immediately afterward. It did nothing toward increasing Britain's reserves of gold or dollars. Without such reserves, it was in no position to play equal partner with the United States in the IMF or in financing the reconstruction of the rest of Western Europe. Britain did earn some dollars and gold from limited exports to the dollar area and received huge sums first in the form of relief from the

United Nations Relief and Rehabilitation Agency, the Anglo-American Loan of 1946, and the Marshall Plan. Britain, in fact, was the largest recipient of Marshall Plan aid. But it offset all of this and more by capital exports. Some of the capital went toward reduction of the sterling balances through trade with third parties, some toward building up British military establishments overseas, and some toward restoring British direct investments abroad. Rather than applying American aid directly toward rebuilding export capacity as in the case of Germany and the Netherlands, or toward restoring basic industries such as energy and steel, as in the case of France and Italy, Britain chose to use it to make the process of transition toward peacetime more gradual and less disruptive to the British people.

The sterling strategy—maintaining preferential trade arrangements between Britain and the former colonies while keeping sterling inconvertible with gold and the dollar—helped the British government maintain a sense of control over the twin processes of decolonization abroad and peacetime conversion at home during the critical five to seven years after the war. Both decolonization and conversion proceeded more gradually and with less political trauma for Britain than it might easily have had to endure otherwise. The pound sterling was maintained unchanged as the unit of account not only for the British economy, but for the entire sterling area as long as the sterling area lasted (until 1958). Currency reform along either the French or German models was avoided, as was Italian-style inflation. Colonies were lost, true, but without Britain's suffering casualties on the order that had become all too familiar during World War II. On these terms, which after all were paramount to British politicians, the strategy has to be judged a brilliant success.

It did have unfortunate long term consequences, however, in separating Britain economically and politically from both the United States and Europe. British leaders constantly found themselves holding fast to untenable positions against either American or European initiatives and then yielding with bad grace and limited reward for the concessions made. Finally taking the obvious step of devaluing the pound against the dollar in September 1949, for example, it had to devalue the pound fully 30 percent, from $4.03 to $2.80. But with over one-third of its imports and nearly one-half of its exports with the sterling area and with most of Western Europe devaluing as much or more against the dollar, this translated into a mere 9 percent overall devaluation against the currencies of its trading partners. In coming into the European Payments Union at the insistence of the Americans, Britain had to give up its network of bilateral agreements with each European country in which trade deficits beyond certain agreed limits were paid off in sterling. Only when Britain, in effect, was allowed to act as the banker for the entire sterling area in its dealings with any of the European countries was it satisfied with the EPU arrangement. The British obsession with maintaining its preferred trading relationships within the sterling area meant continued resistance to American plans to liberalize trade patterns and reintroduce multilateral settlements of financial imbalances.

It also meant resistance to European initiatives for dealing with the dollar shortage. For example, the Schuman Plan was devised by the French and Germans without any thought of British participation. The immediate casualty of British intransigence was the American proposal for an international trade organization to oversee the removal of non-tariff barriers to trade and the reduction of tariff barriers. In its place, the makeshift arrangement called the General Agreement on Tariffs and Trade, begun in October 1947, had to be the framework for international trade negotiations until it was superseded by the World Trade Organization in 1995. Britain was to pay a high price in later years for this early estrangement from America and Europe.

Domestically, the sterling strategy allowed the Labour government, elected in April 1945, to continue in power until 1951. By that time, it had successfully completed a large part of its initial agenda, which was to implant the fundamental elements of democratic socialism into British society. Labour sought to do this first by enacting the basic elements of the welfare state as spelled out in the prewar Beveridge Report. This recommended "cradle to grave" support of Britain's citizens by the state. This meant, first, a national health system with access based on need rather than ability to pay, and then free universal education and benefits for unemployment, retirement, and death. The national health system was the only part actually installed that placed any demand on government spending during Labour's term in office. And that spending was exceeded by the agriculture and food subsidies the government continued from wartime in order to complement the "sterling strategy."

Agricultural subsidies were needed to decrease food imports and relieve strain on the balance of payments. Food subsidies were needed to placate labor demands for higher wages. In fact, real wages actually fell on average during the Labour government. The explanation for this paradox is that organized labor, represented by the Trade Unions Congress, was willing to soft-pedal demands for higher wages in return for a commitment to the welfare state and acknowledgment of their power to organize at the plant level by individual trades. This created a fragmented and mutually competitive structure of labor unions, any one of which could strike and extract improved working conditions or emoluments for its members, who could be limited to, say, the machinists in a particular plant. The structure of British labor unions fragmented by craft and plant contrasted with the national and industrial unions that dominated in continental Europe. However, in these early years, British labor unions faced with the daunting task of reabsorbing some seven million members of the armed forces were quite content to increase their membership base without insisting on higher real wages. Unfortunately for the future progress of British labor productivity, both the unions and the firms were also happy to expand output on the basis of traditional work practices and plant organization. Later, these practices became entitlements used to resist the technical advances taking place rapidly in continental Europe.

Beyond establishing the welfare state, Labour's leaders were also determined to seize control of the "commanding heights" of the economy. Drawing on the lessons of government control of resources during the wartime mobilization, they sought to accomplish this by nationalizing the basic industries of the nation. They started with the Bank of England in 1946 and moved steadily into coal, gas, and electricity by 1948, with rail and canal transport, telecommunications, civil aviation, and steel thrown in for good measure by the beginning of 1951. Once in formal control of these basic sectors, however, the Labour government seemed to have no particular objective, other than to provide ample employment opportunities and to keep prices of output controlled as part of the overall strategy to avoid inflation. There were no plans drawn up as in the French example to change the structure of the economy.

Overall, what the Labour government did accomplish was to expand output and employment rapidly, while keeping down the level of consumption. This allowed both investment and exports to expand, driving unemployment down to record lows and removing fear of a balance-of-payments problem. Meanwhile, the government's budget tended toward regular surpluses, as tax revenues rose and the costs of the welfare state commitments proved to be for future generations rather than the present. This meant that the succeeding chancellors of the exchequer increasingly saw the budget as a means of controlling the inflationary pressures on the economy by varying the size of surplus. Deliberate manipulation of the budget surplus or deficit to control the state of the economy was initiated by Hugh Gaitskell, Labour's Chancellor of the Exchequer from 1949 to 1951, but was then continued by R. A. Butler, who succeeded him as the Conservative's Chancellor in 1951. This fiscal tinkering to the exclusion of any grand strategy for the economic direction of Britain earned the derisive label of "Butskellism" from the *Economist* magazine.

The "sterling strategy" effectively terminated with the denouement of the Suez Crisis of 1956. This stemmed from the failed attempt to regain joint Franco-British control of the Suez Canal from Egypt, whose President Nasser had nationalized it in 1954. The military exercise combined elements of British, French, and Israeli forces in a joint exercise conceived by the British and French. In the event, it failed, and worse, brought down on the French and British the opprobrium of both the Americans and the Russians, neither of whom had been privy to the military plans, and both of whom felt their military forces were being put to the test and possibly brought into nuclear conflict. In military disgrace, and with gold and dollar reserves rapidly draining away as foreigners withdrew their sterling deposits, Britain was forced to come to terms with U.S. plans for restoring convertibility of sterling, at least on current account transactions, as a condition for receiving support from the International Monetary Fund. The French proceeded to strengthen their European connection without further dealings with Britain by moving the European Coal and Steel Community into the next phase of economic integration, the European Economic Community. Meanwhile, however, British unemployment remained low and economic growth continued at its decorous pace. The last of rationing controls on consumer food products had been lifted in 1954, and in 1958 the Conservative prime minister, Harold Macmillan, could honestly claim in his successful reelection campaign, "You've never had it so good."

OPPORTUNITY KEEPS KNOCKING: 1958–73

The next fifteen years, however, were destined to shake British confidence in its postwar strategy. The war-torn economies of Europe had started their rapid recovery from a much lower base than in Britain, so it had been assumed that their pace of growth would slacken off as they regained prewar levels of output and per capita income, perhaps falling to the British level. Instead, the members of the EEC continued to grow rapidly, enjoying what came to be termed the golden age of economic growth until 1973. Meanwhile, British growth continued at its sedate pace of the 1950s. The result is shown clearly in Figures 12.2 and 12.3. Both use the OECD's base of 1991 U.S. dollars in their purchasing power parity exchange rate with a given country to compare Great Britain's level of gross domestic product and per capita income with that of Germany, France, and Italy for the period 1960 to 1996 (the figure for 1996 is the OECD's estimates made at the end of 1996, which was probably too optimistic for all four countries). In 1960, Britain's total output was already below that of Germany, then fell below that of France in 1970, and even that of Italy by 1979. The relative decline was even more dramatic in per capita terms, given Britain's relatively faster growth in population. Barely behind Germany in 1960, Britain fell below France in 1966 and below Italy for the first time in 1977, and then permanently below all three from 1979 to the present.

Much analysis has gone into uncovering the reasons for Britain's relative

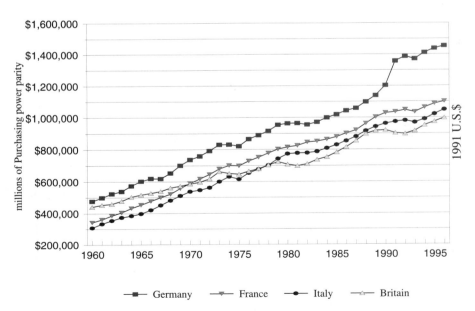

Figure 12.2. Gross domestic product, 1960–96, Germany, France, Italy, Britain.
Source: OECD Economic Outlook diskette.

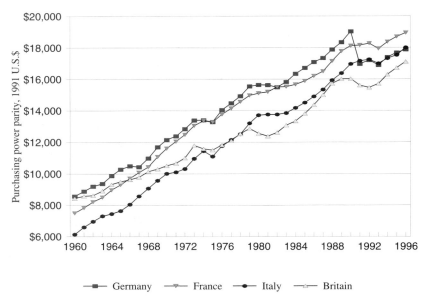

Figure 12.3. Per capita income, 1960–96, Germany, France, Italy, Britain.
Source: OECD Economic Outlook diskette

decline during this period. The first suspect was the relatively low level of investment relative to total output in Britain as compared with the growth leaders on the continent. This gave a very satisfactory explanation for Britain's relatively slow growth during the 1950s and continued to be the favorite villain for British policymakers through the 1960s, even as the close relationship between ratios of investment to output and the rate of growth of output among the OECD countries began to dissolve. Some even persisted with it during the 1970s, when it had disappeared completely.

The consensus in the most recent research is that Britain's rate of investment was not so much to blame as was the low productivity of its investment. Low productivity of the new capital, in turn, has been attributed to the large proportion of it coming from the public sector, especially in housing and in the nationalized industries, which seemed more interested in maintaining large numbers of employees than in increasing productive efficiency. But even in the private sector, new investment proved less productive than in Germany or France. The conjecture here is that the fragmented structure of British labor unions and the ability of each small craft union to protect the jobs of its members by preserving out-of-date work rules prevented the new equipment from being used most efficiently. This made it difficult for even American or Japanese firms to achieve the same levels of productivity with their new plants built in Britain that they were able to reach in their home country. Economic historians have also drawn attention to the likelihood that investment in human capital in Britain was misdirected.[3] Lacking the intensive government-and business-supported apprenticeship programs of Germany and the northern European countries, Britain could not match the productivity of their labor in specialized, small-scale production. Lacking the business training programs that supply skilled managers to American corporations, Britain could not match the productivity of American and Japanese firms in mass production.

Recognizing the power of export-led growth in the cases of both Germany and Italy, Britain took the initiative to found the European Free Trade Association (EFTA) to widen the European market for its own export industries. This combined the traditional trading partners of Britain—Portugal, Denmark, Norway, and Sweden—with the neutral countries in Central Europe, Austria, and Switzerland. A much looser combination of countries with three neutrals and four members of NATO, EFTA had no ambitions for political integration arising from economic integration. Rather, each country agreed to remove its tariffs on industrial imports from any of the other member countries. But each maintained its own tariff schedule against imports from any other country. American policymakers were displeased at this obvious rebuff of multilateral trade relations by thirteen of the sixteen countries it had introduced to the advantages of multilateral clearing in the European Payments Union, following on the Marshall Plan. They had to be content with the restoration of convertibility of each country's currency based on fixed exchange rates, which by itself allowed multilateral clearing of trade imbalances regardless of the differences in trade barriers. Through another round of negotiations on tariff levels in the GATT, called the Dillon Round, the United States was able to extract the commitment by the members of each trade grouping that the average of their new tariff against the rest of the world would be no higher than the original average tariff. The hope remained, then, that reducing some of the tariff barriers within Europe would increase trade and lead to further tariff reductions as the advantages of more liberal trade became apparent.

Looking at a map, the seven countries formed an outer ring around the inner six countries constituting the EEC. All thirteen countries continued to be members of the Organization of European Economic Cooperation, the European organization for administering the Marshall Plan funds, and then the European Payments Union. This organization had little of its original functions left to justify its existence, but the United States was now left out of all European economic policy discussions in addition. In 1960, the OEEC was formally dissolved and replaced by the OECD, the Organisation for Economic Cooperation and Development, made up of the sixteen European members of the OEEC plus the United States and Canada. It remains the main international organization for policy discussions among the rich industrial nations of the world, some of which may lead to policy coordination. More likely, such discussions may lead to some degree of policy convergence as alternative policies to counter similar problems are compared regularly and systematically. In this context, the British could keep closely informed of the increasingly obvious success of the EEC participants and the relatively lackluster performance of its own economy and that of its EFTA partners. Not only had the EEC countries caught up with Britain as anticipated in the 1950s, they were now moving steadily past.

Concern about the relatively slow pace of British growth had started to influence British policymakers already in the late 1950s, especially after the Suez debacle. In addition to the "fine tuning" of the demand side of the economy in the short run through fiscal policy, the Conservative government made an explicit effort at improving the long-run supply-side performance of the economy as well. Until the early sixties, however, these efforts were limited to more vigorous action against restrictive marketing practices that had become endemic in Britain since the rationalization movements in British industry in the 1930s. The Restrictive Practices Court set up in 1956 managed to eliminate overt price-fixing arrangements throughout British industry. Instead of leading to price competition that might have forced increases in productivity, however, it appears the RPC simply encouraged the development of other means of market control. For example, trade associations were very effective in disseminating information on market shares of firms, which could be used to monitor informal agreements. A second form of supply-side encouragement came in the form of government finance of higher levels of research and development expenditures than in Germany, France, or Italy. However, these were mostly for very expensive military projects with nuclear energy and supersonic aviation, which did nothing for industrial productivity.

Impressed by the evident French success in stimulating rapid industrialization, the Conservatives initiated a British version of "indicative planning" by setting up the National Economic Development Council in 1962. Lacking even the access to government-directed finance that the Commisariat du Plan enjoyed in France, however, the NEDC was unable to put any force behind its recommendations of how to raise the rate of economic growth. In fact, the first "plan" proposed by the NEDC in 1963, calling for a target of 4 percent annual rates of growth over the next three years, was quickly followed by a deflationary budget in 1964. This showed clearly that Conservative economic policy was still more focused on demand management to maintain the fixed exchange rate of the pound. Moreover, as achievement of this goal seemed to require keeping down the pressure of rising wages on the rate of price inflation, the indicative planning efforts of the NEDC were accompanied by calls for a stronger "incomes policy." The idea was that increases in wages might be held down but the share of wages in national income could remain the same by agreeing that nonwage incomes would not rise any faster. The Trades Union Congress naturally objected that while union contracts could enforce the wages part of the incomes policy, there was no comparable mechanism for keeping other incomes under control. Moreover, they wanted to increase the share of wages, not just keep it constant.

In 1964, the Labour party came back to power determined to make economic planning a success and, like the Gaullist regime in France, raise real wages as part of the social dividend from achieving higher rates of growth. Figure 12.1 shows how badly they failed, as growth rates, while positive, fell off and unemployment edged up. The basic problems that had confronted the Conservative government remained unsolved by the increased vigor of the Labour government. On the macroeconomic level, the problem was an increasingly overvalued exchange rate due to a fixed rate for sterling and higher rates of inflation in Britain than in its major trading partners.[4] This steadily reduced the market share for Britain's exports while increasing imports, so that the resulting adverse balance of payments became again the primary policy issue. On the microeconomic level, wage bargains struck with the Trades Union Congress had to be offset with increased entitlements or increased power for the individual unions. In the short run, this raised expectations in the financial markets of future inflation, inducing speculative movements out of sterling. In the longer run, this reduced incentives to raise labor productivity by reorganization of shop floor practices much less than by increasing capital stock. In November 1967, the pound had to be devalued at last, from $2.80 to $2.40.

The delay in devaluation was due to a dangerous combination of pride, presumption, and pragmatism. The pride lay in maintaining the role of the pound sterling as a reserve currency for the remaining countries staying in the sterling area, now reduced by the withdrawal of India and Argentina, but still including former African colonies, Hong Kong, Malaysia, and Australia. As long as these countries and colonies maintained their deposits, Britain had a credible claim to maintaining a major role within the IMF, second only to that of the United States. If official holders of sterling thought it would be devalued, however, it was feared the deposits would be withdrawn quickly. Such a run on sterling also concerned the Americans, whose gold stock was now less than the sum of dollars held by foreign central banks. Because a run on sterling might have created a spillover run on the dollar as well, American support for the pound was often forthcoming.

Moreover, there was a presumption among British economists and politicians that monetary policy would have little or no effect on the economy, even if it were freed of the constraint to keep the exchange rate fixed. The Radcliffe Commission was set up in 1959 to examine the British financial system and to assess the benefits of adopting German or Italian-style monetary policy. It reported that the complex British system of specialized banks, other financial intermediaries, and sophisticated capital markets made it impossible for the Bank of England to control domestic credit expansion in the way that the Bundesbank or the Banca d'Italia was able to do.

Finally, the pragmatism lay in the realization that devaluation would immediately raise the overhang of the remaining sterling balances, while any advantage in increasing exports or decreasing imports would take one to two years to be realized. As it developed, the devaluation regained export competitiveness for Britain very quickly and the United States and IMF provided overwhelming credit lines to Britain to defend the pound at the new parity, so no adverse consequences occurred on capital account. The dangers of inflation breaking out with the devaluation were forestalled successfully by imposing wage and price freezes across the board at first, and only gradually relaxing them to allow wage increases in line with rises in the cost of living and in productivity. Pride was maintained, while the presumption was undermined, and pragmatists appreciated the value of capital controls.

Decolonization continued to completion as Britain withdrew its forces first from east of Suez and then from Cyprus and Malta. (Gibraltar remained the last British base in the Mediterranean, much to the continued chagrin of the Spanish.) This helped reduce British military spending to more sustainable levels, a consideration that became increasingly important as the costs of the welfare state set up immediately after the war now began to mount and mount. It also cast Britain clearly as a junior partner of the United States in the western alliance, which did not bother the Labour government particularly when it came back into power in the elections of 1964. But dealing with the United States as supplicant during the successive balance-of-payments crises became increasingly expensive, especially as the expenses of the Vietnam War began to take their toll on the U.S. balance of payments. One way to offset the diminished role of sterling as an official reserve asset for foreign central banks was to encourage the development of the Euro-dollar market in London. This helped restore the leading role of London bankers in the finance of international trade, even if most of that trade worldwide was now invoiced in dollars rather than in sterling. Euro-dollars were simply deposits of dollars made in non-U.S. banks and kept on account as dollars. The advantage to depositors was that the accounts were free from restrictions placed by the U.S. authorities on U.S. bank practices, such as interest rate ceilings and withholding taxes on interest to be paid overseas. The Euro-dollar market developed rapidly in London after 1964. The other offset, pursued by both Labour governments in 1967 and Conservative governments from 1971 on, was to open up the European Economic Community market to British exporters, while subjecting British labor unions and management to healthy competition from the Continent.

The negotiations with the EEC were protracted and at times seem destined to failure as Britain seemed determined to hold on to the advantages of the sterling area as it saw them while France was determined to maintain the methods of operation that had been developed within the EEC. Eventual compromise was reached by Britain extracting a commitment from the EEC to broaden its eligibility requirements for backward regions to receive Community aid, so that regions with low per capita incomes as a result of an industry becoming uncompetitive and declining would be eligible for assistance in addition to regions with low per capita incomes as a result of having no industrial base. This would bring EEC aid, it was thought, into declining industrial regions in the north of England, especially Lancashire, and into southern Scotland and South Wales. The hope was that enough regional subsidies would be forthcoming to offset what clearly would be net outpayments to the rest of the Community for food imports. These would now bear a high variable levy if imports continued from the sterling area and the United States or a high price if they came increasingly from within the Community. Other member states could see that they might also have regions that could become eligible for aid under the new, broadened criteria, and so the British proposals were accepted.

The other concession of sorts that Britain extracted was to broaden the membership of the African, Caribbean, and Pacific countries, so that the poorest of the sterling area countries and colonies could continue to enjoy preferred access to the British market and now to the rest of the European market in addition. New Zealand, however, didn't qualify as a low-income country, so final concessions were extracted to allow continued imports of New Zealand butter and lamb for the five-year transition period allowed for full compliance with the Common Agricultural Policy. The common external tariff, however, had to be imposed around the British market within four years. As it turned out, commitments of EEC resources to the price support system of the CAP were allowed to expand over the next decade, which limited the possibility for expanding regional aid, much less foreign aid, to the less developed countries now included in the African, Caribbean and Pacific countries. All these concerns, however, were put aside over the next decade as much more pressing problems confronted Britain and the other members of the EEC than the distribution among them of the EEC's modest resources.

A SHOCKING PERIOD: 1974–85

The negotiations for entry into the Common Market coincided with the end of the fixed rate regime of the Bretton Woods era, which was terminated by the United States in August 1971, when President Nixon ordered the Federal Reserve System to stop selling gold to foreign central banks, especially those in France and Germany. At home, the Conservative government of Edward Heath was under constant challenge from the labor unions, whose strikes always seemed to bring a new round of pay increases. Drawing on the lessons of the 1967 devaluation, Britain let the pound float in 1972, assuming it would fall relative to the dollar and to the European currencies and so stimulate exports. It did fall, but exports did not rise, while prices and wages did. To keep imports from rising too rapidly, the Heath government tried its hand at an incomes policy. Unions agreed to keep wage demands moderate so as not to push up prices, but only on condition that if prices did start rising rapidly they would be free to catch up. The threshold chosen was 7 percent; a rise in the retail price index greater than that would trigger a wave of wage increases greater than 7 percent by an amount equal to the shortfall of wages behind prices that had accumulated to that point. The effect was that Britain entered the Common Market in 1973 pursuing much the same line of policy as Italy at the time, providing accommodative financing by the central bank to allow nominal wages to rise as much as the price level. As in the Italian case, this made Britain very vulnerable to the first oil shock, and made the shock of entering the continental system even harder.

The first round effect was the same as in the other countries—a sudden, sharp rise in both unemployment and inflation. In the British case, however, the inflationary shock was exacerbated by the Heath government's income policy, because the threshold of 7 percent was quickly exceeded. The Labour government that came to power in 1974, thanks to the support of the labor unions, naturally supported the catch-up wage increases that followed. Given the continued indifference of both Labour and Conservative governments to any thought of controlling the growth of the money supply, these wage increases were readily financed by the banking sector, supported by the Bank of England's policy of keeping interest rates low. So the rise in inflation rates for Britain far exceeded that in the rest of Europe, reaching a high of 27 percent in 1975. Fiscal policy was also lax, as first Heath and then Labour in the first election in 1974 had weak majorities in Parliament, so they kept spending high and taxes steady. Accommodative monetary policy combined with loose fiscal policy in this case did nothing for unemployment rates, which also rose. The excessive inflation rates forced the floating pound to devalue even further relative to both the U.S. dollar and the European currencies. This encouraged speculative attacks on the pound, forcing it lower. IMF assistance was limited in the amount it could offer and even then would be conditional on an antiinflationary policy being imposed.

Even though Britain was formally a member of the EEC at this point, the conditions of entry had factored in four- to five-year transition periods for switching fully to the Common Agricultural Policy or to the common external tariff. The shocks of adjustment to the continental way of doing things were not yet a factor, but it was clear they would only make economic conditions worse in the short run. Consequently, Labour held a referendum in 1975 asking British voters whether they approved of Britain remaining in the European Community on the terms negotiated by the Conservative government. Two-thirds approved. So the remaining way out of the oil shock quandary for the Labour government was to stake everything on developing North Sea oil-producing potential as quickly as possible. To make this pay off, however, required that oil prices remain at least as high as the OPEC cartel had raised them; the costs of exploiting offshore wells in one of the stormiest seas in the world were enormous. Consequently, Britain's interests with respect to dealing with the OPEC cartel were directly counter to those of the European oil importers.

By the end of 1976, the costs of importing the construction materials for North Sea oil facilities had increased the pressure on the balance of payments and the value of the pound to the point that IMF assistance was required. The conditions, as foreseen and already anticipated by the British government, were to impose a more antiinflationary budget but also to remove exchange controls on capital account transactions. This meant freeing up the blocked sterling balances that still remained from the end of World War II. As anticipated, they were rapidly withdrawn. Fortunately, North Sea gas exports began to appear in 1977 and oil exports in 1978. These helped reduce the deficit on current account that might otherwise have occurred, but deficits still existed. Nevertheless, the pound stabilized and even began to strengthen on the basis of strong capital imports.

The cause of these gyrations in the exchange rate of the pound remains an interesting issue for economists. A favorite explanation is that investors anticipated the higher interest rates and future export earnings from North Sea oil that in fact did occur in 1979–81. But economic historians emphasize that the root causes of these phenomena—the second oil shock in 1979 and the Volcker shock in 1980—could hardly have been anticipated in 1977.[5] A more plausible explanation is that removing restrictions on foreigners' deposits in the British financial system made the London capital market that much more attractive as a place for OPEC countries to deposit their excess profits. The Euro-dollar market was a natural focal point for this activity. The British government helped by putting a dollar guarantee on their new bonds. Even though denominated in sterling, their higher interest rates made them an attractive alternative to U.S. government bonds. Whatever the cause, the pound strengthened and official reserves began to rise once again in the late 1970s.

With the external pressure off the government, the labor unions now struck for catch-up pay increases. Resistance to these demands led to the fall of the Labour government and the election in May 1979 of the Conservative government, led by Margaret Thatcher. Thatcher's term as prime minister was extended through two successive elections in 1983 and 1987 until the end of 1990, when internal opposition to her dominating procedures forced her to step down. These eleven years of power made her the longest-serving prime minister in British history since Lord Liverpool after the Napoleonic Wars. But her place in history will be determined less by the length of her term than by the depth of the changes in British society wrought by her economic policy. Her determination was to remove government regulation and interference as much as possible from the decision-making considerations by British producers and consumers so that markets for goods and services, capital and labor could function more efficiently. Toward this end, the first step was to get inflation under control by restricting the growth of the money supply. Later steps required denationalizing the nationalized industries and introducing privatization and market incentives into as much of the public sector as possible.

The beginning of the Thatcher era was shocking, to say the least, and not at all auspicious for the future of the government. Unemployment rose sharply, soon hitting the unimaginably high figure of two million out of work, and then moving on to put a full three million on the dole. The growth rate of the economy was actually negative for two successive years, 1980 and 1981. Inflation rose to nearly a record high in 1980. Even the pound began to decline relative to the dollar again in 1981. Every aspect of British macroeconomic performance that had obsessed governments from 1945 on deteriorated in the first two years of the Thatcher era. Nevertheless, her economic policy remained committed to reducing inflation by controlling the rate of growth of the money supply. True, her economists dithered over how to measure the money supply, and the announced targets were regularly exceeded. But as bad as things were, they seemed no worse than the travails being endured at the same time by the rest of Europe. North Sea oil was now in full production and contributing larger and larger amounts to the current account.

By 1982, the worst was over for Britain, and recovery began to show up in renewed rates of growth, while inflation seemed to stay under control. No progress was made in terms of reducing unemployment, which continued to rise, but in comparison with the continued slow growth in the rest of Europe, the British did not look so bad, and they certainly were not doing as badly as they had become accustomed to doing relative to France and Germany. The success of British forces in the Falklands/Malvinas War of 1982 renewed British pride and no doubt helped reelect Thatcher and the Conservative Parliament in 1983. Without this kind of extra-economic boost to Thatcher's popularity, it is likely she would have been defeated when the next mandatory election occurred in 1984. Then the effects of her reforms would not have had time to show up in increased rates of productivity and rising rates of growth. It was precisely this long lag time required for institutional changes to take effect coupled with the requirement to have new elections at least every five years that inhibited previous Conservative prime ministers from initiating fundamental reforms. It also explains why the Thatcher reforms have not been quickly imitated by other industrial democracies.

After Thatcher's reelection came the Trade Union Bill in October 1983, which was intended to break the power of trade union leaders by requiring them to subject their decisions on strikes or political contributions to direct vote by the union membership. The coal miners struck in 1984 to test the resolve of the Thatcher government and to rally other unions to their support. They failed on both counts, although the battle lasted for some months. The failure of the miners' strike meant that henceforth much of the ability of British labor unions in general to limit reorganization of work practices and the effective use of labor-saving technology was dissipated. As British investment rates rose over the rest of the 1980s, so did the total factor productivity of British manufacturing. Overall, Britain stopped falling behind the rest of Europe and actually began catching up with France and Germany, as Figures 12.2 and 12.3 show.

This supply-side effect of Thatcher's economic policy was reinforced by a commitment to privatization of as much of the nationalized industries and the public sector as possible starting in 1984. Although this could not be done systematically or quickly, given the entrenchments of at least forty years, eventually gas and electricity were privatized, then waterworks as well as coal and steel, aviation, and telecommunications. In most cases, the revenues from the sale of the enterprises were used to reduce the government debt or income taxes, while expenditures in the future were no longer burdened by the need to subsidize inefficient and overstaffed operations. Unemployment rose as a result, but customers and taxpayers were satisfied with the results on the whole. Of course, objections were raised that regulators were allowing prices charged by the utilities to rise too much to benefit the new shareholders and penalize the customers, or, conversely, that prices were being kept too low to benefit customers at the expense of shareholders. As privatization was usually carried out by giving the customers preferred purchase rights to the shares, however, the customers and shareholders tended to be the same people. Consequently, losses suffered in one role were offset on average by gains in the other. Overall, improvements in the quality of infrastructure encouraged private industry to increase its productivity further.

Thatcher's policy with respect to the EC also was controversial. She fought incessantly with the other heads of government at the semiannual meetings of the European Council over most initiatives being proposed. Eventually she won a sizable rebate from the Community in recognition of Britain's substantial net payment into the Community's coffers despite its having a lower per capita income than some of the net recipients. (See Chapter 5 for a discussion of the British rebate in the EU budget.) In return, she allowed the Commission to expand in size by allowing each new member to have at least one commissioner. But she was also one of the prime movers in promoting the Single Market initiative in 1985, as it was consistent with her overall philosophy of reducing the amount of government regulations and imposition of additional transactions costs on the operations of markets. When the momentum from the Single Market initiative was carried on by the Commission to the Delors Plan, which eventually culminated in the Maastricht Treaty of 1993, she raised stern objections. Both the common currency and the additional responsibilities that would be given to the EC's supranational authority in foreign and social policy were anathema to her vision of revitalizing the British economy by freeing its markets of excessive government regulation and interference.

ONLY PART OF THE EUROPEAN UNION: 1986–96

Renewed vitality of the British economy in the early 1980s was achieved while Britain remained out of the European Monetary System. Initially, this made sense, because Britain had become a net oil exporter by the end of 1978. Since oil was invoiced in dollars, it would be to Britain's advantage to see the dollar strengthen relative to the pound, because then the oil earnings in dollars would have more purchasing power for extinguishing British liabilities denominated in pounds sterling. The interests of Germany, France, and Italy as large net oil importers were exactly opposite. As it turned out, the combination of the second oil shock and the Volcker shock greatly improved Britain's situation with respect to the balance of payments as reserves accumulated rapidly. The exchange rate, after strengthening relative to the dollar in 1978–80 as expected from the second oil shock, then weakened in common with the rest of the European currencies during the Volcker shock of the early 1980s, even as the export surpluses continued from North Sea oil. When the third oil shock occurred in early 1986, however, the price of oil fell sharply and the British balance of trade began to weaken. Initially, however, the pound strengthened relative to the dollar even as it weakened relative to the deutsche mark and the currencies of the rest of the EMS countries. As part of the U.S.-led effort to stabilize exchange rates in the late 1980s, the pound stabilized with respect to both the dollar and the deutsche mark. By 1990, as the balance of trade began to improve again, Britain seemed determined to try anything to keep inflation from cropping up again. This finally led Thatcher to agree to commit the pound sterling to a fixed parity with the deutsche mark and the rest of the participating currencies in the Exchange Rate Mechanism of the EMS. If this move had convinced foreign investors that Italy had a credible commitment to stable prices, surely it would convince them of Britain's commitment! However, like Italy, Britain was now poised to participate fully in the economic shock caused by German reunification.

With Italy, Britain was forced to leave the Exchange Rate Mechanism and the EMS in September 1992. Like Italy, the sharp devaluation in its currency relative to those of what were now its primary trading partners created an export-led recovery and a resumption of relatively higher growth rates than in France and Germany. The exit of Britain from the EMS occurred as the discussions over the ratification of the Maastricht Treaty were preoccupying Europe. John Major, who had brought Britain into the EMS in October 1990 as the Chancellor of the Exchequer under Thatcher, was now her successor as prime minister. Reluctant to damage relations with the EU in the way Thatcher had enjoyed doing, he argued for the British Parliament to ratify the Treaty. In deference to his party's concerns that the supranational goals of the Maastricht Treaty might undo or stymie Thatcher's reforms, especially in limiting the power of British labor unions, he had negotiated agreement that Britain could opt out of the Social Chapter of the Treaty, which would have required Britain to harmonize its labor union legislation with that of the rest of the EU. Moreover, by withdrawing from the EMS in 1992 before ratification of the Treaty, he was holding open the options for Britain of whether and when to rejoin the EMS as it progressed toward the Treaty's objective of European Monetary Union.

Parliament approved, narrowly, and Major won reelection in 1992, again narrowly. In the meantime, British unemployment rates began to fall once again as the growth rate of the economy picked up. From an economic point of view, the British had the best of the economic worlds available to members—full access to the markets of the fifteen member European Union for its exports, investors, and work force—without bearing the economic costs they had had imposed on them by the shock of German reunification. For foreign firms seeking access to the enlarged Single Market and the possible extension of it into Central and East Europe in the near future, this meant that Britain was the preferred location for setting up distribution and manufacturing centers. So Britain became the fortunate recipient of increased foreign direct investment as well as being able to maintain its attractiveness for foreign portfolio investment in British securities. As the elections of 1997 came into view, both parties seemed content to continue this state of affairs as long as possible.

CONCLUSION

Today, as for most of its history, Britain is not really sure if it is better off as part of Europe or separate from Europe. Clearly now it is part of the European economy to a much greater extent than it has been since the seventeenth century. But just as it had never been militarily allied with both France and Germany at the same time until the North Atlantic Treaty Organization was established after World War II, and then only with the likelihood of a "special relationship" with the American superpower, so Britain may not be clearly better off politically if it supports the Franco-German architectural design for the continent in the twenty-first century. This dilemma between support for the economic goals and resistance to the political ambitions of France and Germany comes out clearly in Britain's internal conflict over joining the European Monetary Union. There the economic gains seem clear but minor, whereas the political gains or losses are not at all clear but may be major. Until this internal conflict is resolved, Britain will not be able to help the Inter-Governmental Conference of 1996–97 satisfactorily.

In fact, its position is completely opposed to the Franco-German proposals to strengthen the role of the EU's institutions with respect to foreign policy and security. Rather than create any new international institutions, much less combine the Western European Union with the European Union to give a military enforcement instrument to the EU, the British Conservative government insists that any European action in the field of security and defense must be based on cooperation between national governments. Each nation must preserve its capacity to act in defense of its particular national interests without restriction. NATO must remain the primary organization for securing such cooperation, although it may assign particular European theater tasks to the WEU on a case-by-case basis. Under no conditions that can be foreseen by the British government would the EU or any of its institutions play any role in such decisions for military action. Britain backs up its position by offering to strengthen the operational capacity of the WEU, as long as its military role is kept within the NATO structure.

As far as the third pillar of the Treaty on European Union is concerned, Britain, as long as it has a Conservative party government, remains firm in its opt out of the social chapter, as well as from the Schengen Accord to eliminate passport controls among member states. The Labour government, which came to power in the 1997 elections, has endorsed the social chapter, although it will likely hold to positions similar to those of the Conservatives on many of the Inter-Governmental Conference issues. For example, the Conservatives in Britain joined the other major powers in calling for more efficiency in the structure and operation of the existing institutions. This would give more voting power to the larger countries in both the Council of Ministers and the European Parliament, encourage communication on issues between the European Parliament and the national parliaments (but to reduce the number of directives enacted by the European Parliament, not to speed up their implementation at the national level), reduce the number of commissioners, and make sure one of the major powers has the presidency of the European Council each term, letting one of the smaller countries share the presidency with whichever major power held it. Perhaps most provocatively, it has suggested that the Court of European Justice be restricted in its authority, and only give its views retrospectively once the member states have acted. This would prevent the embarrassment that happened when the European Court threw out the treaty that had been signed between the EC and the EFTA countries to form the European Economic Area in 1992, insisting that any dispute arising in the operation of the treaty had to be adjudicated by it rather than any special arbitration committee set up jointly by the EC and EFTA. It would also reduce this major element of supranationalism that exists in the Community's institutions.

While insisting that its membership in the European Union is irrevocable and that it wishes to play a major role in its future development, Britain also insists that the EU should remain a flexible organization capable of containing a wide diversity of nations with distinct national interests. More democratic procedures and attention to the will of the people within the separate nation-states should be developed, so that it can continue to contribute to the peace of Europe. But Britain feels that the EU contribution has been, and should remain, primarily in the economic sphere. Other institutions, NATO in particular, have been much more important for maintaining that peace behind the protective military force projected by the United States and the United Kingdom. These institutions should be maintained, strengthened, and made more efficient so that the peace of Europe will continue.

Endnotes

1. Pressnell, p. 413.

2. The Volcker shock refers to the decision in 1980 by Paul Volcker, head of the Federal Reserve System in the U.S., to focus on restricting the growth of the U.S. money supply to the exclusion of other monetary goals. The result was a sudden skyrocketing of US interest rates, which both strengthened the dollar on foreign exchanges (increasing the effect of the second oil shock on oil-importing countries) and plunged the US economy into a sharp, if short, recession.

3. Steve Broadberry, "Technological leadership and productivity leadership in manufacturing since the industrial revolution: implications for the convergence thesis," *Economic Journal* 104 (1994), pp. 291–302.

4. The real exchange rate between any two countries is calculated by deflating each currency by the price index in that country. To find the real price of the pound sterling in terms of deutsche marks, for example, one should divide the "real" deutsche mark, DM/P_{DM}, by the real pound, $£/P_{UK}$. Rearranging, one multiplies the fixed nominal exchange rate, $DM/£$, by the ratio of price indexes, P_{UK}/P_{DM}. Therefore, if the price level in the United Kingdom rises relative to that in Germany, the real exchange rate of the former has risen, making its exports less competitive compared with those of the latter.

5. James Foreman-Peck, "Trade and the balance of payments," in N. F. R. Crafts and N. W. C. Woodward, eds. *The British Economy since 1945,* Oxford: Clarendon Press, 1991, pp. 141–79.

Bibliography

Alford, B. W. E. *British Economic Performance, 1945–1975.* Cambridge: Cambridge University Press, 1993.

Bean Charles, and Nicholas Crafts. "British economic growth since 1945: relative economic decline . . . and renaissance?" in Nicholas Crafts and Gianni Toniolo, eds. *Economic Growth in Europe since 1945.* Cambridge: Cambridge University Press, 1996.

Britton, A. J. C. *Macroeconomic Policy in Britain 1974–1987.* Cambridge: Cambridge University Press, 1991.

Broadberry, Steve. "Technological leadership and productivity leadership in manufacturing since the industrial revolution: implications for the convergence thesis." *Economic Journal,* 104 (1994), pp. 291–302.

Buxton, Tony, Paul Chapman, and Paul Temple, eds. *Britain's Economic Performance.* London: Routledge, 1994.

Crafts, N. F. R. " 'You've never had it so good?': British economy policy and performance, 1945–60," in Barry Eichengreen, ed. *Europe's Post-War Recovery.* Cambridge: Cambridge University Press, 1995.

Economist Intelligence Unit. *Country Report, Britain.* London: Economist Intelligence Unit, 2nd quarter, 1996.

Floud, Roderick and Donald N. McCloskey, eds. *The Economic History of Britain since 1700.* 2d ed. Vol. 3, "1939–1992." Cambridge: Cambridge University Press, 1994.

Pressnell, Leslie. "The post-war financial settlement." *External Economic Policy since the War.* Vol. 1. London: HMSO, 1987.

Benelux and Denmark:

Economic Unions, Decolonization, and the Perils of Openness

Basic Facts			
Area: **Total**		117,400 km^2	3.6 % of EU15
	Belgium	30,500 km^2	0.9 %
	Luxembourg	2,600 km2	0.1 %
	Netherlands	41,200 km^2	1.3 %
	Denmark	43,100 km^2	1.3 %
Population (1/1/1994):		31,040,700	8.4 % of EU15
	Belgium	10,101,600	2.7 %
	Luxembourg	400,900	0.1 %
	Netherlands	15,341,600	4.1 %
	Denmark	5,196,600	1.4 %
Gross Domestic Product (1993):		$532.9 billion	8.9 % of EU15
	Belgium	$177.5 billion	3.0 %
	Luxembourg	$8.7 billion	0.1 %
	Netherlands	$255.5 billion	4.3 %
	Denmark	$91.2 billion	1.5 %
Per Capita:			
	Belgium	$17,623	109 % of EU15 average
	Luxembourg	$21,898	135 %
	Netherlands	$16,707	103 %
	Denmark	$17,572	108 %
Openness (X + M)/GDP			
	Belgium/Luxembourg	114 %	73 % with EU12
	Netherlands	86 %	70 %
	Denmark	50 %	54 %

Source: Eurostat, *Basic Statistics of the European Union,* 32nd ed. (Luxembourg, 1995).

The Benelux countries (Belgium, Luxembourg, and the Netherlands) have several features in common with Denmark, which justifies treating these four countries as a group. They are all small, both in terms of land area and population; they are all constitutional monarchies (or a duchy, in the case of Luxembourg); they are high income; and they all do most of their trade with Germany. It is in the interests of each of them, therefore, to make sure they have continued access to the German market. Currently all have kept their currencies tightly linked to the deutsche mark, so each has experienced the full impact of the German reunification shock in the early 1990s. While their common interests with respect to the European Union tend to make them vote as a bloc on strategic issues, they quickly diverge on specific matters due to strong differences in their history, language, and location.

The economic fortunes of each country reflect their vulnerability to international conditions, whether they deal with trade, capital movements, exchange rate fluctuations, or immigration flows. Each was forcibly occupied by Nazi Germany during World War II, so it is only natural that each would insist on exercising peacetime political influence in the European Union that is much greater than their small size warrants. This also explains the energy with which their political leaders pursue initiatives that will deepen the economic and political union of a larger Europe that encompasses, and perhaps contains or even controls, their powerful neighbor. The four countries have turned to Britain and France repeatedly for assistance in these initiatives.

Luxembourg, surrounded by France, Germany, and Belgium, decided after World War I to form an economic and monetary union with the weakest of the three. The economics of the union with Belgium (BLEU) are as compelling as the political logic, because Luxembourg's chief natural resource is one of the world's richest iron ore fields, while southern Belgium is located over Europe's deepest coal fields. Combined, the two small countries have created heavy industry that has provided them economic strength, not to mention military capabilities, that belies their small size. After World War II, they quickly resumed their economic and monetary union and profited from Marshall Plan aid to restore their heavy industry. BLEU contributed greatly to the reconstruction of Europe. Luxembourg is too hilly and rocky to think of being self-sufficient in agriculture, which makes up a smaller share of its GDP (1.7% in 1992) than in any other country in Europe other than the United Kingdom and Germany. When the oil shocks of the 1970s made its steel industry uncompetitive, Luxembourg began to develop a large services sector, especially in finance. This trend has continued into the 1990s, with the displaced workers from the steel industry moving into services, especially government. Luxembourg has also benefited enormously from the expenditures of the European Union on its facilities and staff located in the country. With one of their own, Jacques Santer, as president of the European Commission starting in 1995, Luxembourg can expect to continue to profit from the expansion of European Union activities.

Belgium arose as a separate, independent country only in 1830, after a brief period of being combined with the Kingdom of the Netherlands and a long history as the Austrian Netherlands. Created rather accidentally by great power agreement after a revolt against Dutch rule, Belgium has been at the center of European conflicts and compromises since the Battle of Waterloo. Devastated in both World Wars I and II as German armies launched their offensives against France through Belgian territory, Belgians have more cause than most Europeans to create institutions that will resolve Franco-German relations peacefully. The continual construction of new buildings for the EU in the European quarter of Brussels reflects Belgium's commitment to increasing the political capability of the European Union.

The success of the port of Antwerp reflects the economic benefits Belgium has derived from the European Union. It is once again prospering as the major port, along with Rotterdam in the Netherlands, for ocean-going trade with northern Europe. Until the energy crisis of the 1970s, Belgian coal fields created the basis for heavy industry and metal processing, as they had since the Middle Ages. Metals were imported from all over the world to be processed in Belgian factories, including copper, lead, and zinc from its former colony in Africa, the Belgian Congo now known as Zaire, as well as iron ore from Luxembourg and Lorraine, and tin from Saxony and Malaysia. Since the 1960s, however, Belgium, like Luxembourg, has had to expand its service sector to find employment for workers made redundant by the contraction of its industrial sector. Unlike Luxembourg, it has not been able to keep down unemployment rates.

Moreover, divided between Flemish-speaking Flanders in the north and French-speaking Wallonia in the south, Belgium has its own internal conflicts to manage. In its transition to a service economy after its manufacturing base became uncompetitive during the 1970s, both regions have felt abused. Initially, this led to repeated bursts of inflation as competing claims of the Flemish and Walloons were simply bought off by expanding the money supply and increasing the government debt. By the 1990s, Belgium had the highest ratio of government debt to GDP in the European Union, 134 percent in 1995. After committing to the European Monetary System seriously in 1983, however, the internal conflicts could no longer be settled by accommodative finance. As early as 1975 regional parliaments were established, and by 1993, fiscal power had largely devolved to them. The role of Brussels remains confused—it seems to have become the capital of its own country in name only, while it has become the capital of the European Union in every respect but name. The difficulties of governing a conflicted country while forced to maintain a restrictive monetary and fiscal policy are daunting, especially when its major trading partners are stagnating. While the economic pain of cooperating with France and Germany now is great, Belgians have only to look at their many military cemeteries and war memorials to realize the need to persevere.

The Netherlands may be known to tourists for wooden shoes, rounds of cheese, windmills, and tulips, but to economic historians it is known as the world's first modern economy, to demographers as the most densely populated country in the world, and to economists as once again one of the richest economies in Europe. At the end of World War II, the great port of Rotterdam, where the Netherlands has for centuries controlled entry of the world's goods to the entire hinterland of the Rhine river drainage, was completely flattened, save for one windmill that was left as a landmark to guide successive waves of Allied bombers. Taking advantage of Marshall Plan aid and the logistical demands of Allied forces in Occupied Germany, the Netherlands constructed a much enlarged and improved port facility. German economic expansion ever since has led to Dutch prosperity through perfection not only of its entrepôt role but through development of modern chemical plants and high tech industry with preferred transport access to the markets of Europe and the world.

The oil shocks were a mixed affair for the Netherlands. The oil embargo of October 1973 imposed by the Arab members of OPEC hit the refineries and petrochemical plants of the Dutch earliest and most severely. But it also provoked the Dutch government to exploit finally the large natural gas deposits that lay in shallow, readily accessible areas under the Dutch portion of the North Sea. This opportunity, long deferred for fear of displacing coal miners, was now taken up so rapidly that wages rose sharply in the now-booming petroleum sector. As a small country with a relatively homogeneous population and a democratic government committed to communal welfare, the Netherlands could not prevent the high wages in the leading sector from leading to higher wages in the rest of the economy as well. Such high wages in sectors where demand was not rising made the Dutch products and services increasingly uncompetitive. In the short run, then, Dutch wage policy eroded the advantages of a strong currency that the German economy was experiencing. The term *Dutch disease* was coined by British economists to describe this phenomenon, partly to discredit it before it infected the British economy of the late 1970s. Dutch economists, however, have noted that the symptoms of the disease seemed more evident in Britain than in the Netherlands. From the second oil shock on, the Dutch economy has followed very much the pattern experienced by the German economy. In particular, its monetary policy of maintaining a fixed exchange rate with the deutsche mark means it has experienced fully the German economic experience with the reunification shock of the early 1990s. Whether German monetary policy maintains control of an independent deutsche mark or yields to a common European currency such as the euro, one can be sure that Dutch monetary policy will follow it in lockstep.

Denmark, like the Netherlands and northern Belgium, has an historic tradition as an entrepôt, or transshipment, economy due to its location at the entrance to the Baltic Sea. The Danish Sound for centuries was the source of rich tolls for Danish rulers until British naval power enforced freedom of the seas in the nineteenth century. Even then, the entrepôt role continued until the German empire took most of Schleswig-Holstein and built the Kiel canal to link the North Sea directly with the Baltic through all-German territory. Building on a prosperous, well-educated agricultural population, Denmark became an industrialized economy based on export-oriented food processing at the end of the nineteenth century. It was not until the trade restrictions of the 1930s, which limited Denmark's access to manufactured imports as well as reduced its markets for exports of processed foodstuffs, that Denmark began to develop its industrial base. But serious industrialization did not begin until the 1960s. Then, rapid structural change caused social stresses that were eased by extending and deepening the social welfare services provided by the state at the cost of rising public debt. When the oil shocks of the 1970s created large deficits in Denmark's foreign account, foreign indebtedness rose as well. Various incomes policy and price control schemes were attempted by the Social Democrat government and it even joined the European Monetary System in 1978. The second oil shock demonstrated finally the futility of these demand-management approaches to supply-side problems, as unemployment and government spending both rose again while the economy stagnated.

Since September 1982, a Conservative-led government has progressively reduced government expenditures, raised taxes, and suspended wage indexation. Gradually, Denmark's competitiveness has improved until it actually ran an export surplus in 1990. An interesting aspect of the renewed export boom was the increasing importance of trade with Germany and the decreasing importance of trade with Britain, despite its presence in the expanded Common Market after 1973. Due credit for the eventual surplus in 1990 must therefore be given to the increased imports to former East Germany that arose for Denmark's benefit from the reunification of Germany. Despite the obvious benefits they derive from participation in the Single Market and linking their currency to the deutsche mark, the Danish people rejected the Maastricht Treaty in the first referendum held on it in May 1992. Eventually, after a massive publicity campaign and specific reservations that exempted Denmark from necessary participation in European Monetary Union, the Treaty was ratified by the Danish parliament *(Folketing)*. Since this display of political separatism by the Danish electorate, the krone has typically been among the weakest of the EMS currencies, reflecting the concerns of investors that the government may not be able to hold its course with restrictive monetary and fiscal policy. If the common currency is agreed to by France and Germany, however, one can be sure that Denmark will participate as well.

MACROECONOMIC POLICY INDICATORS: 1960–97

Figures 13.1 to 13.3 show the course of growth rates, inflation, and unemployment for the four small, rich countries of Luxembourg, Belgium, the Netherlands, and Denmark from 1960 to 1997. The features common to them show up clearly for each indicator at first glance; closer observation brings out some interesting differences in policy results on occasion. But the final inference must be that policies, and their economic results, rapidly converge for these economies which have so much in common and are so near to each other.

All of them participated fully in the economic miracle growth rates of the 1960s. However, the smaller the population of the country, the more volatile were these rates. This is easily explained by the importance of immigration for increasing the labor force in expansions and the ease of outmigration to decrease the labor force in recession, which was disproportionately greater the smaller the domestic population. The two oil shocks hit all four countries badly, especially Luxembourg in 1975. It is interesting that the Netherlands was un-

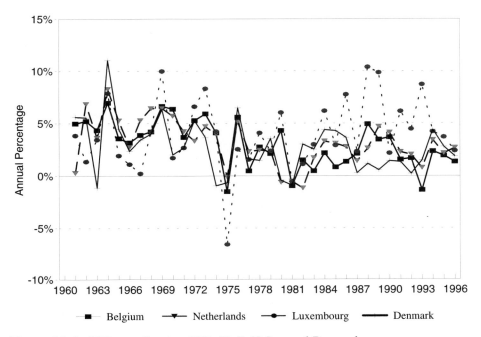

Figure 13.1. GDP growth rates, 1961–96, BeNeLux and Denmark.

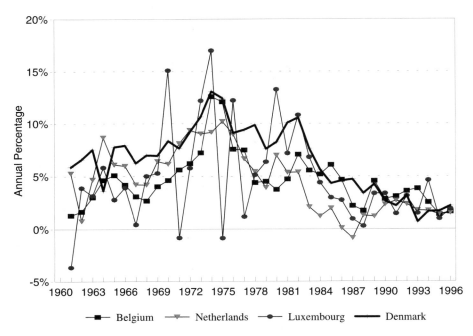

Figure 13.2. Inflation rates, 1961–96, BeNeLux and Denmark.

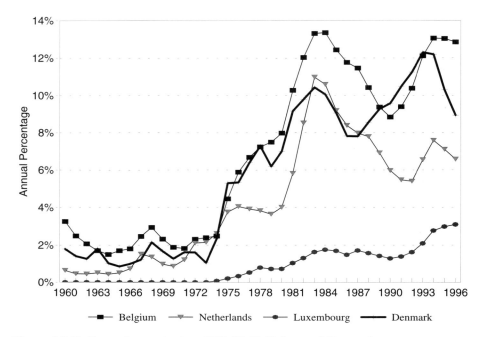

Figure 13.3. Unemployment rates, 1960–96, BeNeLux and Denmark.

able to recover from the second oil shock as quickly as the others, despite the benefits it should have had of natural gas resources coming on line by then. The recovery from "Euro-sclerosis" that occurred with the implementation of the Single Market act was enjoyed by the Benelux countries while Denmark stumbled along at steady but very low rates of growth. The German reunification shock was eventually experienced by all four, although it appears that Denmark was the first to benefit from the increased import demands arising from the reconstruction of East Germany.

A similar congruence of policies can be seen for inflation rates, with tiny Luxembourg's figures creating the only interesting variations from the common pattern. Recalling that the exchange rate of the Luxembourg franc is immutably set at one Belgian franc under the terms of the BLEU, it is clear that inflation rates in Luxembourg cannot long diverge from those in Belgium. Macroeconomists today would say that the inflation rates of the two countries are co-integrated, with the common currency serving as an "error-correction mechanism" that brings them back together whenever they diverge by too much. It is also clear from Figure. 13.2 that the error correction mechanism has been operating much more effectively since the establishment of the European Monetary System in 1978. By the mid-1990s, all four countries participated effectively in the Exchange Rate Mechanism, holding close to their central par rates with the deutsche mark and with each other. Thus tightly linked to the monetary policy of the much larger German economy, they all experienced the low, 2 to 3 percent yearly, inflation rates of unified Germany.

Only someone already attuned to finding common patterns for these four countries would probably find a common pattern in the unemployment rates shown in Figure 13.3. However, it shows clearly the exceptionally low unemployment rates enjoyed by each prosperous little country in the 1960s and the stunning, longer-term rise in these rates with the oil shocks of the 1970s. Tiny Luxembourg again provides an interesting contrast, but only because it was able either to send discharged workers back to their home country, usually Belgium or France, or to employ them in government service. The divergences in the 1980s and early 1990s are really more differences in timing than in permanent levels, Luxembourg again excepted. Denmark's unemployment rate was the first to rise at the end of the 1980s, predating the German reunification shock, while the Netherlands' rate was the last to rise, when even West German unemployment rates began to rise in 1993. The end of the 1990s is projected to show convergence once again, as Luxembourg gradually gives up using the government as the employer of last resort for discharged workers and the Danes and Dutch gradually liberalize their labor markets and reduce the level and duration of unemployment benefits. The political incoherence of Belgium that has been created by the devolution of political decisionmaking to the regional level in the 1990s helps to explain the delay in its convergence, but as past experience indicates it will surely come.

THE DUTCH AND DANES DIVERGE: 1945–58

All four of these small, wealthy countries were occupied by Nazi Germany during World War II, and each played a key role in the New Economic Order proposed for Europe under German hegemony. Prior to the war, all four had suffered economically during the 1930s by being cut out of their traditional export markets for one reason or another. At least some part of each economy proved useful for the Nazi war machine, especially in the intensive mobilization of economic resources that occurred in the years 1942–44, and in that interval each country's authorities tried to placate the demands of the German occupation forces while maintaining the subsistence of their own population as best as possible. The lessons learned in this common ordeal were applied toward mobilizing as fully as possible their economic resources after liberation, but now on their own terms free of Nazi ideology and German domination. Initially, the Belgians did best by establishing an arrangement to keep labor and management cooperating in their heavy industry in southern Belgium (Wallonia) while supporting agricultural improvements in northern Belgium (Flanders). The most successful applications of the lessons to be learned, however, were made by the Dutch, their prize colony of Indonesia stripped away, large areas of their fertile polders flooded, and the key port of Rotterdam demolished. Eventually, the Danes caught on after first casting their fortunes in with the British attempt to reconstitute the sterling area.

The Belgians and Luxembourgers had formed a monetary union in 1935 and reestablished this as the Belgium and Luxembourg Economic Union (BLEU) in late 1944 after liberation. The coal mines of southern Belgium and the iron ore of Luxembourg were natural complements and had been utilized fully by the German war economy. Relatively untouched by Allied bombing, they were in an excellent position to provide the building materials needed for the reconstruction of the rest of Europe. Other raw materials needed for steel alloys or other metallurgical products were made available again from the Belgian Congo, whose rich mines had been exploited by the Allies during the war. Led by Alexandre Galopin, the leading banker in prewar Belgium, the heads of Belgian industry had cooperated with their German occupiers during the war by pursuing what Galopin termed "the politics of production." This meant exporting as much as possible to Germany during the war, subsidizing the exports as needed by loans from the Banque d'Émission to both German importers and to Belgian producers. Belgian industry, therefore, was well positioned to resume exports of its heavy industry to the rest of Europe immediately after the war.

The antagonisms of regional divisions between the Flemish and the Walloons, between the great capitalists and the labor unions, between the socialist government-in-exile and the capitalist Galopin Committee in occupied Belgium, and among the diverse resistance groups had, however, to be resolved before Belgian production could resume. This was achieved by formulation of the Social Pact of 1944, which set up a three-tier system of wage determination throughout Belgian industry in which all of the above-mentioned interest groups would have a voice at one stage or another. "Parity committees" were set up in all sectors and branches of Belgian industry to ensure that wages and working conditions were maintained at an acceptable level in each case. National labor conferences then consolidated these recommendations to the government, which basically accepted them. In this way, Belgium agreed on indexing wages to consumer prices, on maintaining an eight-hour working day and a forty-eight-hour working week, and on an overall incomes policy to maintain an acceptable wage share of national income. With much the same goal of creating a welfare state on the model of the Beveridge Plan in Great Britain, Belgium's weak postwar government had to build a framework for reaching consensus among the conflicting interest groups. This framework has been dubbed "corporatist interest intermediation"[1] and it remained the essential method of Belgian policymaking until it began to be dismantled in the 1990s.

The Netherlands, by contrast to Belgium, was much less industrialized and consequently unable to pursue a "politics of production" during the war much less contribute to the reconstruction of the rest of Europe after the war. By compensation, however, the Dutch emerged from the shared misery of occupation and battle zone destruction with a more homogeneous social basis for dealing with postwar adjustments. Immediate problems were to restore polder lands to production, recover such industrial equipment as had been looted by the

Germans, compensate for the loss of revenues from Indonesia that were never to be resumed, and provide employment for the increased population returning from labor camps and overseas. The famous Dutch economist, Jan Tinbergen, was put in charge of a Ministry of Planning to draw up an overall plan for reconstruction, price controls and rationing were maintained along with a currency reform that reduced the money supply, and agreement was reached between employers' organizations and labor unions to hold down money wages while the economy was rebuilt.

All the elements for a dirigiste, authoritarian system of economic planning were in place, but the unpleasant memories of Nazi occupation prevented them from becoming instruments of state authority. Instead, private initiatives were allowed to preempt state action. These quickly focused on export-led industrialization as the best long-term strategy. Unencumbered by old physical plant in heavy industry, the Dutch were able to develop state-of-the-art industrial facilities in the chemical and electrical sectors and to convert toward petroleum (later to natural gas) as a cheaper, more efficient fuel than the coal on which so much of the Belgian economy relied. Moving toward this goal, however, required imports from Belgian heavy industry. Belgian industrialists, on the other side, needed food imports to keep down the cost of living so their workers would continue to be content with small wage increases. It was natural then to form the customs union for industrial products with the BLEU called Benelux. This soon became an economic union as well, when exchange rates were fixed between the Dutch guilder and the Belgian-Luxembourg franc and free trade in agricultural goods was allowed. (Farmers in both countries were protected from outside competition by a 20 percent tariff wall.)

A further divergence in the economic policy of the Dutch and Belgians occurred with the devaluations of September 1949. Belgium, in a situation of export surplus with the rest of Europe but with a continued dollar deficit with the rest of the world, decided to devalue less than the British against the U.S. dollar. Instead of the 30.5 percent devaluation of the British, Belgium devalued by 12.345 percent, thus revaluing the Belgian franc against the pound sterling. The Netherlands, still in a substantial overall trade deficit even with Marshall Plan aid, devalued by the same amount as the British. Through the rest of the 1950s, then, Dutch exports had a competitive advantage over Belgian exports to the rest of Europe and within the Benelux customs union as well. As a result, Belgian economic growth began to taper off in the 1950s while Dutch economic growth continued at a rapid pace, led by growing exports.

The operation of the European Coal and Steel Community began in February 1953 and began the process of scaling down the Belgian coal industry while consolidating the scattered specialty steel products manufacturers into vertically integrated enterprises on the German model. Belgian coal mines were increasingly uncompetitive compared with both the German and Dutch coal mines, which were able to supply Belgium's fuel needs for its expanding electricity plants and its new steel plants employing electric arc furnaces. Moreover, it became increasingly difficult to staff the mines at the low wages needed to make them profitable. By 1955, over 60 percent of the miners were, in fact,

Italian. Under this duress, Belgian industry began the development of oil refineries and to explore the use of nuclear energy for electric power plants. No doubt it was possible to make a more rapid conversion away from the use of coal, but it would have heightened domestic social tensions, which may have required higher government expenditures than the subsidies to the coal industry entailed. Meanwhile, the Dutch steel industry quickly learned the advantages of locating steel mills by ocean ports so that all the necessary bulky inputs and outputs allocated to them by the European Coal and Steel Community could be delivered cheaply.

Denmark, like Belgium, was able to grow rapidly in the immediate postwar years on the basis of exports from its traditional export sectors, but these were in agricultural processing industries rather than heavy industry. Moreover, foreign demand for Danish food products was kept down by the depressed consumption conditions in both of Denmark's main export markets, Great Britain and Germany. By following Great Britain in devaluing the krone by 30 percent against the dollar in 1949, Denmark tried to maintain access for its goods in the British market and in the sterling area generally. This succeeded in that an export surplus was achieved with the sterling area. But as sterling remained largely inconvertible, the sterling surplus was useless for paying off the import deficit Denmark ran against the dollar area and the rest of Europe. Moreover, to maintain competitiveness in agriculture against the restrictions imposed by its traditional customers in the postwar world of limiting consumption in order to focus on investment, Denmark's farmers had to improve their productivity even further. This released labor from agriculture, creating a larger unemployment problem than existed at the time for either Belgium or the Netherlands.

Like Belgium, then, Denmark found that as a small open economy in the new European economy being created after World War II, it was not sufficient to rely on revitalizing its traditional sectors. A new industrial strategy similar to that of its more successful neighbors would have to be pursued. In the meantime, a Socialist government had kept social peace by providing a Scandinavian-style welfare system. This included wage indexation, pension benefits, health insurance, and generous unemployment benefits. But paying for this required the public sector to grow rapidly in size, with the result that the share of tax revenues in gross domestic product rose quickly in the 1950s. Even so, government deficits began to accumulate, setting a pattern that was to continue until the 1980s.

To sum up, each of these small, open economies occupied by Nazi Germany during the war experienced rapid economic recovery afterward. Each participated in the Marshall Plan and benefited greatly from the provision of scarce capital goods, fuel, or foreign exchange that the United States provided. Each became an initial member of the North Atlantic Treaty Organization as well as of the European Payments Union. Within the European Payments Union, however, Belgium was in continued, although diminishing, export surplus and had to be compensated periodically with net payments of U.S. dollars; the Netherlands was in deficit until the mid-1950s when it began to earn surpluses ending up with a small net payment in U.S. dollars; and Denmark continued to run deficits to the end. Dutch success was clearly identified with developing a complementary role to the economic miracle under way in Germany. Belgian retardation was easily diagnosed as arising from trying to maintain a substitute source of supply for German heavy industry and capital goods, which had become much more efficient. Danish retardation was clearly bound up with the continued difficulties of Britain and its relations with the sterling area. All three were well positioned and motivated to take innovative initiatives in the subsequent decade. Belgium opened up its industry to competition from Germany while inviting in new technology from American firms by expanding the Benelux customs union to include the three major European economies. The Netherlands began to exploit natural gas as both a new fuel and a new raw material for its petrochemical industry. Denmark decided to industrialize while benefiting from the convertibility of sterling earnings from 1958 on. For the time being, it remained out of the Common Market and oriented still to the British and sterling markets.

THE IRON TRIANGLE VS. THE BALTIC TRADES: 1958–73

Both Belgium under the leadership of Paul-Henri Spaak and the Netherlands under the guidance of Johan Beyen were prime movers in establishing the European Economic Community. The economic rationale for the Netherlands was clear, to sustain the export-led industrialization that was complementary to the rapid expansion of the German economy. So the government's initiatives were strongly supported by Dutch industrialists. For Belgium, the economic rationale was more complicated. The Belgian economist, Alexandre Lamfalussy (who in 1995 became head of the newly established European Monetary Institute), in two influential books[2] had identified the sources of Belgium's relative retardation in the 1950s. The first was the strategy of "defensive investment," which was directed toward maintaining the competitiveness of the traditional heavy-industry sectors in the Belgian economy. Not only was this a smaller part of GDP relative to the aggressive investment strategies of the Netherlands and Germany, it was also less productive. The refurbishment of existing plants could not begin to yield the productivity gains available from building entirely new plants with the latest technology. The second was the cost of maintaining control over foreign colonies, essentially the Belgian Congo. While not as severe a drain on Belgium's government as were the British and French efforts to maintain their overseas possessions, the Congo represented a commitment to a trade policy that emphasized secure sources of imports rather than finding profitable markets for exports.

In the event, after suffering a recession in 1958 and a crisis in the coal mining districts in 1958–9, which culminated in the General Strike of 1960, a new Belgian government encouraged investment in new sectors. The response was gratifying, even if it came primarily from foreign multinationals. American and British firms, fearful of being cut out of the European market by the common external tariff about to be set up, and anticipating expanded Belgian exports to France and Italy as their trade barriers against Belgium were eliminated, responded eagerly to the inducements offered by the Belgian government. Moreover, unlike Belgian firms, they could finance their investment at lower interest rates available on the international capital market. The result was very satisfying. Exports increased quickly, especially to Germany and France, and investment levels rose and were directed toward the new growth sectors of chemicals, consumer products, and electronics. Belgium finally was able to participate in the golden age of economic growth that its neighbors had initiated.

The problems of maintaining social peace, however, were exacerbated by the preference of foreign companies to locate in Flanders, the Flemish-speaking north. This enabled them to take advantage of the cheap transport available from the port of Antwerp as well as the cheaper labor available in the less unionized part of the country. Meanwhile, the French-speaking south, Wallonia, suffered further declines in its heavy industry and rising unemployment. Underneath the appearance of rapid economic growth in the 1960s, therefore, the latent regional division of Belgium was being aggravated. Through the 1960s, the government responded by attempting to redirect investment into the south, but this only irritated the Flemish while doing little to relieve structural unemployment in the laggard south. The main effect was to increase government expenditures on subsidies and unemployment benefits at the cost of raising taxes. While government debt was reduced from two-thirds of GDP in the late 1950s and early 1960s to under one-half by 1970, the share of government expenditures in the economy kept rising, from under 30 percent in 1960 to over 40 percent by 1973.

Meanwhile, the Dutch economic miracle continued as its entrepôt role between the EEC and the rest of the world was consolidated on the basis of easy access to the port of Rotterdam, now completely rebuilt and modernized, and then to the rivers draining the "iron triangle" from Liege in Belgium to Essen in the Ruhr to Mannheim in the Saar. Moreover, huge natural gas deposits were discovered, which provided the Netherlands for the first time in the industrial age with the prospect of self-sufficiency in energy sources. Nevertheless, despite the continuity in achieving high growth rates in the 1960s, there were important changes in the way these were maintained. Most important, the cost advantages enjoyed by Dutch exporters due to Dutch labor receiving low wages relative to its productivity were eroded. Unemployment rates had fallen to such levels by 1960 that Dutch labor unions could now exercise more effective pressure in raising wages. In fact, real wages grew more rapidly from 1960 to 1973 in the Netherlands than anywhere else in Europe. The government reduced industry's competitiveness further by reducing the official work week to forty-five hours in 1960–61 and then revaluing the Dutch guilder by 5 percent in 1961. Dutch industry responded by emphasizing labor-saving investment and reducing nonlabor costs.

Dutch wage policy, set within the corporatist framework established after the war, tried to equalize real wages across the entire economy, including both the most competitive and the least competitive parts of the tradables sectors as well as the nontradables sectors, which include most services and most of the labor force. The leading export sectors were faced with labor shortages so they had to pay labor a real wage equal to the high marginal product that labor provided them or they would lose market share. Less productive labor in the lagging export sectors, however, would get the same real wage, which meant that firms would have to reduce the size of their labor force. In the nontradables sectors where productivity tended to grow most slowly or not at all, the same high real wages were insisted upon by the labor unions and the government. Unemployment rates began their upward rise in the mid1960s, while government transfers to households more than doubled as a percentage of GDP from 1955 (8%) to 1970 (18.4%).[3] The increased transfers to households alone accounted for the rising share of government expenditure in the economy over this period. Here lay the seeds of what later became known as the Dutch disease—the phenomenon of high wages in a successful sector leading to unemployment and inflation in the rest of the economy. Whatever it is called, it is an affliction endemic to small, open economies with a commitment to wage parity across different sectors. The Belgian economy had already been weakened by a similar ailment during the 1950s.

In fact, the Danish economy during the 1960s might be an example of the Nordic version of the Dutch disease. This was the decade that industrialization finally took hold for the Danes after several false starts in the twentieth century. Unlike the Dutch case, however, it was not export led and the manufacturing sector did not expand in importance nearly as much as the private service sector and the public sector. In fact, the openness of the Danish economy actually declined in the 1960s as measured by the ratios of either imports or exports to GDP. This was in sharp contrast to the economies of the Benelux countries. The composition of exports did shift more toward industrial products as Denmark's food products were closed out of the EEC market by the Common Agricultural Policy. Imports shifted more toward raw materials and fuel and away from manufactured products as well. Denmark's success in establishing an industrial base, therefore, was dependent on raising the investment ratio for the economy as a whole, from an already high 22 percent to over 25 percent of GDP, and changing the composition of investment away from residential construction toward machinery and equipment. The relative prices of machinery and equipment compared with all other goods and services actually fell sharply in this period, which helped induce the high investment ratio.[4] This was no doubt due to the reduction of tariffs on industrial goods from Great Britain and Sweden, trading partners in the European Free Trade Association, and from Germany and Benelux, due to reciprocal tariff reductions on industrial goods between the EEC and EFTA.

Cheap labor was no longer a source of industrial expansion even though agricultural employment continued to fall. The reason was that the public sector expanded its share of employment enormously. Denmark by 1973 was second only to Sweden in the relative importance of public sector employment in the economy. From one of the least taxing economies in Europe, Denmark became one of Europe's leaders with tax revenues nearing 50 percent of GDP by 1973.

Small wonder that Denmark was eager to join the EEC along with Britain, still its main trading partner overall, when the British application to join was finally taken seriously in the early 1970s. Like Britain, therefore, Denmark suffered the shock of joining the EEC at the same time that the first oil shock hit it. Unlike Britain, however, Denmark benefited quickly from the EEC's Common Agricultural Policy, which helped offset the increased costs of importing oil.

FOUR COUNTRIES, FOUR STRATEGIES FOR THE OIL SHOCKS: 1974–85

Confronting the same effects of a sudden, incredible rise in the price of a vital import that all the rest of the countries in Western Europe confronted, these four, small, well-off countries all pursued separate strategies. The choice of strategy depended strictly on domestic political pressures and specific national assets that could be mobilized. In this, the four simply reflected the general disarray of Europe faced with the common economic threat posed by the actions of the OPEC cartel. Belgium was the hardest hit of the four and the least effective in dealing with the successive oil shocks. Luxembourg's industrial sector was hit equally hard, but the unemployment effects could be largely avoided by sending foreign guest workers back to their home countries. Denmark had the problem of maintaining high levels of government employment against a weakening tax base. Only the Netherlands seemed to have the advantages of efficient agriculture, social harmony, and, most important, valuable deposits of natural gas that could now be exploited vigorously.

There was similarity, however, in that all four felt compelled to participate in the European snake, linking the exchange rate of their respective currencies to the German deutsche mark and then floating with the deutsche mark up against the dollar. In this way, part of the oil shock was mitigated for each as the OPEC-determined price of oil was always in dollars. Belgium added an extra wrinkle by following the French example of imposing a two-tier exchange rate, with the Belgian franc worth more on capital account transactions, which were tightly controlled, than on current account transactions, where it floated. This effectively meant a tax on foreigners holding franc accounts in either France or Belgium, as their bank accounts were considered subject to capital controls. If a foreign depositor wished to withdraw cash, the amount had to be paid out at the overvalued capital account rate, meaning the depositor received fewer francs than had been paid in. Desiring to maintain fixed rates with both France and Germany, Belgium worked hard to resolve Franco-German differences over the operation first of the snake and then of the European Monetary System agreed on in 1978.

Raising the exchange value of their currencies relative to the dollar and pound obviously hurt exports, although the major cause of falling exports was the economic depression that occurred throughout the industrialized world. All four tried to keep up employment, however, by pursuing the expansionary fiscal policies that had tamed cyclical fluctuations through the 1950s and 1960s. The results were successful in keeping down unemployment rates during the first oil shock, as shown in Figure 13.3. However, the price paid for temporary success was to increase the role of government in each case. This produced the rise in the ratio of general government tax revenues to gross domestic product that is shown in Figure 13.4. Although the tax ratios had been rising throughout the 1960s, efforts had been under way to reduce the fiscal pressure on the economy at the end of the 1960s. All thought of this limit to government activity was put aside in order to confront the threat to employment and real wages represented by the OPEC extortions.

By the time of the second oil shock, sharp increases in the ratio of government debt had to occur as well, as shown in Figure 13.5. These were especially marked in Belgium, where any efforts to restrain the growth of government spending or to confine the cost push pressures for inflation led to a fall in the government. Unions managed to keep wage indexation to the successive rises in the cost of living, thereby ensuring a vicious cycle of inflationary pressures to be accommodated somehow. Keeping with the European Monetary System limited the rate of inflation for Belgium and the possibility of government expenses being at least partially covered by seigniorage. The Belgian governments had no recourse politically but to increase their issues of debt and to encourage the financial sector to hold it by paying higher and higher interest rates on it. Efforts were made in the early 1980s in both the Netherlands and Denmark, on the other hand, to control the rise of government debt. The Dutch

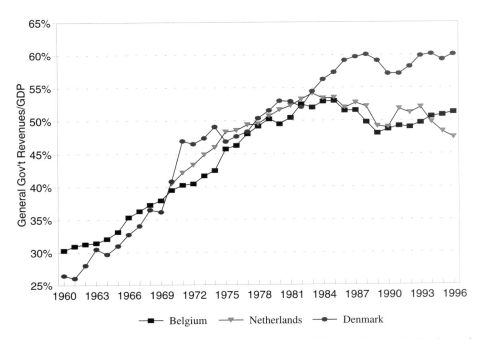

Figure 13.4. Government tax ratios to GDP, 1960–96, Belgium, the Netherlands, and Denmark.

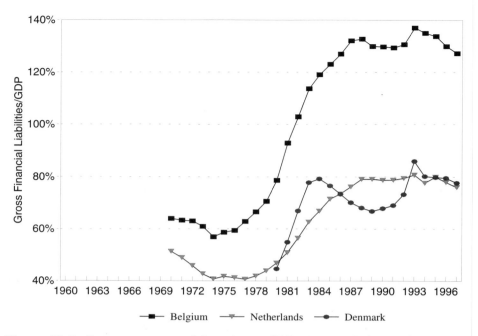

Figure 13.5. Government gross debt ratios to GDP, 1960–96, Belgium, the Nether-lands, and Denmark.

were able to do this by virtue of being net beneficiaries of the second oil shock, by which time they had become net exporters of natural gas. The Danes, alas, were able to do it only by increasing yet further the tax burden on their economy.

ALL FOR ONE, ONE FOR ALL? 1986–96

In this situation, each country was very much in favor of the Single Market initiative of 1985, which promised to revitalize their respective export markets and reduce the pressure on government to maintain social tranquillity by ever-increasing transfer payments. As Figure 13.1 shows, each did benefit from the renewed growth of trade and movement of capital within the European Commu-nity in the late 1980s, and unemployment rates began to fall as well. The associ-ation between increased government deficits and unemployment levels that had arisen at the end of the 1970s was still in evidence as both deficits and unem-ployment rates began to fall. The ratio of the stock of government debt to GDP leveled off and even began to fall for the Netherlands. Recovery was not quite as dramatic as in the poorer member states (see Chapter 14). There was little reason for foreign direct investment to locate in countries with high wages and elaborate state protection of workers' rights, when improved access to the Single Market could be reached equally well from the low-wage countries of Ireland, Portugal, or Spain. Moreover, the reforms made to the operation of the Common Agricultural Policy all tended to the disadvantage of farmers in the rich countries. Their comparative advantage was in livestock and dairy production, which were precisely the areas where reforms were first carried out to limit the potential amount of subsidies. Injury was added to insult as the cohesion funds designed to hasten the economic development of the poorer member states had to be financed by contributions from each member state based on their gross domestic product, which meant a net transfer away from the Benelux countries and Denmark toward the poorer countries. Finally, as very open economies with the best ocean ports in Europe, much of the customs revenues of the European Union had always been collected at their borders. These economic forces tending to make the financial arrangements of the European Union less beneficial to the smaller, more open, and richer countries were held in abeyance, however, by the political power they possessed in the voting arrangements of the EU. As discussed in Chapter 5, these greatly overweighted the smaller countries, tiny Luxembourg being the most favored in terms of voting power and also receiving by far the greatest net transfers per capita from the EU.

Within the EMS, both Belgium-Luxembourg and the Netherlands revalued their currencies along with the deutsche mark in 1986 and 1987. Earlier, Belgium-Luxembourg had revalued in 1983 with the deutsche mark. And the Belgian-Luxembourg franc appreciated against the French franc when it devalued in 1981 and 1982. The Danish krone remained in the middle of the EMS parity grid on each occasion, passively accepting a revaluation against the French franc and the Italian lira when they devalued and equally enjoying a devaluation against the German deutsche mark when it was revalued. By the end of the 1980s, it was clear that all four countries were irrevocably committed to be part of the deutsche-mark zone regardless of the behavior of the British pound sterling or the French franc. Their economic reorientation toward their former military occupier was remarkably complete.

This meant, of course, that all four were very susceptible to the German reunification shock at the beginning of the 1990s. All the progress that had been made toward reducing unemployment, raising rates of growth, and stabilizing the ratio of government debt to GDP was quickly undone. Nevertheless, each of the four has valiantly stayed with the Franco-German plans for a common currency, by keeping their currencies pegged to the deutsche mark. The ultimate advantage their industrialists see is to maintain their preferred access to the largest market in Europe that their fixed exchange rates, zero tariffs, and common technical standards provide. The ultimate gain for their governments will be reduced interest rates on their large stocks of outstanding government debt. As debt service declines, more options open up for governments either to spend more of their tax revenues on redistribution to the lower income groups, use their taxes to reduce the stock of debt as well, or even to reduce taxes overall. Any one of these possibilities should enhance the legitimacy of the national government.

The interesting pattern shown in the comparative figures is that in the mid-1990s it is the Dutch who seem to be making the best progress. If the Dutch disease really did originate in the Netherlands, the Dutch population seems to have acquired general immunity. This shows up in specific legislative reforms passed by the Dutch, which specify that wage increases should be geared to increases in labor productivity for each industry, irrespective of what has happened in the rest of the economy. This effectively breaks the link that ties equal wage increases across sectors with differing rates of productivity advance. It also creates incentives for lower productivity sectors to improve their economic performance. These reforms seem to be having the desired effect, as Dutch unemployment rates have begun to fall below the EU average and both the tax and debt ratios are declining as well. The Danish government is keeping tax ratios high while reducing the stock of debt. The weak, fragmented government of Belgium appears committed to maintaining the redistribution policy that has characterized the Social Pact since 1944. As a result, its unemployment and growth rates show the least improvement.

Unfortunately for the entire group of countries whose economic fortunes are now so closely bound to those of united Germany, it appears that German policymakers have decided to inject the Dutch disease virus into their body politic. This is the effect of agreeing to bring East German real wages in each sector up rapidly to the level of West German real wages, regardless of the much lower productivity of East German workers.

CONCLUSION

The German reunification shock has renewed pressures for each of the four countries considered in this chapter to take separate policy paths in response. Their distinctive policies are demonstrated most vividly by the diverse timing of unemployment patterns for each shown at the right of Figure 13.3. These national policies, in turn, are the outcome of the resolution of differences in comparative advantage among regions within each small country. Each has a politically powerful farming interest; a large public sector staffed by well-educated, highly paid civil servants; national labor unions; profitable multinational firms; and declining industries. These internal regional and sectoral conflicts are much more easily settled in the context of the larger European Union. There, the costs of bringing about a redistribution of privileges or payments can be reduced by using their disproportionate political power in the EU and receiving a net payment that ultimately comes from the major countries. So long as the two largest countries, Germany and France, are committed to making the EU the operations center for implementing their vision of Europe, this strategy may well continue to work.

In formulating their positions with respect to the Inter-Governmental Conference of 1996–97, each country takes, as one would expect, a positive view toward enhancing the supranational functions of the EU as well as improving the efficiency with which it performs its existing responsibilities. All are in favor of backing up the European Economic and Monetary Unions with stronger social protection, environmental preservation, and tax harmonization. To make the EU more effective, they all propose giving the European Parliament a greater role in decision making. They want to establish more firmly the legitimacy of the EU's authority, even if this means losing some of their overrepresentation in it. This commitment to enhancing the EU's authority carries over into supporting qualified majority voting in the Council as well. Moreover, the Commission should have greater enforcement powers while maintaining its role in initiating and formulating EU legislation.

Beyond these rather predictable similarities in their initial discussion positions, however, there are some interesting divergencies on specific issues. These show up in the order of priorities each country has for the issues to be discussed by the 1996–97 Inter-Governmental Conference. Belgium, for example, insists on extolling the virtues of subsidiarity, perhaps using the Belgian model of devolution. Taxing and spending authority has been put down to the regional and communal levels in its internal political reforms over the past decade. Belgium, in fact, has begun the practice of allowing regional ministers to represent Belgium on certain issues taken up in the Council of Ministers. It urges that other countries begin to emulate it. This seems unlikely to strike a responsive chord with any of the other countries, including either the Netherlands or Denmark. But it is consistent with the view common to all of them that all the EU's institutions can be enlarged in numbers, even with the existing membership.

The Dutch, by contrast, declare that German interests should be taken into full account, with primary attention paid to security issues. There, military effectiveness is the most important aspect, so NATO's expansion and authority must take precedence. The EU and the West European Union (WEU) military alliance can expand in membership and functions concerning security issues, but only under the aegis of an expanded and modernized NATO. The Dutch take up seriously the issue of enlargement to the east. They are very cautious about how many countries should enter and how quickly they should participate fully in the EU's redistribution mechanisms. In the meantime, both the structural funds policy and the Common Agricultural Policy need to be examined and reformed. The bottom line is that expansion will be fine, but it should not impose excessive costs on the existing member states. As enlargement proceeds and existing institutions are altered, the Dutch foresee clearly that alternative forms of cooperation will have to be found. The term *differentiated integration* is to describe what they have in mind in preference to phrases such as "variable geometry." While different states can progress at different speeds toward a common goal, none should be allowed to undermine the legal basis on which the EU oversees the operation of the Single Market. This would seem to rule out accepting the British ideal of sovereign nations deciding what to accept and what to opt out of from the menu of EU initiatives.

Denmark, by contrast, seems most sympathetic to British reluctance to impose either a common foreign and security policy or economic and monetary union on the member states. But this may be a reflection of the increased caution with which Danish governments have greeted EU initiatives since the initial defeat of the Maastricht Treaty in the referendum held in spring 1992. One of the reasons given for the negative vote was that the Danish government had distributed the full text of the treaty to each voting household. Unable to decipher what the implications would be for Denmark's citizens given the complexity and obtuseness of the text, Danish voters decided to reject it. Later clarification of how limited would be the constraints on Danish actions under the Maastricht Treaty enabled the government to gain its approval in a second referendum. This amounted to specific opt outs for Denmark on when or whether to join the EMU, on using European citizenship, and on accepting lower environmental standards on EU products than existed in Danish law. Consequently, the Danish government has confined itself to raising the issues that should be discussed in the Inter-Governmental Conference for the benefit of the Danish electorate, without, however, making any concrete proposals for specific changes in voting arrangements, security policy, or administration of justice. Its main concern is that the Treaty of European Union be rewritten in simpler, clearer language that can reduce the final document to a reasonable size. This is defined implicitly as small enough to be distributed once again to all the Danish voters for their approval.

Whatever the outcome of the Iinter-Governmental Conference, these four countries of Belgium, Luxembourg, the Netherlands, and Denmark will continue to play a major and supportive role in the execution of the new programs. They will also be very active within the framework of the revised institutions. They may play a decisive role in their formulation as well to ensure that compromise positions are found that satisfy for the moment the conflicting proposals of the major countries. If Germany and France lie at the center of an integrated, peaceful Europe, these four countries lie at its entrance. Historically, they have all suffered mightily during the conflicts between France and Germany. In the past fifty years, by idyllic contrast, they have prospered beyond their wildest imaginations during the deepening cooperation between France and Germany. This leaves little doubt where their interests lie and where their energies will be directed.

Endnotes

1.   André Mommer, *The Belgian Economy in the Twentieth Century,* London: Routledge, 1994, p. 79.

2.   These were *Investment and Growth in Mature Economies,* London: Macmillan, 1961; and *Investment and Growth: The Case of Belgium,* London: Macmillan, 1961.

3.   Bart van Ark, Jakob de Haan and Herman J. de Jong. "Characteristics of economic growth in the Netherlands during the postwar period," in Nicholas Crafts and Gianni Toniolo, eds. *Economic Growth in Europe since 1945.* Cambridge: Cambridge University Press, 1996, p. 318.

4.   Peder J. Pedersen, "Postwar growth of the Danish economy," in Nicholas Crafts and Gianni Toniolo, eds., note 3, p. 556.

Bibliography

van Ark, Bart, Jakob de Haan and Herman J. de Jong. "Characteristics of economic growth in the Netherlands during the postwar period," in Nicholas Crafts and Gianni Toniolo, eds. *Economic Growth in Europe since 1945*. Cambridge: Cambridge University Press, 1996.

Cassiers, Isabelle. " 'Belgian miracle' to slow growth: the impact of the Marshall Plan and the European Payments Union," in Barry Eichengreen, ed. *Europe's Post-War Recovery*. Cambridge: Cambridge University Press, 1995.

Cassiers, Isabelle, Philippe De Villé, and Peter M. Solar. "Economic growth in postwar Belgium," in Nicholas Crafts and Gianni Toniolo, eds. *Economic Growth in Europe since 1945*. Cambridge: Cambridge University Press, 1996.

de Vries, Johan. *The Netherlands Economy in the Twentieth Century*. Assen: Van Gorcum & Co., 1978.

Economist Intelligence Unit. *Country Report, Belgium*. London: Economist Intelligence Unit, 2nd quarter, 1996.

Economist Intelligence Unit. *Country Report, Denmark*. London: Economist Intelligence Unit, 2nd quarter, 1996.

Economist Intelligence Unit. *Country Report, Luxembourg*. London: Economist Intelligence Unit, 2nd quarter, 1996.

Economist Intelligence Unit. *Country Report, Netherlands*. London: Economist Intelligence Unit, 2nd quarter, 1996.

Johansen, Hans Christian. *The Danish Economy in the Twentieth Century*. London: Croom Helm, 1987.

Mommer, André. *The Belgian Economy in the Twentieth Century*. London: Routledge, 1994.

Pedersen, Peder J. "Postwar growth of the Danish economy," in Nicholas Crafts and Gianni Toniolo, eds. *Economic Growth in Europe since 1945*. Cambridge: Cambridge University Press, 1996.

Ireland, Greece, Portugal, and Spain:

The First Outsiders Rejoin Europe

Basic Facts

Area:	**Total**	799,500 km²	24 % of EU15
	Ireland	70,300 km²	2.1 %
	Greece	132,000 km²	4.0 %
	Portugal	92,400 km²	2.8 %
	Spain	504,800 km²	15.1 %
Population (1/1/94):		62,984,100	17.0 % of EU15
	Ireland	3,569,000	1.0 %
	Greece	10,410,500	2.8 %
	Portugal	9,887,600	2.7 %
	Spain	39,117,000	10.6 %
Gross Domestic Product (1993):		$714.1 billion	11.9 % of EU15
	Ireland	$45.9 billion	0.8 %
	Greece	$84.2 billion	1.4 %
	Portugal	$93.8 billion	1.6 %
	Spain	$490.2 billion	8.2 %
Per Capita:		$11,338	70 % of EU15 average
	Ireland	$12,906	80 %
	Greece	$8,127	50 %
	Portugal	$10,032	62 %
	Spain	$12,545	77 %
Openness (X + M)/GDP			
	Ireland	104 %	82 % with EU12
	Greece	34 %	58 %
	Portugal	46 %	74 %
	Spain	30 %	74 %

Source: Eurostat, *Basic Statistics of the European Union,* 32nd ed. (Luxembourg, 1995).

The four countries treated here are all on the periphery of Europe and all were late coming into the European Community. As the basic data above show, all are relatively poor compared with the rest of the European Union member states. Per capita incomes average only 70 percent of the entire European Union, whose average is lowered by their presence and that of East Germany and southern Italy. Their common poverty has brought them together as a voting bloc within the EU, which has enabled them to obtain an increasing share of the EU budget in the form of regional development funds and, most recently, cohesion funds largely financed by contributions from the richest member states. Their history of progress (or lack of it, in the case of Greece) since joining the EU, however, has shown that their poverty can be attributed in large part to poor economic policies. Membership in the EU has helped them reevaluate their economic strategies, so that a consensus development program may be developing among them. By radically changing policies, Ireland has seen a rise in per capita income to 80 percent of the EU average after it started at close to 50 percent. By not changing policies, in contrast, Greece has seen its per capita income remain at 50 percent of the EU's average. The experience of Ireland and Greece holds out a large measure of hope for policymakers in other backward countries, that selecting the right policy mix can make a difference. Perhaps the transition economies of Central and Eastern Europe can apply some of the lessons learned by these earlier arrivals in the EU.

Ireland's traumatic relationship with Great Britain has dominated its economic, as well as its political, life for centuries. That relationship will continue to be traumatic so long as the island is separated into Northern Ireland, part of the United Kingdom since the Act of Union in 1800, and the Republic of Ireland, separated from the United Kingdom in 1921. Political separation did not lead to economic success for the Republic, however, due to autarkic policies designed to cut trade links with Britain and develop home industry. These policies were first imposed by Britain in the 1920s as a means of obtaining compensation for property taken by the new Irish state. But Irish nationalists eagerly embraced these same policies in the 1930s as a means of eliminating dependence on British manufactures. Ireland remained neutral throughout World War II, so while it received little damage it also received little Marshall Plan aid. Not until 1957 did Ireland join the World Bank and the International Monetary Fund, the twin pillars of the Bretton Woods system set up by the United States and Great Britain. And it took another ten years for it to sign on to the General Agreement on Tariffs and Trade (GATT), the third pillar of the postwar international economic system. By this time, however, Irish trade was expanding rapidly, especially with Great Britain, and economic growth was finally occurring. So it was essential for Ireland to join the EEC when Britain's third application for membership was finally accepted in 1973.

However, there were no oil or natural gas deposits off the coasts of Ireland, so the British strategy for coping with the first oil shock was never considered. Also in contrast to Britain, Ireland benefited greatly from its membership in the EC. The EC's agricultural price supports were extravagantly high for Irish farmers, who were a much larger part of the backward Irish economy than their counterparts in Britain. Further, the increasingly generous disbursements of regional aid helped improve highways and other infrastructure throughout the island. So it was not unreasonable for Ireland to join the European Monetary System in 1978 even while Britain opted out. In the long run, this has proved a wise decision, but in the short run the Irish punt appreciated against the British pound along with the rest of the EMS currencies. For Ireland, this meant a loss of a large part of the British market for its exports at a time when the potential market for its exports on the Continent was stagnant, due to the deep recession afflicting industrial Europe. Ireland was therefore especially hard hit during the second oil shock. The expansionary demand policies pursued by the Irish government only made inflation worse and forced readjustments of the Irish central rate within the exchange rate grid of the EMS. Government debt soared as a percentage of GDP, and unemployment rates were among the highest in Europe.

From the mid 1980s on, Irish governments have cut spending while maintaining faith with the EMS and the tight monetary policy of the Bundesbank. As a result, unemployment has remained high, outmigration has increased, and governments have come and gone much more frequently. However, by the mid 1990s, the cumulated effects of deregulation, reduced interest rates, and foreign investor confidence in the stability of the Irish punt relative to the deutsche mark have encouraged rising investment. This has led to resumed economic growth, rising per capita incomes, and a rapid fall in both government deficits and stocks of debt as a percentage of GDP. Thanks to the large stock of government debt outstanding by 1992, a sharp fall in the interest rate demanded by investors in Irish bonds has meant a sharp reduction in government expenditures on debt service. This has reduced the deficit, and surpluses are now reducing the stock of debt as well. Moreover, as private investment increases, a large part of which is foreign financed, Irish workers are encouraged to stay in Ireland instead of migrating elsewhere. Even those who have sought jobs elsewhere in the EU are induced to return. Labor migration movements ever since the potato famine of the 1840s have exaggerated the ups and downs in Irish growth experience.

The Irish success story is being touted as an example of how restrictive fiscal policy can be expansionary, essentially by crowding in private investment as interest rates fall with the reduction of government debt. But it helps greatly to be a small country with a large part of one's debt held by foreigners in countries with floating exchange rates, such as Britain and the United States, and it helps also to have an internationally mobile labor force when things are going well.

Greece was the next peripheral member state to join the EU, entering in 1980. Its ancient history, unique culture, and above all, strategic location at the eastern end of the Mediterranean and southern outlet of the Black Sea have made its political history increasingly turbulent. At the beginning of the nineteenth century, Western Europe took serious notice of Greece's attempts to break away from the rule of the Ottoman Empire and aided its war for independence begun in 1821. Ever since, Greece has gradually expanded its territory, usually by conquest, but always with the consent of the great powers in Europe at the time. At the end of World War II, both British troops and Greek resistance forces led by the Communists (ELAS) could take credit for the final departure of German troops in October 1944. Armed conflict then broke out between the British troops and the ELAS forces, with Britain prevailing and restoring the prewar constitutional monarchy. Unable to continue meeting the expense of the defense of Greece by 1947, Britain asked for American support. This led to the Truman Doctrine, which in turn initiated the long-term American strategy of lending military support if necessary to ensure Communists would not control the governments in Western Europe. In this perspective, Marshall Plan aid was the necessary economic support to enable non-Communist governments to establish their postwar legitimacy after being in exile during Nazi occupation.

Even with rapid rebuilding of damaged infrastructure, especially the Corinth canal and the various port facilities, Greece's political system remained in turmoil. The monarchy proved increasingly unpopular with the population, which led to the rise of socialist parties in the legislature. This led to either the king or a military junta disbanding the elected government, which provoked more determined opposition from the population. While the rest of Europe was enjoying the golden age of 1950–73, Greece was wracked with political disputes and excessive military expenditures and tossed between the Scylla of repressive regulations of economic life imposed by the military or monarch and the Charybdis of excessive expenditures on social subsidies instituted by the socialists, as these groups alternated in power. Finally, the ruling military junta from 1967 to 1973 was discredited by its failure to incorporate Cyprus into Greece, a failure so abysmal it led to Turkish occupation of the northern part of the island from 1974 to this day. Since 1974, Greece has become a parliamentary democracy. Since its economic policies were similar to those of Ireland described above, and were equally ineffective, part of the motivation for admitting Greece to the European Community in 1980 was to lend it the economic support of democratic Europe and to discourage any thought of resumption of military rule.

Unfortunately for the economic development of Greece, its political elite responded in much the same fashion as described for southern Italy. The generous subsidies and agricultural protection provided by the European Community were directed as political favors inside Greece rather than used as incentives to promote economic growth and efficiency. If Ireland's record is disappointing because it did not do better than the richer countries in the EC until the 1990s, Greece's is truly dismal, because it did not even manage to keep pace. Only in 1996 was there the promise of implementing sounder economic policies that might begin the resurgence of growth that has occurred in other countries whenever they imitate the successful economic policies employed in the rest of Europe.

The Iberian countries, Spain and Portugal, in contrast to Greece, were politically quiescent (i.e., repressed by fascist dictatorships) during the first thirty years after World War II. They were neutral during World War II, albeit Portugal was favored with Marshall Plan aid while Spain was not. For strategic reasons (access to the southern Atlantic from the Azores to Brazil) and domestic political considerations (long-standing mercantile relations with Britain and the United States), Portugal tilted to the Allies. Spain, on the other hand, tilted to the Nazis. In the Spanish case, General Franco had only prevailed in the Spanish Civil War of the 1930s by military aid and advice provided by Nazi Germany and Fascist Italy. Both countries, however, pursued autarkic economic policies as a counterpart to their political isolation from the rest of Europe after the Allied victory in World War II. Portugal's policies were more successful than Spain's, probably because its economic sphere was much broader. Portugal maintained control of its resource-rich colonies in Africa, Angola on the west and Mozambique on the east, until the early 1970s, as well as of entrepôt outposts in India (Goa) and China (Macao) and intensive trade relations with Brazil. Spain, however, had been stripped of its last overseas colonies following the Spanish-American War of 1898, and both Mexico and Argentina, natural trading partners for Spain, were at this time as equally committed as Spain toward achieving a self-sufficient economy.

Spain, however, with American support, began to change policy starting in 1953 when American military aid began to arrive. The radical change of economic policy occurred with promulgation of the Stabilization Plan of 1959. By 1961, Spain had joined the OECD, the successor organization to the Marshall Plan; arranged reciprocal tariff reductions with the EEC; signed bilateral labor migration agreements with France, Germany, and Switzerland; and unified its multiple exchange rate system to begin resuming convertibility of the peseta on current account. If Spanish national income accounts are to be believed, 1960 marks the beginning of a rapid structural transformation of the Spanish economy, as Spain built up a competitive industrial base for the first time since the sixteenth century and finally modernized the agricultural sector. Rapid urbanization ensued, and this brought with it a rising service sector as well as an industrial sector. Spain's economic miracle period is 1960–73.

The death of Franco in 1975 enabled the joint development of a constitutional monarchy and parliamentary democracy. Franco had laid plans to restore the successor to the Bourbon dynasty, Juan Carlos II, to the Spanish throne after his death, which his political heirs carried out in 1976. Meanwhile, the Spanish political and intellectual elite in exile since the end of the Civil War in 1936 returned in order to ensure that a parliamentary democracy would begin functioning. The peaceful and symbiotic relationship between the two forms of government, which exists in most other countries in Europe, was sealed by the dramatic action of King Juan Carlos II in 1981. On national television he donned full uniform, marched alone into the Cortes where rebellious soldiers held the legislature hostage at gunpoint, and ordered the rebels to lay down their arms—a classic act of Spanish heroism that established simultaneously the legitimacy of the monarchy and the parliament.

The oil shocks and the political uncertainty of the transition period from 1974 through 1981 devastated the industrial base that had arisen during the

economic miracle period. Its key elements—iron and steel, shipbuilding, cement—were all energy intensive, so they were especially hard hit by the oil
shocks. The political uncertainty made it difficult for strong remedial action to
be taken, mainly freeing prices of energy to force a reallocation of resources.
Nevertheless, overall economic growth was sustained by the prosperity of agriculture and the rise in commodity prices, the growth of the service sector, and
the return of both exiles and Spanish workers from abroad. The return flow of
Spanish migrants brought with them heavy inflows of repatriated capital, financial as well as human. This helped finance the import deficits created by the oil
shocks. Ironically, and unexpectedly, the oil shocks and political shocks were
to some degree offsetting for Spain.

Growth of industry began again in the 1980s as the political situation stabilized with a Socialist government in power. Nevertheless, the high level of unemployment that had arisen during the previous decade remained implacable,
staying at the highest levels in the European Community. Due to political resistance from France and Italy, Spain's entry into the EC was delayed until 1986
and then the terms were unusually harsh. Full access to the Common Market
would be phased in over seven years and participation in the Common Agricultural Policy for all of Spanish agriculture was phased in over a ten-year period.
Only gradually has Spain been able to disentangle itself from the web of restrictive regulations that bound up its economy for the benefit of Franco's dictatorship. In retrospect, the intermittent spurts of growth and structural change
since 1960 have derived more from state-directed and -controlled initiatives than
from an embrace of competitive markets.

Portugal, the smaller Iberian cousin of Spain, has a very similar economic
and political history in the twentieth century, usually anticipating events in
Spain by a few years. Portugal's experience with a republic began in 1910,
which was overthrown by a military junta in 1926, but without much internal
strife. In 1928, an economics professor, Antonio de Oliveira Salazar, began forty
years of authoritarian rule. Eschewing any connection to the dominant European ideologies of capitalism, communism, socialism, or fascism, Salazar prom-
ulgated "Lusitanian integralism," which in practice looked like Portuguese fascism to the rest of the world. This meant it had an Atlantic, not European,
orientation, but still maintained an autarkic economic policy with extensive regulation of the economy and preferential political favors extended to the regime's
supporters. The policy worked well for Portugal compared with the rest of Europe through the 1930s and 1940s. The 1950s, however, demonstrated the cumulative disadvantages of autarky compared with the economic miracles taking
place in the rest of Europe. Even Spain was doing better, thanks to American
aid.

Portugal, always a participant in the OEEC and Marshall Plan aid, joined
the British-initiated European Free Trade Area when it was established in 1960.
Trade expanded rapidly with the EFTA members, but fell with its overseas possessions. In the early 1960s, revolts in the African colonies of Angola, Mozambique, and Guinea-Bissau led to increasing expenditures by Portugal for devel-

opment of its African resources, even as foreign direct investment rose to the home country from the United States and Portugal's trading partners in EFTA. Tourism receipts increased as well as emigrant remittances to cover a growing trade deficit. Emigration was so important, stimulated both by higher wages in northern Europe and the threat of military service in Africa, that Portugal actually lost population during its growth spurt from 1960 to 1973. In 1968, Salazar stepped down in favor of a hand-picked successor, Marcello Caetano. Caetano tried to liberalize the economy but was increasingly frustrated by political resistance and sharply divided opinion within the ruling class over the appropriate change of strategy for Portugal. Finally, in 1974, a military coup led by younger officers ousted Caetano, withdrew Portugal from the African colonies, and initiated attempts to integrate Portugal more closely with Europe.

To do this on the EC's terms, however, representative democratic institutions had to be initiated and legitimated, which they were by 1977 when Portugal applied for membership in the EC, ahead of Spain. Like Spain, Portugal suffered political upheaval at the same time as it endured the twin oil shocks of the 1970s. But also like Spain, Portugal benefited from the return of large numbers of its emigrant workers bringing their accumulated savings back from abroad. In addition, nearly one million ex-colonials returned to the home country, bringing with them their human and financial capital as well. These capital infusions, plus the advantage of no longer spending large sums abroad to maintain military control of the colonies, helped Portugal weather the oil shocks better than would have been possible otherwise.

Moreover, the EC greeted the application of Portugal very favorably, recognizing the importance of economic advance for stabilizing its infant democratic institutions. Tariffs against Portuguese manufactures were quickly dropped, while Portugal was allowed to lower its tariffs gradually over a ten-year period. Extensive financial aid was also extended to Portugal starting in October 1975. The advantages of the trade arrangements for Portugal quickly elicited renewed foreign direct investment to take advantage of its newly plentiful labor supply as well as market access to all of Western Europe. This was further encouraged when Portugal entered the EC in 1986.

The one encumbrance to rapid economic growth arising from the fall of the Salazar-Caetano dictatorship was the widespread nationalization of basic industrial and financial firms in the initial stages of the revolution. When foreign investment tailed off in the late 1980s, the subsidies required to maintain employment levels in the state enterprises led to inflationary pressures, less investor confidence, and marked slowdown in growth rates. At this stage of economic evolution, it appears that Portugal is now learning a lesson from Spain, rather than the reverse. For example, Portugal entered the Exchange Rate Mechanism of the EMS only in April 1992, over two years after Spain. The result since then has been an increasing convergence in the economic performance of the two countries—Portugal's inflation rate falling toward the low Spanish levels while its unemployment rate soars.

MACROECONOMIC POLICY INDICATORS: 1960–97

Figures 14.1 to 14.3 show the course of growth rates, inflation, and unemployment for the four poorest countries of Ireland, Greece, Spain, and Portugal. The general pattern of high growth rates in the 1960–73 period, low growth rates in the oil shock period of 1973–85, and vulnerability to the shock of German reunification shows up for inflation and unemployment as well as growth rates. Ireland does worst in terms of growth and inflation in the 1960s and then emerges to do the best of the four in the 1990s. Greece shows up as the worst performer in terms of growth most frequently, and by the time it joins the EC, it is clearly the worst case of chronic inflation. From typically low unemployment rates in the 1960s, all four rise sharply during the oil shock period but to quite different levels and with varied patterns. By the 1990s, however, a process of convergence, even of unemployment rates, seemed to be under way.

All of them except Ireland participated in the economic miracle growth rates of the 1960s. Greece and Portugal were the countries hardest hit by the first oil shock, but it was the effect of their political disruptions on top of the oil crisis that accounts for Greece's negative growth in 1974 and Portugal's in 1975. The political changes of direction in all four countries determined when their growth rates were especially low in the second oil shock. Through the 1980s, the inflationary finance followed by Greece, Portugal, and Ireland, which devalued repeatedly within the Exchange Rate Mechanism of the EMS, caused all

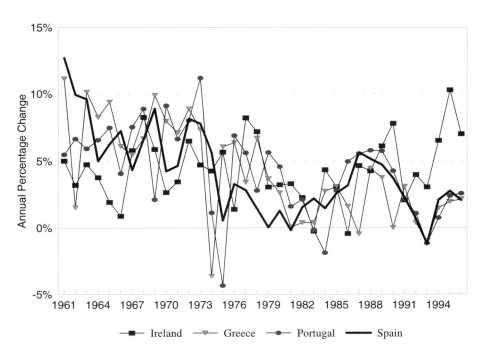

Figure 14.1. GDP growth rates, 1961–96, Ireland, Greece, Portugal, and Spain.

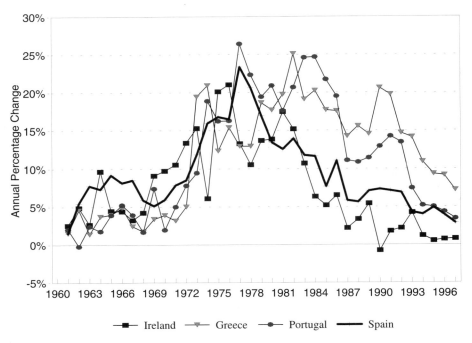

Figure 14.2. Inflation rates, 1961–96, Ireland, Greece, Portugal, and Spain.

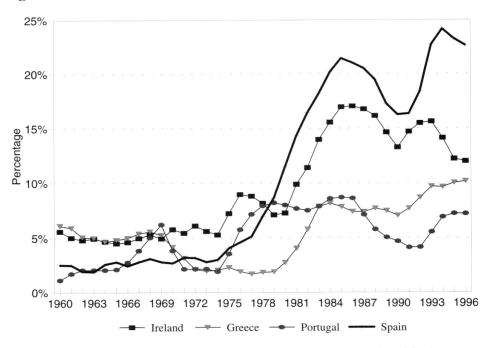

Figure 14.3. Unemployment rates, 1960–96, Ireland, Greece, Portugal, and Spain.

three to have very volatile growth rates. Meanwhile, with its political situation stabilized after the coup attempt in 1981, Spain's growth rates kept increasing until, ironically, it entered the EC. This would seem to give credence to Spain's complaint that it was ill treated in the terms of entry, although the growth rates of the other three also declined in this period. It appears that the reinvigorated growth of the wealthier, more industrialized countries did not spill over to their poorer trading partners.

In the 1990s, Ireland managed to fight off the deleterious effects of the German reunification shock that hampered the other three. As a result, the Irish were finally closing some of the gap in per capita income that had separated them from their British neighbors since the 1940s. Given that Ireland had had the highest ratio of government debt to GDP of any of the four, the rapid payoff Ireland enjoyed to its stringent fiscal policy and stern commitment to the antiinflation policies of the Bundesbank provided an interesting object lesson to the other three, and perhaps to Belgium and Italy as well.

A similar dispersion of policies can be seen for inflation rates. Between the first oil shock and the early 1980s, Portugal and Spain broke their close link and pursued separate courses, with Spain taking the lower inflation route to enter the EC (although it was still high by comparison to the other members of the EC) and Portugal maintaining a high inflation policy. Relaxing the iron grip of the colonels as they entered the land of largesse, the Greeks joined the Portuguese on the high-inflation route. Meanwhile, Ireland fought to lower inflation, eventually achieving rates comparable to those of the richer members of the EMS and well below those of the other lower income members of the EC. It bears pointing out that the central banks of all four had no independence from the financial demands of the government, but first Ireland and then Spain managed to obtain a degree of de facto independence by joining the Exchange Rate Mechanism of the EMS. The object lesson of Irish success, not to mention the terms of the Maastricht Treaty, persuaded Portugal to commit to the Exchange Rate Mechanism of the EMS in 1992, and even Greece announces from time to time that it would like to join.

As in the case of the small, rich countries discussed in the previous chapter, the unemployment rates of the four poor countries diverged sharply in the 1980s and remain far apart in the 1990s. Spain and Ireland stand out as the worst cases in the EU from the early 1980s on. The contrast between the rates of these two and the much lower rates enjoyed by Portugal and Greece stems directly from contrasts in government labor policy. Spain and Ireland provide generous unemployment benefits and require employers to pay significant contributions on behalf of their employees. This discourages workers from seeking any but the best jobs and employers from seeking to hire any but the best workers, prolonging the kind of unemployment that arises from job search behavior. It also encourages both workers and employers to engage in the informal, unregistered labor market, as described previously for Italy. By contrast, both Portugal and Greece have major nationalized industrial and transport enterprises that are committed to act as employers of last resort and as providers of political patronage, which is very important to their relatively young governments. Nevertheless, as these governments start to control expenditures by reducing the subsidies required to maintain excess employment in their nationalized industries, their unemployment rates have begun to rise. Meanwhile, the success of Ireland in raising employment opportunities has gradually reduced its unemployment rates. The conservative economic policies anticipated from Prime Minister Aznar, elected in 1996, may eventually bring down unemployment rates for Spain as well, but only if the adverse policies described above are changed.

THE PERIPHERY CHOOSES SELF-SUFFICIENCY AND AUTARKY

For quite different reasons in each case, these peripheral countries pursued policies of economic autarky after World War II. Their respective attempts to achieve or maintain varying degrees of self-sufficiency effectively excluded them from the stimulating effects of expanding trade that was taking place in the center of Europe. Consequently, they also did not participate in the economic miracles that were taking place. In fact, their growth rates for both per capita and total gross domestic product were below those of Great Britain, the slowest growing of the major economies in Europe until 1960. However, many of the citizens of each autarky did participate directly in one or more of the growth miracles taking place. They did this by migrating either permanently or as temporary workers to a country that would employ them in an expanding economy. The Irish went to Great Britain, the United States, and to the European Continent, usually Germany. The Greeks, Spanish, and Portuguese went to Germany, the Benelux countries, and France. By 1960, each country responded to the opportunities abroad and the pressures of dissatisfaction at home by altering its policies significantly.

The Irish move to autarky was the most unusual, because it ran counter to what was announced Irish policy during most of the period. In the 1930s, Ireland had pursued a deliberate policy of autarky as a way to protest the British government's insistence on diverting Irish export earnings into annuity payments to the British government, various British institutions, and British citizens in compensation for property ceded to the Irish Republic. In 1938, however, the futility of this mutually costly arrangement had been recognized and a new treaty was negotiated to expand trade between the two countries once again. The Irish insisted on the withdrawal of British naval forces from Irish ports, while the British insisted on maintaining Northern Ireland as part of the United Kingdom. To reach agreement, the Irish proclaimed a policy of neutrality in future European conflict. With World War II formally declared in September 1939, Irish neutrality was immediately put to the test. As it was clearly understood on all sides—Irish, British, and German—that any use of Irish territory for hostile action against Britain would bring British sea and land forces immediately back to Ireland, the neutrality was maintained throughout the war. It has become a fact of Irish politics ever since.

Neutrality, however, meant that the prospects of expanded trade with Great

Britain envisioned in the 1938 treaty were never realized. Britain had to restrict food imports in order to divert resources to the war effort and was not about to spend scarce foreign exchange on imports from Ireland, preferring to encourage expanded agricultural production at home or import from an ally, such as Canada or the United States. This meant that exports of fertilizer and agricultural machinery to Ireland were cut off as well in favor of the British farmers. The result was that Ireland's comparative advantage in agriculture was not put to use, unlike the situation in World War I, and wartime conditions were hardly propitious for starting an industrialization program. The British market did not expand for Irish agriculture after the war either. It did, however, provide employment for many of the Irish emigrants who left Ireland, both during the war and after. Because of the value of its neutral status during the war and the importance of the Irish vote in the United States, Ireland did participate in Marshall Plan aid. With a change in government in 1948, however, aid was used for a major land reclamation project in the west of Ireland, historically one of the poorest regions and a prime source of continued outmigration. The possibility of a sustained industrialization policy seemed to have passed by with this diversion of Marshall Plan aid into a backward, and declining, agricultural sector. Ireland devalued with Britain in September 1949, thus maintaining its uncompetitive position relative to its largest market. For the rest of the 1950s, Irish economic policy was to rely on domestic demand to determine the rate and direction of investment. This meant accepting a relatively low rate of investment of less than 15 percent over the period 1949–61.[1] Although it rose to this level quickly after the war, most of the rise was directed toward building houses. Investment in manufacturing continued at a low constant level throughout the 1950s. Without the prospect of expanding exports and with a stagnant domestic economy, there was little incentive for private investment to take place in the manufacturing sector.

Greece also ended up in the 1950s as a relatively autarkic economy with a continued large agricultural sector, but through a dramatically different path. It entered World War II as a combatant on the Allied side in October 1940, when it repelled an invasion by Italian forces. However, the dictatorial government, headed by a monarchy and closely allied to British interests, fled to Egypt with the central bank's gold reserves in early 1941 as German forces moved in to occupy the country. The Greek government in exile arrived back in October 1944, so World War II technically lasted only four years for Greece. But the returning government was not greeted enthusiastically by the population, which had become accustomed to resisting authoritarian power with increasing success by the Greek resistance movements that had arisen during German occupation. These were led most effectively by the Communists, who fought now equally against the reimposition of right-wing dictatorial rule by the prewar government. A civil war ensued, which lasted until October 1949. Initially supported by British troops against the Communist EAM (National Liberation Front in Greek), the right-wing government was sustained from March 1947 on by American support. Thanks to the costs of the civil war, military aid was more important than economic aid and even the Marshall Plan funds went mostly to cover the government's deficit. American administrators insisted that the Greek government do its best to balance its budget, however, and to stabilize its exchange rate while establishing law and order. If the government succeeded in this, not only would American aid be used more efficiently, but eventually the government would reestablish its legitimacy among the Greek people.

This was apparently achieved over the 1950s after the military victory in 1949. However, the long-term costs were debilitating for the future economic growth of Greece. One barometer of the economic difficulties of the period is the exchange rate of the drachma. It was pegged to the British pound sterling in November 1944 at a rate of 600 drachmas to one British Military pound, which implied a rate of 150 drachmas to the U.S. dollar. But thanks to the hyperinflation that had broken out in the last months of Nazi rule, most domestic monetary transactions were already being carried on with gold sovereigns as both the unit of account and the medium of exchange. The government had to declare a drachma value of the gold sovereign as well, which it put initially at 2,850 drachmas. In June 1945, the first of many devaluations of the drachma occurred, falling to 2,000 drachmas to the pound, 500 to the dollar. This was in conjunction with a scheme, typical of a military dictatorship, to limit aggregate civilian demand rather than to increase aggregate domestic supplies. Relying on continued aid from Britain at this time, the government was forced as a condition of British aid to devalue the drachma in January 1946 to 20,000 drachmas to the pound, 5,000 to the dollar. Greece followed the British devaluation in September 1949 along with Ireland and the rest of the sterling area, so the dollar now was equal to 15,000 drachmas. The drachma was now worth 1 percent of its asserted value in 1944. Even so, another major devaluation was required in April 1953, which raised the rate for one dollar to 30,000 drachmas. Similar to the French devaluation in 1958, discussed in Chapter 10, a currency reform was carried out that replaced the old drachmas with new drachmas at a rate of one-hundred old to one new.

The final devaluation in 1953 signaled a determination of the Greek government to open the economy further. At the same time as the devaluation, most import controls and export subsidies were removed. This greatly simplified the process for Greeks who wished to deal with the outside world. The immediate result, however, was to continue reliance on emigrants' remittances to cover the deficit in foreign trade. The government, meanwhile, continued to rely on U.S. military aid to cover its budget deficit. Emigrants' remittances, in turn, seemed to flow into financing housing construction in Greece. While benefiting Greek citizens, an improved housing stock contributed little or nothing toward increasing labor productivity or providing capital stock to potential export industries. To cover the budget deficit, moreover, the government continued to enforce heavy reserve requirements on the banking sector. Regulating the interest rates the banks could pay out to depositors, the government kept them too low to attract domestic saving into the financial sector. Regulating the interest rates the banks could charge on loans discouraged the banks from initiating much lending activity. Consequently, Greece, like Ireland, had a relatively low ratio of investment to GDP, and much too much of the capital formation that did take place was in housing construction or in agriculture instead of industry. Nevertheless, signs of change were occurring as the decade drew to a close: U.S. aid tapered off, the government actually ran a surplus starting in 1957, real interest rates on deposits rose as the rate of inflation tapered off, and domestic savings began to rise and more of them were placed in bank deposits, where they were used to finance increased rates of investment.

Portugal, unlike the rest of the countries in Europe considered to this point, actually benefited economically from World War II. Its neutral status not only removed the threat of physical damage from its European territory, it enhanced the profit it could make by supplying the Allies raw materials from its overseas territories, especially Angola. The war years were the only time in the twentieth century up to then that Portugal managed a trade surplus. Until then, and again after the war through the 1950s, it had covered a chronic trade deficit with remittances from the large overseas community of emigrant Portuguese. The war did expose, however, the precariousness of its overseas connections in case of European conflict. This motivated Salazar to redirect his corporatist autarkic policies toward industrialization. This became a prime goal of the Portuguese state in the 1950s, with a goal of import substitution in the industrial sector. The Portuguese escudo was strong, thanks to wartime prosperity. After Portugal devalued by only 13 percent against the dollar in September 1949, the same as Belgium, the escudo continued to be stable throughout the 1950s. Marshall Plan aid was used to improve infrastructure in electric power and transportation. This, in turn, was supposed to facilitate development of a larger scale industrial sector. Economic growth was quite satisfactory on a comparative basis, around 4 percent annually, if below the spectacular rates achieved by the export-led economies such as the Netherlands, Germany, and Italy. Industry, however, remained confined mainly to traditional sectors such as footwear and textiles, with very small enterprises dominating.

Spain, the Iberian partner of Portugal, could hardly be said to have prospered during the war, despite its neutral status. After the devastation and demoralization caused by its civil war in the late 1930s, however, the relative calm of neutral status during the conflagration consuming the rest of Europe was a welcome respite. The economy managed to recover partially from the shock of the civil war, during which some of the heaviest damage had occurred in the most industrialized parts of Spain. Consequently, the autarkic economic policies imposed on the country by wartime conditions were continued into the postwar period. Moreover, Spain was not allowed to participate in the Marshall Plan. Cut off from the reconstruction efforts under way in the rest of Europe, the economy stagnated during the late 1940s. A great deal of effort was made to achieve self-sufficiency in wheat production, to minimize Spain's need for foreign exchange. Increasingly complicated sets of multiple exchange rates were imposed on top of ad hoc import and export quotas. These were intended to cope with the lack of foreign exchange and the difficulty of earning any within the new international system of trade and finance surrounding it in Europe. Of course, they simply reinforced Spain's autarky and political isolation while thwarting any possibility of sustained economic growth. In the early 1950s, some improvement occurred, but that seemed due mostly to American aid arriving in return for the right to establish major air bases in Spain. Perhaps this did sustain Franco's autarkic policy a bit longer, much as American military bases in Greece provided extended support for that dictatorship. However, just as in Greece, American aid fell off in the late 1950s to lower levels. Meanwhile, Spanish attempts to industrialize under strict direction from the central government led to increasing foreign trade deficits. These placed increased pressures on the central bank's reserves, which constrained the entire economic strategy of the government. Spain reacted with an impressive turnabout in economic policy in 1959. This was aimed at opening up the economy to the rest of Europe by reducing barriers to trade, migration, and capital movements, while strengthening the political power of the regime by maintaining strict controls over the tax system, the labor market, and the financial sector.

THE PERIPHERY JOINS THE GOLDEN AGE OF GROWTH: 1958–73

By 1960, the four peripheral countries realized along with the rest of Europe that autarky was not going to pay off any longer. Trade expansion was the order of the day in Europe. Quantitative restrictions on trade were being removed; currencies were now convertible at fixed exchange rates for the sixteen European countries in the OEEC, tariffs were being removed within the customs union among the six members of the EEC, and mutual tariff reductions between Europe and North America were coming out of the GATT negotiations. It was time to switch from autarky or import substitution into trade expansion and export promotion. All four countries did so by 1960, but each chose its own, distinctive approach to the golden age of growth.

Ireland and Portugal joined the European Free Trade Association with Great Britain, historically the major trading partner for both. Spain joined the OECD and initiated trade agreements with the EEC as well as migration agreements with individual countries including France, Germany, and Switzerland. Greece signed an Association agreement with the EEC and benefited in the early 1960s from preferential trade arrangements. All four made their currencies convertible on current account while maintaining strict capital controls. In each case, the importance of foreign trade expanded rapidly as well as the ratio of investment to GDP. Moreover, investment was directed more into the manufacturing sector. Much of it came in each case from direct investment made by foreign multinational firms, attracted by cheap labor, stable government, and improved access to the expanding European market. In addition, there were always special inducements offered to foreign firms able to install the kind of manufacturing capacity desired by the government. The formulation of plans for improving the economy, which had been required for obtaining American aid after World War II, was now carried over into direction of private investment by both domestic and foreign firms.

Figure 14.4 shows that each country except Ireland was quite successful in converging "unconditionally" toward the higher per capita incomes enjoyed by

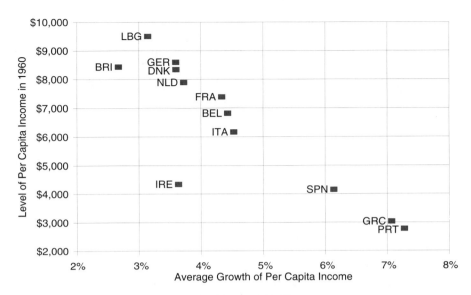

Figure 14.4. Convergence among the EU12, 1960–73.

their richer trading partners in this period. It plots the initial per capita GDP of all EU12 countries in 1960 on the Y axis against the average annual rate of growth of per capita GDP over the period 1960–73. If each country had equal access to the technology of the time and an equal institutional capacity to adopt it, then the poorer countries at the start should systematically grow more rapidly over the succeeding period. This is necessary if they are to catch up to the richer countries, assuming there is no special condition that distinguishes them from the richer countries. It is obvious from the figure that Ireland is a special case. Despite achieving the highest rates of growth since gaining political independence from Britain, Ireland should have been growing faster than France, Belgium, and Italy, all of which started with much higher outputs per capita. The possibilities forgone by Ireland in this period are evident in the much more rapid rates of growth in Spain, Greece, and Portugal. None of them started the "golden age" very far behind Ireland, but all had caught up with or surpassed Ireland by its end.[2]

One obvious clue to Ireland's special condition is the position of Great Britain in Figure 14.4, which also lies to the left of where it should be. Given that its per capita output was less than Germany's and nearly the same as that of Denmark and the Netherlands in 1960, it should have grown at about the same rate they did. Because Ireland's trade expansion was geared primarily to restoring its traditional linkages to Great Britain, which was growing more slowly than the rest of Europe, its trade could not expand as rapidly as that of Greece, Portugal, or Spain. Moreover, Ireland took special care to reduce tariff barriers only gradually. Only in 1966 did it finally agree to establishing full free trade with Britain, and even then it demanded a leisurely transition. In addition, the

industrial policy of the government developed during the heyday of import substitution was still very much alive. Despite the substantial rise in investment in
manufacturing, much of it was directed into areas that were pet projects of the
government but were destined never to be competitive in a freer trade environment. The final special condition for Ireland may well be the rather loose monetary and fiscal policy followed by its government in sharp contrast to the stricter
regimes imposed by the authoritarian governments in Spain, Portugal, and
Greece.

Portugal appears as the fast-growing country in per capita terms over the
period, but it has to be said that it, too, had special conditions. These tended to
push it artificially to the right of the unconditional convergence line. The first,
and probably most important, condition was the continued high rate of emigration from Portugal. It lost an average of 2 percent of its total population to
emigration each year over this period. The second condition was the increased
exploitation of its African colonies. Angola proved to have oil fields and rich
iron ore deposits as well as diamonds. Taking advantage of these for Portuguese industry required sending large numbers of Portuguese workers and
technicians, as well as encouraging foreign direct investments. Rebel movements for independence arose as well in Angola and Mozambique, but these
were met by sending more Portuguese to the area as troops. The costs of the
military efforts by Portugal appear to have been met mostly by increased taxes
or expropriations in the colonies. The government continued to run balanced
budgets with relatively low rates of taxation, and the money supply expanded
only slightly faster than the rate of output. As a result, Portugal had the lowest
average rates of inflation of the four periphery countries during its rapid growth
phase. (See Figure 14.2.) Remittances from the increased numbers of temporary guest workers going from Portugal to Western Europe, especially France,
more than covered the chronic trade deficit.

The economic success indicated by these external measures, however, was
not sufficient to keep the government in power. Salazar had to step aside in
September 1968 as a result of a stroke. His successor, Marcello Caetano, tried
to maintain the thrust of Salazar's policies while establishing his own power
base. Contrary to the thrust of decolonization by the rest of Europe, which was
clearly proving by the end of the 1960s to be very beneficial to the former
colonial powers, Caetano and his supporters insisted on maintaining an African
domain. The increasing costs of this and a series of military setbacks led to a
military coup in April 1974, despite the apparent economic success of the strategy for the Portuguese homeland.

Greece did not have overseas colonies to populate in this period, but like
Portugal it lost large numbers of its population. In the decade 1960–70, over
800,000 people left Greece, almost 10 percent of its average population in this
period. This helped raise its rate of growth of per capita output during the
golden age in arithmetic terms, but the long-run consequences were not beneficial. Despite the government's efforts to encourage agricultural production,
Greeks left the rural areas as soon as they grew up. If they could not migrate
abroad, at least they went to Athens, which grew rapidly and by 1980 held 40

percent of the total population of Greece. One consequence of the high rate of internal migration was that a very high proportion of capital formation had to be devoted to housing construction. Like both Ireland and Portugal, Greece's catch-up spurt to the rest of Europe in this period was short-lived because so little of its capital formation embodied more advanced technology or helped in other ways to improve labor productivity.

Spain's growth spurt, by contrast, seemed directed more toward the manufacturing and services sectors. Investment rates rose along with trade expansion, but more of the increased investment went into the expanding export sectors and less into housing stock. The new technology embodied in Spain's capital formation meant that nearly 60 percent of its growth in output was accounted for by improved productivity, rather than just more capital and labor. The structural transformation of the economy as a result was the most striking among the four countries. Agricultural employment fell from over 40 percent of the labor force to under 25 percent. Two million workers left agriculture in the ten years 1961–70. This provided a potentially elastic supply of labor for the expanding industrial, construction, and urban services sectors as well as a steady stream of migrant workers to France, Switzerland, and Belgium. Relatively little of the labor, however, went into manufacturing due to the regime's maintenance of restrictive controls on the industrial labor force. As a result of government policy, then, most of the increase in industrial output was due to expanded capital stock and greatly increased productivity.

Emigrants' remittances grew as well as export earnings from labor and natural resource intensive products, which helped expand imports rapidly while keeping the current account close to balance. Import deficits did appear more frequently at the end of the period. Meanwhile, inflation was kept under relatively good control, largely due to IMF conditions imposed in the devaluation of the peseta in 1967. At this time, it was changed to 70 pesetas to the dollar from the 60 that had been settled in 1959, when exchange controls were lifted and multiple exchange rates eliminated. The government's budget also went from a chronic deficit to being typically balanced.

THE PERIPHERY CONFRONTS THE OIL SHOCKS WITH REVOLUTIONS AND COUPS: 1974–85

In addition to confronting the economic crisis inflicted by the actions of the OPEC cartel at the end of 1973, these relatively poor and peripheral countries all endured political upheavals during the first oil shock. Starting with the peaceful "carnation revolution" in Portugal in April 1974, continuing with the overthrow of the military junta in Greece in July 1974, and ending with the death of Franco in November 1975, new regimes had to establish their political legitimacy in a vastly different international economy. Ireland had been spared military rule, although the troubles of Northern Ireland were a growing concern from the end of the 1960s on. Nevertheless, it managed to turn over its parliamentary governments even more rapidly than the fledgling democracies on the southern periphery of Europe. The common reaction of each new government during the first oil shock was to increase government spending in order to offset the shock to real incomes imposed by the OPEC cartel. As tax revenues either stagnated or fell, government deficits rose sharply in addition to the trade deficits. The money supply had to expand to finance both deficits so that inflation was even worse in these countries than in the center countries (the British case aside).

Worse yet, the European market for their excess labor supply collapsed. Instead of exporting labor, all four suddenly became confronted with rising unemployment rates and demands for additional unemployment benefits. The change in migration patterns meant slower rates of growth of per capita income in the short run and a reduced flow of emigrants' remittances to cover the trade deficits. On capital account, however, there were some interesting developments that tended to offset these effects. Portugal became a country of net immigration as the colonists sent out to Africa in the 1960s now returned home. In addition, Portuguese, Irish, Greek, and Spanish workers abroad who were dismissed from their jobs returned home with their accumulated savings. Spanish and Greek exiles returned home to participate in the liberation of the society from authoritarian rule. While Ireland lost much of the foreign investment that had recently entered, its capital account tended to be balanced by payments from the EC for regional development aid and price supports to farmers under the Common Agricultural Policy. In sum, these capital account flows helped ameliorate the effects of the oil shock on the current account of the balance of payments.

In the new era of floating exchange rates, the four countries adopted different strategies. Initially, Ireland and Portugal stayed with their exchange rates pegged to the pound sterling, while Greece and Spain devalued. But during the brief recovery from the oil shock, Spain and Portugal had short-lived governments that let inflation rise even more sharply, while Ireland and Greece had equally short-lived governments that tried to impose deflationary policies. When the second oil shock hit, the final pattern that emerged had Ireland and Spain following similar deflationary policies and Greece and Portugal pursuing comparably inflationary policies. Ireland made a serious break from the sterling area by joining the European Monetary System in 1978. This cut the link with the pound sterling that had been maintained since 1826. Spain began its policy of pegging the peseta to the deutsche mark, in an effort to encourage foreign investment from the European core. Part of the idea was that foreign firms might follow their departing Spanish employees back to Spain by setting up plants there. Portugal began a policy of an adjustable peg in 1977, which meant that it would offset the effects of higher than average domestic inflation on its foreign trade by devaluing the escudo periodically. Greece basically allowed the drachma to float so that the government could continue to finance its deficits by a combination of seigniorage from the central bank and financial repression of the banking sector. This loose monetary policy was locked in with the change of government in 1981 that replaced a moderate administration with a leftist regime.

Figure 14.5 summarizes the effects of the oil shocks and the diverse policy reactions of the poor periphery countries relative to the rest of the EU12. Unconditional convergence in the period 1973–85 can only be detected for Luxembourg, France, Belgium, Germany, Denmark, and Italy. The two energy-exporting countries, Great Britain and the Netherlands, were knocked off to the left of the convergence line. This may reflect the costs of shifting their export emphasis from manufactured goods, where continued technical progress and productivity improvements were possible, into natural resource fuels subject to increasing costs of extraction and adverse price shocks. The most dramatic changes, however, occurred precisely with the most backward countries, the poor four on the periphery. Now Ireland seems to have moved over to the convergence line. Despite the mounting unemployment rates and the trauma of cutting loose from the British export market, joining the EC and casting its monetary lot in with the core countries on the Continent proved to be a very beneficial move. By contrast, Greece had the benefits of EC membership only from 1980 on and seemed determined to minimize these as much as possible by countervailing policies. Spain and Portugal clearly had special conditions that constrained them to the lowest rates of per capita growth despite starting the period with some of the lowest levels of per capita output. But democratic regimes had been firmly established in each country and the way forward was clear—join the European Community as quickly and completely as possible.

COHESION At LAST? 1986–96

Spain and Portugal finally became full members of the EC in 1986. Spain, with a population nearly double that of the other three periphery countries combined

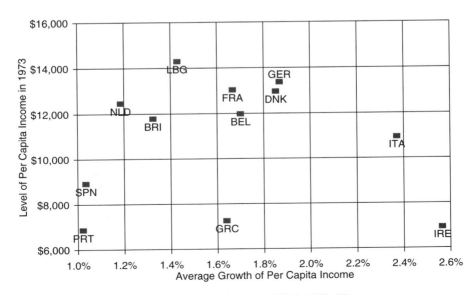

Figure 14.5. Convergence in per capita income, EU12, 1973–85.

and not much below that of the major four countries in the EC, was able to exercise effective leadership in coalescing the four countries as a political bloc within the EC. As a result, they were increasingly able to extract development assistance from the rest of the countries, all much richer and more advanced. The share of the EC budget allocated to structural funds increased even as the share devoted to agricultural subsidies decreased in response to overall budgetary pressures on the EC. The net effect has been to change the basis for supporting the heavily agricultural members of the EC from price supports to income supplements and development projects. This strategy culminated when the "poor four" were able to extract contributions toward a Cohesion Fund from the European Free Trade Association countries as their price for agreeing to the European Economic Area agreement between the EU and the EFTA. All the EFTA countries (Chapters 15 and 16) were wealthier than the average EU country, so their participation in the Single Market widened the gap between rich and poor countries. The Cohesion Fund is intended solely for disbursal among the poor periphery and is now part of the *acquis communautaire* of the EU. Given the small size of the EC budget, however, it is doubtful how effective this redistribution will be in maintaining (or regaining) economic convergence among the EU members. Moreover, Italy's experience of subsidizing the Mezzogiorno for half a century with no convergence in per capita incomes indicates that this kind of regional development policy is not a sensible long-run strategy. One can only hope that as their respective governments mature and become confident in their legitimacy, their political incentives for redistribution within the EC framework may lose force as well.

Figure 14.6 summarizes the convergence experience from 1985 through 1995, when the next three member countries joined the EU. In this latest epoch

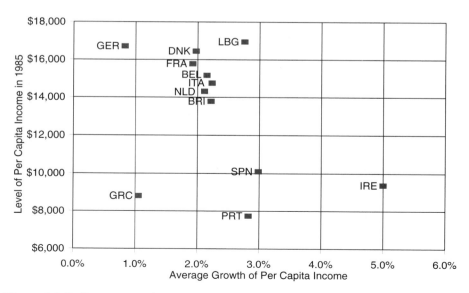

Figure 14.6. Convergence in per capita income, EU12, 1985–95.

it appears that special conditions existed for the two highest per capita output countries, Germany and Luxembourg. Germany has been shoved to the left of the convergence line, thanks to reunification with a much poorer East Germany, while Luxembourg has been pushed to the right, thanks to extraction of economic rents from the EU. Of the four periphery countries, however, only Spain seems to be on the unconditional convergence line. Ireland has moved on well to the right as its "fiscally conservative expansion" continues as described in the opening section of this chapter. Portugal seems to have nearly caught up to the convergence line after belatedly joining the European Monetary System in 1993 and adopting a correspondingly tighter monetary policy. Greece has slipped well behind the others in overall performance. From being at the vanguard of the catching up process that began at the end of the 1950s, it has slipped well to the rear despite enjoying the benefits of EU membership from 1980 on. Clearly, domestic economic policies are still the dominant force in determining a country's economic performance. The value of EU membership is still derived more from imitating successful policies in other countries than from continuing the same policies within a larger arena. A look back at the basic facts summarized at the start of this chapter underlines the willfulness of Greek governments in this period in avoiding the potential advantages of EU membership. With nearly the same population as Portugal and with a greater concentration of population in urban centers, Greece is much less open to foreign trade than Portugal. It is only slightly more open than Spain, which has four times the population. Moreover, despite being within the customs union for over fifteen years, a remarkably small part of its trade is with the rest of the EU. Clearly, domestic policies make a difference, even for small countries on the periphery of the industrialized world's trading and financial system.

CONCLUSION

Internal political problems continue to plague both the Spanish and Irish governments. ETA (Basque nationalists) and IRA (Irish nationalists) terrorists foment domestic political tension for each, which might be alleviated eventually within the larger political context of the EU. Both Portugal and Greece have severe regional imbalances economically, with poor agricultural regions in the north and rapid expansion of the urban population in Lisbon and Athens. Dealing with the political consequences of these imbalances makes it difficult to disencumber themselves of inefficient, large-scale state enterprises. This is necessary, however, if either is to take competitive advantage of the Single Market. All four benefit from tourism and emigrant remittances, cheap labor, and the possibility of inducing further foreign direct investment if the correct policies are pursued. All, however, are nervous about their reduced political influence within the EU as expansion continues into Eastern and Central Europe.

Consequently, there is a remarkable similarity among their positions with respect to the Inter-Governmental Conference of 1996–97. All accept that the EU will expand in membership and that the Economic and Monetary Union will take place as scheduled in 1999. In common with the rest of the member states, they want to see more efficiency and transparency in the operations of the EU, while its democratic legitimacy is enhanced. Only Spain, however, accepts fully that this will require a reduction in the overrepresentation of the small states. Indeed, the smaller the state, the more insistent becomes the emphasis on maintaining the existing system that maintains their full participation in every aspect of decision making. All accept that the new accession states will be even poorer at the outset than they are, and so will have a better claim to the EU's structural funds and the cohesion fund. The common solution offered is to increase the EU's own resources, preferably by introducing a fifth source of revenue, one that would be assessed among the member states progressively according to their ability to pay. Whatever the solution, there should be increased revenue sufficient to maintain the current allotments of aid to the current recipients.

Each of the states, including even Portugal and Greece, insists that it should be part of the Economic and Monetary Union when it takes effect in 1999. Unsurprisingly, Greece argues that the "nominal" convergence criteria should be relaxed or at least broadened to include "real" criteria such as unemployment rates. It is unlikely, to say the least, that this position will be taken seriously by the others. But Greece insists that unanimity must prevail for the recommendations of the IGC to take effect, and it is clear that it is willing to exercise a veto on anything that might undercut its current benefits within the EU. All accept that the Western European Union has to play a larger role in providing for the military security of the EU in the future. Ireland even holds out the possibility of holding a referendum on whether to join NATO, which would reverse its long-standing status as a neutral country (and might shake some noteworthy concessions out of Great Britain!). Greece, given its ever-tense relations with NATO ally Turkey, is unsurprisingly the most enthusiastic of the four about expanding the role of the alternative military alliance, the West European Union. But even here, it is wary that its special security concerns not be overridden by a system of qualified majority voting, whatever means are used to project a common security policy. Given the continued economic backwardness of all four and their current strong political position within the decision-making framework of the EU, and especially within the IGC, it is unlikely that they will give up any of their perquisites within the *acquis communautaire* without being compensated handsomely. It will be interesting to see how handsome and in what form that compensation will come.

Endnotes

1. Kieran A. Kennedy and Brendan R. Dowling, *Economic Growth in Ireland: The Experience since 1947,* New York: Barnes & Noble, 1975, p. 178.

2. Cormac Ó Gráda and Kevin O'Rourke compare Ireland with a variety of OECD countries in various subperiods using several different measures of real per capita output that have been developed by separate investigators. In each case, they come to this same conclusion, although they do not use the precise data used here, which

are OECD estimates in 1991 purchasing power parity U.S. dollars, nor the periodization shown in Figures 14.4 through 14.6. These simply confirm that their conclusion is robust to the adjustments that can reasonably be made to the Irish data. Ó Gráda and O'Rourke. "Irish economic growth, 1945–88," in Nicholas Crafts and Gianni Toniolo, eds., *Economic Growth in Europe since 1945,* Cambridge: Cambridge University Press, 1996.

Bibliography

Baklanoff, Eric N. *The Economic Transformation of Spain and Portugal.* New York: Praeger, 1978.

Cesar das Neves, Joao L. "Portuguese postwar growth: A global approach," in Nicholas Crafts and Gianni Toniolo, eds. *Economic Growth in Europe since 1945.* Cambridge: Cambridge University Press, 1996.

Corkill, David. *The Portuguese Economy since 1974.* Edinburgh: Edinburgh University Press, 1993.

Economist Intelligence Unit. *Country Report, Ireland.* London: Economist Intelligence Unit, 2nd quarter, 1996.

Economist Intelligence Unit. *Country Report, Greece.* London: Economist Intelligence Unit, 2nd quarter, 1996.

Economist Intelligence Unit. *Country Report, Portugal.* London: Economist Intelligence Unit, 2nd quarter, 1996.

Economist Intelligence Unit. *Country Report, Spain.* London: Economist Intelligence Unit, 2nd quarter, 1996.

Freris, A. F. *The Greek Economy in the Twentieth Century.* London: Croom Helm, 1986.

Harrison, Joseph. *The Spanish Economy from the Civil War to the European Community.* Cambridge: Cambridge University Press, 1995.

Harrison, Joseph. *The Spanish Economy in the Twentieth Century.* Beckenham, Kent: Croom Helm, 1985.

Jouganatos, George A. *The Development of the Greek Economy, 1950–1991: An Historical, Empirical, and Econometric Analysis.* Westport, Conn.: Greenwood Press, 1992.

Kennedy, Kieran A. and Brendan R. Dowling. *Economic Growth in Ireland: The Experience since 1947.* New York: Barnes & Noble, 1975.

Kennedy, Kieran A., Thomas Giblin, and Deirdre McHugh. *The Economic Development of Ireland in the Twentieth Century.* London: Routledge, 1988.

Lieberman, Sima. *Growth and Crisis in the Spanish Economy 1940–9.* London: Routledge, 1995.

Ó Gráda, Cormac and Kevin O'Rourke. "Irish economic growth, 1945–88," in Nicholas Crafts and Gianni Toniolo, eds. *Economic Growth in Europe since 1945.* Cambridge: Cambridge University Press, 1996.

O'Hagan, John. *The Economy of Ireland: Policy and Performance of a Small European Country.* New York: St. Martin's Press, 1995.

Prados de la Escosura, Leandro and Jorge C. Sans. "Growth and macroeconomic performance in Spain, 1939–93," in Nicholas Crafts and Gianni Toniolo, eds. *Economic Growth in Europe since 1945.* Cambridge: Cambridge University Press, 1996.

Salmon, Keith G. *The Modern Spanish Economy. Transformation and Integration into Europe.* London: Pinter Publishers, 1991.

Tamanes, Ramon. *The Spanish Economy: An Introduction.* New York: St. Martin's Press, 1986.

Austria, Finland, and Sweden:
Part of the Outer Circle Joins In

Basic Facts			
Area:	**Total**	871,000 km²	26.1 % of EU15
	Austria	83,900 km²	2.5 %
	Finland	337,100 km²	10.1 %
	Sweden	450,000 km²	13.5 %
Population (1/1/94):		21,838,000	5.9 % of EU15
	Austria	8,015.000	2.2 %
	Finland	5,077,900	1.4 %
	Sweden	8,745,100	2.4 %
Gross Domestic Product (1993):		$349.7 billion	5.8 % of EU15
	Austria	$140.3 billion	2.3 %
	Finland	$70.5 billion	1.2 %
	Sweden	$138.9 billion	2.3 %
Per Capita:		$16,013	99 % of EU15 average
	Austria	$17,654	109 %
	Finland	$13,926	86 %
	Sweden	$15,903	98 %
Openness (X + M)/GDP			
	Austria	50 %	63 % with EU12
	Finland	50 %	46 %
	Sweden	54 %	54 %

Source: Eurostat, *Basic Statistics of the European Union,* 32nd ed. (Luxembourg, 1995).

INTRODUCTION

On January 1, 1995, the fourth expansion of the European Union took place, adding Austria, Finland, and Sweden. These three countries, all members of the Organization for Economic Cooperation and Development (OECD) and the European Free Trade Area (EFTA), are small, open economies, the bulk of whose trade has been with the EC since the end of the 1960s; within the EC their main trading partner has been Germany. They finally decided to be part of the decision-making process of the European Union rather than merely continuing to accept whatever terms and conditions the EU decided were appropriate for economic relations with them. In other words, they were not satisfied with the terms of the European Economic Area (EEA), which had been dictated by the EU. The decision to join took as long as it did because each of the three had carefully maintained a neutral position between the United States and the Soviet Union. None belonged to the North Atlantic Treaty Organization (NATO) or the Western European Union (WEU), the two military alliances for Western Europe. With the collapse of the Soviet military threat, however, all three felt that their neutral status would not be jeopardized by joining the EU. (However, they will surely opt out of any military arrangements that arise from implementation of the European Union's third pillar dealing with foreign affairs and security.) All were welcomed as valuable members of the EU, for each was a relatively well-off country with highly developed economic relationships with the West. Some reluctance was shown by their farmers, who would get lower subsidies under the EU's Common Agricultural Policy, but each new entrant was allowed to top up the EU's support payments over a transition period of several years. Some resistance was also shown by the poorer, peripheral countries of the EU, who were afraid of being outvoted on issues dealing with regional aid to backward regions of Europe. This was overcome when the new entrants agreed to add to the cohesion funds of the EU, in addition to paying subsidies to their own farmers.

Were the costs of joining the EU, basically on the terms set by the EU, worth paying for the benefits expected? While these countries' leaders and voting population clearly thought so, it is also true that the voters in Norway and Switzerland rejected the possibility of joining the EU, despite the wishes of their leaders. All of the EFTA countries were affected adversely by the Single Market initiative, the terms of which excluded them from any role in deciding how nontariff barriers were to be lowered with respect to non-EU members. And all of them have suffered from the German reunification shock, as Germany is their largest single trading partner. Finland's other major trading partner was the Soviet Union, so Finland experienced the shocks that shook both Western and Eastern Europe.

Austria's desire to join the EU was long-standing and it was only its treaty commitment to remain militarily neutral that prevented it from applying for membership in the 1960s. Benefiting from Marshall Plan aid and the clearing arrangements of the European Payments Union, not to mention the restoration of its traditionally close trading ties with both Germany and Italy, Austria was one of the economic miracle countries of the 1950s. Growth slowed in the 1960s as it felt the disadvantage of being excluded from the customs union that included its two largest trading partners. But along with the other members of EFTA, it received mutual tariff elimination on industrial products with the EC in 1972, which revitalized its export trade. The end of the Bretton Woods era forced Austria, along with all of the European countries, to make a strategic decision on the proper exchange rate policy to follow. Luckily, as it turned out, it decided to peg the Austrian schilling to the German mark, but only after the mark had revalued relative to the dollar and all the other European currencies by 10 percent in 1969. Thereafter, the mark and the schilling were inseparable, to the extent that Austria immediately joined the Exchange Rate Mechanism of the EMS upon its membership in the EU. It may be noted, however, that following German monetary reform in 1948, the schilling had depreciated sharply against the deutsche mark through the early 1950s. In 1945, one schilling equaled one mark; since 1969 the rate has been set at 7 AS to 1 DM.

The oil shocks were met initially by an expansionary policy, despite the decision to peg the currency to the strengthening deutsche mark. Predictably, this led to severe balance-of-payments deficits, although the docility of Austrian labor unions combined with the commitment of Austria's nationalized industries to maintain employment helped keep down both inflation and unemployment relative to much of Europe. By the second oil shock in 1979, Austria decided to maintain the peg to the deutsche mark and forgo expansionary monetary or fiscal policy. Instead, emphasis was placed on gradual liberalization of labor and commodity markets and some partial privatization to increase the efficiency of the state enterprises. Nevertheless, its growth pattern was determined by that of Germany from 1979 on thanks to the exchange rate policy.

Sweden likewise benefited from Marshall Plan aid and the restoration of traditional strong trade ties with Germany after World War II. Justifiably proud of the success of its welfare state established in the 1930s as a "middle way" between capitalism and socialism, it perfected the redistributive mechanisms of its society while enjoying high growth rates in the 1950s and 1960s. It ensured the continuation of Swedish-style socialism with political reforms in 1970, which provided shorter terms of office and a single-chamber parliament elected by proportional representation. Unfortunately, the rigidity of the institutions for redistribution made it very difficult for Sweden to find a suitable response to the successive oil shocks. Like Austria, it tried to peg its currency, the krona, to that of its major trading partner. Unfortunately, it chose the European basket currency, the ECU, rather than the deutsche mark. As a result, it experienced more of the oil shock in terms of dollar prices than either Austria or Germany.

Moreover, the Swedish government provided increased employment opportunities directly, rather than through state enterprises as with Austria. Giving public employees strong unions with rights to strike then made it impossible to impose the efficiency-enhancing reforms that were possible in Austria. Worse, it actually nationalized companies in the hardest hit sectors such as steel and shipbuilding, increasing the burden of subsidies for the state. A mounting crisis showed up as wages continued to grow rapidly in response to wage procedures that effectively institutionalized the "Dutch disease" in Sweden. As in the Netherlands in the 1970s, wage increases won by the most productive workers in Sweden, typically in the export-oriented multinational firms, were the standard for wage adjustments for the rest of the labor force, especially in the growing public sector. As wages rose, labor productivity grew more and more slowly, even more slowly than in the EC, probably because the high interest rates needed in Sweden to keep the krona in line with the ECU raised the cost of capital required to modernize Swedish industry. By 1991, Swedish per capita income had fallen from third place among the OECD countries to fourteenth. At this time, Sweden had the largest public sector of any country in Western Europe, at 60 percent of GDP and a third of the labor force employed by the state.

In 1992, the conservative-oriented government of Karl Bildt began privatization and tax reform and reduced welfare entitlements, as well as formally announcing that the krona would be linked to the ECU again after several devaluations in the 1980s. The exchange rate crisis of 1992 that took Britain and Italy out of the formal Exchange Rate Mechanism (ERM) also took Sweden and Finland out of their informal commitment to it. Despite joining the EU in 1995, neither Sweden nor Finland has committed immediately to lock their exchange rates to the deutsche mark again. For Bildt's troubles, which also included negotiating terms for Sweden's entry into the EU, his government was voted out of power in 1994. Entry into the EU was still approved, narrowly, by the electorate, but the dismantling of the rigid redistributive mechanisms of the state sector have been put on hold for the time being. The new prime minister, Goran Persson, has nevertheless continued the tight monetary and fiscal policy initiated by Bildt. By the end of 1996, Sweden announced its intent to join the ERM and participate in the common currency of the EMU starting in 1999, despite increased grumbling at the weakening of welfare benefits.

Since World War II, Finland managed to maintain an uneasy independence from the Soviet Union, basically by providing the Soviets with whatever raw materials and access to Finnish waters they wanted and by preparing to make the Soviets pay a very high price in blood for any military takeover. Not only did Finland make it a point to pay off its war debt to the United States after (long after) World War I, it also paid off a huge reparations demand after World War II to the Soviets by 1952. This helped force industrialization to occur and also made Russia the major market for Finnish trade, even as its trade with Western Europe expanded in the 1960s. Imports of fuel from Russia were vital for Finnish industry since 90 percent of its oil, 50 percent of its electricity, and all of its natural gas came from there. Finland joined the OECD in 1972, but unlike the rest of the OECD countries, managed to weather the oil shocks relatively well thanks to its barter arrangements with Russia.

The collapse of the Soviet empire in 1990, however, brought all these economic advantages for Finland to an end. Beginning in January 1991, the Soviets imposed market-related prices for its deliveries of energy to Finland, which created a major balance-of-payments deficit for Finland and cut off its major export market as well. Finland plunged into a deep recession. Tying its fortunes to those of the EU at that time proved not to be successful, and its currency, the markka, was forced to devalue sharply in 1992. Nevertheless, the Finnish population was the most enthusiastic of the populations voting on membership in the EU, and trade has rapidly grown with its western neighbors, especially Sweden and Norway. Moreover, with per capita income below the EU average and being committed to encouraging industry and tourism in its northern regions, Finland will benefit from structural funds provided by the EU. While the loss of the Soviet market was very damaging in the short run to the Finnish economy, the elimination of the Soviet military threat will be very beneficial in the medium and long run. Indeed, by October 1996, Finland's balance of payments had recovered to the extent that it joined the Exchange Rate Mechanism, fixing the exchange rate of the markka to the deutsche mark.

MACROECONOMIC POLICY INDICATORS: 1960–97

Figures 15.1 to 15.3 trace out the growth rates, inflation rates, and unemployment rates of the three most recent members of the EU from 1960 on. The growth rates of real GDP[1] should be very familiar to readers of the previous chapters: the economic miracle of the 1960s, the two oil shocks of the 1970s, and the gradual reprise of the 1980s until the German reunification shock show up clearly for each country. It may be surprising that the growth rates of each were so closely correlated. Both Austria and Sweden had very similar economic

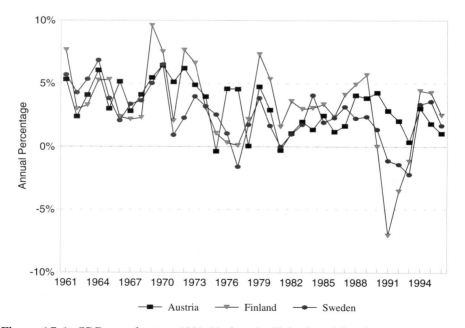

Figure 15.1. GDP growth rates, 1961–96, Austria, Finland, and Sweden.

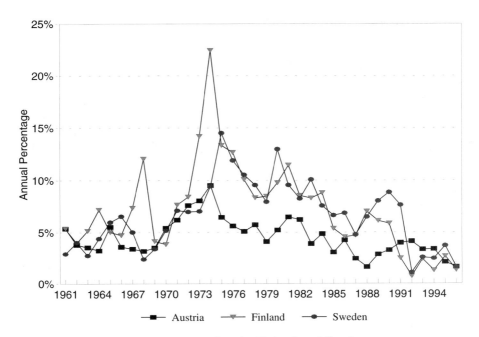

Figure 15.2. Inflation rates, 1961–96, Austria, Finland, and Sweden.

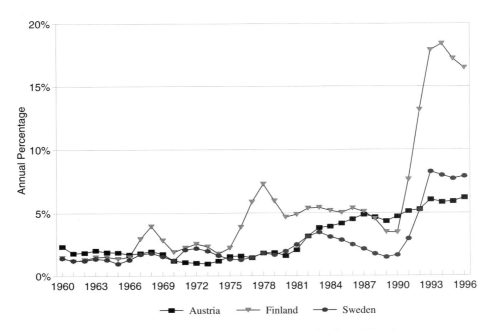

Figure 15.3. Unemployment rates, 1960–96, Austria, Finland, and Sweden.

strategies, and both, as small open economies, had their fortunes tied closely to those of their common major trading partner, West Germany. Finland's window on the west was Sweden, with whom it maintained very close and mutually beneficial economic relations. There are only three disturbances to this common pattern of growth among the three. The first occurred with the first oil shock, when Austria followed an expansionary policy that worked to keep up growth for a couple of years until the balance of payments difficulties brought it back to reality. The second is the dramatic fall in Finland's GDP as it was hammered by the Soviet Union's collapse, in addition to suffering the shock that German reunification inflicted on all three. The third is the much sharper recovery in growth for Sweden and Finland in 1993. The reason is that both devalued sharply against the deutsche mark at the end of 1992. Exports and the trade balances for both countries rose quickly and sharply in response. Even small, open countries with heavy reliance on their trade with Germany may, it seems, find the burdens of a common currency a net encumbrance.

The inflation rates, by contrast to the growth rates, show the effects of quite different strategies. Finland's rate exploded with the breakup of the Bretton Woods system, coming shortly after it entered the OECD and loosening capital controls. From 1975 on, however, Finland pegged the markka to the Swedish krona and thereby locked its monetary fortunes to those of Sweden. The inflation rates of the two countries match up very closely thereafter, falling over the 1980s until they match up with those of Austria (and Germany) by the 1990s. This is not surprising, given that the ECU, to which Sweden pegged the krona, gradually behaved more like the deutsche mark, especially after 1985. The devaluations of Sweden and Finland in 1992, as beneficial as they were for their exports, did not do any harm to their inflation rates. As a result, by the summer of 1996 both currencies had stabilized and their central bankers were talking confidently of joining the EMS shortly in order to qualify for the common currency regime in 1999.

The unemployment rates show unusually low rates throughout, save for the explosion in Finland's rates in the early 1990s. The expected rise in rates during the oil shocks and the hysteresis effect that kept them high during the 1980s show up in each case, but in heavily dampened form compared with what happened in the other countries. But the long-term costs of maintaining unproductive workers on jobs in the public sector (Sweden) or in state enterprises (Austria) are penalizing the long-term growth rates of both. One might hope that the restructuring forced on Finland will pay off with renewed catch-up growth that will bring it up nearer the level of Swedish per capita income—unless Sweden turns around its economic policy as well and resumes higher rates of growth.

PART OF EUROPE'S RECONSTRUCTION: 1945–57

All three countries had played an important role in the German war economy: Austria as part of the Nazi Reich from the economic union with Germany in

1938 until the end of the war in 1945, Sweden as a neutral but supplying important steel products and iron ore to Germany, and Finland as an ally from 1941 to 1944 when it resumed its war of defense against the Soviet Union with German support. The different political status of each with respect to Nazi Germany determined the different ways each participated in European economic recovery after the war. Austria began like Germany, divided and occupied in four zones by the Allied powers. Unlike Germany, however, it was allowed to act with its own government in 1948 when the Organization for European Economic Cooperation was formally established. After Marshall Plan aid began arriving, industrial production rose rapidly. From a level in 1948 that was only 85 percent of the 1938 output, it had shot up to 148 percent by 1951. Finland, subjected by the Soviet Union to stiff reparations payments and a contraction of its eastern border as the price for not being invaded by the Red Army, had to decline the invitation to join the Marshall Plan. It was then forced to concentrate on building up a heavy industry to meet the Soviet demands for reparations in kind. Western demand for its timber products helped provide Finland the hard currency needed to build up its industrial base. Sweden participated in the Marshall Plan on condition that it could maintain its neutrality as well as its trade with the Soviet bloc. From the comfortable position of supplying Nazi Germany with vital material for its war effort, Sweden now moved easily into the comfortable position of supplying Western Europe with construction materials and capital goods as well as trading actively with Finland and the Soviet bloc on the Baltic.

In each case, recovery was rapid, with a continued high rate of investment as a share of gross domestic product combined with stable wages and low unemployment rates. Government policy was given credit for a successful outcome in each country, but some key differences in economic strategies led to longer run divergences. Austria took care of its monetary overhang by inflation, which was brought under control only at the end of 1951, well after stabilization had occurred in West Germany. Forced to commit to a fixed, uniform exchange rate for trade with Western Europe as part of the European Payments Union, it still had to devalue the schilling in 1953. It had already devalued relative to the rest of Europe in the general devaluations of September 1949. Sweden maintained extensive price controls as well as exchange controls on the krona, sticking to strategies that had proven successful starting in the 1930s and that had carried it through World War II. Finland, burdened by reparations to the Russians that were either denominated in dollars convertible to gold at $35 to an ounce or imposed in terms of specific goods, and faced with the expense of relocating thousands of Finns displaced from territory ceded to the Russians, had no choice but inflation and a repeatedly devalued markka. Nevertheless, loans from the West as well as expanded exports of building materials to the West enabled Finland to complete reparations payments by the end of 1952; in fact, from 1949 on it had become a net capital exporter. Like Austria, it devalued not once, but twice, during 1949. Repeated bouts of inflation followed in the 1950s, leading to another devaluation in 1957. In sum, fighting inflation was not a priority for any of the three neutrals during the 1950s. While all participated in the adjustable peg system of fixed exchange rates adopted by the rest of Western Europe, none hesitated to devalue to regain competitive advantages in foreign trade once they had been lost by excessive domestic inflation.

It was in employment, rather, that each excelled, although by using different strategies. Immediately after the war, Austria nationalized all large firms, mainly to remove all vestiges of Nazi and German control. Under the conditions of military occupation, which lasted until 1955, there were no private interests willing to purchase the firms. To this day, Austria has the largest proportion of nationalized industry in Europe, which has stymied development of a stock market and stultified the lending skills of its banks. With governments controlled by a coalition of the Socialist party and the People's party, the nationalized industries were committed to maintain high employment opportunities. In the private sector, meanwhile, small and medium-sized firms were encouraged. Their growth in numbers also increased employment, especially in the services but also in manufacturing.

Finland became a large exporter of labor during the 1950s. Mechanization in its agricultural and forestry sectors released large numbers of families from the land. They either crowded into the cities on the southwestern edge of the country or migrated to Sweden. Expansion of industry and services in the cities took place rapidly. Sweden intervened with social legislation designed to help relocate and retrain workers displaced from its rural areas into the urban economies in the south of the country. This enlightened social policy meant that the costs of transition in making the structural changes to a modern industrial society were borne by the taxpayers at large rather than by the individuals forced to move.

The movement of labor out of agriculture occurred in all three countries at a rapid pace. But in each case, an aggressive price support program for the agricultural sector encouraged mechanization. This kept agricultural production rising rapidly enough to achieve close to self-sufficiency overall. Even Finland, with the shortest growing seasons in Europe thanks to being the northernmost country, managed self-sufficiency in grains most of the time. Although there were fewer days in its growing seasons, each day had more hours of sunshine than in countries to the south. Nevertheless, each country has a comparative advantage in livestock production and dairying rather than cereals, and the composition of agricultural output changed in this direction as per capita incomes rose.

Overall, the growth rates of all three were sufficiently high and sustained during the 1950s that they, too, were participating in the golden age of growth. Figure 15.4 compares their GDP indexes as calculated by Angus Maddison with those of the members of the European Coal and Steel Community, later to become the EEC. Compared to their levels of real GDP in 1939, only Sweden and Finland came out of the war at a higher level than before. But thanks to the general expansion of trade with a rapidly rebounding Western Europe, their economies continued to grow at high rates through the 1950s. Meanwhile, Austria was growing at nearly the same rate as Germany from 1946 on, with the exception of its slowdown during the Korean War. There appeared to be a vari-

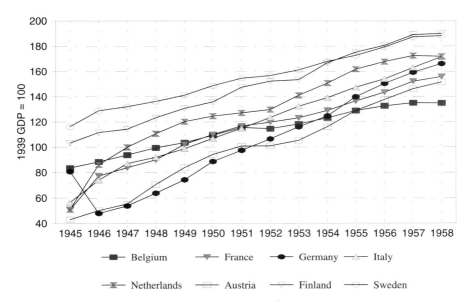

Figure 15.4. Europe's postwar growth: GDP Indexes, 1945–58.

ety of arrangements possible in a country's economic affairs, ranging from how it dealt with the foreign sector to the way it handled industrial relations, that would allow it to share in the bounty of the golden age of growth. At least, this was the case in the 1950s.

ON THE OUTSIDE LOOKING IN: 1958–73

All three countries were necessarily excluded from the EEC by reason of their commitment to neutrality. But in addition, each had an important steel industry that had grown rapidly with an export orientation during the same period that the European Coal and Steel Community had come into operation. Excluded now from the furtherance of trade expansion envisioned for the EEC, Austria and Sweden responded quickly to Britain's initiative in forming the European Free Association in 1959. Finland by now was enjoying the benefits of being an intermediary in trade between the West, where it earned hard currency, and the East, where it could barter technologically superior products for fuel and raw materials on advantageous terms. It managed to maintain the best of both worlds by joining the EFTA as an associate member in 1961.

This was clearly a second best alternative. While all three countries continued to grow at rates equal to or even slightly better than those in the 1950s, their growth was no longer export led. The ratio of exports to gross domestic product leveled off for each country before being forced up again during the oil shocks of the 1970s. Instead, growth was sustained by continuing the process of modern industrialization by improving the technology used by firms and the infrastructure available to them. The latter required increased investment by the public sector. The outcome was that while the ratio of investment to GDP remained high in each case, the share of public investment rose relative to private investment. In addition, an increasing share of capital formation in each economy was being absorbed by housing construction, which did little to improve the productivity of the labor force beyond maintaining its morale. Sweden tried to maintain the rate of investment by its most productive firms by allowing all firms to shelter earnings from taxes if they were placed in an investment fund. The investment funds were earmarked, however, only for capital formation by the firm itself, not for investment in other firms' projects. This limited the extent to which capital resources could be reallocated within the Swedish economy. The long-run consequences of structural rigidity in the allocation of capital were very harmful when the international economy was subjected to the shocks of the 1970s and 1980s.

The continuation of growth on a par with the rest of Western Europe in the 1960s, however, encouraged the government in each country to solidify its techniques for maintaining social harmony in the face of continuing structural change. Wage settlements were determined by nationwide unions, whose leaders met regularly with the heads of the major corporations and state enterprises. Decisions were made jointly, and usually without open conflict. Even Finland's last major round of strikes was in 1959, after which the government aided unions and business to reach settlements amicably. The agreements reached were then presented to the government, which accepted them because the central bank could provide the necessary financing to accommodate the increases in nominal wages and the price hikes that followed them. As each country had a small, quite homogeneous population, wage increases granted to workers in the major unions were quickly imitated for nonunionized workers and especially employees in the public sector. Indeed, Sweden had formalized this into a model of wage determination where the initial wage increases would occur in the most competitive export industries. There, they would be determined by the rate of international inflation faced by the exporters plus the rate of increase in their labor productivity. These wage increases, when passed on to the rest of the economy where there were lower rates of increase in labor productivity, would force firms there either to increase labor productivity or release labor to the higher productivity sectors. This may have worked as intended in the 1950s, but starting in the 1960s the overpaid workers released from less productive sectors of the private economy tended to go into the public sector rather than into the leading sectors in the private economy. To absorb them, taxes were increased, beginning their rise that was eventually to make Sweden the most heavily taxed economy in Western Europe. As with capital, Swedish policy in the 1960s made it increasingly difficult to reallocate labor toward the more productive parts of the economy.

In Austria, the issue of labor absorption was met more by reducing the rate of labor force participation. Extending the years of schooling required of both men and women reduced the participation rate at the younger ages, while increasing the attractiveness of state-funded pensions lowered the retirement age, sharply reducing participation rates among the population aged over 60. The continued expansion of demand for labor in the growing sectors, especially construction and urban services, was met by importing foreign labor. By the time of the first oil shock in 1973, foreigners made up over 8 percent of the Austrian labor force. Meanwhile, a steady 3 percent of the domestic labor force was employed in other countries, mainly Germany and Switzerland. The release of labor in Finland from agriculture and forestry became absorbed primarily in Sweden. By the beginning of the 1970s, both countries included provisions for this labor migration in their economic planning.

The upshot for each economy was that unemployment rates remained satisfactorily low throughout the 1960s (Figure 15.3). While inflation rates were above average (Figure 15.2), periodic devaluations could offset the effects of these on international competitiveness. Growth rates were high on average, but becoming more volatile when measured in purchasing power parity terms, as they are in Figure 15.1. This kind of volatility, however, was obscured for policymakers at the time because it did not show up in the real growth rates calculated only on the basis of domestic price indexes. All seemed well, but the policy structure being constructed was to prove inflexible and inadequate for the challenges that lay ahead.

THE THREE OIL SHOCKS: 1974–85

The oil shocks seemed to have been weathered quite well by all three countries, at least in comparison to the experiences of the twelve member states of the European Union at the time. Unemployment rates remained low in Austria and Sweden, and Finland managed to reabsorb many of the workers who previously had gone to Sweden with only a comparatively small rise in unemployment. Growth rates were reduced close to zero at the worst point of each of the two oil shocks but they were able to rebound quickly and strongly. Despite the similarities in outcomes, however, the underlying strategies were quite different.

In the case of Austria, a blend of monetarism with respect to the foreign sector and Keynesianism with respect to the domestic sector was developed, which became labeled Austro-Keynesianism. After letting the deutsche mark revalue twice in the 1960s relative to the Austrian schilling, the Austrian authorities had decided to keep their exchange rate fixed at 7 AS to 1 deutsche mark as part of their trade agreement with the expanded EC in 1973. They maintained this rate throughout, even though they expanded their money supply more rapidly than did Germany and permitted higher rates of inflation. The apparent contradiction in external and internal monetary policy was resolved by the influx of capital imports. Foreign investors were attracted by the combination of higher interest rates in Austria and a reliable exchange rate with the deutsche mark, which was appreciating relative to sterling and the dollar. Austria's trade account went into continued deficit throughout the 1970s, but this created no loss of reserves because the commitment to a fixed exchange rate with the deutsche mark continued to attract capital imports from abroad. Like Germany, Austria also reduced the price shock of the OPEC rate increase by appreciating its currency relative to the dollar.

Finland found that its careful cultivation of countertrade with the Soviet Union now paid off handsomely. By setting up long-term barter arrangements with the Soviet Union in which Finland did large projects on Soviet territory in exchange for guaranteed supplies of petroleum and natural gas, the Finns were able to avoid much of the price shock inflicted on the west by the OPEC cartel. Meanwhile, they could take full advantage of the increased commodity prices on their exports of forestry products and iron ore. While this did not solve their unemployment problem, it did raise their growth rates persistently above those of both Austria and Sweden.

Sweden was not as lucky as either Austria or Finland. Like Austria, it set a nominal anchor for its currency by pegging the krona, but instead of choosing the highly visible and steadily appreciating deutsche mark of Germany, it chose a basket of the currencies of its chief trading partners. This created more uncertainty among foreign investors about the exchange rate risk, so Sweden's current account deficit was not offset by a surge of investment funds on capital account. Meanwhile, by increasing unemployment benefits and indexing not only wages but also pensions, children's allowances, minimum wages, and transfer payments in general to the inflation rate, Sweden created an inflation machine. The consistently higher rates of inflation than those of its trading partners forced it into repeated devaluations, twice in 1977 and again in 1981. Government debt shot up from 20 percent of GDP in 1973 to over 60 percent in the early 1980s. Worse, Sweden's vaunted export industries began to export licenses to firms abroad so they could produce Swedish products with Swedish technology but with foreign labor and capital. Devaluations were not enough to offset the increased costs of Swedish labor and the stiffer tax rates imposed by the government, so Swedish multinationals began placing their production facilities offshore.

Figure 15.5 shows the dramatic divergence in openness of these three small, open economies from 1979 until the reconvergence of the mid-1990s took place. Openness is measured as the percent share of exports and imports of goods and services to gross domestic product. The figure shows the stability of the foreign sector in all three economies during most of the 1960s, as their export-led growth ceased. The upward thrust in openness for them corresponds to the increase in international inflation that began in the late 1960s and predates the collapse of the Bretton Woods system in 1971. The two oil shocks pushed up international price levels in turn and raised the openness of each small economy in corresponding stages. Starting in 1981, however, the varying domestic policies began to have their effect.

Austria stabilized at the higher level of openness, much as did its role model, the much larger economy of West Germany. In the transition to a steady state, it had a short-lived trade surplus, corresponding to the deficit on capital account as foreign investors withdrew their capital to the higher returns avail-

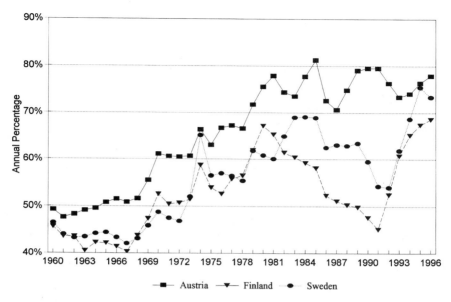

Figure 15.5. Openness (XGS + MGS)/GDP, 1960–96, Austria, Finland, and Sweden (XGS = exports of goods and services; MGS = imports of goods and services).

able in the United States and Great Britain in 1981–83. Finland began to drop back toward 1960s levels starting in 1981 as the depressed state of the Western industrial economies reduced the possibilities of trade intermediation between the Soviet Union and the West. In 1986, it reacted by becoming a full member of the European Free Trade Association. Not only did this increase its potential markets among the EFTA countries, it also allowed Finland to take advantage of any trade concessions wrung by the EFTA group from the EU in the negotiations to establish the European Economic Area. By 1985, Sweden's openness also began to fall, just as the Single Market initiative began to pick up trade within the European Union. In the case of both Finland and Sweden, the fall in the importance of the foreign sector was due to their own loss of competitiveness, caused by their insistence on maintaining higher inflation rates than those in their trading partners. Any effort to peg their exchange rates with respect to their main trading partners in the EU would naturally be offset by their higher inflation rates. These had the effect of raising their real exchange rates, making their exports less competitive and forcing them to cut back on imports in response, Only Austria, with its rate of inflation now corresponding to that of West Germany, was able to keep its real exchange rate stable relative to the EU, as well as its nominal exchange rate fixed with the deutsche mark. Eventually, the lesson was absorbed by its inflation-prone partners in the European Free Trade Association.

FROM SINGLE MARKET TO UNITED GERMANY: 1986–96

Left out of the Single Market initiative along with the other members of the EFTA, all three countries were forced to reconsider their relationship with the EC. The tough negotiating stance of the EC with EFTA demonstrated that the only way for these small countries to improve their trading opportunities with the EC was to join it. EFTA, as a free trade area but with different tariff schedules maintained against the rest of the world by each individual member state, could not negotiate tariff reductions, much less reductions in nontariff barriers, with the EC. Instead, each member of EFTA was put in the position of negotiating with the EC. Once the member states of the EC had finally agreed on a common position, after much discussion and numerous side deals among members, it was nearly impossible for the EC to modify it at the negotiating table. Even the United States was discovering this in its negotiations with the EC during the Uruguay Round at the same time. If a single, powerful trading partner such as the United States could not get the EC to budge on how to reduce nontariff barriers and bring agriculture into the GATT treaties, there was no chance at all for EFTA.

Inside the EC, on the other hand, alliances could be formed with the other small countries, and if their political weight proved greater than their economic size alone would warrant, they could have much greater impact. Austria could get pollution and noise controls on Greek trucks passing through its alpine valleys on their way to markets in northern Europe. Finland could get regional aid for its frozen northern forests and access to the rest of the European labor market for its displaced farmers and foresters. Sweden could argue for common technical standards that would allow its high-quality specialty goods to enter all of the Single Market in preference to comparable products from the United States or Japan. Other small countries had done well within the EC; the EFTA alternative was clearly played out while the EC market was in course of expanding and reinvigorating its members' economies. Negotiations to complete the European Economic Area completely on the terms dictated by the EC were wound up in 1991 and four of the EFTA members—Austria, Finland, Sweden, and Norway—made formal application to join.

To show their commitment to the deepening process under way within the EC, which culminated with the Maastricht Treaty on European Union, the Scandinavian applicants joined Austria in pegging their currencies to the German mark. The collapse of the Soviet Union over the period 1989 to 1991 also encouraged three of them to rethink the terms of their neutrality—was it still necessary for Sweden and Finland, in order to reassure a formerly dangerous superpower that there was no threat of an invasion being launched from their waters or over their land? Was the 1955 agreement between the Soviet Union and the United States that led to the withdrawal of all foreign troops still binding for Austria? Moreover, given the example of Ireland, wouldn't it still be possible to maintain the reality of neutrality even as a member of the EU? By mid-1996, all three and Ireland, comprising the four neutral member states of the EC, had carried this line of thinking to the extent that they agreed they could provide troops for peacekeeping missions decided on by either the United Nations or the European Union.

In the event, their informal commitment to the EMS made them fully vulnerable to the German reunification shock. Only Austria was able to persist in pegging its currency to the deutsche mark in the foreign exchange market crisis of summer 1992. At one point, the Bank of Sweden even raised its discount rate to 500 percent to show dramatically its commitment to defending the krona and restricting the growth of the domestic money supply. Of course, no one borrowed at that rate, so no funds could be attracted from foreign lenders. Instead of showing commitment, the ridiculous rate showed the total lack of effective tools to control the domestic money supply and the rate of inflation. First Finland, and then Sweden followed quickly by Norway, were forced to let their currencies float. Finland's problems were compounded by the even more devastating shock of the political and economic collapse of the Soviet Union. This eliminated immediately the market for a large part of its exports, while the Russian insistence on receiving world prices for deliveries of natural gas and oil that previously had been part of countertrade agreements created a serious balance-of-trade deficit.

When serious negotiations began for accession starting in 1993, then, the four applicants were in an even weaker bargaining position that they had been as members of the European Free Trade Association. As a result, all four had to agree to lower their agricultural price supports immediately to the level of the Common Agricultural Policy and open their markets to the agricultural surpluses still available from the EU12. If they wanted to sustain their farming populations, the applicants could make income supplements available to them out of their own budgets during a limited transition period. As high-income countries, each had to agree to pay a supplement into the cohesion fund created to benefit the four poorest countries, a blatant political payoff to get agreement from them for the accession. Norway had to agree to bring its offshore fishing grounds under the regulation of the common fisheries policy. This would mean giving access to Spanish and Portuguese fishing fleets, whose activities were already causing Iceland and Canada to fear depletion of their fisheries. As onerous as these terms were, membership in the club, once gained, would enable them to offset these costs in other ways. Each country's government signed off on the terms, waiting until the last moment to convince the voters back home that they had wrung the last possible concession from the EU negotiators.

Then the British almost wrecked the entire venture for them. When the terms of the political accommodations that would be made to the new entrants were brought back to the twelve members for approval, the British objected that the same number of negative votes in the European Council as before the expansion should still suffice to block legislation. The European Commission, by contrast, had kept the qualified majority needed to pass legislation as close as possible to 70 percent, the same as before. With an increased number of votes to be cast in the Council, ninety compared with the previous seventy-six, this meant that a blocking minority now would have to have twenty-seven votes, four more than the twenty-three previously needed. Eventually, the British and

Spanish were satisfied by having the entire issue brought up for final discussion in the Inter-Governmental Conference of 1996. The British proposal, if accepted, would have enhanced the political power of the new small countries entering the EU. But at the time it was made, it actually jeopardized the entire accession process for the applicants.

The referendums that followed in the applicant countries were scheduled in descending order of popular enthusiasm for entry among the voters. Austria voted first and approved accession overwhelmingly; Finland followed and approved by a substantial majority. Then came Sweden, where the population, still attached to the "middle way" of corporatist capitalism and Scandinavian socialism, barely approved the terms of accession. Finally, came Norway. By design, it was hoped that the momentum created by one after another of its erstwhile EFTA trading partners abandoning it for the embrace of the EU would sway the reluctant Norwegians to join up this time around. Instead, they seemed more impressed by the smaller and smaller margins of approval as the referendums came closer to them and, once again, voted against the accession on the terms their government had extracted.

The economic results led to a dramatic rebound in the openness of both Finland and Sweden. Inflation rates remained low, while growth rates picked up and the first signs of falling unemployment rates began to appear. Clearly, after all the delay, disturbance, and distraction, entry into the EU was a sound move for these three perennial outsiders. In the short run, however, it has not proved any kind of panacea. The problems of slow growth and high unemployment in the rest of the EU limit the growth of trade for the new entrants, just as they do for the original members as discussed in the preceding chapters. Austria finds that as a member of the EU it is limited in the extent to which it can restrict the entry of foreign labor, who are entering the EU wherever and however they can from Eastern and Central Europe. Its traditional role as a way station for refugees from the Soviet Union is now being overwhelmed by the apparently permanent refugees from the former Yugoslavia. Its farmers scattered in alpine pastures are finding that income supplements are not as satisfactory as high price supports. In the first elections for its members of the European Parliament, held in October 1996, a majority of those elected were pledged to withdraw Austria from the EU! Sweden's government continues to antagonize Swedes now confronting reductions in benefits that had been taken for granted for generations. Only Finland seems fully committed to reorient its trade to the West as fast and completely as possible. In October 1996, its government rejoined the Exchange Rate Mechanism of the EMS, the first to do so since the disruptions of 1992.

CONCLUSION

Given the disparate routes which each of the three new members has taken to enter the European Union, it would be surprising if they had the same attitude toward further expansion of membership or increased efficiency in its existing operations. Finland and Sweden appear eager to include the new members from Central and East Europe as quickly as possible, including the Baltic states on the same terms as the others. Austria seems more reserved in its enthusiasm for enlargement, perhaps reflecting the current tensions it has with an enlarged foreign population. All three are explicit that the rights of full representation of small states must be preserved and not jeopardized by an effort to increase efficiency in the operation of the EU's decision-making processes. Even if the number of commissioners is reduced, for example, each country should be able to nominate a commissioner, presumably to reserve right of access to the Commission by each member state, no matter how small. The numbers in the European Parliament can be allowed to increase as well with the new member states.

All three of the neutrals are especially concerned about the common foreign and security policy. If the EU were to strengthen its role in preserving the security of Europe, this would allow the neutrals to have a voice in security arrangements affecting their national self-interests without forcing them to join NATO. But any decisions taken for joint action by the member states would have to have unanimous approval. In other words, they still will not cede determination of their foreign policy as neutrals to a supranational organization that may not be strictly neutral. In the development of organizational structures for Europe's future security, therefore, they seem fully in accord with the British view that intergovernmental cooperation is the proper route to take. But that view applies only to foreign and security policy. On other issues, such as the Economic and Monetary Union, reform of the Common Agricultural Policy, or arranging the finances of the EU for the next five-year period, these new, small member states want to strengthen the supranational apparatus of the EU that is already in place and functioning. Austria, in particular, feels that Britain has to be forced to accede to the social chapter of the Maastricht Treaty, while Sweden has no real problem with each country adjusting its social policy at its own pace toward a common set of standards. All three are concerned that environmental issues become part of the mission of the EU, because they are downwind (Finland and Sweden) or downstream (Austria) from concentrations of heavy industry in the EU.

Despite histories of imperial glory for both Sweden and Austria, neither country seems eager to take on the political problems of dealing with economically backward neighbors. It may be some time before even Finland can restore its economic relations with the former Soviet Union to the level that existed at the beginning of the 1980s. While willing to approach the economic opportunities that are opening up to the east for them, the new members in the EU will do so only gingerly and gradually. Their first priority is to embed their own economies more firmly into the existing structure that has been created by the European Union. Once safely in this prosperous redoubt, they will join in the common, cautious effort by the EU member states to further the development of peaceful, democratic, and market-oriented economies to the east.

Endnotes

1. Due to the volatility of foreign exchange rates, all international economic comparisons are now made in purchasing power parity exchange rates, which adjust for the different price levels within each country. In the early 1980s, the U.S. dollar was overvalued in the markets compared with its domestic purchasing power, while in the early 1990s it was undervalued. Using the market exchange rates to compare the United States with Europe, it appears that the U.S. economy has slowed down markedly compared to the EU. Adjusting for the large swings in the exchange rates that are not passed on to domestic price levels, however, shows that the U.S. economy has grown faster than the EU economies over the past decade. The PPP exchange rates used in this book are the 1991 U.S. dollar equivalents as calculated by the Organization for Economic Cooperation and Development in Paris.

Bibliography

Böhm, Bernhard and Lionello F. Punzo, eds. *Economic Performance, A Look at Austria and Italy.* Heidelberg: Physica-Verlag, 1994.

Child, Marquis W. *Sweden: The Middle Way on Trial.* New Haven, Conn.: Yale University Press, 1980.

Economist Intelligence Unit. *Country Report, Austria.* London: Economist Intelligence Unit, 2nd quarter, 1996.

Economist Intelligence Unit. *Country Report, Finland.* London: Economist Intelligence Unit, 2nd quarter, 1996.

Economist Intelligence Unit. *Country Report, Swede.* London: Economist Intelligence Unit, 2nd quarter, 1996.

Hartmann, Jürgen. "Social Policy in Sweden (1950–80)," in Roger Girod, Patrick de Laubier, and Alan Gladstone, eds. *Social Policy in Western Europe and the USA, 1950–1980. An Assessment.* New York: St. Martin's Press, 1985.

Henreksen, Magnus, Lars Jonung, and Joakim Stymne. "Economic growth and the Swedish model," in Nicholas Crafts and Gianni Toniolo, eds. *Economic Growth in Europe since 1945.* Cambridge: Cambridge University Press, 1996.

Lindbeck, Assar, Per Molander, Tosten Persson, Olof Petersson, Agnar Sandmo, Birgitta Swedenbort, and Niels Thygesen. *Turning Sweden Around.* Cambridge, Mass.: MIT Press, 1994.

Maddison, Angus. *Monitoring the World's Economy 1820–1992.* Paris: Organisation for Economic Cooperation and Development, 1995.

Singleton, Fred. *The Economy of Finland in the Twentieth Century.* Bradford, England: The University of Bradford, 1986.

Starck, Christian C. *Foreign and Domestic Shocks and Fluctuations in the Finnish Economy 1960–1988.* Helsinki: Suomen Pankki, 1990.

CHAPTER 16

Norway, Switzerland, Iceland, and Turkey:

The Opt Outs and the Locked Out

Basic Facts			
Area:	**Total**	1,247,700 km²	37 % of EU15
	Norway	323,900 km²	9.7 %
	Switzerland	41,300 km²	1.2 %
	Iceland	103,000 km²	3.1 %
	Turkey	779,500 km²	23.4 %
Population (1/1/1994):		73,711,600	19.9 % of EU15
	Norway	4,324,000	1.2 %
	Switzerland	6,968,500	1.9 %
	Iceland	265,100	0.1 %
	Turkey	62,154,000	16.8 %
Gross Domestic Product (1993):		$547.4 billion	9.2 % of EU15
	Norway	$83.7 billion	1.4 %
	Switzerland	$146.2 billion	2.4 %
	Iceland	$4.5 billion	0.1 %
	Turkey	$313.0 billion	5.2 %
Per Capita:		$7,426	46 % of EU15 average
	Norway	$19,414	120 %
	Switzerland	$21,079	130 %
	Iceland	$17,111	106 %
	Turkey	$5,262	32 %
Openness (X + M)/GDP			
	Norway	55 %	57 % with EU12
	Switzerland	68 %	65 %
	Iceland	45 %	67 %
	Turkey	34 %	46 %

Source: Eurostat, *Basic Statistics of the European Union,* 32nd ed. (Luxembourg, 1995), and *Economic Outlook* (December 1995), data diskettes (openness for Switzerland and Turkey).

Switzerland, Norway, Iceland, and Turkey have nothing in common, except they all have close economic relations with the EU and on grounds of economic self-interest alone should be members. Instead, political factors have kept each one out of the EU to date, and none is being seriously considered for inclusion in the next group of entrants. Iceland is considered one of the world's oldest democracies because its parliament, the Althing, dates to the tenth century, although it did not become fully independent from Denmark until 1944. While it is heavily dependent on exports of fish to supply its needs and two-thirds of its exports go to the EU, it prefers to deal with access to its fishing grounds as a separate, sovereign state than as a small voting member of the EU. Norway gained its independence from Denmark during the Napoleonic Wars at the beginning of the nineteenth century, but was not separated from Sweden until the beginning of the twentieth century. Like Iceland, Norway has a special interest in maintaining national control over access to its seas, especially because of the large reserves of oil and gas in its part of the North Sea, but also because it has an important fishing industry. The EU accounts for over two-thirds of its exports and one-half of its imports. On three separate occasions, 1961, 1972, and 1994, Norway applied for membership in the EU. With Britain, it was rejected the first time, and the last two times the Norwegian electorate narrowly rejected joining. Despite the desire of the government and the business community to join the EU, the resistance of the electorate means that Norway is not likely to apply again for some time, although it remains a member of the European Economic Area with Iceland. Switzerland, now the "white hole" in the center of the map of the EU, has prized its independence and sovereignty since the Middle Ages. Relying on the EU for over half of its exports and two-thirds of its imports, it has resisted joining the EU, or any other international organization, in order to preserve the advantages of neutrality within a war-torn Europe. Only after the collapse of Soviet hegemony in Eastern Europe did Switzerland join even the United Nations and the IMF, although it had had observer status from the beginning of those two international organizations. In 1992, its government applied for membership in the EU, along with the other members of EFTA (save for Iceland and Liechtenstein). But in 1993, its electorate voted against joining even the European Economic Area. With that, the Swiss government withdrew, for the time being, its application. Maintaining its sovereignty may help it to preserve its alpine beauty against the pollution of EU truck traffic, keep exceptionally high subsidies to its dairy industry, and maintain control over the number of foreign (mostly Italian) workers in its service sector. But being landlocked and completely dependent on imports for petroleum supplies, it must maintain open economic relations with the EU that now surrounds it.

Turkey, one of the early associate members of the EEC, signing an agreement in 1962, has very little chance of ever becoming a full member of the EU. With probably two million workers already present in the EU, Turkey has many more potential emigrants, who would readily take advantage of the EU's terms of free mobility of labor among member countries. This would undermine the efforts of the member states, especially Germany, since 1974 to reduce the numbers of Turkish workers in their economies. Moreover, the

Greek opposition to Turkish membership continues unabated. The second best alternative, joining just in the customs union aspect of the EU, has been held to Turkey as compensation if it would not oppose the entry of Cyprus into the EU. This was finally approved on both sides in 1996, twenty-three years after the first agreement to bring Turkey under the Common Customs Tariff was signed in Ankara.

MACROECONOMIC POLICY INDICATORS: 1960–97

Figures 16.1 to 16.3 show the course of growth rates, inflation, and unemployment for these four outsiders to the EU. The general pattern of high growth rates in the 1960–73 period, low rates in the oil shock period of 1973–85, and vulnerability to the shock of German reunification shows up for the series on gross domestic product, inflation, and unemployment, if one looks hard enough. However, despite the common dependence these countries have on the economic events in the EU, it is clear they respond in quite separate and diverse ways. There is little correlation among their respective growth, inflation, or unemployment rates within the four epochs we have identified for the European economic experience after World War II. Because all are small economies— Iceland, Norway, and Switzerland because of their small populations and Turkey because of its low per capita income—their growth rates are unusually volatile,

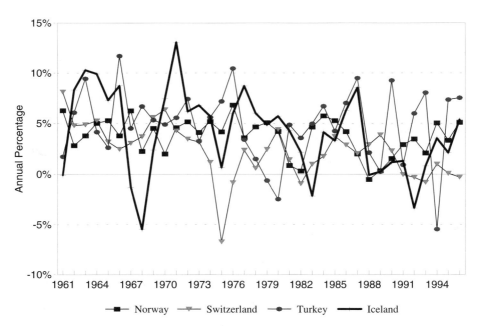

Figure 16.1. GDP growth rates, 1961–96, Norway, Switzerland, Iceland, and Turkey.

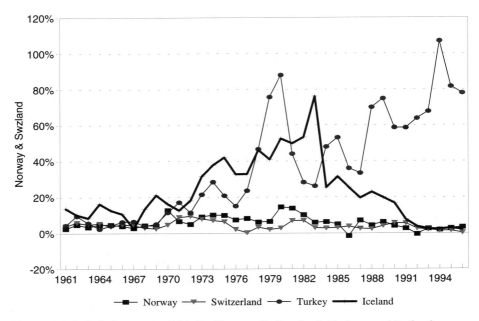

Figure 16.2. Inflation rates, 1961–96, Norway, Switzerland, Turkey, and Iceland.

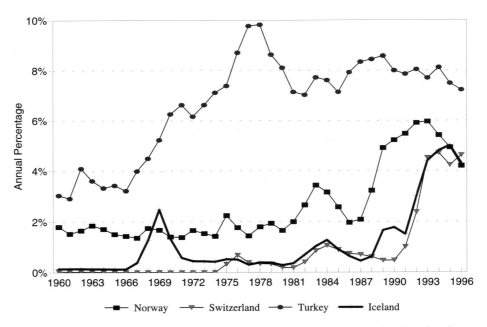

Figure 16.3. Unemployment rates, 1960–96, Norway, Switzerland, Iceland, and turkey.

especially so for Iceland and Turkey. These two economies also had the worst inflation rates of all the OECD countries during the oil shocks of the 1970s. Turkey has failed to get inflation under control even now in the 1990s, while Iceland managed to get in line with the other members of EFTA and the EEA by the beginning of this decade. The unemployment rates, on the other hand, were unusually low by European standards even through the 1970s and 1980s, except for Turkey. Even Turkey's unemployment rates are no worse than the European average, despite its volatile experience with growth rates and its losing battle with inflation. However, it also has no unemployment insurance, so there is much less incentive for workers to declare themselves unemployed or to be selective about the jobs they will accept.

All of the countries participated in the economic miracle growth rates of the 1960s. Switzerland was hardest hit by the first oil shock, and Turkey by the second. Switzerland's restrictive monetary policy led to a sharp appreciation of the Swiss franc, much like the deutsche mark. This should have led to a reduction in the dollar price of imported oil, as a stronger currency did for Germany, but the costs of getting oil to a landlocked, mountainous country rose as well. Moreover, tourism and the export markets for Switzerland's high value goods were hit especially hard. In the second oil shock, Turkey's proximity to the conflict between Iraq and Iran and drop in its remittances from its workers abroad were damaging factors. Growth rates held up well for each of the countries during the early 1980s, in contrast to the Euro-sclerosis that was afflicting the EU member states at that time. However, the Single Market initiative was a worrisome thing for these peripheral economies. The threat that the Single Market was merely a euphemism for "Fortress Europe" was very appreciable to these countries because each one had its own set of nontariff barriers that were vulnerable to attack. But the economic motivation should have been strongest for Switzerland and Iceland.

Even in the 1990s, Switzerland and Iceland have been staggering along at very low growth rates. These rates have provoked Iceland into serious fiscal reforms to try to emulate the Irish experience. By reducing government deficits and inflation it hopes to reduce interest rates and encourage investment, both domestic and foreign. Investment on a large scale is needed if Iceland is ever to exploit its one natural resource—geothermal energy. To date, only one aluminum plant has been constructed to take advantage of this source of electric power (aluminum is the favorite way for any country to export cheap electric power). But aluminum still accounts for less than 20 percent of Iceland's exports. Switzerland has responded to the Single Market and its low growth rates by negotiating as a single country with the EEA and the EU for improved access to the EU's markets, especially for its pharmaceutical and special engineering products. These are precisely the areas where technical standards and government procurement preferences become very important as a possible form of nontariff barrier, so Switzerland's bargaining position is inherently weak. Increasingly, Switzerland is being forced to make concessions with respect to its banking sector and its role in Europe's common financial market.

Meanwhile, Turkey has had high rates of growth, but low compared with what should be implied for a low-income country in the process of catching up to the standards of its wealthier trading partners. Domestic political problems have kept it from pursuing a consistent growth strategy, despite the successes enjoyed initially in the 1980s when President Özal began an export-promotion policy. Overcoming internal political turmoil was necessary before Turkey could be too concerned about nontariff barriers; first it had to deal with the tariff barriers that still existed. Norway's abundant oil supplies have enabled it to continue a high rate of growth despite maintaining an even more elaborate social welfare system than its Nordic neighbors, Denmark and Sweden. Moreover, it has exploited its excellent fjord harbors and cheap hydroelectric power at the head of the harbors to create a prosperous manufacturing industry. It had second thoughts about being out of the EU in the late 1980s, but this was due more to the drop in oil revenues than to fears of losing access to the EU market. The political decision to opt out of the EU, first in the 1970s and now in the 1990s, has had no adverse economic consequences for Norway and is not likely to so long as its export industries have access to the EU market and the price of oil remains firm.

Inflation rates display more dramatic differences in levels and patterns than even the growth rates. Norway and Switzerland track each other's rates quite closely, with the striking exception of the oil shocks in the 1970s. At this time, Switzerland followed a tight money policy, which drove up the value of its currency in terms of dollars and lowered the real cost to it of importing all of its petroleum-based fuel. This was a sensible economic strategy for a country totally dependent on imported oil. Norway, by contrast, followed an easy money policy, which facilitated construction of its North Sea oil platforms, but also depreciated the krona in terms of dollars. This, too, was a sensible strategy for a country that rapidly became a net exporter of oil, which was priced in dollars. Norway's export earnings were enhanced as a result of the devaluation of its currency. By the time of the third oil shock in the mid 1980s, however, the monetary policy, and the inflation rates, of the two countries had converged to typical European levels. Norway and Switzerland each made efforts at the beginning of the 1990s to peg their respective currencies, the krona and the Swiss franc, to the ECU even though neither was a member of the EU. Both abandoned that policy in 1992, Norway under pressure to devalue and Switzerland under pressure to revalue. As a result of the opposite movements of their currencies, Norway's export earnings have been enhanced, while Switzerland's have been harmed.

Turkey and Iceland both lost control of first their government budgets and then their domestic money supplies. Inflation rates soared as a result, rising to levels far above those in the other OECD countries and approaching hyperinflation in Turkey by 1978. Changes of government were needed in both countries to bring budgets under control. Turkey imposed a military caretaker government for three years and began the painful switch from its long-standing import substitution policy to one of export promotion for encouraging the growth of industry. The political costs were substantial, however, and inflation has never been brought back fully under control as a result. Iceland decided to stay in

NATO and benefit from American military expenditures, resting content to be a nuclear-free zone. Maintaining a Scandinavian-style welfare state in an economy whose national income is dependent on each year's fish catch, however, makes it impossible to stabilize government budgets. Sporadic eruptions of volcanoes do not help matters either.

The unemployment rates of the four outsider countries are interesting, especially when contrasting the reasons for their differences with those given for the three recent insider countries considered in the previous chapter. There, it was argued that Austria's low unemployment rates stemmed basically from its determination to use its state-controlled enterprises as stable, long-term employers who would not lay off workers even when they became increasingly redundant. High unemployment rates existed in countries like Finland that relied on private enterprise to determine the level of employment. Iceland, Norway, and Switzerland all have low unemployment rates right into the 1990s, but none has extensive state enterprises. Rather, each relies on internationally competitive firms to maintain employment levels, and the state steps in to subsidize employment in firms that become uncompetitive. Examples of this are Switzerland with its textile industry and Switzerland, Iceland, and Norway with their dairy industry. Turkey, by contrast, exemplifies an economy dominated by state enterprises, used to maintain political patronage and protected by the state. Its unemployment rates, however, start to rise already in the late 1960s before the oil shocks that drove it to typical European levels. Since the second oil shock of 1979, rates fell to below 8 percent and only rose sharply at the time of German reunification. The shock here may be in part from the return of Turkish workers from Germany, especially from East Germany, but mostly from the internal political stresses it has been enduring. Discord seems endemic over how to deal with the Kurdish dissidents in the southeast and how to deal with its Middle East neighbors. Iraq and Syria, for example, are rightly concerned about the implications of Turkey's projects to build dams on the Tigris and Euphrates rivers, possibly reducing the supply of irrigation water to both.

THE OUTSIDERS TAKE ADVANTAGE OF STRATEGIC LOCATION

All four countries were in on the ground floor of the Marshall Plan, since each sent representatives to the first meeting of potential recipients held in 1947. Each had played quite different roles during the war, however, and so their claims on reconstruction aid were very different as well. Although legally part of Denmark when the war began, Iceland was quickly occupied by British and then American forces. It served as an important base for American planes when air coverage was finally established for the protection of Atlantic shipping convoys in 1943. In 1944, it voted for independence, which it has maintained ever since. Norway was occupied by the Nazis early in the war, which provided German submarines and airplanes a secure flank from which to harass Allied convoys. Wartime destruction was severe in terms of loss of population, bombing of port installations, and German destruction of housing and infrastructure in the initial invasion and final withdrawal from northern Norway. But Norwegian aluminum production was vital to the German war effort, so extensive construction of hydroelectric facilities, aluminum plants, and mines as well as the related infrastructure for transport and communication had taken place. Switzerland and Turkey maintained an uneasy neutrality throughout the war, bolstered by intensive mobilization of their military forces. The economic development of both countries was stifled during the war as a result, even though the foreign reserves of both increased as they provided goods and services to the Axis forces.

Iceland's aid, amounting to 5 percent of its annual prewar GDP in the first year of operation of the Marshall Plan, was devoted mainly to machinery and equipment. This was used to improve mechanization in both its farming and fishing sectors, although the fishing fleet had already more than doubled in size in the two years after the war. Improved productivity in its traditional export areas (99 percent of Iceland's exports were agricultural products in 1951[1]) helped Iceland regain export earnings to cover its essential imports of manufactured goods and fuels. Norway's aid, amounting to nearly 6 percent of its prewar national income, went partly for importing machinery and equipment and especially for building up its merchant marine. Although Norway's substantial foreign reserves at the end of the war derived mostly from the shipping services its state shipping line, Nortraship, had provided Britain and the Allies during the war, over one-half of its shipping had been lost during the war. A substantial part of U.S. aid was used to import foodstuffs from the United States, as Norway, like Britain, continued food rationing and price controls well after the war. Price controls were not lifted on food until 1952, but rationing and price control on automobiles lasted until 1960.[2] Switzerland's participation was mainly intended to ensure it did not get eliminated from the network of trade that was reemerging in Western Europe, on which its economic success relied. Shut off from the traditional markets for its luxury exports during the war, it benefited from a surge of pent-up demand immediately after the war, especially for watches. Its dollar earnings as a consequence were sufficient to cover its import requirements from the dollar area. Turkey's aid was used to mechanize its agriculture and to facilitate further expansion of its cultivated area into land being settled by demobilized troops and refugee Turkish families from surrounding countries.

The American and British motivations for bringing all four countries into the Organization for European Economic Cooperation were clearly driven by strategic military considerations. Iceland and Norway lie astride the main access lanes to North Atlantic shipping that were used by Soviet submarines operating out of the White Sea. Both countries remain strategic assets for the NATO alliance. Turkey's control of the link between the Black Sea and the Mediterranean had already brought American and British aid to counter the possibility of Soviet expansion from either Iran or Greece, where Communist forces were present after the war. Switzerland proved a useful staging area for postwar reconstruction efforts and recuperation of prewar gold reserves of central banks that had belonged to the Bank for International Settlements. Its fabled banking services were vital for financing much of the resumption of foreign trade and capital flows for the rest of Europe.

The motivations of the four countries for participating in American-led reconstruction efforts, however, were quite different. Initially, all four clung to the idea of maintaining neutrality in the postwar political environment. Switzerland and Turkey had benefited relatively from neutrality during the war and saw no reason to discontinue the policy. The governments of Iceland and Norway were initially more concerned with regaining a sense of national identity than with maintaining a military establishment. Iceland, Norway, and Switzerland all depended on trade with Western Europe, however, and they were eager to cooperate with the rest of Europe in any efforts to expand trade. The increasing hostility of the Soviet bloc toward trade with the West confirmed their need to participate in the OEEC. Indeed, by 1949, when the North Atlantic Treaty Organization was formed, both Iceland and Norway were charter members. Turkey had enjoyed relative economic success during the 1930s and the war by pursuing a policy of autarky, in common with Spain and Portugal. Moreover, as the recipient of large amounts of U.N. aid and then American military aid, Turkey saw no particular need to participate in the OEEC. With Greece, Turkey's aim was to prevent American aid from being diverted from Turkey back into the Western European reconstruction effort.[3] From these quite different positions, all four countries were united in arguing against a political agenda, much less a military one, for the OEEC. They were consistent in keeping the OEEC's efforts strictly devoted to improvement of the economic functions of the member states and divorced from any integrative political purposes or military alliances. While Turkey eventually joined NATO in 1952, so that three of the four countries have also been members of the Western military alliance, to this day none of them has joined in the European Union.

From 1952 when the Marshall Plan ended until the present, all four have shared in the economic experiences of Europe while remaining apart from the political formation of an integrated Europe. In the parlance of economists, they have been free riders, taking advantage of the efforts of others without making the sacrifices required to create and maintain a public good. The public good in this case was the expansion of multilateral trade among the recovering European industrial nations as they worked to overcome the havoc and hatred wrought by the most devastating war in human history. The political framework that made this possible was created only with great difficulty and frustrating delays, as it seemed every conceivable alternative was explored until found wanting. The reasons each of these four countries stood aside from this process are so disparate they must be analyzed separately. We take them in descending order of per capita inome.

SWITZERLAND

The 1950s era of high, smooth growth rates was shared by Switzerland, which had a slightly lower than average growth rate for per capita income. This was understandable given that it began with much the highest per capita income in Europe. It continued to raise its standard of living, however, by maintaining historically high ratios of investment to GDP and exceptionally high rates of growth of GDP as population grew only moderately. The agricultural sector was modernized to increase total output in order to approach self-sufficiency, and industries whose prewar trade patterns had shown they had a comparative advantage were encouraged to expand their production facilities. The Swiss franc participated in the Bretton Woods system of fixed exchange rates and devalued with the British pound in 1949 by the same 30.5 percent that the pound devalued relative to the dollar. Switzerland, however, maintained lower rates of inflation through the 1950s and 1960s than its trading partners. Effectively, then, its real exchange rate was devaluing, which made its exports increasingly competitive.

In 1960, it responded favorably to the alternative proposed by Great Britain and Sweden to the formation of the European Economic Community and became a charter member of the European Free Trade Association. When Britain and Denmark abandoned the EFTA in 1973, Switzerland benefited from the reciprocal tariff reductions negotiated between the EEC and the remaining countries in the EFTA. These were limited, of course, to trade in manufactured goods, so Switzerland was free to maintain its protected agricultural sector. Swiss cheese, as a manufactured product, enjoyed preferred access to the Common Market, and Swiss dairy farmers prospered accordingly. Overall, Switzerland's growth pattern was remarkably close to the OECD average in terms of average rates of growth, investment ratios, and structural change away from agricultural employment into first industry and then services.

Moreover, its balance of payments was typically in equilibrium. Although its rate of inflation was slightly higher than the OECD average, it was close to the U.S. level so there was no change in the real effective exchange rate of the Swiss franc in this period. Exports were mainly in high value-added products, primarily watches and pharmaceuticals. Imports were mainly in raw materials, food, and low value-added intermediate products. In a European environment that still constrained the mobility of capital across national boundaries and levied progressively higher taxes on rentier incomes derived from dividends and interest coons, Switzerland's banks were in a position to attract large amounts of foreign capital. Their secrecy laws on revealing details of customers' accounts to anyone, including foreign tax authorities, combined with a low tax rate on interest payments due to a weak federal government made the Swiss Alps a potential tax haven for the rest of the world.

It was not until the latter half of the 1960s, however, that this "natural" advantage of Switzerland began to be exploited. From 1964 on, Switzerland began to enjoy rising levels of net capital imports, which rose as a percentage of GDP from under 3 percent in the 1950s and early 1960s to over 7 percent by the end of the 1980s.[4] This must be due to the rising importance of the Eurodollar market initially and then to the rising value of the Swiss franc after 1971. But the effectiveness of capital controls worldwide before the rise of the Eurodollar market must be credited for the delay in Switzerland's exploitation of its

financial advantages. On the negative side, the increasing ability to finance imports of goods and services created by the rise in capital imports may account
for the failure of Swiss industry to recognize its gradual loss of technological
leadership in the watch industry and in machine tools. As the Union Bank of
Switzerland put it in 1986 when Switzerland had the highest density of computers in the world, "Switzerland . . . has not missed the bus of new technology.
At the most it jumped on a little late."[5]

Hard hit by the oil shocks of the 1970s, Switzerland managed, partly by
design and partly by luck, to survive fairly well. The key both to the initial
shock and the eventual success was the rising value of the Swiss franc in the
period of wildly fluctuating exchange rates that followed the collapse of the
Bretton Woods era in 1971–73. This is contrasted in Figure 16.4 with the trade-
weighted exchange rate indexes of Norway and Turkey, just to highlight the
contrasting responses of each quite different country to the repeated oil shocks.

Switzerland pursued its hard-currency policy partly by design, partly by accident. The design part came as the central bank restricted the growth of the
domestic money supply in order to keep down the domestic rate of inflation. If
this were less than the rate of inflation in its trading partners, and it certainly
was less than inflation rates in France and Italy, the real exchange rate of the
Swiss franc would be devalued, helping its trade balance. For example, while
the price of the Swiss franc rose in terms of Belgian francs, the price in Swiss
francs of Swiss chocolate did not rise while the price of Belgian chocolate in

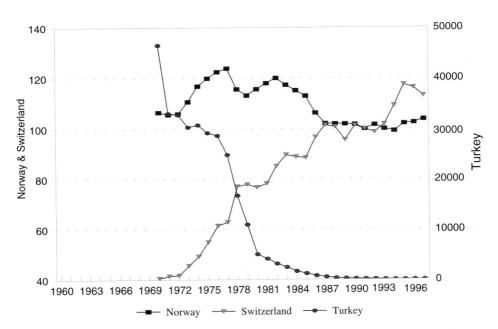

Figure 16.4. Exchange rate indexes (1991 = 100), Norway, Switzerland, and Turkey.

Belgian francs did. So the relative prices of Godiva and Toblerone chocolate did not change nearly as much for French or German consumers.

The accident part came from the influx of foreign capital seeking the tax advantages provided foreign depositors in the Swiss banking sector. Switzerland's leading role in the development of the Euro-dollar market in the late 1960s now proved greatly to its advantage as it became a premier financial center for recycling petro-dollars in the 1970s. OPEC exporters would deposit their oil dollars in Swiss banks, which then could lend them at high, but still relatively favorable, rates to the European importers. Service charges and the interest rate spread on an enormously increased volume of transactions made the financial sector Switzerland's leading sector in the 1970s.

All told, the appreciation of the Swiss franc had less effect on its export earnings than did the drop in consumption demand in its export markets. It did have an effect in hastening the change in composition of Swiss exports toward high-value products intended for high-income consumers, however. Moreover, unemployment was kept minimal by the simple expedient of sending most of the foreign workers, who at one time amounted to 20 percent of the Swiss labor force, back to their home countries—primarily Italy and Spain. Much of the foreign labor force was engaged in the tourist industry, especially restaurants and hotels. The strong Swiss franc discouraged tourism and made the dismissal of foreign workers all the easier.

Swiss multinationals at this time began to move their production facilities out of Switzerland, which decreased employment opportunities for lower skilled manufacturing workers. They continued, however, to maintain their headquarters in Switzerland, where they managed their financial affairs, carried on research and development, and developed marketing campaigns. This maintained employment, therefore, in higher paying white-collar positions, already predominantly held by Swiss nationals, while reducing employment in lower paying, blue-collar jobs. Even though the growth of Swiss GDP in purchasing power parity terms was reduced dramatically in the period 1973–85, the Swiss population as a whole continued to enjoy rising per capita incomes, and they certainly benefited from the increased purchasing power of the Swiss franc in their consumption of imported goods.

Nevertheless, the Single Market initiative by the European Community posed a distinct threat to the continuation of Switzerland's privileged position at the Alpine crossroads of Europe. Much of Switzerland's economic success over its history has derived from performing the role of middleman in transactions between hostile countries. It was not merely happenstance that led to the League of Nations establishing its headquarters in Geneva after World War I, or the Bank of International Settlements in Basel in 1930, or the United Nations Economic Commission of Europe in 1945. The latter's annual economic survey was divided into two sections, one for Western Europe and one for Central and Eastern Europe, which epitomized the middleman role of Switzerland in a divided Europe. If the Single Market succeeded fully, what further need would there be for a middleman? The Swiss government certainly felt the danger of being excluded from the ongoing process of defining technical standards, say on pharmaceutical products, which would raise nontariff barriers to Swiss companies while eliminating them for French and German firms. Government procurement might be widened among firms within the EU, but now discriminate even more against Swis firms. Swiss banks would have to merge with counterparts already operating in the EU if they were to continue to have access to the emerging common financial market. Consequently, the Swiss government joined the other EFTA countries in the final agreement to establish a European Economic Area jointly between the EFTA and EC countries in 1991. The government also determined that Switzerland's longer term interests would be better served as a member of the EC and made formal application to join. In the event, the Swiss population defeated the ratification of the EEA treaty, which was the first step to joining the EC, so the Swiss government let its application for membership in the EC lapse.

It must be said that subsequent events have not been kind to Switzerland, which was affected by the German reunification shock in ways similar to those already observed for member states of the EC who participate in the European Monetary System. Its growth rate fell to zero and below in the early 1990s, and for the first time ever its unemployment rate began to rise. After a brief period of pegging the Swiss franc to the deutsche mark, the Swiss gave it up, not because of a run on the Swiss franc, but because as foreign investors sought a safe haven from the exchange rate uncertainties in Europe they tended to go more to the Swiss franc than even the deutsche mark. As markets become convinced that the mark will be replaced by the euro in 1999, the Swiss franc has been appreciating further. The increased value of the Swiss franc creates more serious problems for the Swiss exporters than the remaining nontariff barriers that confront them in Europe, annoying as these may be in particular cases.

NORWAY

Also a charter member of the IMF, Norway, unlike Switzerland, kept inflation rates slightly higher than the OEEC average through the golden age of growth, so that with fixed nominal exchange rates its real effective exchange rate kept rising. This made their exports less and less competitive, which helps to explain why Norway's rate of growth began gradually declining relative to the rest of the OEEC countries. When the EEC was formed, Norway readily joined Switzerland and the others in forming the European Free Trade Association in 1960. This helped to maintain its already high degree of openness to foreign trade, but it did not increase it the way the EEC increased openness for its members. Throughout the golden age of growth, Norway was governed by the Labor party, which was bent on perfecting the welfare state by keeping full employment, equalizing incomes, and sustaining economic growth. To perfect its management of the economy it established an elaborate system for a planned capitalist economy. This was headed by an Economic Coordination Council, where representatives of government, industry, farming, fishing, and labor would recommend a consensus course of action to the government. The national budget would then be drawn up by economic experts, with special attention paid to the amount of government spending required to achieve the policy goals.

Norway's economic experts, led by the distinguished economist Ragnar Frisch who shared the first Nobel Prize in Economics with Jan Tinbergen of the Netherlands in 1969, were adept at applying the principles of Keynesian economics. They pursued a mixed strategy of export earnings promotion and substitution of domestic production for vital imports. On the export side, the merchant marine continued to be built up in order to restore Norway's preeminence in ocean shipping, hydroelectric resources were developed further, and the fishing fleet was modernized. On the import side, price supports were supplemented with income guarantees to farmers to encourage as much agricultural output as possible, even if 50 percent of Norway's grain needs still had to be imported. A steel works begun shortly after the war continued to be supported with additional infrastructure created to supply it with coke, iron ore, and electricity despite increasing evidence it was a white elephant. Private firms were induced to locate their factories in remote areas where intensive housing projects had been completed in the previous decade, thus starting a policy of bringing jobs to people that was to create serious problems of labor immobility in coming years. The upshot of Norway's strategy was to maintain growth rates at average OECD rates, but at the cost of an exceptionally high ratio of investment to output, averaging nearly 33 percent.

Various explanations have been offered for this evidence of low capital productivity, given that Norway also enjoyed one of the highest levels of per capita income in the world. In common with Great Britain, Norway devoted a large portion of its domestic capital formation to rebuilding and relocating its housing stock. Housing does not contribute directly to further increases in output, and to the extent it is placed where industry finds it uneconomic to locate, it may hinder the growth of output. For strategic reasons to maintain protection of its borders with Sweden and Russia, much of Norway's housing investments were located away from the southeastern part of the country, where business has always tended naturally to locate. A second explanation of the high investment ratio was the expense of construction in a northern climate. This was a problem shared with Canada, Sweden, and Finland, all of whom had higher than expected investment ratios given their average rates of growth in this period. Even adjusting for these two factors, however, Norway was still an outlier in terms of its average rate of growth.

The final explanation may lie in the enormous importance of shipbuilding in the Norwegian economy combined with the importance of shipping and fishing. Increasingly, Norway's shipyards concentrated on very large ships, culminating with their famous VLCCs (standing for Very Large Cargo Carriers). Expenditures on building these ships over a period of two to five years, many destined for export to other shipping nations, are counted as domestic investment expenditures. Eventually, their sale increases domestic output. But this increase in output is offset largely on foreign account by the import of smaller ships destined for coastal shipping and the fishing fleet. The imported ships, however, are also counted as part of domestic capital formation, as they are clearly capital goods added to the nation's stock of capital. Ships, whether exported or imported, count as capital formation and raise the numerator in the I/Y ratio. When they are both exported and imported, however, their effects on the denominator tend to cancel out. Ships were never less than 20 percent of total capital formation in Norway until the end of the 1960s. At that time, housing rose to nearly 20 percent. The two combined made up anywhere from one-third to over 40 percent of Norwegian investment from the end of the war to the first oil shock.[6]

In the first shock of the 1970s, the collapse of Bretton Woods and its regime of fixed exchange rates, Norway at first devalued due to its continued high rates of government spending and domestic inflation. With the oil shock, Norway's oil potential in the North Sea became economically feasible and its currency began to appreciate against the dollar. Figure 16.4 shows that it didn't appreciate much, at least not by comparison with the Swiss franc. This was thanks to the government's enthusiasm in spending the oil dividend before it actually arrived.

Norway's situation was most enviable. Foreign investment began pouring in to provide the infrastructure needed to exploit its proven oil field at Ekofisk, which lies at the extreme southwest of Norway's North Sea jurisdiction. The Norwegian government, still controlled by the Labor party, immediately began planning how to spend the oil dividend. It succeeded in spending it all on its primary goal—maintaining employment for every Norwegian in the labor force at a high-paying job in his (or much less frequently, her) present location. This policy had two unfortunate consequences for Norway's economic future. One was that it froze the potential mobility of the Norwegian population to respond to future changes in economic structure and in the location of attractive employment. The second was that it created a phenomenon called wage drift by the Norwegians. This arose from the two-stage process of wage determination practiced in Norway. The first stage, in common with the procedure in the rest of Scandinavia and northern Europe, was to negotiate a general wage package between the national association of business firms (Norwegian Employers' Federation, or NAF) and the national union organization (Norwegian Federation of Labor, or LO). Given the prosperity foreseen from the forthcoming oil bounty, these wage settlements became increasingly generous in the early 1970s. The second stage of wage determination, however, mimicked in some ways the British practice, in that it allowed individual firms and their local unions to make supplementary agreements. Because skilled, highly paid workmen were in exceptional demand thanks to the construction demands from the North Sea oil fields, they could bargain successfully for additional pay increases. Wage drift over the period of the two oil shocks amounted to two-thirds of total wage increases in Norway.[7] To accommodate these increased wages, the government was forced to increase both its spending and the domestic money supply. It was forced to raise domestic taxes from just over 40 percent of GDP in 1970 to over 50 percent by 1980 and increase its foreign indebtedness from 11 percent of GDP in 1970 to 33 percent in 1980.[8] Moreover, the actual output from the initial

North Sea concession fell short of the anticipated levels and the government had failed to license other concessions for several years. Fortunately for the government, the second oil shock in 1979–80, which doubled prices again, increased its oil revenues so it could sustain its funding of its welfare-oriented policy. Unfortunately for the productivity of the private sector, this continued to decrease the international competitiveness of Norwegian manufacturing. At the level of individual firms, moreover, the wage compression between unskilled and skilled workers was decreasing the incentives for workers to acquire human capital. This constrained firms further from implementing effectively new technologies.

Norway's problems with slowing GDP growth and rising unemployment began in the 1980s well before the reunification shock that created similar problems for the rest of northern Europe. Norway's problems were clearly due to what might be termed now the third oil shock, the collapse of oil prices after 1985. Norway's reliance on the oil dividend depended very much on the price of oil remaining high, because it had strictly limited, through licensing arrangements, the amount of oil that could be produced. This led the government to enter wholeheartedly into the negotiations that established the European Economic Area and to peg the krone to the deutsche mark until the exchange rate disturbance of 1992. By 1995, however, new concessions in the North Sea had begun producing as the original Ekofisk field began to dry up. Thus the oil dividend was replenished. By 1996, the price of oil on world markets had risen as well so that Norway's economic position seemed quite enviable once again to the rest of Europe. Only those few economists worried about the basis in Norway for longer run growth based on technological advances were concerned about Norway's prospects.

ICELAND

Iceland after its independence found it had preferred access to a common pool resource, the rich fishing grounds off its shores. Lying next to the main route for Soviet submarines and supply ships to enter the North Atlantic from their bases in the White Sea conferred a double advantage. The Americans spent large sums of money building and maintaining an airbase at Keflavik to monitor Soviet shipping movements, while the Soviets set up barter arrangements with Iceland, trading fuel for fish, to supply their fleets. At one point in the mid-1950s, American military spending accounted for one-fifth of Iceland's national income! Exports of fish kept growing to the entire OEEC market and kept Iceland's tiny economy growing at the same high rates enjoyed in its export markets. In common with Norway and Switzerland, Iceland's tiny, open economy shared in the benefits of increased trade taking place with a rapidly growing European economy.

When the EEC was formed, however, Iceland remained apart from both it and the EFTA alternative. Part of the motivation was to insist on its independence from Denmark, which was one of the charter members. In addition, however, it had begun a fishing dispute with both Germany and Great Britain, which ruled out any amicable association with either the EEC or the EFTA at the time. This led eventually to common acceptance of the twelve mile limit off a country's coast as the exclusive fishing grounds for any country's fishing fleet, but at the time it disrupted Iceland's fishing activity, leading to large deficits for both the government and the balance of payments. A new government came to power in October 1959. Led by the Independence party, it won the election on grounds that it would put both the economy and the government budget on a sounder basis.

Toward this end, two devaluations of the krona followed in short order: from $1.00 = 16.286 kr in February 1960 to $1.00 = 38.00 kr, and then in August 1961 to $1.00 = 57.00 kr. A 300 percent devaluation was adequate to restore Iceland's competitiveness for its main export—frozen fish. At the same time, the new government insisted on exclusive fishing rights for the Icelandic fleet within twelve miles of Iceland's shores. After some skirmishes with British warships, agreement was reached with Britain and Germany that this would become effective within three years and in the meantime other fishing boats, mainly the British, could approach within six miles of Iceland. Fish exports resumed their growth, the Icelandic fleet expanded, but the fish population stock failed to grow. By 1968, a serious shortfall in the fish catch occurred, which forced a sharp fall in Iceland's GDP as well (Figure 16.1). This forced Iceland to reconsider its outsider status from the European markets. It reached agreement in December 1969 with the other members of the EFTA to join, which it did in March 1970. In 1972 it signed a trade agreement with the EEC, which eliminated tariffs on about 70 percent of Iceland's exports, mainly fresh and frozen fish. Beyond entering into the spirit of multilateral trade liberalization more than a decade later than the rest of Europe, Iceland's policy responses were the same as ten years earlier. First a devaluation, this time to $1.00 = 88.00 kr, and then an attempt to expand its exclusive fishing rights from twelve to fifty miles offshore. This provoked a more serious confrontation with British warships, which were called in to protect the British fishing boats trawling between twelve and fifty miles offshore. The confrontation also led to a further devaluation of the krona against the dollar in December 1972, to $1.00 = 97.25 kr. The final period of golden growth for Iceland thus began and ended with devaluations and successful attempts to expand the country's exclusive fishing grounds. Having depleted the supply of herring in the first fifteen years following independence, Iceland's fishermen proceeded to deplete the supply of cod in the next fifteen years.

When the Bretton Woods system of fixed exchange rates collapsed in 1971, Iceland had first devalued as part of the adjustment necessary to continue high rates of government spending and contain domestic inflation. But as fish harvests rose with settlement of the Cod War, as it was labeled by the British press, and prices began to soar for Iceland's fish thanks to much greater access to the EC market, its currency began to appreciate relative to the dollar. Further, as the Soviet Union was its primary supplier for petroleum and did not price according to OPEC standards but rather on the basis of long-term countertrade agreements, Iceland was relatively insulated from the price shocks. So Iceland confronted the first oil shock with an appreciating currency. As a small, open economy, however, it was still subject to the income shocks in its trading partners. Countering the decline in export earnings and employment by increased subsidies to the agricultural and fishing sectors, the government kept increasing deficits and financing them with increased money supply. This led to a raging inflation. In Figure 16.2, it has to be plotted on the same scale as Turkey's, and by the early 1980s actually exceeded the rate in Turkey.

Nevertheless, the government's primary objective was achieved; unemployment rates remained low throughout the turbulent 1970s. By 1979, however, it had to take recourse yet again to the policy action that had brought Iceland through the crises of the late 1950s and the late 1960s. This time, it claimed an exclusive fishing zone for its fleet within two-hundred miles offshore! By 1983, Iceland's fishing fleet, having exhausted the stocks of first herring in the 1950s and cod in the 1960s, now proceeded to deplete Atlantic salmon. This kept growth rates up in the mid-1980s, counter to the typical European experience. Iceland's fish catch dropped off again at the end of the 1980s as the result of constant overfishing. Iceland's response, predictable by now, was to send its fishing boats into the hitherto sacrosanct waters around Svalbard Island. This frozen bit of territory well above the Arctic Circle was made an international zone by a Treaty of Paris in 1920, which placed it under Norwegian protection. Iceland claims that since Denmark was a signatory to the treaty and Iceland was part of Denmark at the time, it has access to the international waters around Svalbard and their still undepleted fishing grounds. Norway, in its role as protector of the territory (and of its own fishing fleet) disagrees, having made Svalbard part of its reserved fishing grounds at the beginning of the 1980s. (Svalbard is roughly 1,000 miles from either Oslo or Reyjkavik.) No doubt this will be solved to Iceland's advantage as the smaller country, because Norway would not like to see the EU's fishing fleets become involved in the settlement of the dispute.

TURKEY

Turkey stayed quite apart from the phenomenon of export-led growth as its new parliamentary democracy, installed in elections of 1950, maintained the basic strategy of import substitution that had proven successful in the 1930s and 1940s. The ruling Democrat party built up an agrarian power base by expanding the agricultural sector both in terms of acreage under cultivation and of the number of smallholders engaged. This simply emphasized and completed a policy begun earlier with the Land Distribution Law of 1946. During the first period of redistribution, 1947–54, approximately 3 million acres of farmland and common pastures were brought into cultivation by 142,000 rural families. Many of them were refugees from Bulgaria. In the next five years another 5 million acres were brought into cultivation from public lands. Construction of roads and electrification in the new farming areas accounted for much of the capital formation in the economy, in addition to the intensive mechanization that took place. The number of tractors increased from about 1,000 in 1946 to nearly 42,000 in 1960. While this was a dramatic increase, it was far less than the number of new farm households, which meant that most smallholders still had to content themselves with the traditional oxen.

The rapid growth that persisted was financed by continued deficits both on the government's account and on foreign account. Unlike the other participants in the European Payments Union, however, Turkey began to reverse its liberalization of foreign trade by 1954. From then until the military takeover in 1960, it engaged in an increasing variety of import restrictions, export subsidies, and exchange controls, quite in opposition to the removal of quantitative restrictions and the move toward full current account convertibility of currencies that was taking place in Western Europe. The foreign exchange crisis caused by Turkey's inability to follow the other countries into convertibility in 1958 led to a stabilization program under IMF guidance beginning in August 1958. As with nearly all future IMF programs, devaluation of the lira to a sustainable rate was required. But the recalcitrance of the Turkish government stretched out the process for nearly three years, by altering first the exchange rate on imports and then the rate for exports. Finally, in August 1960 the official rate was increased from LT2.80 to LT9.00, a devaluation of over 300 percent!

The military government in power in 1960–61 also imposed draconian reductions in government spending. This terminated the first phase of Turkish growth. Expansion of the cultivated area ceased, although nearly 40 percent of the rapidly growing labor forced continued to be in the agricultural sector. Improvements in mechanization dropped off sharply. Emphasis turned toward investment in state economic enterprises, but since these were primarily capital intensive projects, they created few employment opportunities. While the Democratic government had passed a good deal of progressive social legislation, providing pension plans for government employees and improved health care, it never enacted unemployment insurance. The solution for unemployment by workers displaced from agriculture thus became migration abroad.

In the next phase of the golden age of growth, 1960–73, Turkey continued to remain outside both European sets of arrangements to expand trade. However, it was not immune to economic developments in Europe. The restoration of democratic government in 1962 led to a change in economic policy, but the change was to improve the rationality of the import-substitution strategy by adopting national plans similar to those that seemed to be so successful in Europe. Attributing the successes of France and the Netherlands to the implementation of their successive five-year plans, Turkey invited the distinguished Dutch economist, Jan Tinbergen (who shared the first Nobel Prize in Economics with Ragnar Frisch of Norway), to help design comparable plans for Turkey. The resumption of high rates of growth in the 1960s, then, in Turkey as in the other countries of Europe, was based on the same strategies that had begun in the 1950s, but that were now implemented with greater confidence and care.

Turkey's planned economic development produced typically high growth rates for GDP, averaging over 5.5 percent in the period 1960–73. But more and more of its investment, still very low as a proportion of GDP at under 18 percent, was directed to white elephants. Fifty percent of investment had to be in the public sector, and much of the remainder in the private sector was directed to firms ancillary to the large state enterprises. Moreover, population continued to grow rapidly, the rate averaging over 2.5 percent annually in the period 1960–73. This was by far the highest rate of population growth in the OECD at the time. Given its very low level of per capita income at the outset, therefore, it should have seen much higher rates of growth of per capita income. A large part of the explanation for this unsatisfactory performance must lie in the failure to move labor out of the agricultural sector and into industry or urban employment. Nearly three-quarters of Turkey's labor force was in agriculture as late as 1960, and even after the first oil shock, 54 percent were still in agriculture as late as 1977.[9]

If Turkish development plans could not absorb the growing labor force, European industry could use it. Over the period 1960–73, millions of Turkish male workers went to Western Europe, mainly to West Germany. Intended as temporary guest workers, the most able became long-term residents of Germany as their firms hired them permanently. Earning far higher wages than was possible in Turkey, these men remitted large sums in total back to Turkey. These covered at times up to one-third of Turkey's imports and were far more important than the total of foreign aid or investment credits provided it by the OECD countries. This period of laggard development was brought to an end by a military government once again assuming power in the period 1971–73. Again, it had to remedy the accumulated problems created by foreign and government account deficits. It also put on hold any thought of Turkey enjoying closer economic relations with the EEC. Its democratic government had applied for membership as early as July 1959 and had been granted associate member status at the end of 1964. This was intended to lead to full membership, much as the current wave of Association agreements with East and Central European countries are supposed to do.

With the first oil shock in 1973, Turkey continued its import substitution policy, but now had to protect its state economic enterprise employees from a fall in real wages. This increased further the traditional government deficit. Meanwhile, it had to meet a vastly increased import bill for fuel while losing a large part of emigrants' remittances as Turkish workers were sent home as fast as possible by their host countries. By the middle of 1974, all the bilateral agreements for the use of temporary labor in the EC had been terminated. Turkey's experience overall was perhaps the mirror image of Switzerland's, much as the inverse patterns of their exchange rate indexes appear in Figure 16.4. With a strong central government committed to import-substitution policies through support of state economic enterprises, Turkey's policy response could be expected to be the exact opposite of Switzerland's to any external shock. While Switzerland sent back its foreign workers, Turkey had to receive large numbers of returned guest workers. Even Turkish workers who remained in Germany stopped sending remittances back. There was too much exchange rate risk in dealing with the fluctuations of the Turkish lira and the government's unpredictable impositions of exchange controls. Many Turkish workers solved the problem by bringing their families to join them abroad.

Typically, the government responded by spending more money. From 1974 on, it was clearly public sector spending that drove the Turkish rates of inflation ever higher, culminating in hyperinflation when the second oil shock hit in 1979–80.[10] Despite the spending, unemployment continued to rise along with inflation. Finally, the government had to accept terms set by the IMF in 1978 to obtain relief on its balance-of-payments deficit. Both debt service and import payments had risen while emigrants' remittances had dropped off sharply and the excessive inflation rates worked to overprice Turkish exports. The IMF insisted the government reduce spending mainly by cutting subsidies to state enterprises, devalue the lira sharply, and move toward export promotion while lifting quantity restrictions on imports. The immediate result was a sharp decline in Turkish GDP, an adverse balance of payments, and, with continuing rapid population growth, a drastic drop in per capita income. The government fell, but the draconian policies were pursued by a caretaker military government, which assumed temporary power for the period 1980–83. Maintaining the course toward export promotion and letting production respond to market signals, a turnaround in economic fortunes was evident by 1981 and continued into the mid-1980s.

The architect of this remarkable turnaround was Turgut Özal. As a staff economist at the IMF in the 1970s, he was very familiar with IMF practice and with the logic of the standard IMF stabilization programs. Put in charge of implementing the program by the coalition government elected at the end of 1979, he instituted the radical reform program put into effect in January 1980. The military takeover followed in September, but Özal was kept in charge of the economy. A new constitution was enacted in 1982 and in elections held on the basis of the new constitution, Özal was elected as prime minister of Turkey in the restored civilian government, a position he held until he became president of Turkey in 1989. He died in office in 1993.

Özal's export promotion policy certainly proved successful on its own terms. Exports expanded rapidly as a share of Turkey's GDP, which resumed growth rates in the neighborhood of 5 percent per annum. Structural change began to increase overall productivity again as more of the labor force moved out of agriculture into manufacturing. Manufacturing's share of GDP rose as it should in a country that is developing successfully. Closer examination of Turkey's export performance, however, raises some interesting questions. The destination of Turkey's rising exports was not the rich industrial countries of the West so much as it was the newly rich OPEC countries in the Middle East. In 1970, developed countries took 75 percent of Turkey's exports and less developed countries only 10 percent. By 1984, developed countries took only slightly more than 50 percent while the less developed countries' share had risen to over 40 percent.[11] Closer examination of this counterintuitive change in the pattern of exports shows that much of the rise took place to two countries in particular, Iran and Iraq. It will be recalled that the two were at war with each other throughout the initial period of Turkey's liberalization. Moreover, much of the expansion in exports to the Middle East was in food products, not manufactures. On the import side, there was an increase in the share of raw materials, including fuel, which may indicate one way Iran and Iraq were financing their war against each other. While export promotion obviously had the desired effects at the macroeconomic level, it is more doubtful that it had the desired effects at the microeconomic level of stimulating technological change and productivity as well as of transferring resources from agriculture to manufacturing.

With both economic growth and democratic government restored in the mid 1980s, Turkey welcomed the Single Market initiative. In fact, its continued civilian rule and continued move toward successful trade liberalization renewed Turkish optimism that its long-standing application to join might be renewed. While both the governments were in agreement on the desirability of joining the EC, the idea was a nonstarter and remains so to this day. There is no country currently in the EC that is actively in favor of Turkey joining, not even Britain, which might be expected to promote it in order to expand the free trade area while diminishing the political cohesion of Europe. There are at least two countries actively opposed, Greece, where the government and population agree on this, and Germany, where the electorate definitely oppose the idea despite the deliberately noncommittal approach of the government.

Turkey's alternative to membership in the EU was suggested in 1994, which was to proceed with a customs union arrangement implementing at last an agreement that had been signed in Ankara in 1973! This is a unique approach to association with the EU for it implies that Turkey will eventually have the same low external tariff on manufactured goods with the rest of the world that the EU currently has. This would be a necessary step toward eventual membership in any event, and Malta and Cyprus are included currently in the customs union as well. But in Turkey's case it appears to be a substitute for membership. Full membership would imply the right of Turkish workers to seek employment anywhere in the EU, and that is not attractive to any of the current members. They are all agreed that it is much better to substitute trade flows for migration pressures. This means encouraging German and Swiss manufacturers to set up plants in Turkey and export their products back to the EU instead of importing Turkish workers to their plants in Western Europe.

The unanticipated effects of the oil shock of 1973 on the EC economies was the primary reason the customs union was put on hold. In the interim from then until 1996 various incidents further delayed its implementation—the Turkish invasion of Cyprus, its military regimes in 1980–83, and the EU membership of Greece. Even in the original version, tariffs were to be reduced only very gradually, one set over twelve years and another over twenty-two years. It was clearly Özal's initiative as president of Turkey that led to the final breakthrough in negotiations. This was based on Turkey not raising any objection to Cyprus entering the EU in return for proceeding with the customs union agreement. In return, Greece lifted its veto on the customs union agreement going forward. As of late 1996, however, it had not lifted its veto on granting "financial cooperation" to Turkey to compensate it over several years for its loss in customs revenues that would occur. Moreover, the European Parliament failed to ratify the agreement until Turkey demonstrated more care toward the civil rights of its Kurdish minority. The fall of Tansu Çiller's government in 1996, which had tried to carry on the Özal policies, did not help move matters along. The Islamist party that did come to power began by emphasizing the improvement of political relations with its Middle East neighbors rather than with Europe. When Poland, Hungary, and the Czech Republic were invited to send observers to the Inter-Governmental Conference in 1996 because their interests as potential new members would be at stake, it was noteworthy that Turkey was not invited. The limits of Europe may have been expanded eastward and northward with the collapse of the Soviet bloc, but they had already been reached in the eastern Mediterranean.

CONCLUSION

To sum up, these perennial outsiders to the process of European integration stayed outside the EC and the attempts at exchange rate stabilization within Europe throughout the most traumatic period for economic growth in the West. Their absence, or rather exclusion in the case of Turkey, did not help them confront the shock initially any better, or worse, than the countries already in the EC. Their eventual recovery from the shock and resumption of satisfactory growth rates was helped, in fact, in each case by not being part of the EC's economic structure or political process. Membership would have hindered each of the outsiders in taking the route toward recovery that each finally adopted, different as they were. It is not clear that membership would have offered any of them more attractive alternatives either.

With the Single Market initiative begun in 1985, however, the EFTA countries at least were faced with a potential threat to the continuation of their successful strategy. They responded by considering seriously the possibility of joining forces with the EC in forming an even larger Single Market, known now as the European Economic Area. When the negotiations highlighted their complete lack of negotiating power outside the political framework of the EC, the governments of Switzerland and Norway prepared applications to join in order to defend their interests in alliance with other small countries inside the EU. The Swiss electorate, however, defeated the idea of joining even the EEA in a referendum held in 1993. The Norwegian population defeated the referendum on accepting the terms of joining the EC in 1994. Just to complete this picture of each government's view of its national interests being at odds with the opinion of their electorate, we should add that Iceland's government was always opposed to the idea of EC membership despite public opinion polls that show a sizable majority of Iceland's citizen are in favor of joining. Turkey renewed its long dormant application to join the EC in 1987, and to date has received no positive response.

The policy paths of these four outsiders have never had much in common and there is less and less reason for them to converge as time goes on. The interesting question is what economic costs might be borne by these nations for the political benefits they sense are derived from staying outside the EU's institutional framework. The answer to this question will be observed with interest by the rest of Europe's nation-states, whether they are in or out of the EU. To date, the economic costs do not seem serious for any of them

Endnotes

1. Alan Milward, *The Reconstruction of Western Europe, 1945–51,* London: Metheun, 1983, p. 441.

2. Fritz Hodne, *The Norwegian Economy, 1920–1980,* New York: St. Martin's Press, 1983, pp. 144–45.

3. Milward states, " . . . it would be fair to say that most of the other members (of the OEEC) thought they [Greece and Turkey] were a thorough nuisance throughout." Milward, note 1, pp. 68–69.

4. Jean-Christian Lambelet, *L'Économie Suisse,* Paris: Economica, 1993, p. 18.

5. Union Bank of Switzerland, *The Swiss Economy, 1946–1986. Data, Facts, Analyses,* Zurich: Union Bank of Switzerland, 1987, p. 29.

6. Hodne, note 2, p. 190.

7. Walter Galenson, *A Welfare State Strikes Oil. The Norwegian Experience,* Lanham, Md.: University Press of America, 1986, p. 24.

8. Hodne, note 2, pp. 247, 258.

9. Bent Hansen, *The Political Economy of Poverty, Equity, and Growth: Egypt and Turkey,* New York: Oxford University Press (published for the World Bank), 1991, p. 358.

10. Hansen, note 9, p. 372.

11. Ibid., p. 394.

Bibliography

Economist Intelligence Unit. *Country Profile, Iceland, 1995–96.* London: Economist Intelligence Unit, 1996.

Economist Intelligence Unit. *Country Profile, Norway, 1995–96.* London: Economist Intelligence Unit, 1996.

Economist Intelligence Unit. *Country Profile, Switzerland, 1995–96.* London: Economist Intelligence Unit, 1996.

Economist Intelligence Unit. *Country Profile, Turkey. 1995–96.* London: Economist Intelligence Unit, 1996.

Economist Intelligence Unit. *Country Report, Iceland.* London: Economist Intelligence Unit, 2nd quarter, 1996.

Economist Intelligence Unit. *Country Report, Norway.* London: Economist Intelligence Unit, 2nd quarter, 1996.

Economist Intelligence Unit. *Country Report, Switzerland.* London: Economist Intelligence Unit, 2nd quarter, 1996.

Economist Intelligence Unit. *Country Report, Turkey.* London: Economist Intelligence Unit, 2nd quarter, 1996.

Galenson, Walter. *A Welfare State Strikes Oil. The Norwegian Experience*. Lanham, Md.: University Press of America, 1986.

Hansen, Bent. *The Political Economy of Poverty, Equity, and Growth: Egypt and Turkey*. New York: Oxford University Press (published for the World Bank), 1991.

Hershlag, Z. Y. *The Contemporary Turkish Economy*. London: Routledge, 1988.

Hodne, Fritz. *The Norwegian Economy, 1920–1980*. New York: St. Martin's Press, 1983.

Katzenstein, Peter J. *Capitalism in One Country? Switzerland in the International Economy*. Ithaca, N.Y.: Center for International Studies, Cornell University, 1980.

Körner, Heiko and Rasul Shams, eds. *Institutional Aspects of Economic Integration of Turkey into the European Community*. Hamburg: Verlag Weltarchiv GmbH, 1990.

Lambelet, Jean-Christian. *L'Économie Suisse*. Paris: Economica, 1993.

Nas, Tevfik f. and Mehmet Odekon, *Economics and Politics of Turkish Liberalization*. Bethlehem: Lehigh University Press, 1992.

Nelsen, Brent F., ed. *Norway and the European Community: The Political Economy of Integration*. Westport, Conn.: Praeger, 1993.

Schwock, Rene. *Switzerland and the European Common Market*. New York: Praeger, 1991.

Tschudi, Hans-Peter. "Swiss social policy since 1950," in Roger Girod, Patrick de Laubier, and Alan Gladstone, eds. *Social Policy in Western Europe and the USA, 1950–1980. An Assessment*. New York: St. Martin's Press, 1985.

Union Bank of Switzerland. *The Swiss Economy, 1946–1986. Data, Facts, Analyses*. Zurich: Union Bank of Switzerland, 1987.

CHAPTER 17

The Next Expansion:

From the Mediterranean to the Black Sea to the Baltic

Basic Facts

Country (date*)	Area	Population	GDP (1994)	Per Capita
Cyprus (7/3/90)				
Greek	5,895 km^2	602,656	$7.3 billion	$12,500
Turkish	3,355 km^2	133,980	$0.5 billion	$3,500
Malta (7/16/90)	320 km^2	369,609	$3.9 billion	$10,760
Hungary (3/31/94)	93,030 km^2	10,318,838	$58.8 billion	$5,700
Poland (4/5/94)	312,680 km^2	38,792,442	$191.1 billion	$4,920
Romania (6/22/95)	237,500 km^2	23,198,330	$64.7 billion	$2,790
Slovakia (6/27/95)	48,845 km^2	5,432,383	$32.8 billion	$6,070
Latvia (10/27/95)	64,100 km^2	2,762,899	$12.3 billion	$4,480
Estonia (11/28/95)	45,100 km^2	1,625,399	$10.4 billion	$6,460
Lithuania (12/8/95)	65,200 km^2	3,876,396	$13.5 billion	$3,500
Bulgaria (12/16/95)	110,550 km^2	8,775,198	$33.7 billion	$3,830
Czech Republic (1/23/96)	78,703 km^2	10,432,774	$76.5 billion	$7,350
Slovenia (6/10/96)	20,296 km^2	2,051,522	$16.0 billion	$8,110

*When applied for membership in EU.

Source: CIA, *World Factbook 1995,* http://www.ocdi.gov/cia/publications/95fact.

These thirteen countries have even less in common than the outsider countries considered in the previous chapter. But each has applied for membership in the European Union and each will be considered seriously as soon as the Inter-Governmental Conference ends in 1997. Most (the last ten listed) are in the process of transition from centrally planned economies under Soviet military domination and ruled by the domestic Communist party. There is no question that they want and expect to be included in the European Union and to share in the economic success exhibited in the West. There is also no question that the European Union requires them to enter if its political vision of the future of Europe is ever to be realized. But there are questions—many difficult questions—as to when, how many, and under what terms they should enter.

The situations of Cyprus and Malta are similar with respect to the European Union, but quite unlike those of the transition economies. Both are small, open economies heavily dependent on amicable trading relationships with the EU and both are strategically located athwart the heavily traveled shipping lanes of the Mediterranean. Each can easily be absorbed within the customs union and the Common Agricultural Policy. Only the per capita incomes of the Turkish part of Cyprus are sufficiently below the EU's average to warrant extensive subsidies from the structural funds. But the political problems are difficult. Any kind of representation for them on the terms currently in effect for voting in the Council and the Parliament and positions as commissioners would replicate the gross overrepresentation currently possessed by Luxembourg. Malta's population is roughly the same as Luxembourg's and Cyprus's is twice that. Moreover, Cyprus has been physically divided since Turkish military intervention in 1974 into a Turkish part in the northern one-third of the island (known, but not legally recognized by the international community, as the Turkish Republic of Northern Cyprus) and a Greek part in the southern two-thirds (legally recognized by the EU and other international organizations as the Republic of Cyprus). Peacekeeping forces of the United Nations have been in place ever since to monitor and stabilize the situation. Presumably, the EU would have to take on these delicate responsibilities if it admitted the Greek Republic of Cyprus. The responsibilities would be especially difficult given the perpetual tension between Greece and Turkey. Greece could exercise veto power on any EU decision regarding the terms of separation or of reunification. Turkey could carry out its threat to incorporate the TRNC into Turkey proper if convinced it would always remain excluded from serious consideration for EU membership. Economically, membership for Malta and Cyprus is a clearly feasible and on-course no-brainer; politically, it is a non-starter unless the poorer, smaller members of the EU willingly yield power in the new political structure of the EU that emerges from the IGC of 1996–97 and the EU takes on foreign policy obligations of the member states. Neither course is likely.

By contrast, the political motivations for including the transition economies of Central and East Europe are decisively in their favor. This is especially the case with Poland, Hungary, the Czech Republic, and Slovenia. These are the most advanced countries economically and the ones already contiguous to the current makeup of the EU. The Baltic states of Estonia, Latvia, and Lithuania cause some concern about possible frictions with Russia. (Poland and Lithuania control land access to the major Russian naval base at Kaliningrad.) The ethnic conflicts and political uncertainty of democratic institutions in Slovakia, Romania, and Bulgaria also pose some concerns. And note that none of the former Yugoslavia states embroiled in the Croatian-Muslim-Serbian conflicts is in the queue or likely to enter in the near future.

While the political calculus varies across the transition nations, the potential economic costs to the EU of each are remarkably similar in kind. Obviously, all of them qualify for structural funds, whether from the cohesion fund, the regional development funds, or the Common Agricultural Policy. Each has a very low level of per capita income currently and none is likely to reach above the 75 percent of the EU average for quite some time. Each has a much higher percentage of their population engaged in agriculture, and agricultural productivity is far below that attained in the EU. The infrastructure is in worse shape than the disgracefully backward capital stock that the West Germans discovered was characteristic of East Germany. But if the political motives are paramount for the EU and the economic motives paramount for the applicants, and the bargaining power is strictly on the side of the EU, as indicated in all the accessions to date, then accommodations can certainly be made to allow entry of all of the Central and East European countries.

Transition periods of typically five, but as long as ten, years have been arranged for some of the policies of previous entrants. Longer transition periods are certainly a plausible possibility, for these are all clearly "transition economies." Periodic reassessments would occur to determine how each country had progressed in completing the transition to a market economy on the EU model. The Common Agricultural Policy is already moving toward an income supplement scheme rather than price support policy, and the supplements for the new entrants could be geared to previous levels of income in each country, rather than to the EU average. Moreover, the total of subsidies is limited to 50 percent of the budget in any case. Regional funds are predicated on matching funds from the national government of the recipient. However, a reassessment of the cohesion funds would be necessary. The new countries will certainly lower the average per capita income of the EU, so that Ireland, for example, would no longer qualify for sharing in the cohesion fund. And the share of the remaining recipients currently would fall sharply. So long as each new entrant is required to have the unanimous approval of all the existing members, it will be increasingly difficult politically for the EU to expand its membership. So the altered political structure of the EU's institutions that emerges from the IGC of 1996–97 will be critical in determining the speed and terms of accession for the current group of applicants.

MALTA AND CYPRUS

Malta said goodbye to a long-standing British naval base in 1979 and began to pursue a policy of neutrality, which it enshrined in its constitution in 1987. But like Austria, Malta did not feel that its neutral status prohibited it from joining the EU after the collapse of the Soviet Union. In July 1990 it applied for membership in the EU, and this will be considered seriously by the EU starting in 1997. Elections in 1996, however, led to a withdrawal of its application as the opposition party, the Malta Labour party, came to power. On the economic side, however, Malta continues to abolish tariffs and to enjoy tariff-free access to the

EU. Its foreign trade, both for exports and imports, is made up mostly of machinery and transport equipment as well as manufactures and semimanufactures. Both exports and imports are mainly with Italy, with Germany and the United Kingdom a distant second and third place in importance. Since 1989, the central bank has pegged its currency, the Maltese lira, to a basket of currencies made up of the dollar, the pound sterling; and the ECU. The economy has shown strong growth since the mid-1980s, which has continued into the mid-1990s despite an appreciation of the Maltese lira against the Italian lira.

Cyprus signed an Association Agreement with the EU in 1973, which was intended to lead to a full customs union over a period of ten years. But the division of the island in 1974 postponed this indefinitely. Again, in May 1987, another agreement was signed for a customs union to be achieved in two stages, the first one lasting ten years and the second for four or five years. In 1990, the Republic of Cyprus applied for full membership, introduced a value-added tax, and pegged the Cyprus pound to the ECU. The European Commission has approved the entry of Cyprus, subject only to concern over determining the future of the Turkish-occupied part of the island. The Mediterranean members of the EU support entry promptly, whereas the United Kingdom and Germany prefer to see the status of the Turkish part settled before Greek Cyprus enters. One plausible scenario, based strictly on economic self-interest, would provide for reunification of the island with due compensation to property owners previously displaced and serious accession negotiations for Turkey. The impoverished Turkish Cypriots would benefit from access to the labor market in Greek Cyprus, and Turkey would benefit from access to the labor market of the EU. Needless to say, this economically rational scenario is quite vulnerable to political obstacles that can, and have been, raised in Cyprus, Greece, and Turkey.

Since the mid-1980s, the Cyprus economy has enjoyed rates of growth well above the EU average. However, keeping the Cyprus pound pegged to the appreciating ECU has gradually slowed growth in the 1990s. The trade patterns are strongly oriented to the EU, which takes 40 percent of its exports, mainly light manufactures, and provides over 50 percent of its imports, mostly intermediate inputs for manufacturing, but also capital and consumer goods. The Arab countries of the mid-East are an import-export market as well, but account for less than 5 percent of imports. In recent years, the Republic of Cyprus has tried to replace Lebanon as a regional financial center. Toward this end it has increasingly deregulated the financial sector to allow interest rates to vary and to permit capital movements in and out of the country. Entrepreneurs from the states of the former Soviet Union are among the first wave of foreign businesses to respond to this initiative. As a result of the influx of foreign capital in response to these initiatives, the Cyprus pound has tended to strengthen even relative to the ECU. This has dampened somewhat the traditional sources of export earnings, especially tourism. If the political obstacles to entry are cleared, the economic situation will be mutually beneficial for Cyprus and the EU.

TRANSITION ECONOMIES

It is natural to deal with the transition economies in terms of how advanced they are in the process of switching over from the typically inefficient and nearly self-sufficient centrally planned economy under Soviet domination and achieving a self-sustaining process toward market-driven allocations of resources and effort. This is measured by determining, first, whether the economy has regained its pretransition level of total production and employment and is beginning to enjoy the high "catch-up" rates of growth expected of low-income countries; second, whether it has reduced the rate of inflation to levels that are manageable by Western standards of fiscal and monetary policy; and third, whether the government is able to maintain a balanced budget by reducing the extent of subsidies to state enterprises and raising taxes on sales revenue and income generated in market activity. These measures of performance show how well a given transition economy has progressed toward reaping the potential fruits of liberalization, privatization, and macroeconomic stabilization. Consensus was quickly reached by all Western economists that these three processes had each to be carried out for a command economy to turn itself into a market economy. However, they disagreed on the proper pace and sequence of these processes. This was partly because of domestic political factors, which varied in each country, and partly due to the natural fractiousness of economists. But mostly it was due to the necessary uncertainty over how people in the countries affected would react to each policy change. From previous experiences in the West when the command economies imposed during both World Wars I and II were dismantled and the prewar market economy reinstated, a minimum transition period of five years could have been predicted. Given that the command economies of East and Central Europe had become embedded for fifty years and that there had been only fleeting experience with a market economy before World War II for most of them, the transition period for them might reasonably be expected to last decades.

THE VISEGRAD FOUR: POLAND, HUNGARY, CZECH REPUBLIC, AND THE SLOVAK REPUBLIC

These four countries began the transition process earliest, Poland in the political sphere and Hungary in the economic sphere, while still under Soviet hegemony. Beginning in 1989, each moved to complete its political independence and to begin the process of economic transformation. The strategies decided on by each of the three (the Czech Republic and the Slovak Republic were still united as the Republic of Czechoslovakia in 1989) were quite different in both speed and sequence. Poland began a "Big Bang" strategy, simultaneously removing price controls, putting up state enterprises for sale to private investors (but retaining managerial control with Polish citizens), and moving government finances toward Western models of taxation and spending. Hungary had already begun some price liberalization, which it continued, but its first priority was privatization of large state enterprises, and foreign investors were actively solicited. Gradual reform of state finances was to be financed by the proceeds of privatization. Czechoslovakia was the slowest of all to proceed on privatization, deliberating between the equitable privatization sought by the Czech half of the country and the maintenance of employment in the large military production plants sought by the Slovaks. So it proceeded with liberalization of prices, worked then at macroeconomic stabilization, and only after three years began serious privatization.

Figures 17.1 to 17.3 show the dimensions of the transition shock for the Visegrad Four in terms of the drop in the level of measured real GDP from 1989, inflation rates from 1990, and unemployment rates. Some analysts feel the GDP figures exaggerate the drop in actual output because they miss the increased use of the informal market that had to arise during the collapse of planned distribution systems. But as the informal market avoids taxation as well as measurement, the figures do reflect accurately the problems facing the governments of the transition economies. It is clear that Poland's output fell soonest and fastest, but also began to recover soonest. Polish output began to rise after 1991, while the output of the other three continued to fall until 1993. Moreover, their loss of measured output was even greater than that for Poland. By 1995, Polish output had regained its 1989 level and was growing faster than any of the other transition economies. But both the Czech and Slovak Republics

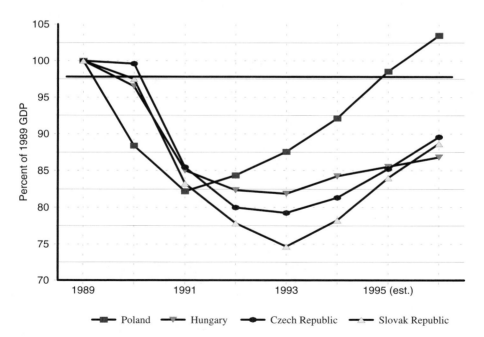

Figure 17.1. GDP in Transition, Poland, Hungary, Czech and Slovak Republics.
Source: European Bank for Reconstruction and Development, *Transition Report 1996.* London: EBRD, 1996.

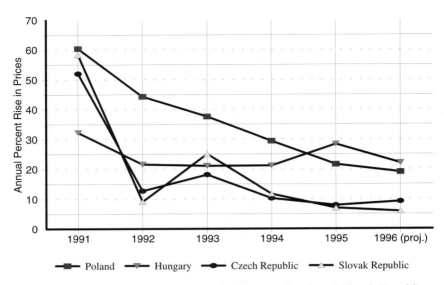

Figure 17.2. Inflation in Transition, Poland, Hungary, Czech and Slovak Republics.

were catching up fast. Only Hungary seemed to be stalling out. Observers have attributed these differences in recovery patterns precisely to the differences in the transition strategies used by each country.

Poland's experience was chaotic economically and disheartening politically. But the experience of the other transition economies has been worse. This observation has led to a consensus among IMF and World Bank officials that each transition is painful, so it is best to make it as short as possible. In other words, imitate the Polish strategy. The political possibility to begin reform started in September 1989, when the Solidarity party took power while inflation was soaring as the government printed more and more money to cover its expenses. Immediately banking reform began as the "monobank," the National Bank of Poland, was converted to a Western-style central bank and its numerous branches throughout the country were privatized. This enabled the shock treatment to begin in January 1990, with deflationary measures decreed by the finance minister Lescek Balcerowitz. While maintaining liberalization of prices and removal of trade barriers, he attempted to reduce inflation by defending a nominal exchange rate that was subject to the influence of both trade flows and capital movements. This required reducing government expenditures, which undermined his political support. By July 1990, a newly elected government agreed on the first stages of privatization, which basically privatized immediately small and medium-sized state enterprises. But it put off the difficult problems of dealing with large state enterprises such as coal mines, steel mills, and shipyards. Government finances could not really be brought under control until these state enterprises were sold off. Investors, whether foreign or domestic, were unwilling to pay much for state enterprises. The investors lacked cost

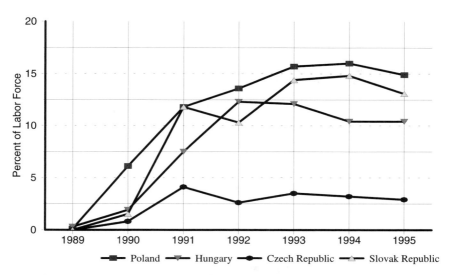

Figure 17.3. Unemployment in Transition, Poland, Hungary, Czech and Slovak Republics.

accounting records to evaluate the past operations and the existing capital stock and equipment, and they were uncertain about the future market potential. Wealthy foreign investors might have been willing to risk a small part of their capital just to establish a position in the Polish economy. But two factors discouraged even risk-takers. One was Poland's reluctance to cede managerial control over large enterprises to foreigners. Another was its large stock of existing foreign debt owed to Western governments and financial institutions. To give these prior creditors first claim on foreign reserves, Poland had to maintain strict capital controls. So foreign investors would not be able to repatriate their funds once they were invested in Poland. Moreover, the Polish currency, the zloty, was depreciating rapidly due to the high rate of inflation, so foreign investors faced additional risks of losing badly on the exchange rate even if they did find a way to repatriate earnings. Without privatization proceeds and burdened by large amounts of foreign debt, the Polish government had to resort to seigniorage (the proceeds from creating new supplies of money) to cover its expenses. This created a vicious circle of rising inflation, which exacerbated the problem of collecting taxes (the longer people delayed paying, the lower the real burden to them and the less use to the government). It also increased the uncertainty facing potential investors in privatized state enterprises.

Inflation soared, unemployment rose, and total output fell sharply. Political unrest manifested itself in a proliferation of small parties. These, in turn, created political gridlock in the newly formed parliament, which only exacerbated the economic problems. Nevertheless, the political momentum created by the Solidarity party's long years of preparation for overthrowing Communist rule carried the reforms forward. A deep recession occurred, worsened in 1991 by the collapse of the Comecon trading arrangements with the other Central and Eastern European countries. Russia also began charging all its trading partners in hard currency at world market prices, which drove up sharply the costs of fuel, especially natural gas. The one bright spot for Poland in 1991 was the debt forgiveness arranged by Western governments and international agencies. These so-called Paris Club arrangements deferred repayment until 2001, when repayment will be required to make up for lost interest. These also set the stage for the London Club in 1994 to reschedule debts owed to private banks. These agreements were important to allow new capital imports to occur without fear of being displaced by the prior commitments to repay previous debts incurred under the Communist regime.

Recovery was taking place, meanwhile, without great assistance from the European Union. Concerned about excess capacity itself in textiles, steel, coal, and shipbuilding, not to mention agricultural products, the EU maintained strict quotas against the very goods in which Poland had specialized while it was in Comecon. Other export goods were sought by Polish and Western entrepreneurs to exploit the trade opportunities that remained. Not too surprisingly, fresh elections in September 1993 brought the reformed Communists back to power in the parliament. Moreover, a former Communist, Aleksander Kwasniewski, defeated the Solidarity icon, Lech Walesa, as president in November 1995. Despite these apparent political setbacks to the process of reform, the economic transition continued apace. More and more of the economy steadily went to the private sector, as small and medium-sized enterprises flourished and the large state enterprises largely languished.

In 1994, the EU finally made a formal Europe Agreement with Poland that provided gradual relaxation of import quotas against Polish products. This replaced the five-year Trade and Economic Cooperation Agreement signed between the EC and Poland in December 1989. While including a clause pledging reciprocal Most Favored Nation treatment to each other, this first agreement was nonpreferential and maintained extensive quantitative restrictions against imports from Poland, which were to be gradually abolished by 1994. However, in January 1990, the EU suspended all nonspecific quantitative restrictions and liberalized all specific quantitative restrictions, exception made for Portugal and Spain to protect their textile and footwear industries. In October 1991, the European Coal and Steel Community signed a protocol on coal and steel products, which increased imports of crude steel and coal from Poland in exchange for exports of finished steel products from the ECSC. It also provided for aid to help modernize Polish coal and steel works. The Europe Agreement was signed in December 1991, ratified by the Polish Parliament in July 1992, the European Parliament in September 1992, and finally by the twelve member state parliaments in December 1993. So it entered into force in February 1994, which shows some of the political frictions that hamper the economic integration of the transition economies into Western Europe.

Fortunately for the continued economic recovery of Poland, the EU instituted the trade provisions of the Europe Agreement by means of an Interim Agreement starting in March 1992. This provided for a free trade area to be established between the EU and Poland over a period of ten years, while all quantitative restrictions are to be abolished, and both parties pledged not to introduce new barriers to trade. Poland was allowed to maintain some degree of tariff protection for its newly established manufacturing firms. By 1991, the EU had become Poland's largest trading partner, and both exports and imports have continued to grow rapidly. In 1995, the EU took over 70 percent of Poland's exports, mainly agricultural products and raw materials or semifinished goods, and provided 64 percent of its imports, mainly manufactured goods and capital equipment. Poland has also increased again its exports of machinery and finished manufactures to the East. By 1994, Polish growth was being driven mainly by increases in exports and investment, rather than increases in consumption.

This was a healthy sign, which augured well for its continued convergence to a Western-style market economy. Inflation continued to be high, however, by western standards, falling from 40 percent in 1993 to 30 percent in 1994, 22 percent in 1995 and ended at under 20 percent in 1996. Unemployment, also high by Western standards, was also falling gradually, from 16 percent in 1994 to 15 percent and 14 percent in 1995 and 1996. And it appeared that internal political resistance to reform had disappeared. A telling example of this was the results of the referendum on privatization that then President Walesa ordered in February 1996, hoping to show public dissatisfaction with the privatization schemes voted in by the leftist Parliament. On the contrary, voters were overwhelmingly in favor of rapid privatization, using the proceeds to make up previous freezes in pensions and public service wages and to support new pension funds. The only objection they had was to allowing the new National Investment Funds to bid on more state enterprises than originally planned. Moreover, the new president retained as minister of finance the outspoken Western-style economist, Grzegorz Kolodko. He pressed for continued reduction of tariffs and greater control over inflationary pressures by the central bank sterilizing the capital inflows, which were actually driving up the value of the zloty on the foreign exchanges. In sum, the economic confusion created by the multiplicity of changes initiated in Poland from September 1989 to July 1990 seems to have had the felicitous effect of causing enough political confusion that no effective resistance to reform could be mounted. Certainly by 1994 and probably by 1992, enough promise of good things to come from closer relations with the EU had convinced a working majority of the Polish electorate to continue the course.

Hungary's experience was perhaps more rapid in the initial stages of reform, based on a longer period of introducing price liberalization under the Communist regime and promoting exports to the West. This experience also allowed Hungary to encourage rapid privatization of its state enterprises, principally by offering excellent terms to foreign investors. As a result Hungary quickly garnered more foreign investment than any other transition economy. Unfortunately for its further progress, many of the state enterprises were simply handed over to the politically savvy apparatchiks who managed them. This entrenched their political influence in the government. Exercising political influence proved to be their comparative advantage compared with modernizing their plants and marketing their products. Off to a promising start, with only moderate rates of inflation and unemployment that peaked around 14 percent at the end of 1992, Hungary's economic decline nevertheless continued through 1993. Even when things began to pick up in 1994, when it was treated by the EU on the same basis as Poland, growth turned out to be disappointingly low. The explanation lies partly in the relatively poor performance of exports, but mainly in the failure of the privatized state enterprises to modernize.

Instead, they have continued to press successfully for subsidies from the state. The government, in turn, has run a much higher budget deficit than the other three members of the Visegrad Four, running between 7 and 8 percent of GDP from 1994 to 1996. Consequently, inflation has begun to rise again, actually surpassing that of Poland by late 1995. The decline in unemployment rates also ceased in 1995 and threatened to start rising again. Moreover, the government, dominated by former members of the Communist party, maintained high levels of spending on health and social security. Not only did this make it difficult to bring down the ratio of the government's deficit to GDP, it increased demand for imports. In 1993 and 1994, Hungary was running substantial deficits on current account in addition to deficits in the public sector. The IMF, as a result, held up disbursement of promised loans, which slowed down the rate of foreign investment by private parties as well. The transition process had clearly begun to stall out.

Encouraging signs, however, were seen in 1995 as the political situation began to stabilize and consensus emerged that it made sense to follow the Polish example. The government's economic policy now focused on macroeconomic stabilization, reducing the government deficit, and controlling the rate of devaluation of the currency, the forint. In 1995 it also renewed privatization of large state enterprises, especially telecommunications and natural gas distribution networks. Growth slowed and inflation remained stubbornly high, but foreign direct investment resumed on a large scale, showing that investors had renewed confidence in the economic strategy being followed.

By 1996, Hungary had greatly expanded and redirected its foreign trade so that about two-thirds of both exports and imports were with the EU. Hungary's trade relations with the EU were actually formalized a year earlier than Poland's. A ten-year Trade and Economic Cooperation Agreement was signed in September 1988, one year before that with Poland. Since then, however, the two countries have been treated equally with the establishment of the PHARE program (Poland and Hungary: Aid for Reconstruction of the Economy) at the end of 1989. Initially designed for just Poland and Hungary to give them grants and technical assistance for specific modernization projects, PHARE has since widened its scope to include all of the Central and East European countries. Through 1995, PHARE had distributed nearly 5.5 billion ECU to the eleven partner countries. This made it the largest grant assistance program for these transition economies. In 1993, the EU decided to offer all these countries Europe agreements with the intent of preparing them for eventual membership. Each project funded by PHARE is supposed to help the recipient cope with the competitive pressure and market forces it will encounter once it is a full member. Poland and Hungary have received the most funds to date, but Romania is a close third.

The *Czech* and *Slovak Republics* enjoyed the most peaceful transition from Communism during the justly celebrated Prague Spring of 1990. Led by the charismatic idealist and former playwright, Vaclav Havel, Czechoslovakia seemed the country most likely to maintain the political stability necessary to carry out the wrenching transition from plan to market without violence. It had no foreign debt, unlike Poland, and it had begun limited liberalization of prices and encouragement of private plots following the Hungarian example. Moreover, it had a skilled labor force and a reputation for high quality manufactures. But then Czechoslovakia was hit by two shocks. First, in 1991 it had to deal, like the rest of the Central and East European countries, with the sudden rise in costs of imports from the Soviet Union as it began charging world market prices in hard currency to all its customers. Second, it found increasing conflict between the Czechs and the Slovaks, which created a political gridlock over the course of privatization and the sequence of reforms. The Czechs enthusiastically endorsed privatization of small and medium-sized enterprises, while the Slovaks were concerned about maintaining employment in the large arms factories located in the eastern, Slovakian, part of Czechoslovakia. Unlike the tragic case of Yugoslavia, however, the two parts of the country agreed to separate peaceably at the end of 1992. However, the secondary transition costs of creating separate currencies and border controls for trade created a further setback economically in 1993.

By 1994, however, the Czech Republic was able to continue privatization of large enterprises, employing a unique two-tier voucher scheme. A limited number of investment trusts were allowed to bid on the state enterprises to be auctioned off. The trusts, in turn, were obligated to sell shares to Czech citizens in return for the vouchers that were distributed to them. The vouchers would then be used to pay for the state enterprises, each trust bidding for the set of enterprises it thought would make a complementary set of investments for its principals. Each Czech then had the opportunity to buy shares in the trust especially interested in his or her place of employment or to diversify across other possibilities. And the trusts competed with each other to offer the best prices they felt possible to the voucher holders. The Slovaks, by contrast, preferred to give preference to the employees at the state enterprises, who could then be assured of maintaining their place of employment. The disadvantage of the Czech scheme was the delay in privatization caused by the time required to distribute the vouchers, authorize the trusts, and explain the unusual scheme to the population to gain their support. The disadvantage of the Slovak scheme was the lack of clear market incentives to increase efficiency at obsolete plants.

Surprisingly, the two countries have had very similar economic outcomes even after separation. Both have enviably low rates of inflation and of recorded unemployment, and similarly low rates of economic growth relative to Poland. But the Czech Republic is much more highly privatized than the Slovak Republic and is considered the leading transition economy in this sense. The only concern is a very large trade deficit in 1994 and 1995, but this is the necessary counterpart of its successful privatization, which has drawn in increasing flows of foreign portfolio and direct investment. Its application for membership in the EU is considered very favorably by the EU and was late in arriving due to some doubts by the Czech prime minister Vaclav Klaus over the federalist tendencies of the EU since Maastricht. Klaus' doubts, however, are not shared by the Czech population, who have expressed overwhelming support in favor of joining. The Slovak Republic is a surprising economic success, in part by restoring its export markets at least partially to the former Soviet Union. Its prime minister since December 1994, Vladimir Meciar, however, has caused concern in the West by his reversion to Soviet-style exercise of leadership. He was suspected of arranging a bizarre incident, which resulted in the kidnapping of the son of President Michal Kovac and spiriting him to Austria where he could be arrested on charges of fraud. Whatever his role in that escapade, he has pushed through a law that allows him to exercise police-state powers incompatible with a democratic state. As a result, he has jeopardized Slovakia's chances for early entrance into the EU.

THE BALTIC STATES: ESTONIA, LATVIA, AND LITHUANIA

These three tiny states have little in common save their small size, location on the Baltic Sea, and intense desire to be rid of the Russians and to join the EU. Given their small size, their poverty, and their remoteness, however, the EU was not enthusiastic about extending open arms to them. It was not until 1993 that the PHARE program described above under Hungary was extended to the Baltic States. But the accession of Finland and Sweden in 1995 has added two more vigorous voices in favor of accepting them and they have been allowed to join the queue. All three have much in common from an economic point of view, but the differences in economic policy pursued by each have taught some interesting lessons about the economics of transition.

The modern Baltic States came into existence as independent nations only after World War I, each establishing a separate constitution and currency in 1922. They were ruthlessly occupied by Nazi forces during World War II and equally ruthlessly reoccupied by the Soviet Union, which incorporated each of them as Soviet Socialist Republics. While this act was never formally recognized by the Western powers, nothing was ever done about it either. So all three became heavily industrialized, with their smallholder agriculture transformed into huge collective farms and their cities inhabited by a large number of Russians. Moreover, as small economies with large industrial plants and collective farms, up to 70 percent of their output was exported, almost all to the Soviet Union. In return, almost all of their imports—fuel, raw materials, and intermediate goods—came from the Soviet Union. In common with the rest of the Soviet Union, their economies faltered at the end of the 1980s. Unlike the other applicants to the EU, however, their independence was not recognized by the Soviet Union until September 1991, after the failed coup attempt against then President Gorbachev. Consequently, their attempts to form a coherent transition policy were stymied until then. Moreover, the economic collapse of the Soviet Union cut off both the markets for their exports and the sources for their imports. Finally, the Russian insistence on world prices in convertible currencies for deliveries of natural gas by Gazprom made their most vital import very expensive. As a result, their collapse in total output, explosion of inflation, and rise in unemployment was by far the worst for any of the transition economies considered here. (Figures 17.4 to 17.6)

Faced with these catastrophic events in common, each Baltic state pursued its own course of action in both the political and economic spheres. From Estonia in the north, close to Western markets in Finland, to Lithuania in the south abutted by Belarus and the Russian naval base at Kaliningrad, the policies ran from more market oriented to more plan oriented. The differences are captured most succinctly in the exchange rate regime chosen by each. Estonia was the first to abandon the Russian ruble and establish its own currency in June 1992, the kroon (EEK), which it had been called before World War II. It was then set by law at a fixed exchange rate of 8 EEK per 1 DM. It has been able to maintain this rate (at least through August 1996) because its supply of kroon is governed by a currency board, rather than by a central bank. The currency board is restricted by law to issue kroon only in exchange for gold or foreign exchange that is convertible into deutsche marks. Moreover, it began its initial issue based on a large amount of gold reclaimed from West European central banks where it had been deposited when World War II broke out. Finally, Estonia deliberately undervalued the kroon at 8 EEK to 1 DM in order to promote exports to the West. (Recall that the West European countries all tried to overvalue their currencies after World War II to increase their imports!) Given that the nominal exchange rate cannot be altered, the real exchange rate can only

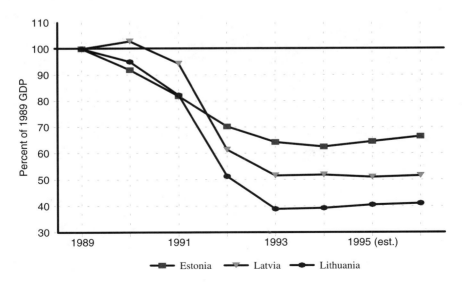

Figure 17.4. GDP in Transition, Estonia Latvia, and Lithuania.

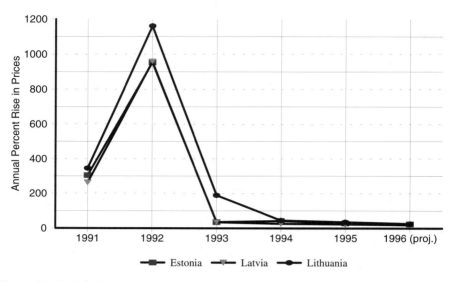

Figure 17.5. Inflation in Transition, Estonia, Latfvia, and Lithuania.

fall by Estonia running lower rates of inflation than in Germany, which has been difficult to do.

Latvia was the second country to drop the ruble as the domestic medium of exchange. First it introduced a transition currency, called the Latvia ruble (rublis), in May 1992. This was pegged initially to the Russian ruble, but given Russia's highly inflationary monetary policy at the time Latvia was quickly flooded with rapidly depreciating Russian rubles. So the Latvian rublis was floated, made legal tender, and rapidly strengthened relative to the Russian ruble until the national currency, the lat (also the name of the pre-World War II currency), was introduced in May 1993. Latvia chose to regulate the supply of currency with an independent central bank, initially headed by a strongly antiinflationary governor, rather than using a currency board. Part of the reason was that it did not have nearly as much gold to be repatriated, so some other means of building up foreign reserves was required. A strong central bank able to maintain high interest rates to attract foreign reserves and committed to fixed targets for the supply of money it will create can have the same restrictive effect on the supply of money as a currency board. But in addition it can take proactive steps to increase the supply of foreign reserves, which a currency board cannot. Finally, like Estonia, Latvia, while floating its currency, tried to keep it undervalued. This policy was formalized in February 1994 when it de facto pegged the lat to the Special Drawing Right (SDR) of the IMF at 0.8 lat to 1 SDR. This is a basket currency similar to the ECU, but with the dollar, yen, and several other non-European currencies weighted in. As with the Estonia kroon, the Latvian lat was undervalued at this rate, which it maintained at least until mid-August 1996. But as the SDR has depreciated relative to the deutsche mark, so inflation in Latvia has been lower than in Estonia from 1993 to 1996.

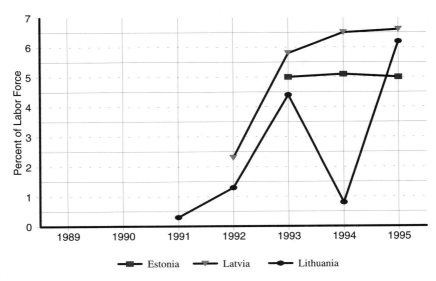

Figure 17.6. Unemployment in Transition, Estonia, Latvia, and Lithuania.

Lithuania was the last country to stabilize its currency and to bring inflation under control. It had a weak central bank, which was forced to accommodate the financing demands of a strong government, relatively stable compared with that of either Estonia or Latvia, until April 1994. So it didn't break with the Russian ruble until October 1992, when it introduced the talonas as a transition currency, which was allowed to float in the foreign exchange markets. By summer 1993, Lithuania had regained 5.8 tons of gold from Western banks where it had been placed at the outbreak of World War II and had accumulated another $200 million of hard currency reserves. It then introduced the lit (again, the same name as the interwar currency), and tried to peg it to the dollar, again undervaluing it deliberately. However, the weak central bank had little control over the money supply and the lit quickly appreciated, but in terms of the nominal exchange rate rather than more rapid rates of inflation. So in April 1994, Lithuania finally caught on and introduced a currency board modeled on Estonia's successful example. It pegged the lit to the dollar, which had been depreciating against both the deutsche mark and the Special Drawing Right, at 4 lit to $1.00.

Pegging one's currency to that of one's major trading partners is a sensible policy for a small, open economy, as discussed in the chapter on the European Monetary System. Unfortunately, a sensible monetary policy, even when combined with a sound fiscal policy as it has been in the Baltic States, is not sufficient for a smooth transition from plan to market. All three states were hit by serious bank failures, first Estonia in 1993 and then Latvia in 1995 and Lithuania at the end of 1995. Estonia let the shareholders and depositors bear the full brunt of the losses for its failed banks. Counter to fears that this might lead to a systemic shock drying up all sources of credit in the country, this "let the weak fail" policy actually reassured depositors in those banks that remained open. While Estonia's transition was delayed, its recovery soon outstripped that of either Latvia or Lithuania. At the other extreme, Lithuania seemed committed to bailing out its failed banks, at least to some extent. The continued uncertainties over the degree of fraud among its banks and the extent of bad loans outstanding have prolonged Lithuania's drop in GDP. All three countries need to supplement their financial sector with active capital markets, trading both stocks and bonds in privatized state enterprises, and each is moving in that direction.

The EU signed its standard Trade and Economic Cooperation Agreements with all three Baltic republics on May 11, 1992, and they entered into force on February 1, 1993, for Latvia and Lithuania and on March 1, 1993, for Estonia. The one-month delay for Estonia was done at the request of the European Parliament in order to display its displeasure at Estonia's behavior toward the Russian minority. The agreements were expanded to speed up the reduction of EU tariffs against their exports with free trade agreements that began in January 1995. Then on June 12, 1995, Europe Agreements were signed with all three, which will put them on course for eventual accession—when they are fully ratified (not yet by July 1996). In 1993 a fisheries agreement was signed with Latvia, with agreements to follow with Estonia and Lithuania. However, even by 1996 Latvia was having disputes with both Estonia and Lithuania over the proper division of fishing rights in the Baltic. In 1991 all three received some assistance from the EU under the program designed for the former Soviet Union, and since January 1992, all three have received continued aid from the PHARE facilities. In addition, occasional humanitarian aid as well as balance-of-payments support have been granted, not to mention commitments by the European Bank for Reconstruction and Development and the G24. All told, the EU had granted and committed well over $1 billion toward aid for the three Baltic states by the end of 1993 to facilitate their transition from being part of the Soviet Union to becoming part of Western Europe once again. By 1996, trade of all three had shifted in favor of the West, with the EU taking over 50 percent of exports from each and accounting for over 50 percent of imports. Nevertheless, for each state, Russia remained the single largest trading partner, both as a market for exports and as a source of imports.

In terms of both political and economic criteria, Estonia seems well on track toward entry into the EU, while Lithuania is the laggard and Latvia falls somewhere in between. The economic indicators of output, inflation rates, and unemployment are all consistent with this assessment. It is interesting and possibly meaningful that Estonia's political leadership has been the weakest and most divisive, reflecting in part the diversity of the country's population, while its economic transformation has been the strongest and most consistent. By contrast, Lithuania's political governance has been the strongest (and possibly most corrupt), reflecting a relatively homogeneous population after the withdrawal of Russian troops. However, its economic course has been weak and vacillating.

THE REMAINING THREE: BULGARIA, ROMANIA, AND SLOVENIA

These three applicants represent not only distinct transition policies but particular challenges to the EU. As independent states, each suffered immediately from the breakup of Communist-ruled planned economies in 1989. So, unlike the Baltic States, but similar to the Visegrad Four, their output began to drop immediately after 1989, inflation soared and unmployment rose. (Figures 17.7 to 17.9) True, Slovenia's output began to recover after 1992, and by 1996 it seemed well on its way to recovering pretransition levels. However, this was a full year after Poland's recovery began. Slovenia's turnaround was delayed by the confusion created by the dissolution of Yugoslavia in 1991 and then the military conflicts that arose. By 1992, Slovenia had successfully removed itself from the arenas of conflict in Croatia and Bosnia-Herzegovina as well as from the effects of the embargo on trade with the newly declared Republic of Serbia and Montenegro. Recovery could then begin. Bulgaria and Romania, by contrast, continued to decline until 1993, and even then the recovery process appeared weak through 1996. Moreover, the cumulative fall in their output was greater than that for either Hungary or Czechoslovakia. Caught between the military conflict in the former Yugoslavia and the confusion over access rights to the Black Sea, as well as embroiled in their own internal ethnic conflicts with minorities, these two countries appear to have a long and arduous transition path before them.

Slovenia, as part of the former Yugoslavia, has the longest economic relationship with the EU. As early as 1970, the EC signed a limited trade agreement with Yugoslavia and a full-fledged Trade and Cooperation Agreement in 1980.

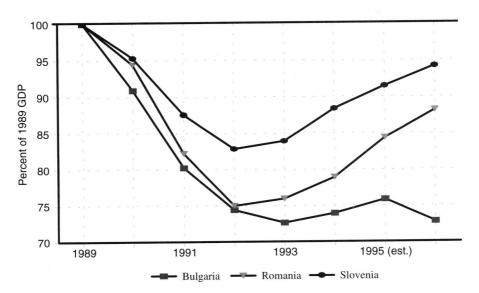

Figure 17.7. GDP in Transition, Bulgaria, Romania, and Slovenia.

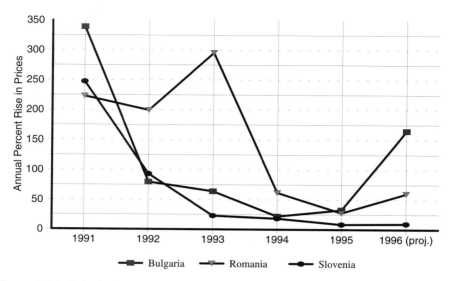

Figure 17.8. Inflation in Transition, Bulgaria, Romania, and Slovenia.

Even earlier, individual member states such as France, Belgium, and Germany had signed guest worker agreements with Yugoslavia in the 1960s. All of these, however, were suspended in 1974, never to be resumed. Once the military conflict broke out (Slovenia fought off an assault by Yugoslav forces in June-July 1991), the EC suspended the trade agreement in November 1991. But this was an excuse simply to exclude Serbia and Montenegro, as the NATO powers agreed to an embargo against Serbia. Trade relations with Croatia, Macedonia, Bosnia-Herzegovina, and Slovenia were continued, but only Slovenia was formally recognized as a partner state. This occurred in January 1992 and since then only Slovenia has been party to the Trade and Cooperation Agreement, which explicitly stated that a Europe Agreement would be forthcoming. This was initialed in June 1995, but implementation was delayed due to conflicts over property claims with Italy.

In October 1991, Slovenia formally declared its independence and issued its own currency, the tolar. Initially, the tolar depreciated rapidly, but by 1993 it was depreciating only gradually relative to the deutsche mark and the dollar. This reflected sharp drops in inflation rates, which by 1996 were in single digits. Both the trade balance and the general government fiscal balance were slightly in deficit, but these were very healthy even by comparison with those of the EU member states, much less by comparison with those of the other transition economies. It helped, no doubt, that recognition by the EU and acceptance into the major international organizations quickly followed after independence. Almost immediately in 1992, Slovenia's foreign trade doubled, mostly with the EU, which in 1994 accounted for roughly 60 percent of Slovenia's exports and imports. Trade with the rest of the Eastern bloc was minimal. By the time Slovenia

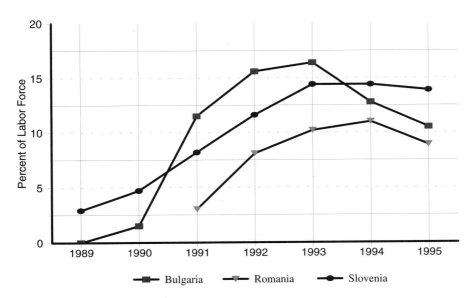

Figure 17.9. Unemployment in Transition, Bulgaria, Romania, and Slovenia.

formally applied for membership in the EU (June 1996), it was clear that its economic orientation was firmly toward the west and north.

Bulgaria lies at the other extreme of transition paths. Dominated by the ex-Communists and uncertain over its orientation as well as its transition strategy, Bulgaria has floundered in the meshes of its planned economy. Its plan was among the last to be instituted in the Eastern bloc and it may be the last to be dissipated. In common with the Baltic States, Bulgaria's plan starting in the 1970s focused on building up a strong, specialized industrial base and providing labor released from the agriculture sector by collectivizing farms. Up to the mid 1980s, Bulgaria was considered one of the success stories of Soviet-style economic development as its industrial output soared and urbanization took off. In common with the rest of the Soviet bloc, however, output leveled off in the late 1980s leading up to the final collapse in 1989.

Unlike the other countries, Bulgaria had no public consensus on how to proceed out of the plan. Restoring property rights to the previous smallholders in agriculture after the collapse of Communism proved time consuming, to say the least. Given the uncertainty over access to the land, agricultural output dropped. Worse, similar disputes occurred in the industrial sector, further delaying privatization. In fact, only by the end of 1995 had Bulgaria finally settled on a privatization scheme, which was a blend of the Czech two-stage and the Russian one-stage coupon disbursements and subsequent auctions. But it was dubious how well this would be carried out, given past internal disputes. Indeed, by the summer of 1996, the Bulgarian lev had depreciated once again by half. The immediate source of problems was that the central bank tried to bail out the failed Vitosha Bank for Agricultural Credit and then became involved as well with the First Private Bank, the largest private bank in the country. A weak central bank, apparently more interested in bailing out overextended banks than in regulating them, was both cause and effect of Bulgaria's lack of political will for undertaking the transition. The collapse of the government that followed in 1997 may allow it to get back on course.

Nevertheless, Bulgaria and Romania both had signed Europe Agreements with the EU in 1993, which had taken effect by February 1995, well ahead of those of the Baltic States. By 1994, Bulgaria's trade was predominantly with the OECD countries, with nearly 40 percent of both exports and imports occurring with the EU. Trade with Russia was still important, but mainly on the import side for fuel and raw materials. As one of Bulgaria's designated industrial products within the former Soviet Union had been inferior copies of Western personal computers, this market was lost entirely as trade with the West opened up. The other major industry, small arms, was hampered by the arms embargo against former Yugoslavia, which it had to agree to in order to maintain relations with the EU.

Romania applied for membership in 1995 shortly after its Europe Agreement with the EU had come into force (February 1995). But the trade terms of the Europe Agreement already took effect in May 1993. That is also the year that Romania's GDP began to recover, albeit accompanied by a fresh spurt in inflation. While the EU accounted for half of Romania's exports and imports by 1994, its foreign trade overall had not grown as rapidly as in the other transition countries. Part of this was due to historical legacy, part to the slow pace of transition.

Communist control of Romania began in 1947, but Soviet troops were expelled from the country in 1959. But the unique characteristics of Romania began with the assumption of power in 1967 of Nicolae Ceaușescu. This egomaniac and dictator managed to pursue a Soviet-style development strategy that was more Soviet than the Soviets. Not only did he insist on building up an industrial base consisting of very large scale plants, but he also attempted to achieve self-sufficiency, even avoiding trade with the rest of the Soviet bloc as much as possible. His idiosyncratic economic policy was tolerated by the Soviets since the army was kept relatively weak and Romanians paid full price for their fuel imports from Russia. Ceaușescu pursued ties with the West, mainly to obtain technical assistance and capital goods for his industrial policy. The policy was enforced by his personal security force, but any gains from it were captured by Ceaușescu's family. Economic growth stagnated in the 1980s, especially by comparison with Bulgaria. By 1989, the average Romanian was the worst off among all the Central and East Europeans. Romania's economic policy under communism was notable for the high degree of centralized control over the plan, its emphasis on heavy industry, and the persistence with which it was pursued, continuing long after other countries, including the Soviet Union, had altered their strategies.

As a consequence, the collapse of the regime was the most violent within the CEEC. Ceaușescu and his family fled for their lives in December 1989, were caught, summarily tried, and promptly executed. The disaffected Communist leaders assumed power, renaming their party the National Salvation Front. Elections were held in 1990, which the NSF won, and economic reforms began to get under way in March-April 1991. These included establishing a weak central bank and signing a deal with the IMF for stabilization loans conditioned on fiscal reforms and devaluation of the national currency, the leu. Fresh elections were held in fall 1992 based on the constitution adopted in November 1991. Again, the NSF dominated. As with the case of Lithuania discussed above, the relative stability of political control has slowed down the movement to a market economy.

Romania's transition process has been more gradual than in the other countries, mainly because of the slow pace of privatization. This only began to get under way in October 1995, with a two-stage process similar to that successfully demonstrated earlier by the Czech Republic. Vouchers were issued to the public at nominal prices, and then could be used to purchase shares in various mutual funds authorized to bid on state enterprises put up for auction. The expansion in output, which began in 1993 and has continued since, has been unusual in that the most rapid increases have not been in services, as in the other transition economies, but in consumer goods. This reflects the relatively miserable consumption standards endured by the Romanian people under Ceauşescu's rule. But it also reflects the changeover in Romania's industrial base from heavy manufacturing to light manufacturing, which is directed toward satisfying pent-up domestic demands rather than finding export markets in the surrounding region.

Eventually, Romania's best hope is to find markets in Western Europe, which is clearly recognized by the political leadership and the mass of the Romanian public. As an example of its eagerness to establish ties with the West, Romania was the first transition economy to apply for membership in NATO and offered peacekeeping troops in Bosnia-Herzegovina. One of the legacies of Ceauşescu's craze for monumental construction projects is the Danube–Black Sea–Rhine canal. This provides a secure, cheap transportation route for oil produced in the Caspian Sea fields and shipped to the Black Sea to be carried into the heart of the European Union. Moreover, this would reduce the pressure on the EU to admit Turkey in order to maintain access to the Black Sea through the Bosporus. Romania's location is its best asset to date and the strongest argument for its accession to the EU.

CONCLUSION

Confronted by similar challenges in making the painful transition from plan to market, each of these new applicants for membership to the EU have responded in unique ways, determined to seek out the policy path most congenial to its political situation as well as appropriate for its economic condition. They each present special challenges to the existing set of the EU's economic policies— the Common Agricultural Policy, the Regional Development Funds, and the European Monetary Union. However, they also present political opportunities for creating a peaceful, democratically governed Europe that would finally put paid to the legacies of World War I and World War II. The economic policies of the EU have proven to be seriously flawed, moreover, and will have to be altered in any event. It will be economically beneficial to the existing member states to amend the EU's policies to allow speedy accession by these applicants. The political reforms necessary to achieve this are even more important for the prospect of peace and prosperity for Europe that lies tantalizingly within reach. This is the mission of the EU's Inter-Governmental Conference of 1996–97.

Bibliography

Economist Intelligence Unit. *Country Profile, Bosnia-Hercegovina/Croatia/Slovenia, 1995–96.* London: Economist Intelligence Unit, 1996.

Economist Intelligence Unit. *Country Profile, Bulgaria/Albania, 1995–96.* London: Economist Intelligence Unit, 1996.

Economist Intelligence Unit. *Country Profile, Czech Republic/Slovakia, 1995–96.* London: Economist Intelligence Unit, 1996.

Economist Intelligence Unit. *Country Profile, Estonia/Latvia/Lithuania, 1995–96.* London: Economist Intelligence Unit, 1996.

Economist Intelligence Unit. *Country Profile, Hungary, 1995–96.* London: Economist Intelligence Unit, 1996.

Economist Intelligence Unit. *Country Profile, Poland, 1995–96.* London: Economist Intelligence Unit, 1996.

Economist Intelligence Unit. *Country Profile, Romania, 1995–96.* London: Economist Intelligence Unit, 1996.

Economist Intelligence Unit. *Country Report, Bosnia-Hercegovina/Croatia/Slovenia.* London: Economist Intelligence Unit, 2nd quarter, 1996.

Economist Intelligence Unit. *Country Report, Bulgaria/Albania.* London: Economist Intelligence Unit, 2nd quarter, 1996.

Economist Intelligence Unit. *Country Report, Czech Republic/Slovakia.* London: Economist Intelligence Unit, 2nd quarter, 1996.

Economist Intelligence Unit. *Country Report, Estonia/Latvia/Lithuania.* London: Economist Intelligence Unit, 2nd quarter, 1996.

Economist Intelligence Unit. *Country Report, Hungary.* London: Economist Intelligence Unit, 2nd quarter, 1996.

Economist Intelligence Unit. *Country Report, Poland.* London: Economist Intelligence Unit, 2nd quarter, 1996.

Economist Intelligence Unit. *Country Report, Romania.* London: Economist Intelligence Unit, 2nd quarter, 1996.

European Bank for Reconstruction and Development. *Transition Report.* London: EBRD, October 1995.

European Bank for Reconstruction and Development. *Transition Report.* London: EBRD, November 1996.

European Bank for Reconstruction and Development. *Transition Report Update.* London: EBRD, April 1996.

International Monetary Fund. *Financial Sector Reforms and Exchange Arrangements in Eastern Europe.* Occasional Paper No. 102. Washington, D.C.: International Monetary Fund, 1993.

International Monetary Fund. *Road Maps of the Transition: The Baltics, the Czech Republic, Hungary, and Russia.* Occasional Paper No. 127. Washington, DC: International Monetary Fund, 1995.

Website:http://www.ebrd.com for the latest update on transition progress from the European Bank for Reconstruction and Development.

Index